Calaveras County

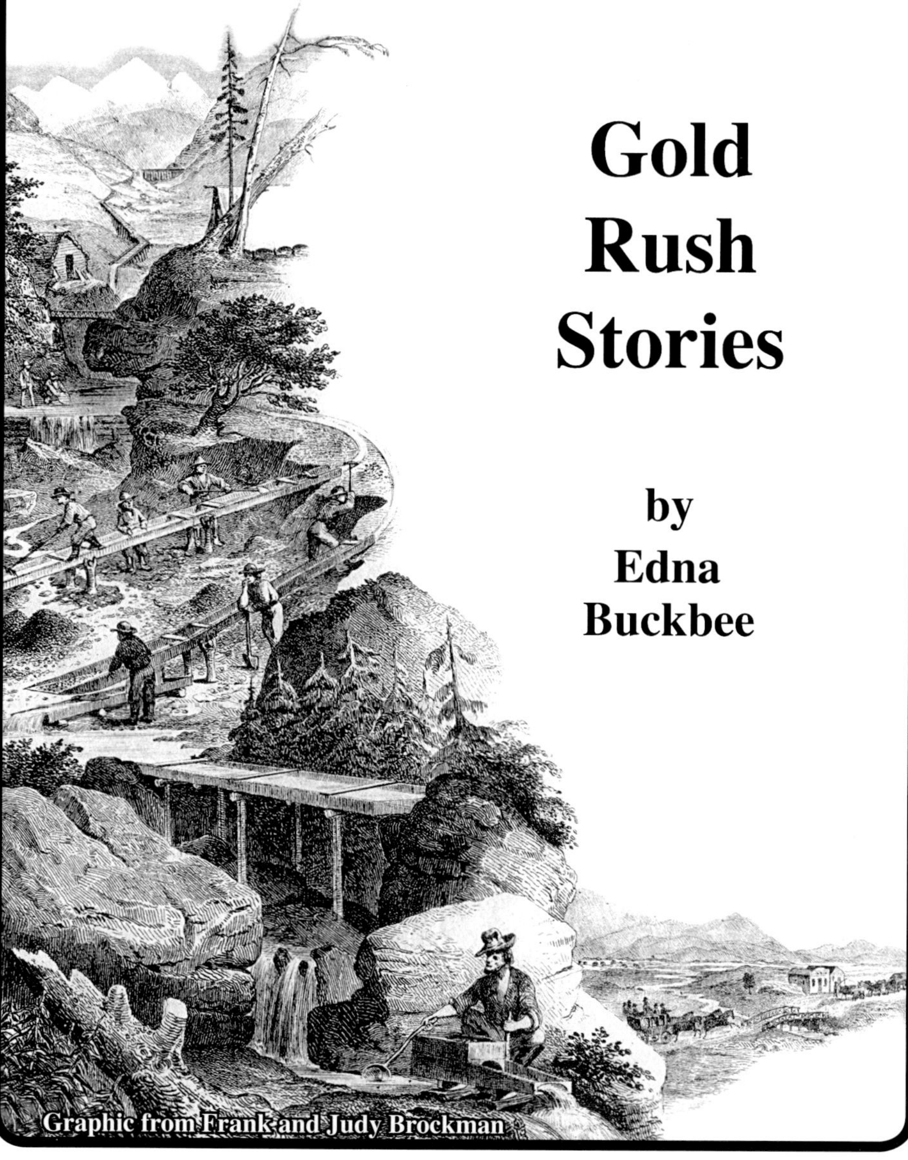

Gold Rush Stories

by
Edna
Buckbee

Published by
Calaveras County Historical Society
30 N. Main St
Post Office Box 721
San Andreas CA 95249
www.calaverascohistorical.com

Editor
Wallace Motloch

Library of Congress Cataloging-in-Publication Data
Buckbee Edna Bryan
Calaveras County, Gold Rush Stories
Includes bibliographical references

ISBN 0-9773744-0-8
1. Gold Rush, Gold mines and mining, California, Calaveras County, History, 19th century.

First Printing

Printed in Canada

CONTENTS

Printing of this book was supported financially by:

The Calaveras County Historical Society
Lane Family
Sender Family
Steve and Pat Wilensky
Frank and Judy Brockman
Suzanne and Lincoln Russin
D. Margaret Studley Foundation
Rosemary Bosse Faulkner
Phil Alberts Family
Wally Motloch

Note of Thanks

There are many people and institutions that need to be thanked for making this book possible.

On behalf of The Board of Directors of the Calaveras County Historical Society, I wish to thank:
Posthumously, Mrs. Edna Bryan Buckbee for all the years of work that must have had gone into writing and preserving our early history. Many a historian will find this information extremely valuable and a general reader will find it informative and entertaining. Her keen eye for detail and her way with words makes this work a classic, Buckbee classic.

My sincere thanks goes to the California Historical Society in San Francisco for granting permission to compile and publish this material from Edna Bryan Buckbee Papers, [193-]-1954 (MS273). Much gratitude goes to Ms. Mary Morganti, Director of Library and Archives and the staff of the Society's North Baker Research Library for being particularly helpful and generous with their time. They assisted me in locating related collections and made copies of many fragile pages.

I am grateful to the Board of Directors of the Calaveras County Historical Society for their support and encouragement. To the office staff of the Society, but especially to Ms. Cate Culver, for her help with photographs, proofreading and her quiet guidance that kept me focused. To Shannon Van Zant, County Archivist, Shannon Mason, Elizabeth Webber, Jo Sanders and Lillian Browning for all their help. To Bill Fuller, Phil Alberts and Salvatore Manna for being on the lookout for accuracy and the style of this book.

Lastly, to Lillian, my wonderful partner, for all her help with proof-reading, tea and cookies, without these, my life at the computer would have been a lot harder.

Thank you

Wallace Motloch
Editor

Introduction and Explanatory Notes

While I was hunting for "history nuggets" at the California Historical Society's North Baker Research Library in San Francisco, quite by accident I came across Mrs. Edna Bryan Buckbee's notes and typescripts. I was delighted to find some pertinent information about my own town, Mountain Ranch. Soon I realized that there, in among the folders and dividers were pieces of a manuscript notes dealing with Old Calaveras. It was with a child's excitement that I searched through files of material that had been donated to the California Historical Society in 1954. These were not just any stories but local history with people's names, places and dates, exactly the kind of Gold Rush narrative I had been hoping to find. This was a very rich "pay dirt" indeed!

There was an added reason for my excitement. Historians in this county have been at a disadvantage because, unlike other counties, a truly comprehensive history of Calaveras has never been published. To illustrate this point, in 1932 the editor of the California Historical Society Quarterly wrote to several people looking for historical information about Calaveras County.

He wrote:

"I find that there is very little published material on that county, and am therefore finding it rather difficult to obtain accurate information."

The California State Librarian replied:

" There is no other history of Calaveras other than the one you mention in your letter, [and that history source] is exceedingly meager"

Edna Buckbee was a daughter of California pioneers, Joseph (Joe) Turner Bryan and Elvira Ellis who married in Sonora in 1854. Her father had ridden to California with a group of horsemen five years before the Gold Rush, in 1845. A skillful reinsmen, later he was the top driver for Vogan Stage covering the company's longest daily run of 120 miles from Sonora to Sacramento.

Edna was born in San Andreas in 1876, some 27 years after the Gold Rush. She lived in Sheep Ranch, Angels Camp and San Andreas. As a child she heard many of the Old Calaveras stories first-hand and knew some of the characters personally.

As far as can be ascertained, she was married in 1900 and had no children. She went to Alaska with her mining engineer husband. He died in 1905 leaving her to support herself. As a lover of Western History, she immersed herself in research. While not formally trained as a historian, she devoted the remainder of her life to this passion. No armchair researcher, she "lived" in archives, museums and libraries. She interviewed hundreds of people and kept notes of every historical detail. As such, she had her own view of history, sometimes in contradiction to accepted beliefs. Notable local historian like Coke Wood and Emmett Joy frequently quoted her.

She wrote many and varied historical items. Here is a quote from the April 29, 1928 Los Angeles Times:

> "CALIFORNIA FIGURE APPEARS IN LIBRETTO
>
> Mary Carr Moore, well known composer and Edna Buckbee an authority on Californiana and a writer, are collaborating on an opera to be written about the life of Lola Montez, famous dancer of the blazing 50s. Edna Buckbee who has written a number of books, short stories, articles and poetry on early California figures, will provide the libretto."

For many years Buckbee gathered material for two historical books, one book on Tuolumne County and the other on Calaveras. Press of the Pioneers in New York published in 1935 The Saga of Old Tuolumne a 530-page book.

The Tuolumne book was published first but already in 1932 she had submitted a list of chapters and an outline to the same publisher for her Old Calaveras book. However, in reviewing her letters, there were problems with the royalty payments from the publisher for the Tuolumne book. With regards to the Calaveras book, in a letter to a friend dated October 1935 she writes:

> " I am heartily sick of Western history, however, I thank you for your suggestions about Old Calaveras, but the manuscript, so far as I am concerned, can furnish paper for lighting this winter's fires."

The publishing company delayed paying her for three years and in the end they went bankrupt. Financially strapped, Buckbee became bitter and disillusioned.

For various reasons, the Old Calaveras manuscript was never turned into a book. Edna died in San Francisco in 1956 and is buried in the Bryan's Plot at Peoples Cemetery in San Andreas, Calaveras County, the county she loved and knew so well.

In her effort to make a living as a writer, Buckbee reused some of the Calaveras material for other works or as magazine articles. The reader will soon realize that chapters in this book have two distinct styles. There are the long drafts and the short, more finished articles. Since the complete working draft was not recovered, this book is a mixture of both styles. Some of our chapters were just research notes. Yet, even in these notes there is useful historical information and that is why they are included here.

Her stories reflect the customs of Gold Rush times. To preserve authenticity, no effort was made to sanitize these or make them more "politically correct." Some of the descriptions of lynchings and murders are gruesome and despicable by today's standards.

Every effort has been made to preserve the original text, words and style. Except for spelling and minor grammar corrections, the text is pure and original Edna Buckbee. The editor, in an effort to make this book more palatable to the modern reader has added square brackets, footnotes, maps, photographs and appendices.

There are many references to the price of gold or amounts of gold found. These numbers are expressed in "Gold Rush Dollars." Consider that miners received about $14 per ounce for unrefined gold that they traded for supplies. Today gold sells for approximately $420 per ounce. To get a better understanding of the "Gold Rush" numbers in terms of value in 2005, the reader should multiply each amount by 30. For example, $100 in 1860 has a value of $3000 in 2005 ($100 x 30 =$3000)

Readers are encouraged to provide corrections, additional photographs or helpful information that may be incorporated in future editions of this book.

In the end,

This is Edna Buckbee's Old Calaveras material, finally published, some 70 years after she had worked on it.

Editor

Foreword

This story of Old Calaveras County can but "scratch the surface" as the gold washers themselves would say. Beneath its contour of dates and facts must necessarily be left undisturbed vast deposits, filled with the "color" as alluring to the writer as was the gleam covered by that term to the first gold miners.

Ferreting out the tales of Old Calaveras' hair-raising days and danger has been, for me at least, an agreeable task. Those chance-taking pioneers of ours had dreams that the men and women of this generation have never dared to dream. Therefore, if I have failed to interpret them convincingly, I can but hope that my efforts to collate correctly will help in a measure, to make up for this lack.

Myself a daughter of early settlers in this county, I have not been wanting in sympathy for those men and women who were frequently made to experience the dangers and hardships of pioneer life. They lived with torments of famine, stormbound winters and suffered the dreadful ravages of smallpox and cholera that more than once threatened to depopulate many of the towns and camps of the county.

San Andreas, the old Mexican town in which I was born, and Angels Camp and Sheep Ranch where I attended public school have voices of their own. Always, wherever I happened to be, I kept hearing in my memory their voices.

Until finally, I have returned to the scenes, so familiar to me in childhood, in my girlhood. Here, surrounded and encouraged by family and friends, I wrote this story, which I trust, is a faithful portrayal of our first settlers and the camps and towns they founded.

Edna Bryan Buckbee

[This Foreword may have been written by Mrs. Buckbee in 1932 for the original Old Calaveras manuscript.]

1

OLD CALAVERAS

Full of brave echoes of Gold Rush days, Calaveras[1] is a picturesque ground and its history is more exciting than can be found elsewhere in California. The unbelievable tales of gold, mobs, banditry, lynching and bull and bear fights that used to characterize the early days in the Southern Mines are gone. No longer heard are these from pioneer lips. Other happenings, as colorful as the stage trappings of the troupers who invaded the mining camps for the purpose of entertaining the gold washers, are constantly occurring. There is no other county in California where one may step so completely out of the flatness and drabness of daily life as one can in Calaveras. No other county in which, in the mind's eye one may envision the historic pageant of the past, sweep so unashamedly through a complex, machine burdened age.

The story of Old Calaveras goes back to the time of Lieutenant Alferez Gabriel Moraga, a California Indian fighter and explorer with the Mexican Army. In 1806 say the records, Moraga in a search for marauding Indians and suitable mission sites, blazed a trail from El Pueblo San Jose de Guadalupe into the Sierra foothills. His expedition is credited with having reached, crossed and named the Merced, Mariposa, Tuolumne, and Laquisimes [Stanislaus] rivers. Traveling northward they came to another river along whose banks were skulls and other human bones scattered in heaps. This stream Moraga called El Rio del las Pasion [River of the Passion]. Later it became known as El Rio del Calaveras [River of the Skulls] and from it, 44 years later, the county derived its name.

The banks of this river, Moraga thought, gave mute evidence of once having been the scene of a fiercely contested battle. Moraga knew that the Indians of the foothills had made annual pilgrimages to the San Joaquin River, so it was likely that they came by way of the Calaveras River. Moraga also knew, that at an earlier date, his adventurous father, Captain Joaquin Moraga, named this larger river. His father had not only discovered but had bestowed upon it the name of San Francisco. Later, Gabriel, desiring to honor his father, renamed the river to San Joaquin, by which name it has since been known.

There came a season when the Valley Indians refused the Sierra tribes the privilege of hunting and fishing in their swampy domain. In retaliation, the inhabitants of the "Shining Plain" [San Joaquin Valley Indians] were not permitted to speed arrows, gather seeds, acorns and pine nuts in the foothills. So it was, in the opinion of the Mexican soldier Moraga, that feuds between tribes continued for countless centuries. It is not difficult to imagine warriors wearing head pieces made of eagles' feathers and necklaces of bears' claws, gathered on some quartz boulder where pipes may have been filled but not lighted. The chiefs of the various tribes had never been able to establish a permanent peace. Many a desperate battle had no doubt been fought on the banks of El Rio del las Pasion. That is why, on a lonely reach[2] near this river the explorers found numerous human skulls, left there, by the victors for the summer sun and winter frost to bleach and whiten.

In the general histories of California but a slight mention is made of the territory out of which Calaveras County was formed. In spite of endless hazards, an occasional trapper visited the lower Mokelumne River section, but not often, for the Indian of this region watched with jealous eye the intrusion of strangers for any purpose.

On May 8, 1840 the Mexican Governor of California Juan B. Alvarado, granted to Teodocio Yorba eleven league of land[3]. This foothill land grant was known as El Arroyo Seco, it extended in an easterly direction to the Sierra Nevada Mountains. Lying between the Consumnes and Mokelumne rivers, Mount Diablo was its base or meridian. But it is not to be supposed that Don Teodocio or any other native Californian had ever set foot on this land. He may never have seen it except from some far-off peak of the Coast Range.

Those frontiersmen who accompanied John A. Sutter of New Helvetia [Sacramento] in his campaign against the Mokelumne Indians in the autumn of 1840 may possibly have seen the "Lyon" or "Jim Martin Hills" twenty miles eastward. James Alexander Forbes, Alta California agent for the Hudson Bay Company, in his history of California stated:

"As early as 1840, all attempts to raise cattle on the east side of the San Joaquin had been utter failure, the Indians invariably driving off the stock and destroying the ranches."

Manuel Micheltoreno, a newly appointed Mexican Governor of California, on December 29,1843, granted to Francisco Rico and Jose Antonio Castro eleven leagues of land, known as El Rancheria del Rio Estanislao. The records of Old Calaveras tell us that this princely grant was bound on the east by the Sierras, on the west including all the land, on the south by the Stanislaus River, on the north by the Lomira Hills (presumably the Bear Mountain Range). On March 8, 1853, Don Jose sold his half interest to Manuel Castro, his brother, for the paltry sum of $5,500.

Prior to the discovery of gold by James Wilson Marshall on January 24,1848, the Calaveras locale was a vast forest, extending from the San Joaquin Valley to the Sierra Summit. Here and there were lush and green valleys. In the rock-ribbed upper ranges marched the yellow pine, fir and cedars, while on the lower slopes flourished stately oaks, cottonwood, madrone, maple and aspen. Between the boles, in a wild entanglement were weeds and bears' mat (miner's rose) giving to the landscape the appearance of a park. So careful had been the Indians in their destruction of all objectionable undergrowth that the result must have seemed to the first settlers like thousands of years of peaceful occupation. At every turn of the Indian and deer trails, followed by the men of 1848-49 watchful eyes, undoubtedly glanced about half expecting to see wood nymphs shocked and astonished at the bold intrusion of leather booted men. Entering this sylvan land, they had felled the superb trees, stripped the dirt off boulders, leaving them stark and bare. The generations as yet unborn might marvel at the energy and determination displayed by the resolute gold hunters.

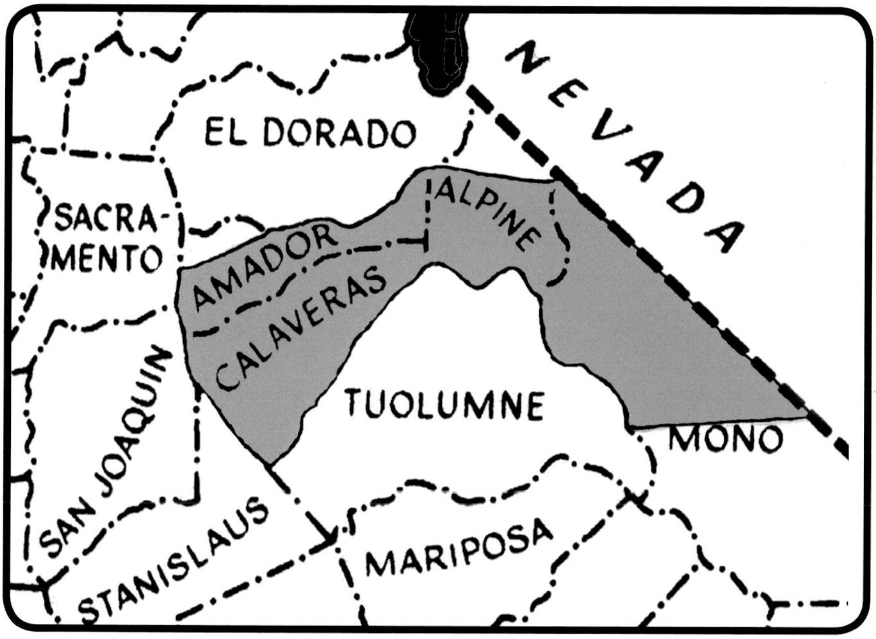

Shaded area shows the original size of Calaveras County

In Monterey, Bennett Riley, United States Military Governor, was in charge of civil affairs in California and by an expressed wish of the people desiring protection of their property rights, called a convention at that place for the purpose of drawing up a constitution. The meeting opened in Colton Hall, in Monterey on September 3, 1849.

Laws for California were made and the boundary lines fixed. An election was called. By vote of the people under the laws of the United States Government, Peter H. Burnett was chosen the first governor of California[4]. The following year it was Governor Burnett himself who, after the arrival of the steamer "Oregon" in San Francisco Bay, leaped into the saddle and thundered out of San Francisco to announce to the people of San Jose that the bill admitting California to the Union had been sent to President Fillmore who had signed it on September 9, 1850.

Calaveras County, one of the original twenty-seven counties, was created by an Act of the First Legislature on February 18, 1850. Its original area was nearly four times its present size. During the first two years three acts were passed in an effort to define the boundaries of this county.

> The act of 1851 gives the clearest definition of the lines as they first existed. It reads as follows:
>
> "Beginning at the corner of Sacramento and San Joaquin counties, thence to the middle of Dry Creek to its source, thence following the summit of the dividing ridge between the Mokelumne and Cosumnes rivers, thence due east to the state boundary line, thence in a southerly direction along the boundary line of the state to the parallel of thirty eight degrees of north latitude, thence due east to the summit of the Sierra Nevada, thence in a westerly direction along said summit to the north fork of the Stanislaus River to a point one mile north of Knight's Ferry, thence along the eastern boundary of San Joaquin County to the place of the beginning."

Questions as to the line dividing the Northern Mines from the Southern Mines are frequently asked and may be answered thus: The line separating these mines may be considered the ridge on the north side of the North Fork of the Cosumnes River. Several points along this stream and its reaches are generally regarded as belonging to the Southern Mines. All the rivers of the Southern Mines are effluents of the San Joaquin River and those of the Northern Mines are of the Sacramento River. The principal rivers of the former are the Cosumnes, Mokelumne, Calaveras, Stanislaus, Mariposa, and Merced. These streams, like those of the northern mines, each has its north, south and middle fork.

The seat of Calaveras County has been shifted three times. In 1850 it was located at Pleasant Valley or Double Springs or Two Springs Ranch, as one wills. Four miles west of San Andreas, today Double Springs [early 1930s] is best known as Wheat's Ranch. The original owners of this ranch were H. M. Guild and Charles L Peck. It consisted of 160 acres of land. Peck took possession under his "pre-emption notice" in 1847[5]. In 1849 the ranch became the scene of unusual activity. Situated at the junction of five different

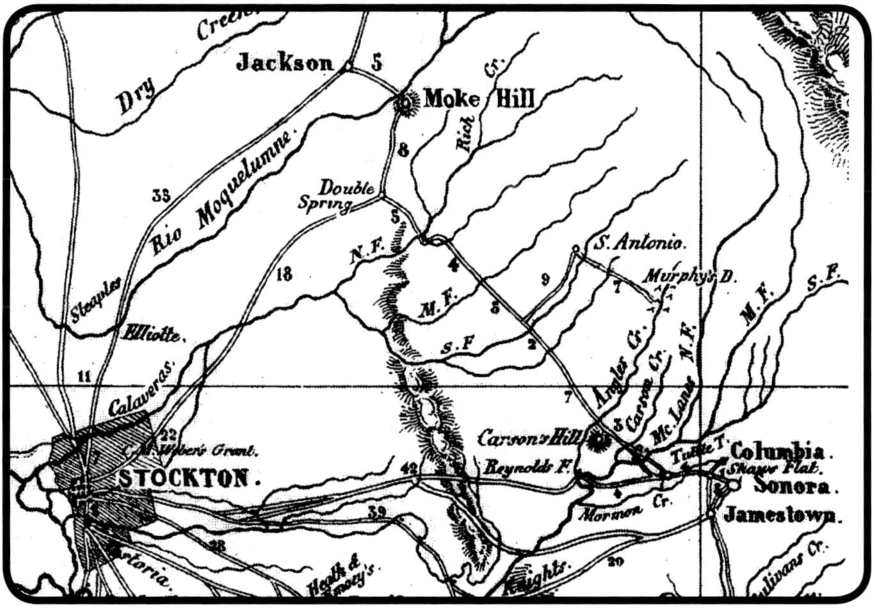

Detail from "Map of the Southern Mines" by C.D. Gibbes 1852.

Courtesy of Calaveras County Historical Society.

roads, it soon became a community devoted to the breeding of livestock and politics. A political hotspot, its population was desirable, progressive and democratic in persuasion. In May 1850 a Stockton Company purchased several small ranches in Pleasant Valley and attempted to found a town, "a new and a beautiful one." In fact, D. F. Small, a surveyor, laid off a portion of the land into town lots. Thomas B. Van Buren, a former resident of Double Springs, in his real estate office on "the Levee" in Stockton, made a brave attempt to promote this project. The lots were no drag on the market nor were the colorful and informative maps of the "New Town of Pleasant Valley".

The first thing the men of 1848 did after reaching a rich spot was to look for desirable camp ground, locate claims and set up a few brush shelter huts. The usual number of men in each camp was from two to six. During the summer they slept outdoors under the trees. Often, the sleepers were awakened by an ox or mule upsetting their rude table or nosing into their bags of sugar, flour and salt. The campers soon discovered that cabins, for security and comfort, were superior to brush huts and cloth tents. There is no sense in attempting to describe the outside of a miner's cabin as a number of books are reamed with accounts of the exterior but seldom a mention is made of the interior. At first, the ground served the miners for a floor on which in winter, the men wrapped in blankets, lay with their feet towards the fireplace. Finally, when one man, handy with a saw and hammer built a bunk for himself, his messmates did likewise. In order to separate one tier of bunks from the other, potato and gunnysacks were hung. Wild hay, fern brakes, pine and cedar boughs furnished the foundation for comfortable beds. Washing gold in some stream involved wet clothing, a roaring fire in the rock fireplace soon dried out the garments.

The Democratic Party in Calaveras County was first organized in the New Town on April 26, 1851, with Wm. Fowle Smith as the president and Lewis Collier[6] the secretary. Those attending were: A. H. Putney, James L. Trask, A. H. Midge, Dr. John Y. Lind, A. W. Mitchell, J. A. P. Weeks, Col. G. W. Platt, Joseph Palmer, Daniel Lattimer, James Laurence, James Broome Smith, Daniel W. Murphy, W. F. Marshall, R. King Read, James Blackburn, A. P. Jordan, Abner Allen, S. B. Morris, and G. C. Robins.

First County Seat was in Double Springs. Photo taken in 1930's of the remains of the first Courthouse. This building was the first mobile or "pre-manufactured" home in Calaveras County. Made of camphor wood panels imported from China in 1849. See footnote 7.

Courtesy of Calaveras County Archives.

The first County Court House, a collapsible building, was erected from wooden panels imported from China in 1849 by Jothan P. Blanchard who established a trading post, saloon and tavern under its roof[7]. Wm. W. Beckham, John G. Dudley, Charles A. Swift, D. D. Hubbell, John Dillon, and Thomas B. Van Buren were occupying tents and patronizing Blanchard's liquor bar, holding inducements that nothing this side of heaven was able to resist.

The first Grand Jury of Old Calaveras held its Sessions under the green branches of an oak tree, while the Court convened in a long cloth tent imported from China, which was about ten feet wide. The first county officers were William Fowle Smith, County Judge; Lewis A. Collier, County Clerk; John Hansen[8], Sheriff; J. B. Mudge, Treasurer and James Foote Smith, County Attorney.

The county's first Book of Records tell us that on May 20,1850 or three months before California was admitted to the Union, it was ordered by the County Judge that a public notice, signed by the County Clerk, be posted.

It read;

"The first term of the Court of Sessions will be held at the county seat on Monday June 10th, next."

In accordance with Judge Smith's order, notices were sent to the various towns and camps. The first townships of the old county were established:

No.1, Jackson, South Fork of Jackson Creek to Clinton and Secreto, inclusive. Middle Fork of Jackson Creek to within six miles of Volcano. North side of Mokelumne River from White's Bar, inclusive, to a point opposite Winter's Bar and Sutter Creek.

No. 2, Dry Creek, Rancheria Creek to point eight miles above the town of Rancheria, Amador Creek, New York Store, Boston Store, and Ione Valley and Mokelumne River, for a point opposite Winter's Bar, to the eastern line of the county.

No. 3, Middle Fork of Jackson Creek, from the boundary line of Township No. 1, to the eastern line of the county; Dry Creek from the eastern line of Township No. 2 to its source, and the north side of the Mokelumne River, including the North Fork and the north side of the Middle Fork, down to White's Bar.

No. 4, South side of the Mokelumne River from James' Bar to the western line of the county; Turnersville or Campo Seco, and south of Campo Seco to the Mokelumne River.

No. 5, Commencing at the junction of the Jesus Maria and Esperanza branches of the North Fork of the Calaveras, thence down the North Calaveras to the main river, thence down the main river to the boundary line of the county, the highland dividing the water running into the Stanislaus to be the southern boundary line.

No. 6, Beginning at the forks of the Mokelumne, running down the south side of same to James' Bar, inclusive, thence along the eastern line of township No. 2, to the Calaveras River thence up the north Calaveras to the junction of the Jesus Maria and Esperanza branches, thence to Esperanza.

No. 7, Commencing at the junction of the Jesus Maria and Esperanza branches of the North Calaveras and running south east to San Antone Creek, to a point a mile above the town of San Antone, thence in an easterly direction to the Stanislaus River, again commencing at the junction of the Jesus Maria and Esperanza branches of the north Calaveras and running up the middle of the Esperanza Branch to its source, thence across the fork of the Mokelumne, and up the middle of the Middle Fork to its source, including the South Fork of the Mokelumne, McKinney's Humbug and El Dorado.

No. 8, Carson Creek, Angel's Creek, and the Stanislaus River, including the camps located on water running into either of the above streams, which are not otherwise specially defined.

No. 9, Included these camps, Murphys New Diggings, Vallecito, San Domingo, Douglas Flat, and Spring Garden Camp.

The petition of William L. Martin and Aristide L. Pench, for a ferry across the Mokelumne River at the Middle Bar of that stream, was the first to be reviewed. Favorably considered, the Court fixed the rate for ferriage as follows:

> "For each passenger, fifty cents, for each horse, mule, jack or jenny or other animal, fifty cents, for each empty wagon, six dollars, for each loaded wagon six dollars and fifty cents for each hundred weight of freight. For every horse, mule, jack or jenny with cargo, one dollar."

At this session the Court ordered that a poll tax of five dollars be levied upon every man residing in the county between the ages of twenty-one and fifty. Also, that each hundred dollars worth of property within the county be taxed fifty cents.

Also present at the Court of Sessions were George H. Wyatt and William L. Dudley who acted as Associate Justice of the Court.

The second session of the Court of Sessions was held on August 12, 1850, at which time Judge Smith ordered Sheriff Hanson to serve notice on twelve men, thus:

> "You are hereby commanded to summons twelve good and
> lawful men from the body of the County of Calaveras,
> to serve as jurors of the present term of the Court of Sessions."

In obedience to this command the following men, the first to act as jurymen in the county were duly sworn: George H. Davis, Stephen Shore, Nicholas Starke, Sylvester Cummings, John Winslow, Joseph Ashby, Simson Anthony, Robert Crook, Oliver French, F. M. Tate, George Brightman and C. M. Pease. Joseph Ashby acted as foreman of the jury.

The first criminal case was that of the people against Alexander A. McElroy, who stood trial for assault and battery upon the body of William

McGilvery. The second offender was Charles McEnaugh, charged with a misdemeanor. Next, came the petition of John W. Robinson and Stephen Mead for a ferry across the Stanislaus River. The rates for crossings were as those fixed for Martin & Pench. At this time James L. Trask, a lawyer, was appointed public auctioneer for Jackson Creek. Samuel Bennett, born in England, received his citizenship.

The first bridge to span the north fork of the Calaveras River, near Moore's Ranch, was commenced by Stevenson & Pirie, of Double Springs, on December 9, 1850.

Justice at Charley Peck's Ranch was anything but a blind goddess during the year 1850. Contradictory too, were the reports regarding the characters of the several county officers. Judge Smith, New York State man, had his friends who believed he was honest and fearless. On the other hand, many said he was crafty and cowardly. Lewis Collier's eccentricities were well known and magnified, especially by Judge Smith. Anyhow, between these men a mutual antipathy had long existed which, seemingly could not be bridged. According to the law enacted in 1849-1850 whenever a majority of the voters of any county in the state petitioned for an election fixing the county seat, the County Judge, if he desired, could order an election at thirty days notice. Late in 1850, an election was held by order of Judge Smith.

The towns contesting for the Seat of Justice were Mokelumne Hill and Jackson. When the County Clerk made the first count of votes, Mokelumne Hill was favored. The jubilant citizens of then the most important mining town in the Southern Mines, wildly excited over their victory, sent a swift team to Double Springs to remove the county's property to their prosperous town.

In the meantime, a second counting of the votes, under the personal direction of Judge Smith, put the prize package in Jackson's lap. The Mokelumne Hill politicians, disgruntled and sullen, screwed up their eyes, uttered savage curses and loudly accused Judge Smith of dishonorable and fraudulent practices.

Double Springs, contrary to the expectations of the promoters of that newly plotted town, had not gained in population. Jackson and Mokelumne Hill were rival towns with the latter, in standpoint of fabulously rich diggings, well to the front. Jackson regarded its bustling town as a more suitable location for the seat of government. They made no bones about saying that. In 1849 gold crazy Mokelumne Hill was Lewis Collier's stamping ground. Since the County Clerk viewed that place with steadfast eyes and its citizens were anxious, they decided to wait for a third counting of the votes.

Charles Boynton, with a sharp eye on Jackson, cooked up the plot to capture the county records. A newspaper writer, his method of seizing documents proved as near a farce as any illegal happening ever gets to be.

Jothan [Jonathan] Blanchard was boastful of his fine wooden building, which was still answering for a courthouse, saloon, tavern, and gold dust exchange. This tavern was Colonel Collier's home in which he sometimes made his presence felt. A native of Virginia, brave as need be, Lewis Collier was pompous and reckless. Those men who knew him best, hesitated to cross his imperious will for when in a towering rage, he used strong language against Judge Smith, going so far as to threaten to "cut out his gizzard".

Naturally, the County Judge strode around Two Springs Ranch, with his five-shooter loaded and ready for any emergency.

On a warm July morning in the year 1851, Lewis Collier sat in the courthouse, fumbling a gold nugget. On this sultry morning nothing of importance had happened to destroy the peace of the tented settlement, that is, until Charlie Boynton and Theodore Mudge swaggered up to the liquor bar. They tossed down a few coins, a proper thing to do in the flush days, invited the "boys" to step up and have a drink. Fond of a racy story, Colonel Collier was even fonder of liquor and on this morning while he quaffed brandy, Boynton glibly engaged him in light banter. Then to the tune of glass, Mudge ambled to the custodian of the archive's desk, seized the records, rushed outdoors, tumbled them into a buggy, and together with Charlie Boynton headed for Jackson, their horses running at full speed.

The loquacious Collier, finding that the one and only Book of Records had been stolen, swore a mighty oath portending no good to those who had violated the dignity of his office.

In Colonel Jackson's camp, a shake shanty roofed with hides, stood at the foot of a trail, which at once received the name of Court Street. A flimsy structure hastily put together, the precious Book of Records was deposited within its four walls. The thirst of the assemblage being very great that day, Jackson was soon celebrating its victory over Mokelumne Hill. Three hours after the seizure of the records, Collier all riled up, reached Jackson from Double Springs. Judge Smith with judicial smile induced the County Clerk to issue the proper papers, dated at Jackson, this being for the convening of a Court. Collier obliged, then for the next few weeks, affairs inside the courthouse progressed without the brandishing of knives and guns.

At Volcano Valley on August 16, 1851 Broderick Stowell stabbed Nimrod Skelton with a "certain American Bowie knife". Stowell was brought to trial before Judge Smith at the third term of the Court, which was held in Jackson, with Henry A. Carter serving as a prosecuting attorney.

An election for county officers was soon in the offing. Joseph Douglas was popular in Jackson and was a candidate against Lewis Collier for the Clerkship. Election day was full of roar, with Douglas coming out first. Collier, to hold on to his office, locked the returns of the contest in his desk. He gave as his reason the need for his opponent to be qualified, but until then, Collier's official seal was attached to the results.

The next day while Collier was absent from his office, Judge Smith broke open the clerk's desk, counted the votes and promptly issued the Certificate of Election to the winners, among whom was Joe Douglas. The Judge's insolent act served only to renew old and bitter hostilities.

Judge Smith had frequently accused Lewis Collier of pocketing the fees received in his official capacity, leaving Smith to collect his salary as best he could.

It was spring and the County Judge stood warming himself in the sunshine, grumbling:

"Lewis Collier has naturalized sixty foreigners
for which he charged each man,
one ounce of gold dust,
putting the same in his own pocket for his own use."

This accusation, carried back to Lewis, further provoked him. After the candidates had been informed of their election to the various offices, Collier, in a sizzling tirade, again threatened to use a knife on his enemy. Smith was soon reloading his five-shooter. Frowning savagely, he thundered out of the courthouse to wreak a swift vengeance unrestrained.

At the lower end of Court Street, Smith saw Collier -
Here his weapon spat fire.
A second shot,
The lean and lanky Lewis Collier unarmed,
Fell at the base of an oak tree.
Dead!

Although not made to stand trial for the homicide, the public opinion was strong and forced Smith's retirement and to George H. Campbell of Jackson, fell the impetuous Judge's mantle. A Volcano pioneer who had witnessed the shooting, afterwards said:

"Smith was a northerner and Collier a southerner.
The people took sides accordingly,
Foreshadowing the dreadful conflict of ten years later."

A Theologian by training, Wm. F. Smith, after leaving Jackson mined with success at Poverty Bar. His pile made, he returned to his home in New York City where, say the records, his preaching of the Gospels created a stir

Tuesday Morning 8 O'Clock 19th August A.D 1851

The Court met pursuant to adjournment.

It is ordered by the Court that the following ~~precincts~~ Counties Comprise the the different ~~Districts~~ Townships of the County as revised by the Court.

~~District~~ No. 1
Township — Jackson, South and Middle forks of Jackson, Sutter, the Butte, Middle and Columbia Bar, and James Bar.

Township ~~District~~ No. 2.
Dry Creek, Rancheria, Amador, New York Store. Benton Store and Ione Valley ~~[illegible] Store~~

Township No. 3.
Volcano and Fort John

Township No. 4.
Fremontville, Winters Bar, and Lower Mokelumne

Township No 5.
Iowa Log Cabin, San Antonia, Lower Calaveras and Double Springs

Township No 6.
Mokelumne Hill, Willow Bar, Big Bar. Upper Mokelumne, Rich Gulch and South fork of Calaveras

Township No. 7.
O'Neils Bar, San Antonio, McKinneys Humbug Santo Domingo. San Antonio Creek, El Dorado Camp

Township No. 8.
Carsons Creek, Angels Creek and Stanislaus ~~Spring Garden~~, Camp Coyote [illegible]

Township No. 9.
Murphys New Diggings ~~Coyote Flat~~ Diggs. [illegible] Biagatus Diggs Garden

Copy to [illegible] Brown. Deputy
Copy to the Sheriff. delivered 20th Aug

List of Election Precincts in Calaveras County. Page 53 from Minutes of the Court of Sessions, Book June 1850 to October 1851.

Courtesy of Calaveras County Archives

amongst spiritually minded people.

Henry A. Carter a prosecuting attorney was born in New York City in which city he practiced law before coming to California in 1849. A witness to the squabble over the records, he took no part in it. Preferring to advise warring factions to settle disputes without resort to law militated against his success as a lawyer. A valuable citizen, the turmoil of politics soon drew Henry Carter from Jackson to Ione Valley to cultivate the soil.

Sheriff John Hansen, a native of Maine, for an unknown reason disappeared from Double Springs on April 6,1851. A document dated July 18, 1851 reads:

> "Benjamin Marshall, of Murphys Diggings, was appointed to fill the vacancy, caused by the unauthorized absence of John Hansen."

John Hansen, whose natural bent was mining, made a rich haul on the Mokelumne River. The year 1879 found him in San Francisco, a prosperous businessman.

The county seat remained at Jackson until 1853, when by vote of the people; it was transferred to Mokelumne Hill. That year, in the production of gold, that town topped all other mining towns in California. On October 12, 1866, the county records were again removed and San Andreas became the Seat of Justice.

Double Springs is now a legend. While Double Springs was designated as the original Seat of Government, Jackson was the first to be mentioned in local history as having enjoyed that honor.

Footnotes

1 In this book, "Old Calaveras" refers to the area of the present day Calaveras and Amador County. (See map page 3) Much of this text refers to times before Amador County disunited in 1854.

2 Historians say that, the location of the bones was near the town of Waterloo on highway 88 in San Joaquin County.

3 Eleven league of land converts to 48,857 acres.

4 Peter Burnett took an Oath of Office Dec.20,1848. Also see, Apendix A page 332 for a 1850 letter from the town of Jesus Maria to Governor Burnett.

5 Apparently, Charles L. Peck located the land in 1847! This seems an unlikely date because one year before the Gold Rush there were no known non-Indian settlements or people in the foothills. However if he did, this would beg the question, "What was he doing in this area at such an early date and did he know about the gold before James Marshall did? " Marshall's discovery date is January 24, 1848. Nevertheless, Coke Wood in *Calaveras, Land of Skulls* says the 1847 claim was filed with the Alcalde of San Francisco. This pre-emption notice was recorded on September 19,1850 on page 59, in Record B, 3rd Archives, San Francisco.

6 Collier or Collyer

7 According to Coke Wood, *Calaveras, The Land of Skulls*, Footnote 14 in Chapter IV. This building was imported from China by Sam Brannan for his store in Sacramento. In 1849 a man named Dudley bought the houses, which were made of panels and erected them at Double Springs. In the Placer Times, August 11, 1849, appears this advertisement:

"Daily expected on the schooner 'Petrol' from Hong Kong four wooden houses, 12x24 feet, 2 rooms each. Also window glass, 4 couches, 6 tables, 1 chair, 10,000 lbs. rice, 7500 lbs. of sugar, 3 cmt. paint. Apply to Sam Brannon & Co." Three of these houses formed the courthouse in one long structure, twelve by seventy two feet. The court was held in one end, the recorder's office came next, and then came the living quarters of the County Judge and Recorder. Apparently Judge Smith and Recorder Collyer owned the building, for the county records show that Smith sold his half interest to Boileau and Shall for $500, on February 18, 1851; Collyer sold his half to Boileau and Shall for $300 on August 26, 1851, after the county seat had been moved to Jackson in July 1851. Part of the old building still stands behind the old A. R. Wheat house in Double Springs.

8 Hansen or Hanlon

2

AS LUCK WOULD HAVE IT.

The story of Busters Gold.

Gold washers, on the Calaveras River in the summer of 1850 gathered large quantities of dust and nuggets as easily as farmers in the San Joaquin valley gathered kernels of corn. Of the numerous bars in this stream, the one called "Red" was perhaps the richest. Anyway, it was at Red Bar that Daniel Buster, a Mississippian, outfitted as though he intended to spend the rest of his life digging for gold, began his career as a placer miner. Daniel not only brought gold scales with him but his faithful slave, who after setting up camp and getting things in ship shape, went outdoors to helped his master dig. Besides laboring at the water's edge, he cooked food, washed clothes and kept the camp spotlessly clean inside and outside.

Gold Miners slucing on the Calaveras River in 1853. Note use of long toms.
Courtesy of Mary Etta Segerstrom

Just when everything was running along smoothly, the long-toms were ready to be set up, the wooden cradle was down at the river bar waiting to be rocked, as luck would have it, Daniel Buster was seized with incurable homesickness. Armed riders dashing hither and yon had helped to cure him of gold fever but in their boldness and persistency had increased his present malady. Now that he had made his "pile" he decided to return to his parental home in Natchez. Before shaking the dust of Calaveras County off his boots, he rewarded his hard working slave by giving him complete freedom and his "wet diggings" chock full of the yellow metal. A few days later when Daniel rode from Red Bar, he left behind him a namesake Dan Buster, a free and grateful young Negro.

In the year of '52 the southern mines were fraught with danger. In Calaveras County along the banks of rivers and creeks, bandits were plentiful that year. Dan Buster, a peaceable Negro, dreaded to even think about a Mexican saber lest he be made to feel as other gold washers at Red Bar. He broke camp, loaded his whitish-grey burro with gold, camp equipment, mining tools and left Red Bar for Mokelumne Hill.

In this greatest of gold rush towns, together with several others of his race he mined on Nigger Hill. There the "color" shimmered in every ounce of soil he shoveled up. Here Dan Buster mined a second fortune and having more faith in Mother Earth than in mankind, he buried his gold in the secret ground.

Dan wasn't one of those hangers-on of the wild days. When the precious metal was no longer to be found on Nigger Hill, he again loaded his burro with camp fixin's and packed out of the lively mining town to try his luck elsewhere. His wanderings finally led to the San Antonio Ridge country and right there he remained for the rest of his life.

He built a cabin for himself near Calaveritas, one room, a kind of lean-to affair. It was nothing to boast about, except the fireplace, which contained crystals from a mine near Mokelumne Hill. His aversion to "white trash" being very great and there being none of his own kind on the ridge, except for an occasional visit from Caleb Johnson[1], a former Mississippi slave, was alone and companion less.

Caleb, now a gold hunter owning a placer claim on McKinney Creek below the ridge, was lacking in honesty and industry.

Dan occasionally rode to Mokelumne Hill in broad daylight. The return trip was invariably made under the cover of darkness. Jim Smiley, who cabined close-by, often wondered just what it was that Dan brought back with him, that couldn't stand sunlight. Had anyone told Jim that Dan's burro's back was burdened with treasure on the return trip from Mokelumne Hill, he wouldn't have believed him at that time.

Dan, usually as silent-tongued as an Indian, let his secret out of the bag one evening. He was in a jovial mood. His friend Caleb Johnson had

Raggio [Dughi, Brockman] Adobe, El Dorado Town [Mountain Ranch] Calaveras County. Looking up Washington Street to the Rodesino Adobe on Garabaldi Street. Imagemaker- W.H. Knowles- May 1936.

Courtesy of California Historical Society.

trudged up the hill from his brush shanty near Humbug on McKinney Creek and in his hand had a forked stick strung with speckled trout that he had angled from that stream.

"Lordly me, Cale,
you'all made a fine catch, yo' did", Dan greeted.

The "fish fry" spiced with Caleb's fabulous tales about gold strikes and the wild doings in El Dorado Town [Mountain Ranch], put Dan in a mood to talk. So in a burst of confidence, he told Caleb about his decision to remove his gold from Mokelumne Hill to San Antonio Ridge. Caleb, a crafty self-seeking Negro, offered to give Dan three lead-lined Chinese tea boxes which he on his own back would be glad to tote up the hill the very next day. True to his word, Caleb lugged the tea boxes up the trail and deposited them in front of Dan's fireplace. He even helped Dan pry up the rocks forming the hearth-stone, helped him scoop out red dirt, place his gold in the tea boxes, bury them deep in the ground, refill the hole and reset the hearthstone rocks.

A few years later, in the dead of night, four desperados entered Caleb's bush shanty near the Humbug. After giving the lone Negro a rightful beating, robbed him of his gold. The robbers thinking that their victim was dead rode back to El Dorado Town, each feeling certain that he would never be accused of having taken part in the outrage against "Old Cale"[2].

Dan Buster could hardly believe his ears when Henry Angel, a prospector on the ridge, dropped into his cabin to tell him about his friend's misfortune. Fearful that he too might be molested, Dan ripped up rocks that very night

Bar in the Raggio-Dughi Adobe in El Dorado Town in 1906 [Mountain Ranch]

Courtesy of Calaveras County Historical Society

and dug up the tea boxes, carted them outdoors where he buried them again. Nobody except himself, know exactly where he secreted these.

Painfully and slowly, Caleb dragged his cruelly beaten body to George Nichols[3] Cave City Hotel to make report of the robbery. A full moon flooding his shelter hut had made it possible for Caleb to get a good view of the four intruders whose names he whispered into George's sympathetic ear. George Nichols, a native of Athens, Greece, at once reported the crime to the authorities in Mokelumne Hill.

Vincenzo Raggio

Courtesy of Barbara Kathan

Ben Thorn the Sheriff, mounted on a fleet dappled grey, rode alone the next morning from Mokelumne Hill to El Dorado Town. In his pockets were handcuffs with which he intended to bind the wrists of the four criminals. The complaint lodged against Bill Holt, Andy Keegan[4], Jim Collins, and Dave Parks by Caleb wasn't the only one chalked up against their names. Holt was wanted for murder and all four had committed robberies singly in pairs and together.

Inside of Vincente [Vincenzo] Raggio's combination grocery store and a saloon[5], Ben Thorn found waiting for him Ned Bushyhead, a full blood Cherokee, who was the Constable of that township. Exceedingly brave and of striking appearance, Ned Bushyhead was a true marksman. After exchanging greetings the two officers walked together to the bar at one end of which Keegan, Collins, and Parks were shaking a dice box and drinking whiskey.

Edward (Ned) Bushyhead, Constable of El Dorado Mining District in 1850's

Courtesy of C.C.H.S...

"Where is Bill Holt, Collins?" asked Ben Thorn.

"At the Flat, I suppose," he answered grudgingly.

"I'll go down and bring him up," Ben said to Ned.

"I'd better go along, hadn't I?" Ned queried.

"No. But you can help put irons on these men."

Under Ben Thorn's steady eye each offender, taken by surprise, submitted to arrest.

Ben Thorn, County Sheriff

Courtesy of C.C.H.S.

Bill Holt was a squaw man. Ben could see smoke curling skyward from the rock chimney of his cabin on Colton Flat. A moment later, he knocked on a flimsy plank door. The wooden bolt on the inside was drawn back and the door partially opened by a young and comely squaw, whose emotionless black eyes betrayed neither a surprise nor fear.

"Hello, Lily", greeted Ben quietly.

"Hello" she mumbled hanging her head.

"Tell Bill I want him",

Lily. "Bill, heem no here.

Heem go way, long time now,"

Lily, loyal to her man, lied.

"Come out, Bill!

I'm here to take you!" Ben shouted.

And since Bill didn't come out, he shoved open the door, brushed past Lily and stalked into the room where he forced Bill to surrender his weapons, in fact, placed him under arrest.

With Ned Bushyhead's help all four prisoners were taken to the Mokelumne Hill where Ben Thorn lodged them in the jail. For long years thereafter, these men walked a chalked line under the watchful eyes of the guards in the State's prison at San Quentin.

Shortly after the episode on McKinney Creek, Caleb straddled his burro and rode up to the ridge to pay a visit to Dan. Dan may have told him about the removal of his gold and he may have pointed out to him the exact location of his underground treasure. Those persons, who knew Dan Buster best, often surmised this to be the case.

Old Cale, no longer able to find gold in his claim, left the Humbug for Old Woman's Gulch near Mokelumne Hill. In this gulch he washed sand without ever laying his eyes on a nugget or a single speck of gold dust. The small amount of dust garnered on McKinney Creek, which he had banked against the lean days, sufficed only to stay his hunger. This state of affairs continued until 1866[6], when in his cabin on the ridge, Dan Buster died. Thereafter, stories tinged with mystery concerning Old Cale were freely circulated and were far reaching. The removal of large amounts of dust and nuggets from San Antonio Ridge to Old Woman's Gulch was the charge brought by Dame Rumor against Caleb Johnson's name.

News of Dan Buster's death caused quite a stir especially amongst treasure hunters. Shortly after, men were flocking to his cabin, their objective being buried gold. In their frenzy they tore down the fireplace, yanked up the hearthstone and dug up the dirt floor. Every so often gold seekers of another generation, may be found on the Ridge, searching vainly for Dan Buster's buried treasure. Mexicans, who believed that on nights of a storm, little fires burned over buried gold, would go out into the darkness, to search for "gold fires", which like Dan Buster's hidden fortune, they never found.

There were those persons who believed that Old Cale had an under ground treasure vault. Although he owned no mining claim and never did a stroke of work afterwards, yet in Mokelumne Hill he spent freely in the stores and paid for all purchases with gold dust. When asked by a merchant why he no longer mined in the gulch, he replied,

"On 'count of de rheumatism."

Flower and vegetable gardens surrounded his shabby and squatty home. Non-social with those of his own color he asked favors of no man and confiding in no man, he lived alone. If a Negro attempted to settle near his cabin, he raised a rumpus and ran him out of the gulch. Once Old Cale's

Tom Brockman, Grandfather of Frank Brockman of Mountain Ranch. This photo shows the tools and equipment necessary for a gold miner to work his claim.

Courtesy of Frank and Judy Brockman

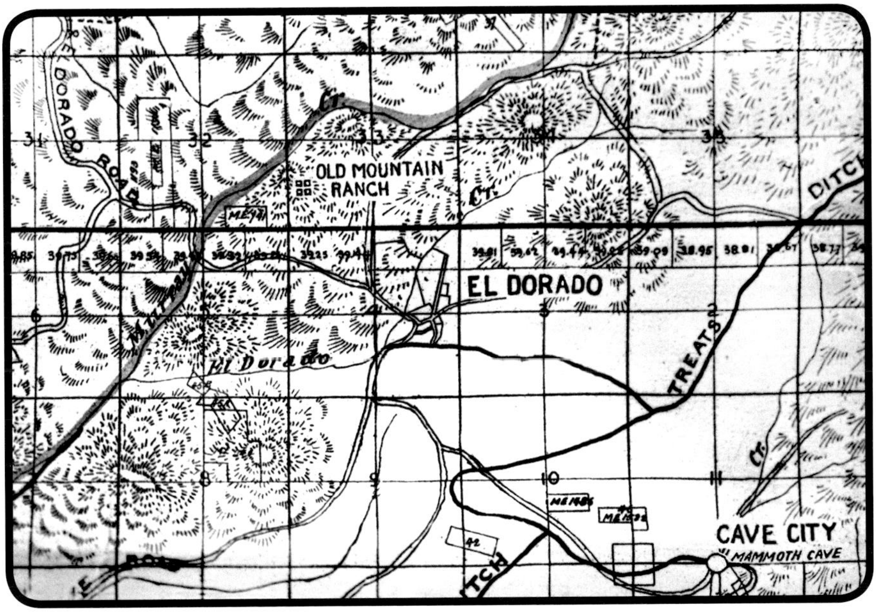

Detail of an early map of Mountain Ranch area. Note location of the original site of Old Mountain Ranch. McKinneys or McKinney's Humbug was located half way between El Dorado and Cave City.

Courtesy of Calaveras County Historical Society

African blood was aroused, he would become a man to fear. A Negro Sam Millegan, built a cabin on government land on this gulch and the "master of the gulch" Old Cale, made things so hot for him that he was obliged to abandon his home and go elsewhere.

Ben Joiner, another of his race, attempted to mine in Old Woman's Gulch, but Johnson wrathfully disputed his right to do so. Joiner insisted upon his right to mine with fatal results. The humble colored man Joiner was slain by the opulent Negro Johnson. Arrested on a murder charge, he entered a plea of self-defense and in a civil court was exonerated.

That Caleb Johnson considered himself the heir to Dan Buster's gold was no doubt true. When on his deathbed he was asked to reveal the exact location of his underground gold cache, instead of divulging his secret, he gestured to a spot outside his front door and in a feeble voice said,

"No sah, I's goin' ter
Let m'gol lie out dar in de groun'
Whar I'se a-goin'."

Footnotes

1 Caleb Johnson was known as "El Dorado"

2 O.C. Treleaven in *Old Men in the Sun* states, "Ben Thorn, he never dogged it. I remember one time, Thorn had to go out and bring in a man named Long-Haired Brown. You see, this Brown and Bill Holt, that's the same Holt that Fernell killed in the doorway of the Mitchler Hotel in Murphys. They had robbed a Negro called El Dorado. "That's the only name anybody ever called him, that I ever knew of. Well, this El Dorado, he was supposed to have around $600 hid in his cabin and a lot of gold dust- nobody ever said how much was buried outside in the ground in the Dutch oven".

3 In a manuscript *Stories of the Olden, Golden Days Of California* by Kate Emily (Pillsbury) Ham the name of George the Greek is spelled as George Nicholeus.

4 Ibid., the name is spelled Andy Kiggan.

5 This Raggio store was located in the Raggio-Dughi adobe building across from the present Post Office. Later this business was conducted under the name of Dughi & Co. with Mr. Raggio being a silent partner.

6 Historian, Coke Wood says Feb.1863 and Desire Fricot says 1872.

3

ALCALDE TALIFERRO'S STORY

In 1849 the Mexicans for the most part were a thieving, bloodthirsty set of gamblers and cut throats[1]. There were, of course, a few honest men amongst them. The Mexicans did not like the Americans. Americans had just whipped them and taken California away from them. We found the rivers, creeks, and gulches with gold and were filling up the place with an enterprising population.

We suffered immensely from their depredations as just about every good horse that was brought into this county [Calaveras] was sooner or later stolen by them. They rifled our flumes, appropriated our property and eluded all our means of detection. Some of our companions would disappear very suddenly. We knew that they had been secretly shot or stabbed by a Greaser, but it was only by a mere chance, that a hot trail was ever discovered.

Whenever suspicious eyes lighted upon one of them, it usually went hard with him. He was lucky if he escaped with his life. Many an offender bore the marks which sundry whippings, chokings and ear-droppings had inflicted upon his carcass. Now, as I look back to those days, I think we sometimes made mistakes, but then, the aggravation we endured was very great. If both sides could be toted up, it would be, I think an even thing between us. There was no law in 1849, except such as we made. Every man carried his life in his hand and I believe we did the best that could be done.

The Mexicans learned how to mine before coming here and excelled in gold digging. Daily, they made new and valuable discoveries. If we found anything it was by accident, but we had come to California to find gold and were determined not to be thwarted.

One night David Lattimer, known as "Dad", Captain Jim Box, James Harris, Charles Bray, Captain Gilson, Ned Morgan, Hubert Ide, Frank Forest, Joe Abbott, and myself, were encamped on rich placer ground near San Andreas. Long about midnight thirty Mexicans passed by silently like buckskin booted Indians. Captain Box was doing guard duty that night. Box who understood the Spanish language, heard one Mexican say to another:

"We must kill the first man that comes into camp."

"But, they can kill us too," replied the other.

"Well,

we have all ready put one of the cursed Gringos out of the Way."
"What Gringo?" he queried.
"The one that was a Captain at the Battle of Monterey."
"What did you do with his body?"
"We buried it in a tent in San Andreas."

Captain Ben Osborne, popular with the "Boys" had been missing for several months. He was a soldier in the Mexican War and was prone to brag. A free drinker, he had the habit when only half drunk, of fighting old battles. He found pleasure in relating, within hearing of the Mexicans, his feats of valor at the battle of Monterey and the dark, scornful looks they cast his way, had seemed to please Ben.

His friends frequently warned him of the consequences of his ill-timed mirth and brag but he would laugh at their fears. He had bragged on so many occasions that, among the Mexicans, he was designated only as the "Captain in the Battle of Monterey"

In San Andreas, in 1849-1850, a Chilean man and woman operated a Fonda, famous for it's chili con carne de Colorado of which Captain Osborne was very fond. He spent many of his evenings in this Fonda, flirting and dancing with its sparkling eyed hostess. They would be playing Monte, drinking and feasting on chili con carne. He was there one night in December 1849 and was never again seen. Besides a large amount of gold dust he had with him $300 in gold coins. His friends who had suspected that he had been roughly treated made a diligent search for him but were unable to find him. Then, finally, in 1850, after the confab between the two Mexicans was overheard by Box, our boys lost their desire to dig fortunes. Possessed with a determination to apprehend the murderers of their comrade, they made a close observation of the men whose talk had revealed the crime. They tracked the one that was leading a packhorse and the other leading a black donkey. The two Mexicans, followed by Box and a few of our companions, halted near McKinney's Humbug[2].

A short distance from a limestone cave, our boys fell back and hid themselves in brush. After breakfast, Charlie Bray rushed into the main camp with a message from Box to Taliferro[3]. Alcalde[4] Taliferro and a few others spread the word through all the placers. It resulted in raising a company of forty volunteers to aid Box in making a capture. The volunteers were well armed and met at Henry Schroebel's trading post in San Andreas at ten o' clock at night. An hour later, under the guidance of Charlie Bray, they left for McKinney's Humbug and arrived there the following morning. Among the others were: Taliferro, Knapp, Broughton, Captain Gilson, John Morrison, Ned Morgan, Hubert Ide and Joe Abbott.

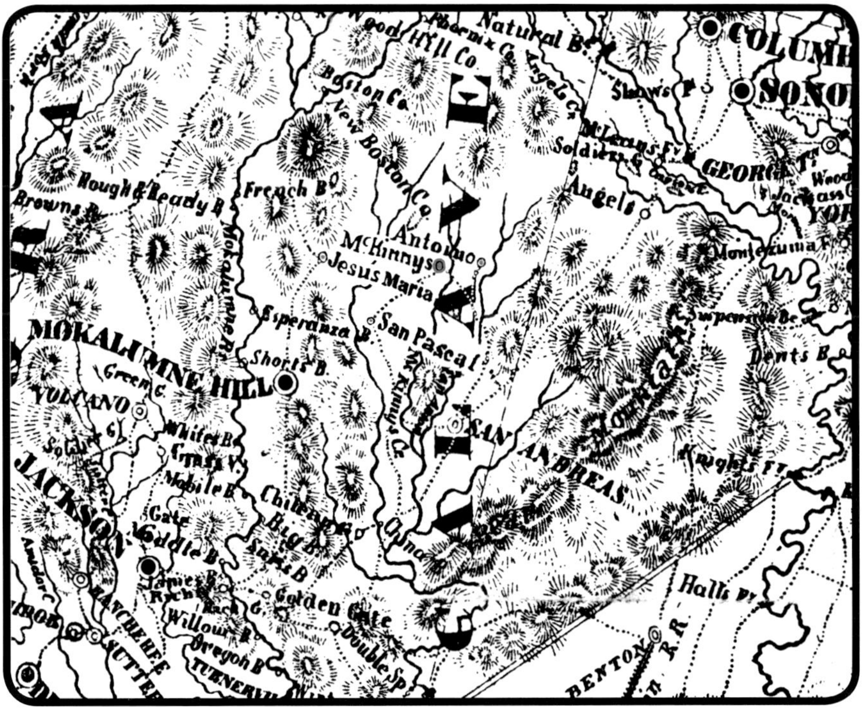

**Detail of "Topographical map of the Mineral Districts of California"
Map printed in 1853, the information gathering stage must have taken more than two years since the Calaveras County section is shown as it existed in 1849-50. Note location of McKinnys between Jesus Maria and Antone.**

Courtesy of California State Library

By arrangement Taliferro, Box and Harris were to visit the Mexican camp while the others were to remain on a hill overlooking the camp. The firing of a gun was to be a signal to tell them when to make a dash to join the main group. When three of our boys reached the camp several of the Mexicans were busy preparing breakfast and the others were still in their blankets. There were seemingly two parties of Mexicans, camped about 200 yards apart. Box soon spotted the one, whom he thought, was the chief speaker in the midnight conversation. Under a pretense of shooting a jay, he fired his gun. At once 38-armed men rushed down the steep hill and into the camp of the Mexicans.

The approach of the armed company brought to each copper-hued face an expression of fear. The little company formed a picket guard round and enclosed the camp:

"It is my duty," said Taliferro to the Mexicans,
"To inform you that you are all under arrest.
A crime has been committed and we have reasons
For believing the perpetrators of it are in this camp."

The silence that followed was deathlike. The Mexicans exchanged terrified glances but made no reply. Finally, one after another avowed his innocence. In those days next to murder, horse stealing was the greatest of crimes, one for which the Mexicans were noted. Each Mexican said the he was a hard working honest miner.

The questioning at the first camp was interrupted by a loud yell from James Harris, who while visiting the second camp had found the horse and black donkey observed by Dad Lattimer. Convinced that they had arrested the wrong men, our boys apologized and went to the other camp where the scene at the first camp was reenacted:

Taliferro made no bones about the nature of the crimes.
"We have no charge of horse stealing against you," he told them.
"One of our comrades has been murdered and his murderers
Or persons, who know about them, are in this camp.
We are here to find them and bring them to justice".

The nine prisoners were disarmed, formed in a line and with their hands bound back of them, were marched off under an armed guard. The Mexicans of the first camp offered us assistance, which we declined. Our object being to find both the murderer and the remains of our comrade, we resolved to the following expedient.

Where three small streams came together, we set up a tribunal before which the prisoners were placed, the line addressed in the Spanish language by Captain Gilson.

"You are," he said,
"Very near the end of your earthly career.
We have evidence that some of your number either killed Ben Osborne, or know who committed the deed.
He was our friend, greatly beloved by us.
Some of the men here, related at midnight
The circumstances of the murder in a Fonda in San Andreas.
And since the knowledge of our comrade's murder is in your keeping,
It is our intention:
To hang each of you with this single exception,
The man who will tell us how, when, where and by whom
Ben Osborne was killed and where he was buried,
He shall escape punishment and to him, we pledge our honor".

Then with a view of impressing the prisoners with the seriousness of our intentions, four of our boys went to the opposite hill to prepare some trees for hangings.

When Gilson had finished his address, a handsome, intelligent looking young man, not a day over 24, was asked to reply to the charge. His lips quivered with emotion and his eyes filled with tears when he said:

"Gentlemen, I am a Cuban, born in Havana where my parents reside. I am in California to make a fortune digging gold and for no other purpose. I reached San Andreas only ten days ago. Previous to that I was a clerk in Mr. Sanderson's store in Stockton. I am not a Spaniard, only speak the Spanish language. Naturally, I sought associates with whom I could converse and they were only Mexicans. I have been well raised. I was taught to fear God and live honestly. This is the first time I have ever been accused of a crime. It is hard gentlemen, that I should suffer for the crime of another. And that my name should be blackened with so infamous a charge as that of taking the life of a fellow man. Gentlemen, I am innocent!"

We were convinced of the truth of this statement but desiring to appear unmoved by his appeal, ordered him to resume his place in the line.

An old man about forty was next addressed. From his dark eyes a calm resignation beamed forth. He seemed not to be afraid of the fate before him and said:

"I have nothing to say to you.
I know nothing about this murder.
My companions here know me to be an honest and hard working man. My wife and daughter are living in Jesus Maria Campo,
There I have been working, they are very dear to me."

Then, turning to his companions, he added:
"Bear to them from me, my dying blessing.
Tell them that, I die with a clean conscience and innocent.
My only regret is, that I am forced to die without the rites of the church."

We marched him over the hill to the scaffold, placed him under it, and asked him if he would seize the opportunity to escape.
"I will not," he replied.
"I know nothing.
Your treatment is cruel and if not here,
Then in Almighty God's Kingdom.
You will be made to account for it."

Impressed with his sincerity, we sent him over the hill beyond and gave him assurance that no harm will come to him and in like manner, two others were disposed of.

Our fifth prisoner, a sharp-eyed young fellow aged 24, displayed so much bravado that we removed him to the scaffold the stout pine limb, put a rope around his neck and were ready to jerk on it, when he became greatly alarmed and consented to tell us all he knew.

He went into detail about several murders, some upon hearsay others that he had witnessed, but made no mention of Osborne. The sharp crack of a rifle brought our inquisition of him to an abrupt close. We sent him to join the others while we hurried the camp. On our way down the hill we saw one of the prisoners running toward a little valley with several of our men in hot pursuit. Taliferro, Broughton and Gilson mounted their horses and gave chase. The fellow, reaching a ledge of quartz inaccessible to the horses, escaped. On returning to camp, the remaining prisoners were ordered to lie down, their faces to the ground. The young Cuban alarmed, prayed with earnest devotion for relief.

During our absence, one of our prisoners took the chance of running for his life and another more closely guarded, attempted to make a dash for liberty but he failed. The runaway was fired at and wounded in the shoulder. These two men were the very ones whose midnight conversation had aroused our suspicions. We conducted the one in custody to the gallows. An obstinate wretch, instead of talking, he dug into his pocket and brought out a large sack of gold dust and handed it to us saying:

"Here, gentlemen, is this what you want.
Take it and give me my freedom."

To this, Taliferro replied:

"You have mistaken our men.
We are neither robbers nor highwaymen.
We are convinced that you know all about the murder of our friend.
Take back your gold and give us the information we seek, or
It shall be buried with you."

John Morrison, holding the hemp rope, resented the impudent Mexicans remark and urged:

"Come on boys, let us choke him a little anyhow."

So, the rope was put around his neck and pulled by John to a dangerous tension.

"Wait a minute," begged the man with a noose around his neck,
"Let us talk this matter over.
If I tell you where the Capitan is buried,
You say that you will spare my life.
Now, what assurance do I have that you will protect me?
My countrymen will kill me for making this exposure and
To shield me from their vengeance will be most difficult for you".

"We will use precaution to prevent any leakage of your information," promised Taliferro.
"We will take you into our camp or if
You wish to leave San Andreas for your safety,
We will furnish you with means of an escort.
Our honor is pledged to this statement."
"Well, on those conditions, I will talk. Your friend, the Capitan, went to his favorite Fonda in San Andreas, got drunk, made a great display of his gold dust and boasted about the number of Mexicans he had killed at the Battle of Monterey. While he was bragging and eating chili con carne, the beautiful Chilean woman told her husband to kill him and take his gold and money. He refused. She insisted. So, he stabbed him in the heart. But how to dispose of the body the murderer did not know. The woman laughed at him while closing and locking the doors of the Fonda. She picked up a mattress lying on the dirt floor and ordered her husband and another man to dig a hole where the mattress had lain. When the hole was deep enough, they laid the Capitan's dead body in it and covered it with dirt. The grave was leveled and the remaining dirt swept up and emptied into San Andreas gulch and the mattress on which the woman slept that night, was replaced. If you wish, I will disguise myself and go with you to the Fonda and stand in the corner where the Capitan is buried."

When this prisoner saw that no harm had been done to the other Mexicans, he regretted having fallen into the trap we had set. The confession made, we removed the rope from his neck and brought him with us into camp. We prepared a good breakfast and the entire company sat down and ate heartily. Breakfast over, we turned to the Mexicans and expressed our regrets for the harsh measures we had employed and parted with them on friendly terms. We made up to the young Cuban who had impressed us so favorably; by a handsome purse which with expressions of gratitude, which he accepted.

We said goodbye to the Mexicans and started with our prisoner for San Andreas. When we arrived within two miles of the town, we stopped because our man insisted that we had misunderstood him and that he didn't know where the Capitan was buried. So, we resorted to hanging a second time, but thinking the information sufficient, we again removed the rope and marched into town with a full and well armed force.

In San Andreas, we found the escaped Mexican spreading the wildest sort of reports one being that we had hanged all his comrades and that only he escaped with a gun shot wound in his shoulder. San Andreas at that time was full of gamblers who were on the friendliest terms with their patrons, the Mexicans. The gamblers not only censured but also defied and threatened us as well. We stood our ground and went in a body to the Fonda only to find it vacant. The Chilean and his wife had suddenly fled from the town.

That day, underneath a shabby tule mattress, we found the body of our murdered comrade. We made efforts to apprehend and arrest the murderers, but they having a full day's start and we having no telegraph or railroad to stop them could not prevent their reaching San Francisco and their native Chile.

That day in San Andreas, we set our prisoner free. Few gentle instructions as to his future conduct were given. These, to the last day of his life, he observed to the letter.

description of McKinnies Humbug.

"This place is situated on the north fork of the Oneil branch of the Calaveras (river) and 16 miles southeast of Mokelumne Hill and was first discovered by James McKinnie.

"He reported the mines in the vicinity to be very rich and a large number of men came here in the winter of '50 and '51 and worked here.

"But the most of them scarcely made their board and in consequence they pronounced it a humbug and it goes by the name of McKinnies Humbug.

"I left the Humbug in Jan. 1852, completely humbuged out of my winter's work besides about $600 in hard cash. Such has been my d–n luck so far in this land of golden dreams, dreams never to be realized by me, I am afraid.

Thomas Pitt 1852 Diary. **Published in Stockton Record Feb. 21, 1971**

Footnotes

1 Editors - This comment and others to be found elsewhere in this book reflect the highly negative attitudes toward Mexicans and Indians that were prevalent amoung the California gold-seekers. These should not be read as a reflection of realty.

2 McKinney's Diggings, later called McKinney's Humbug was an very early community of miners. It was located on McKinney Creek about half way between El Dorado Camp and Cave City, a distance of one to two miles northwest of the cave.

3 Taliferro, Taglifrerro or Taliaferro. State of California Census of 1850, Theophilus W. Taliaferro is listed as follows: Age 30 yrs, Male, Miner, and Native of Alabama. He was a Justice of the Peace prior to 1855. He went to San Francisco; there he became a Judge.

4 An Alcalde was a Mexican official whose duties combined those of Mayor, Justice of the Peace and a Constable.

4

EL DORADO TOWN

Situated halfway between San Andreas and Hay Press Flat [Sheep Ranch], the town was an exciting place in the first years of its existence. Lawless men took refuge in El Dorado[1] and from here in their efforts to elude the law they followed the Indian trails and "deer cuts" to safer ground.

Downtown El Dorado in 1892. Mr. Alfonse Rodesino is third from left and John Rodesino is fourth.

Courtesy of Alberts Family.

Giovanni (John) Rodesino

Courtesy of Alberts Family

In 1851 El Dorado had every appearance of a town. Flags were flying from restaurants, hotels and trading posts. The saloons were prosperous and at the gambling tables large amounts of dust was wagered. The most popular of the games being Monte, Lump o'gold and Stud Poker. Men, many with tousled hair covering their heads and long shaggy beards, resembling those of Babylonian soldiers from history books, poured dust upon the green felt until their buckskin pokes were empty. Come sunrise they were at work on the claims. Mexicans, with serapes [Mexican ponchos] thrown carelessly across their shoulders stood by, each anxious for a chance to display four aces. At the crude bar, liquor was poured three fingers high for fifty cents. In a far corner of the room idlers gathered to listen to some "old toper" fiddle and sing:

"Get me down my high top boots, and my tall silk hat."

In El Dorado's flamboyant days, when barkers in raucous voice yelled,
"Inside gentlemen,
Inside is the Monte bank that will add
weight to your bags of dust"

The waists of ten out of every twelve men there were ornamented with California jewelry in the way of six-shooters and dirk or Bowie knives. The native Californian too was much in evidence. Proudly he strode from hitching post to fandango, the top of boot revealing the silver handle of his never absent boot knife.

William (Bill) Irvine
Courtesy of C.C.H.S.

William Irvine came to El Dorado early and did his full share towards promoting prosperity in this community. Able and energetic Bill Irvine was quarrelsome and vindictive, demanding a voice and a blow in all public affairs. In 1852, he erected at his quartz mine, a short distance east of El Dorado. This was California's first stream ore crusher. We next find Bill Irvine in San Andreas and a little later on at Carson Hill.

D.F. Lovelace circa 1905
Courtesy of C.C.H.S.

In the days when Spanish and "Jay Eye See" [J.I. Case] bits brought horses, their mouths bleeding to El Dorado Town, the permanent settlers were Adolphus Coulter, Frank McPherson, John Walker, Giovanni Rodesino, Martin Rodesino, Henri Renaud, Vincenze Raggio, Bartolomeo Dughi, William L. Henderson, Robert Bowen, W.W. O'Neil, Hugh Gallagher, H.N. Butterfield, David Badgley, Dan Fillippini[2], Jesus Gomez, F.

Comeres, David Billa, J. McCellon, Thomas Stark, William Lloyd, and L. Hastings.

Rodesino building was aquired by the Sender Family in early 1940. This building was destroyed by fire December 1968. In its place there is now a well stocked, modern grocery and hardware store.

Courtesy of Alberts Family

El Dorado Town's adobe buildings were the largest and best to be erected in Calaveras County[3]. Colonel D. F. Lovelace in 1850 established this settlement's first trading post and was considered a rich man but something went wrong, for soon we find him driving a stage for Tom Matteson of Murphys and still later he was a member of the Board of Supervisors of Calaveras County. While handling the leather ribbons, Lovelace's tall yarns, which he delighted in spinning, won him countless friends. When he died in his cabin on San Antone Ridge his mining partner was heard to say:

"Few were,
In the old days as kind and
As large-hearted and
As free from fault as was Colonel Lovelace."

Edward (Ned) Bushyhead, born in the Cherokee Nation, was the Constable of the El Dorado Mining District which included Chee Chee Flat, Broderick, Mountain Ranch, Lava Flats (Tom Martin's ranch), Cave City and Colton Flat.

Vincenze Raggio, B. Dughi and G. Rodesino were the leading merchants for this and the surrounding settlements.

William H. Clary in 1850, located claims and established a trading post

Children at play in El Dorado Town. Tisher building on the left and Rodesino on the right, circa 1920.

Courtesy of Gladys Matson

at Broderick, a short distance from El Dorado Town. He was alone in his cabin one night when it was entered by bandits who demanded his gold. Bill Clary, brave as the bravest, refused to surrender it but after the robber had stabbed him with a Bowie knife, he produced his gold sack. In the dead of night, the wounded man made his way from trading post to El Dorado Town and all the way along the Broderick trail he grimly held together a deep gash, which at any moment, threatened to disembowel him.

William Jersabold Knight was in his cabin at El Dorado Town when he was shot and killed by Andy Keegan, who in this instance, appears to have acted in self-defense. Knight was buried on the day of his death in the public graveyard[4] in El Dorado Town. Knight was a miner and it was said that he possessed considerable property. However, his funeral expenses were as follows:

Lumber for coffin	$1.50
Coffin trimmings	$2.25
Digging Grave	$2.00
Shroud	$5.00
Total	$10.75
Cash on person	$5.00
Unpaid	$5.75

El Dorado Town, now called Mountain Ranch, is a quiet place, full of reminders of the Gold Rush days. The old adobes are still in excellent condition and in constant use.

Dan Filippini on his farm in El Dorado along Whiskey Slide road.

Paul Lewis Photo courtesy of Wally Motloch

Attilio Dominghini freighting supplies to customers near El Dorado.

Courtesy of Calaveras County Archives

Mountain Ranch Hotel in El Dorado Town

Courtesy of Gladys Matson

El Dorado Days Parade in Mountain Ranch in 1966.

Courtesy of Alberts Family

Footnotes

1 During the early Gold Rush days, this El Dorado of the Calaveras County was also called El Dorado Camp like Angels Camp or French Camp. Henry O. Mace in his book Between the Rivers states that there were a least seven towns in California called El Dorado.

2 The proper spelling is Filippini.

3 In Mountain Ranch today one can find some of the best examples of Gold Rush architecture, Joses Ranch house (1852), Dominghini-Alberts adobe (1856), and Raggio/Dughi-Brockman adobe (1861) All three of these buildings are used to this day (2005) and are in excellent shape of preservation.

4 This El Dorado-Mountain Ranch Cemetery is located behind Sender's Store. Many of the original settlers are buried there. The cemetery is in very good shape, well worth exploring.

Denig's Express from San Andreas to Upper Calaveritas, every day except Monday. On Wednesday, Friday and Sunday to Old Gulch, Washington Ranch, El Dorado Camp, Mountain Ranch and Chee Chee Flat. On Saturday to Indian Creek and San Antone Camp. Persons receiving letters or packages by mail or express can have them attended to by leaving their orders at Foster & Roweth's Saloon, Upper Calaveritas; Thompson and Bencroft's Store, Old Gulch; Barker's Saloon, Washington Ranch; Rodesino's Store, El Dorado; Molmes' Store. Mt. Ranch, and MsGowan's Store, Chee Chee Flat; office in the drug store of M. Burkhardt, San Andreas.

Cave City Hotel. Cave City, Calaveras County, Calif., George Nichols, proprietor. (The Cave.) The most celebrated curiosity on the Pacific Coast is now in a condition to receive visitors and none should fail to visit this wonderful work of nature while an opportunity offers.

Early newspaper, circa 1852, an ad in Emmett Joy Scrapbook.

Courtesy of C.C. Archives

5

CAVE CITY

In October 1849 James R. McKinney [in 1850 census, he is listed as James B. McKinnie], while out prospecting, discovered a cave. Later it was called Cave City[1] the cave attracted many people, especially those in search of scientific information.

THE HOTEL.

In 1853 it was taken up, under a pre-emption right, by Messrs. Magee and Angel, who erected a large and substantial hotel adjoining the cave, for the convenience of the public, at a cost of about four thousand five hundred dollars. This hotel is commodious and comfortable, and we shall long remember the enjoyment of our visit, and the personal attention we received from the agreeable and enterprising proprietors.

VIEW OF THE HOTEL AT THE CAVE.

Clipping from a old newspaper, undated and unidentified.

Courtesy of Wally Motloch

In March 1852 one caver wrote as follows:
"I have no words with which to describe this great curiosity. We entered through a small doorway, blasted out of a ledge of rocks, sufficient in size to permit a person to enter. One after another we

John Fairchild of the California Caverns is shown here conducting a tour of the undergroung cave complex at Cave City. The caves are a true wonder and are well worth exploring. Open to public during the summer season.

Photo Wally Motloch

crept slowly along a narrow and difficult passage some 30 or 40 feet long. In order to reach a room called the Council Chamber we were often forced to stoop down.

The Cataract is a room well deserving of its name. Another cavern, the Cathedral, the roof of which is 60 feet high is awe-inspiring. The vast space of about 100 feet square was terrifying. Beyond the Cathedral is another imposing chamber; where in the center of the floor stands an excellent likeness of a Roman Bishop in full robes of state. This curious object has no head.

Climbing and holding fast to our sputtering candles, we soon reached the most splendid sight of all – the Bridal Chamber, in which is a fairy stairway. The candlelight revealed a scene of indescribable beauty. Myriads of weird stone figures were to be seen with folded draperies. The solemn stone images resembling pagan gods glorified the archaic edifice.

Thousands of pendants glistening like translucent alabaster were remindful of fine wooden carvings and silver filigree work. Angels with snowy out-spread wings were represented in this strange underground vault.

The Music Room is connected with the Bridal Chamber by different openings. The former room, so called by reason of its having some singular formations, in appearance like sounding boards. A number of stalactites arranged in a line, gradually slope from large to very small ones and these if properly struck will produce musical tones ranging from a common bass to the highest tone known to the human ear."

On the walls of the caves there are literally thousands of signitures of visitors and well known personalities with dates to 1850's

Photo Wally Motloch

Like the cave in Volcano, heedless persons eventually destroyed this wonder of its day in Old Calaveras. At Cave City it was the gold washers themselves who were responsible for the obliteration of this limestone cavern. The miners of this section permitted the slime and tailings from their claims above to fill up the passageway leading to the cave's entrance, over which now grows the mountain laurel, manzanita, and wild rose thickets.

George Nichols born in Athens Greece and his wife, Juana [Johanna], a native of Hermosillo Mexico, were among Cave City's first settlers. Their little rose-embowered inn was famous throughout the Southern Mines for the excellence of the food Juana prepared for her guests. The custodian of the cave Mr. Nichols, whose nickname was "George de Greek" was respectful of Nature's handiwork, but he was obliged to stand by helplessly and watch its destruction.

Heinrich Diedrich, known to his partners as the Flying Dutchman, mined at McKinney's Humbug near by in 1850. The "Coyote" holes he dug and quickly abandoned still honey comb the ground.

The young Herculean blacksmith Abraham Vandling born in Buck's County, Pennsylvania, left Murphys with Captain Hornsby to try their luck at McKinney's camp. Vandling failed to hang up a record for panning gold at McKinney's. However, after lugging a long tom on his back from the cave to

Johanna (Juana or Chonna) Nichols, owner of the Cave City Hotel and a caretaker of the Caves. Circa 1885

Courtesy of C.C.H.S.

Establishment of Roads

In the matter of the petition for a public highway to commence at Moquelumne Hill and running to Murphy's Camp, via Mountain Ranch, McKinney's Humbug and Cave City.

In this matter the Board ordered that notices be posted up along the proposed line of said road notifying all persons owning land or otherwise interested, to appear at the next session of the Board and make known any objections they may have to the said road being declared a public highway.

Emmett Joy Scrapbook, undated and untitled newspaper clipping. [info 1851?]

Courtesy of C.C. Archives

his cabin in Murphys diggings, the strength and endurance he displayed furnished material for many a conversation.

Hosea G. Allen, a native of New York, washed gold at Cave City in 1853 and from a single pan of dirt took out dust valued at $150. The ground here was not uniformly rich, the gold pockets here and there, soon petered out, the gold washers cleared out. Mere memories now, at Cave City and McKinney's Humbug, the deer's brush and chaparral choke the footpaths along which hopeful men once trudged.

Footnotes

1 This account of cave discovery and birth of Cave City is not supported by other historical accounts. Today, the Cave City's Caverns are open to public during summer season and are most impressive to visit. Located near Mountain Ranch, now called the California Caverns, Historical Landmark #956

6

LONG-HAIRED BROWN MEETS THE LAW

Ben Thorn, a Calaveras County Deputy Sheriff not only had the respect of his fellow officers but that of the criminal element. He rode from the County Seat in Mokelumne Hill astride a chestnut sorrel. Six shooters thrusted into leather holsters, immaculate white linen shirt, black string tie precisely bow-knotted and "plainsman's" hat set firmly on his head, in a day of professional sheriffs, he was a formidable officer.

Ben Thorn, Calaveras County Sheriff. c. 1900
Courtesy of Calaveras County Archives

No gang or mob however well organized was ever able to wrest a prisoner for the purpose of hanging him. To Ben's way of thinking, trees were never intended to be so desecrated. A grimly stoical man when occasion demanded drastic action. He would meet any other obligation to the public in the same cool way. He did not hesitate to shoot.

A handsome specimen of mankind, this native of Plattsburg, New York, came overland to California in 1849. Six feet tall, slim, straight with dark hair and olive complexion, he had unflinching eyes. There were those persons who contended that Ben Thorn[1] possessed a hypnotic eye by the power of which he was able to bring criminals under control. True or false the fact remains that Ben always brought back the man he went out to get.

When hairy-backed coyotes prowled for prey on San Antonio Ridge, quick life rode high and dangerous waves there. When things got too hot in the larger towns for murderers, safecrackers, high-graders, Botany Bay "clipped-ears", thieves, pickpockets, gamblers, and other lawbreakers, they frequently sought safety in this camp. It was a camp, fast in tempo and loose in morals. It was here that Benjamin Kent Thorn in 1851, in search for yellow metal, dropped his roll of blankets. As a gold washer, he was nothing to brag about. While on the ridge, the pay streaks he followed always petered out on him and his was never the experience of finding a gold pocket but in spite of bad luck as a placer miner he became one of the most outstanding sheriffs in California.

After Charles Clark, High Sheriff of Calaveras County appointed Thorn a Deputy Sheriff in April 1851[2], his first act was to locate and arrest John Phipps, an American who had murdered for gold a Mexican Pedro Morales the previous year. Phipps was tried and found guilty. He was hung in the county jail yard in Mokelumne Hill. In San Antonio Camp on the ridge, Pedro Y Barro hacked to death a man and his wife using a broad axe. Thomas Titcomb was shot and killed by J. Bratton. Howard Maupin cruelly murdered Thomas Dill. On Indian Creek a German miner, met death at the hands of four Mexicans who made off with his gold dust. These are only a few of the criminals who had skipped out of Calaveras County, their debt to society unpaid. One by one Ben brought these men back to answer for their misdeeds, some going to the gallows and others to San Quentin prison[3]. His official career if fully narrated would fill many pages of a large-sized tome.

Ben's greatest achievement on San Antonio Ridge was his capture of a notorious criminal known throughout the southern mines as "Long-haired Brown". On this occasion his reputed hypnotic grey eyes may have had something to do with his success.

June 1855 Sam Brown, a desperate character and Bunty Owens a would-be gambler, were partners in a Monte game played against Chilean gamblers in a fandango and gambling hall in Calaveritas. A dispute soon arose between the South Americans and their opponents. A few carambas uttered by the losers and blood was dripping downward through cracks in the plank floor. Without losing any time, Sam Brown wiped the blood off his boot knife and left the scene with Bunty Owens close at his elbow.

Of Chileans and Peruvians there were a-plenty on the Ridge, each of whom was quick to avenge a wrong done his countryman. Of this fact, both Sam and Bunty were sharply aware. So, in their desire to escape before having murder charges brought against their names, they mounted swift horses and galloped away to find safer ground.

The Chileans too, were soon in their saddles giving chase. They were gaining on the fleeing gamblers when Long-haired Brown, turning in his saddle fired a shot that mortally wounded one of the pursuers. The shooting so depressed the spirits of the South Americans that their leader decided to call a halt. He had suddenly thought of a wiser, surer way, of capturing the North Americans. Ben Thorn was on the Ridge that day, so the leader dispatched a messenger to San Antonio Camp to notify the Deputy Sheriff of the crimes committed against his countrymen.

Ben receiving the news in his usual calm way, summoned Edward Hopkins[4] a miner, to his aid and with him rode to Calaveritas. Here at Ben's request, Orrin Spencer, Justice of the Peace, promptly issued the warrants necessary for arrests. The documents safe in Ben's coat pocket, the Deputy and the gold washer, their horses traveling shoulder to shoulder, headed for Tunnel Hill (Fricot City). Ben paused at this point just long enough to search a few vacant cabins but finding nothing, the two riders pressed onward to Big Hill.

EL DORADO Man Shot by Robber

San Andreas Register, Apr 6, 1865: Man Shot Near El Dorado--Mr. Jenkins, from Spring Valley, was shot by a robber near El Dorado, on Thursday last. He was about half-a-mile from town, when a man came up and stopped his team and demanded his money. He put his hand in his pocket, as if going after his money, drew a derringer and fired at the robber, and started his team, when the robber fired two shots at him, one of which took effect in the back of the neck. He then fell from the wagon and his team passed on, and the robber made good his escape, without getting his money...Dr. Ford. thinks his wounds will prove fatal. San And. Reg., Apr 6, 1865

John Hicks' cabin on O'Neil's creek was a mile north of Hay Press Flat [Sheep Ranch]. Sam, Ben thought, would seek shelter there. Ed thought differently, he thought that Sam was more apt to make a dash for El Dorado Town and from there strike out on the Old Secreto Trail, follow it and eventually reach West Point or perhaps the Blue Mountain. Night was falling when Hay Press Flat was reached and instead of continuing their search, they took refuge in the camp of sheepherders. They were tending the flocks of a courageous sleuthhound, Henry Schroebel, himself.

At sunrise the following morning, while eating breakfast with the herdsmen, Ben was told by one of them that Bill Bean, while on the way to his claim, had stopped at the camp that morning to tell him that Long-haired Brown and Bunty Owens were down at John Hicks eatin' his grub. They weren't alone, for four other gamblers, had joined them at sundown, the evening before. Bill Bean's word in this community, being as good as his ability to locate rich quartz ledges, Ben and Ed were soon examining their weapons. Straddling their mounts, they galloped along a "deer-cut", rather than the regular trail, which led from the sheep camp to O'Neil's Creek, close to, which was situated John Hick's cabin.

John Hicks, a hardy pioneer, was a shake maker and honest as day is long. A former fur trapper and grizzly bear hunter, he took pride in the fact of never having shot a buck unless the animal was running full speed. A doe or fawn, he had never killed. And although winter-starved cougars, whose blood-curdling shrieks had made many of his nights hideous and had ripped the heart and lungs out of his burro, they had never attacked him. His combats with grizzlies had left his hands badly scarred. His days of hunting and trapping past, he now lived alone in solitude, his nearest neighbors being the sheepherders at Hay Press Flat. A kindly, sparsely educated but thoughtful man, when leaving his cabin for his shake pile in the forest he always hung his latch-key on the outside of his door. About this woodsman's habit, Sam Brown no doubt had heard.

Ben and Ed cantered their horses to within a few yards of the shake cabin, and then halting, each took a hurried glance at his surroundings. Sam Brown, his long yellowish locks sweeping his powerful shoulders, suddenly bobbed up from the back of a dogberry bush, a rifle in hand. Raising his weapon, he aimed it at Ben.

A competent judge of both good and bad men, Ben thought that he had nothing to fear. Sam Brown in his opinion, was too bold, too fearless a criminal, to fire upon one whom he had not previously hailed. Ed, not sharing his companion's confidence in Sam's chivalry, wheeled his horse around and found protection in the brush flanking the stream.

Ben dismounted. Sam lowered his rifle. "Surrender your gun, Brown!" the deputy ordered in a stern voice. Ben fastened his eyes on the man in front of him and waited. Sam, after a few minutes of hesitation, handed over his rifle and other weapons. Ben then clamped the iron bracelets around his strong wrists and marched him into the cabin, where he disarmed Bunty and the four gamblers.

John Hicks was mixing biscuit dough when Ben with Sam in tow entered the room. Turning to John, Sam said in his bantering way,

"Thorn got here in nick o'time.
Bunty and I were just about to skip the county"
John smiled.

In shackles, the angelic haired Brown watched the shake-maker slide a pan of biscuits into his rock oven to bake. Since Brown was all muscle,

John was wondering why the gambler had allowed himself to be taken without putting up a fight.

He pressed:
"Why, Sam,
When you had the drop on Ben,
Why didn't you draw a bead?"

"Well, John", he drawled,
"I just couldn't bring myself to the point of wanting
To kill so brave a man as Ben Thorn."

One of the most spectacular criminals ever to set foot in California, Sam Brown was a law-defying gunman and knife wielder, ready to shoot and stab at the drop of a hat. He was in Lancha Plana on the Mokelumne River in 1850; the jeweled hilt of a blade was always showing above his Spanish-heeled boot top. Proud of his long golden hair, he was scornful of headgear. With beaver hat in hand, he flaunted a full-sweep circular cape, in vogue in his day with gamblers on the Mother Lode. Courageous as he was dangerous, he wore his pistols and blades for all to see. In Camp Opera near Chili Junction, in a stabbing affray that year, he slashed at a miner inflicting a painful wound, for this assault he barely escaped being lynched by infuriated gold washers.

That morning, covered by Ben Thorn, John Hicks' uninvited guests sat unshackled on three legged stools around his pine table and ate the food. They ate speckled trout caught in the creek flowing past the cabin, biscuits, wild honey and coffee that he had prepared. They ate in silence and they ate slowly.

The last drop of coffee drained from Sam's tin cup, Ben handcuffed them a second time. Ed, having heard no shots, changed his mind about danger and was at the hitching post, cinching the girth around the belly of his blue roan mustang. Bunty and the four gamblers were told by Ben to saddle up and get ready for the ride to Calaveritas.

Sam, after climbing into his saddle, urged Ben to remove the handcuffs from his wrists. The Chileans, he thought, might be lying in ambush. Ben, perceiving his fear of being seized by his enemies, removed the irons, permitting him the free use of his hands and arms. Sam, caught between the Law and a mob, Ben surmised, preferred to go to jail rather than to some tree.

Keeping their prisoners in sight, Ben and Ed, their weapons handy, after an uneventful ride, reached Calaveritas. Since no charge had been made against them, the four gamblers were released. Sam and Bunty, both in irons, were at once taken to Judge Spencer's courtroom for arraignment.

The preliminary examination lasted two days and created intense excitement. That Long-haired Brown had been taken into custody was highly gratifying to the law and order element, but there were others on the Ridge who resented his capture, especially his fellow gamblers.The inside walls of the mud and stone courtroom were bullet riddled, for at this time, Calaveritas was one of the most dangerous spots of the southern mines. Around this building on the second day of the hearing were milling more than a hundred angry Chileans. They were, friends and acquaintances of the two men Sam had slain and they were out to take the prisoners from Ben Thorn, none knew it any better than Ben himself.

Sam and Bunty had their friends too, ready to shed blood on the slightest pretext. Like the misguided Bunty, a "tin horn" gambler, they had tangled with professionals. To their dismay, men had come to Calaveritas all the way from Jesus Maria, Esmeralda, Dog Town, Yaqui Camp and San Andreas; some of them came on foot and others on mule and horseback.

Open hostility between the two factions soon become noticeable. Leather-booted and heavily armed men were ready to spring at each other's throats at a moments notice. They kicked and scuffed at each other, swore mighty oaths and openly abused in words Ben Thorn.

Of the many men in Calaveritas that day, Ben Thorn was the calmest. Strong of will, self-controlled, he had his mind fully made up to see that the law was not broken in Judge Spencer's courtroom.

Twilight fell, the atmosphere cooled but the temper of the mob reached fever-heat. Ben Thorn's presence in the camp that evening prevented a bloody conflict. He was thinking that things were quieting down when word was noised that a large group of professional gamblers were on the grounds and had joined forces with Sam and Bunty's supporters. Ben had friends in Calaveritas too, many of whom had been drawn to the scene to be on hand, they assured him, should he need help. Few hours later, he needed help and needed it badly; he called upon his supposed friends to remain near him during the fast darkening night. Instead of standing by him, they found obscure places in which to await the outcome. When one considers the character of Sam Brown's defenders it is easily understandable why Ben's lukewarm friends acted as they did. Ben, it may be said to his credit, did not hold that against them and forgot the desertion incident.

The two prisoners were held in the courtroom. Outside were two mobs, one bent on lynching and the other determined on freeing a fellow gambler. In order to prevent the sale of liquor outside the courtroom and to defeat the intentions of the two mobs, Ben sat outside the court room on a cracker box the whole night long, undaunted, alone, his only companion being a six-shooter.

The next morning, in the Court Room while the commitments were being made, Lafayette Choiser, a French renegade, attempted to pass a loaded pistol to the fair-haired Sam. Ben, springing forward, grabbed the weapon and with its butt, struck a blow on Choiser's head knocking him to the floor senseless.

Alfred Richardson, a sharp trick gambler, then swore out two warrants on false accusations against two Mexican horse thieves, both of whom were expert dagger hurlers. Richardson thought that when Ben would attempt to arrest these men, they would overpower him and possibly slit his throat.

Orrin Spencer the deputy, issued warrants and placed them in Ben's hand. He then jostled his way; gun in hand to the side of the illegally accused Sonorans. Ben, did one better, he served the warrants and lined his prisoners along side of Sam and Bunty. In the mean time, men fearful of stray bullets and flying daggers, made a mad dash for the open doors, while others leaped out of back windows.

The next day at sunrise, Ben, assisted by two Hay Press Flat sheep herders, took his four prisoners on horseback to Mokelumne Hill, where in the county calaboose, he lodged them back of iron bars. In due time, Sam and Bunty each pleading self-defense, stood trial. They were found guilty in the first instance of second-degree murder and in the second of abetting a crime. Charles Creaner, Judge of the District Court, gave each prisoner a short sentence, five years for Sam and three years for Bunty, to be served in San Quentin.

After his release from the State Penitentiary, Bunty took a new lease on life and respectability. Returning to his former home in the Washington Flat Mining District, he became a useful citizen. His old diggings not far from Cave City are known today as Bunty's Gulch[5].

Sam Brown, once his freedom was regained, went back to his profession, juggling and shuffling cards. In Jackson, Amador County, he soon got himself mixed up in another cutting scrape. Using a boot knife, his favorite weapon, he made a savage attack upon a young and popular gold washer. He was arrested and brought before the Bar of Justice. The Presiding Judge set his bail at two thousand dollars. Sam, not having that amount, was returned to the cell in the county jail. Resourceful, he managed somehow to break loose, crossed the Sierra summit to the boomtown of the Comstock Lode, Virginia City. Thus it was, that California got rid of a killer who made no bones about saying that he, up to that date, had slain twelve men.

During Virginia City's flush days, the Long-haired Brown with bright golden tresses and cold sapphire-blue eyes was shot and killed in a barroom brawl by John Van Sickle. Van Sickle, like the gambler whose heart he had pierced with a bullet, was forever in shooting scrapes at a gambling table. His record too, was a bad one. During his wild career in the Far West he had ended, he unashamedly admitted, the lives of seventeen men, beating Sam Brown's record by five. Violence at last caught up with John Van Sickle and he left this world his boots on and all.

CALAVERAS WEEKLY CITIZEN

SATURDAY..........JULY 16, 1887.

ON Friday evening, the 8th inst., a shooting affray occurred in El Dorado. A young man named John Stevens was at Bennett's residence, and at about 10 o'clock P. M. James Delaney came to the house and commenced shooting at Stevens The latter who was unarmed started on a run for home, Delaney continuing the shooting. Five or six shots were fired from a revolver; none of them, however, hitting the intended victim. About 1½ hours afterwards, Stevens who was still unarmed, met Delaney in El Dorado in front of Rodesino's store. Delaney said "who is there" or words to that effect. Stevens answered, giving his name, thinking the person addressing him was Rettagliata. Delaney said "stand back" and inst ntly fired both barrels of a shot gun at him, over 120 No. 5 shot taking effect in his left arm and abdomen.

Stevens was brought to San Andreas and is rapidly recovering.

Nothing was seen or heard of Delaney until Tuesday, when he came to San Andreas and gave himself into the custody of the Sheriff. He had in the meantime shaved off his mustache. His examination will take place Monday at 10 o'clock.

Footnotes

1 Ben Thorn born Dec. 22, 1829.

2 April 1855 is the recognized date.

3 At California State Archives, the San Quentine Prison Register show an entry "Samuel Brown, SQ 762, arrived Oct. 18, 1855, crime: manslaughter, sentence: 2 years; county sent from: Calaveras; discharged Oct. 6, 1857"

4 Edward Hopkins was employed by Thorn at his mine.

5 Bunty's Gulch mining camp was situated between San Antone Ridge and O'Neil's Creek, some 2 miles directly south of Cave City. In his Diary of Leonard Withington Noyes, Noyes describes a voting scene at Bunty's Gulch. In a county election, at this gulch 75 miners managed to cast 450 votes, thereby changing the outcome of this election. When the Elections Judge was asked how this was possible - he replied: "Them votes were all cast and I received them. My clerk put down the names of the voters"

7

SAN ANDREAS

San Andreas[1], originally a Mexican campo, sprung up like a mushroom, in a single night. Don Andres Pico's mining company was the first to light camp fires on San Andreas Gulch in 1848. In less than a month after Don Andres' gold discovery in this gulch there were hundreds of Mexicans, Chileans and Americans. Where today stands the beautiful town of San Andreas, the records say, Gabriel Moraga, a Mexican army officer and an explorer, in 1806, regarded the area as a fitting site for the establishment of a mission. If any such project was ever commenced it was abandoned, probably by reason of the hostile attitude of the Indians.

Andreas Pico
Courtesy of C.C. Archives

Among the first Americans to arrive in San Andreas were David Lattimer (Dad), Captain James Box, James Harris, John Morrison, Charles Bray, Captain Gilson, Captain Ben Osborne, Edward Morgan, Hubert Ide, Frank Forrest, Joseph Abbott, T.W. Taliaferro, Knapp, Broughton, Henry Schroebel, and James R. McKinney. Taliaferro was elected to the Alcalde's office and Henry Schroebel was the first to establish a trading post. The cloth tents of the Americans quickly replaced the brush remadas [made of straw or branches a place to eat, a rest stop] mud huts and hide shanties of the first gold hunters. With horn spoon they had scooped up the gravel and washed it in wooden bateas [pan for washing gold]. The population largely Mexican and native Californian, numbered about 1,500.

Near San Andreas Gulch, amongst brush arbors, mud, stone, and hide shelter huts, stood a white canvas tent—St. Peter's Roman Catholic Church, later known as St. Patrick's and still later as St. Andrews. The altar of the tent church was draped with gaudy cotton cloth, the kind of cloth that the traders exchanged for the gold with the Indians and Mexicans. Candlesticks of wrought iron, pewter and wood were arranged alongside the California candlesticks champagne and claret bottles, bearing labels of famous European vintners. Each mid-morning the miners laid aside their picks, pans and went inside the tent to listen to the officiating priest, a Frenchman[2] who spoke to his congregation in the Spanish language. An early day writer chronicled "at the close of the service the Mexicans dispersed to spend the remainder of the day in the gaming houses and dance halls."

Dr. Archibald Osborne and his wife Eliza and the latter's four children located permanently in San Andreas in the early spring of 1851. While crossing the plains, the wagon train of which the Osbornes were members was attacked by hostile and savage Indians. Sarah Ellis, Mrs. Osborne's oldest daughter, in great fright, leaped from the tailboard of a wagon and landed in the path of the rampaging redskins. When rescued the girl's legs were partially paralyzed, from which misfortune, she never entirely recovered. During the summer of 1851, Osborne erected the San Andreas Hotel. The only major hotel in the town, it was owned and managed by Dr. and Mrs. Osborne. This hotel, near San Andreas Gulch, on the south side of Main Street, was destroyed by fire in the middle fifties. Dr. Osborne, "a genial, long-legged Missourian doctor," after a few years grew tired of mining camp life and returned to his home in St. Louis. Eliza Osborne, however, continued to live in San Andreas, in the home she had established for herself and children and in which, in 1866 she died.

Christoral Noriega and Carlos Benito were among the first gold washers in San Andreas. Native Californians, Benito drifted away from the place at an early date. In May 1866, Christoral, while attending a turkey shoot on Jenk's Ranch at Old Bend, near San Andreas, stabbed to death Antonio Berumes. He was brought to trial. When a jury found him "not guilty" Christoral too disappeared from the county.

Carlos and his wife, Joaquina (Moraga) Noriega, lived contentedly in their home on Court Street in which they conducted a Fonda [Café or an eating place]. Joaquina never made any bones about saying that, on more than one occasion she had protected Joaquin Murrieta. She knew him in her childhood, in Hermosillo Mexico. That was before misfortune overtook him in California.

Because of his excessive thinness, the Mexicans called John Brown, Juan Flaco [lean John]. He washed gold in San Andreas in 1851 but with poor results. Brown, a native of Sweden, fought in South America under Simon Bolivar's command. During the siege of Los Angeles in 1846, he was a member of Captain Archibald Gillespie's garrison. When the Americans found that their stronghold was being threatened, Juan Flaco Brown, presented himself to his superior officer and offered to ride through enemy country to Yerba Buena [San Francisco] to inform Commodore Robert F. Stockton of the hard pinch his countrymen were in. Captain Gillespie pointed

SIEGE AND CAPTURE OF LOS ANGELES, SEPTEMBER, 1846.

Courtesy of Chispa Parlor #139 Native Sons of the Golden West- Murphys, California.

out thatsuch an undertaking could end only in his death. This soldier of fortune was not easily discouraged. He left Los Angeles at eight o'clock on the evening of September 24, 1846, hotly pursued by a troop of California Lancers. Tied in Brown's long hair was a number of cigarettes, each paper, stamped with Gillespie's official seal, it bore the inscription "Believe the bearer." Near Cahuenga Pass, Brown's horse was shot from under him. Finally, the dangerous experience ended, he reached Yerba Buena at eight p.m. on the 28th. Lean John's ride of 630 miles[3] through some of the most unfriendly country and his ride is the most notable ride in California history records. This unsung hero, John Brown, left San Andreas to take up residence in Stockton in which city, in 1859, he died and was buried.

Erected in 1851, the Bella Union was San Andreas's first frame building. It served as a saloon, gambling and dance hall as well as Judge Taliaferro's courtroom. About the time of its completion a rich discovery was made near Golden Gate Peak[4], drawing a large number of miners from the town to the new diggings. The stampede, of short duration, ended during the following autumn and once again San Andreas was a flourishing town.

Each year on St. Andrew's Day, the Mexican settlers raised a large wooden cross on a southwestern hilltop. Then, led by the parish priest,

Main Street, San Andreas, Calaveras County, c.1892
Courtesy of Calaveras County Historical Society

men, women and children filed up the hillside. They offered prayers at the foot of this flower-entwined cruciform. The cross, about twelve feet high, was garlanded with gay flowers, the same wild flowers that brightened every gulch, flat and field for miles around.

In the spring of 1851 a rich strike was made on Gold Hill, at the edge of the town. That same year J. Banque a French merchant arrived and was soon to supervise the erection of the town's first brick building[5]. In 1872, Cyprien J. Agostine, a pioneer merchant of Old Gulch, purchased Banque's old store on the south side of Court Street. He later added an adobe wing to each side of the main structure. The iron rings, inserted in the front wall for tying patrons' horses, are remindful of the days of boots, spurs, and saddles.

James Harris, following J. Banque's example, erected a one-story brick store on the northwest corner of Main and St. Charles streets. The bricks for the Harris building were brought around the Horn as ballast for a sailing vessel and were transported to San Andreas by mule train. The original iron doors and shutters are a thrill to see. This old building is today one of San Andreas' pioneer landmarks.

Joseph Zwinge in 1854, erected a building in which he established a restaurant. Fronting on Main street, the Zwinge building, afterwards known as the American Hotel, was constructed of brick and cut-stone. A few years ago the walls of this old landmark were crumbling and the roof was sagging. The iron doors and window shutters remained intact and permitted the frontage to present a fairly good appearance. In 1936 Mr. Desire Fricot, a public spirited citizen of Calaveras County, realizing the need for a museum,

American Hotel and Restaurant, Main St. San Andreas, c.1900
Erected in 1854 by Joseph Zwinge. Restored by Desire Fricot and given to the county. In 2005 this building houses the Calaveras County Archives.
Courtesy of Calaveras County Archives.

purchased the pioneer building, remodeled it from top to bottom, filled it with historic relics and generously presented it to the people of his county[6].

Arnold Friedberger, a native of Lauphein, Germany, reached San Andreas in 1851. A year later in partnership with Jacob Sellner established a General Merchandise store. These partners in 1854 erected a rock and adobe store at the southwest corner of Main and Court streets. This quaint, picturesque building was destroyed by fire several years ago[7].

The Masonic Lodge that was organized in San Andreas in 1853 lost the last of its charter members, when Arnold Friedberger died in Stockton on January 9, 1908.

Daniel D. Vezey, a Kentuckian, was a cabinetmaker. He built a long pine counter or bar for the Bella Union Saloon. Later, this highly skilled craftsman made tables, chairs, sofas, cupboards and bureaus for household purposes. He also made desks and filing cabinets for offices. For the miners, Vezey built wooden pumps, patent riffles, rockers, long toms, flutter and overshot water wheels for use in the mines.

LOCAL ENTERTAIMENT.

The roughly plastered inside walls of the first saloons were covered with broadsides announcing rewards offered for offenders and other attractions. The more grotesque, called attention to features such as "necktie parties" [public executions, death by hanging].

One day, in the autumn of 1853, a "bill-sticker" arrived in San Andreas with a large yellow hanger that stated:

"There will be exhibited for one day only,
At the Stockton House,
The head of the renowned bandit, Joaquin[8],
And the hand of Three-fingered-Jack,
The notorious robber and murderer."

By this method were heralded: grand balls, wagon show performances, horse races, prizefights, foot races, horseshoe pitching, ten-pin contests and circuses.

A "throw around" handbill that is still in existence in Calaveras County, stated:

"Mr. A. J. Tait, proprietor to the Kentucky House,
Will give a grand ball at Third Crossing,
Three miles southeast of San Andreas.
On Saturday evening, January 17, 1856.
Floor managers:
Gordon E. Sloss, Dr. Archibald L. Osborne,
W. Miller, P. Brodwell, and Mark McNickels."

During the years 1853-1854 San Andreas made but small progress and it was not until the summer of 1855 that things took a fresh start. That summer Kohlburg & Company erected a handsome stone building using stone quarried at John Huberty's Ranch. Others to use the same type of building material were Thomas Cochoran and Sullivan & Gallagher. The upper story of Sullivan & Gallager's building was used for a ballroom and the lower floor served as a store. This two-story building at the northeast corner of Main and St. Charles streets is now in use as a public garage[9].

In 1856 the Odd Fellows' Lodge erected a two-story brick building. This building is now the property of Calaveras County. Its original iron doors open and close daily. In it are located the offices of some of the county officials[10].

On Wednesday, September 24, 1856, the first edition of the "Independent," a weekly newspaper, was run off the press. Published by George Armor, the "Independent" was financed by the miners of San Andreas. They, it is said,

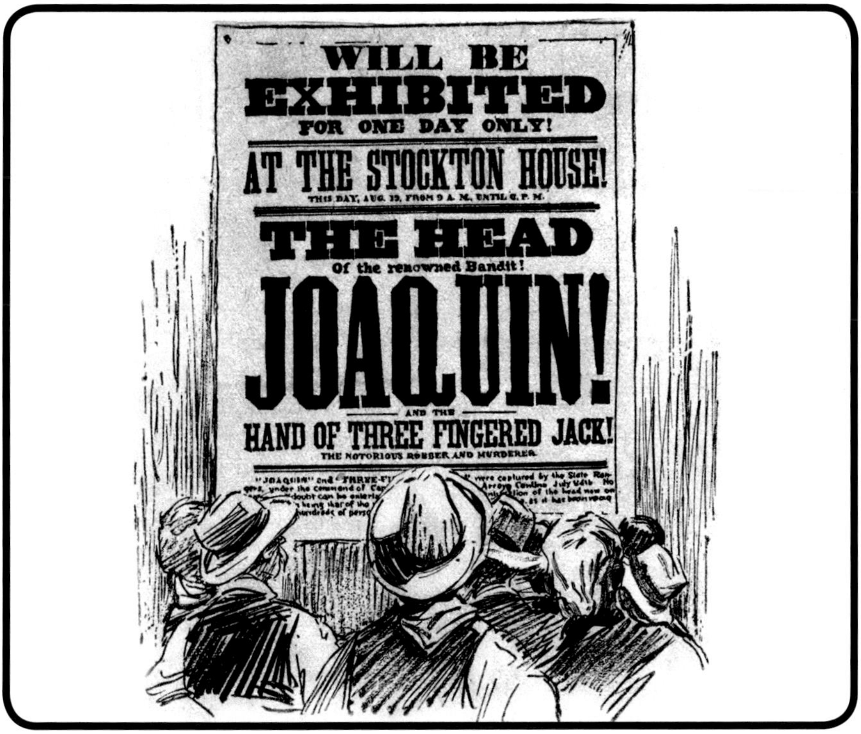

There were five robbers in Calaveras County with the name Joaquin. Joaquin Murieta was the most notorious. Some believed that it was his head that was exhibited but others claimed he moved to Mexico. Interestingly, the name Murieta is not listed on this poster.

Courtesy of Calaveras County Archives

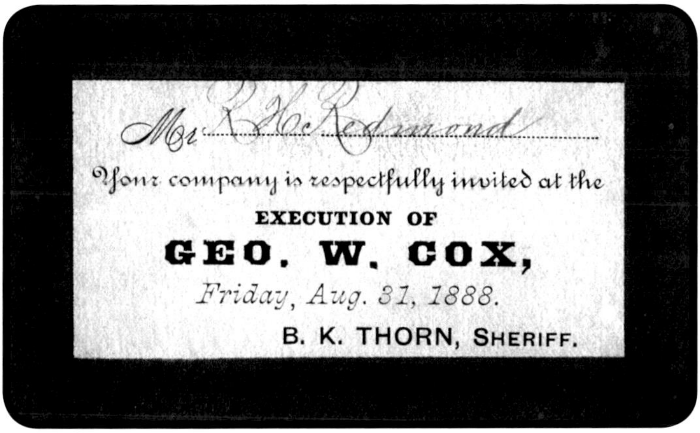

Sheriff Ben Thorn sent out 250 of these invitations to the hanging of George Cox in the County jailyard, all trimmed in black.

Courtesy of Calveras County Archives

were desirous of giving publicity to a miners' ditch for the conveyance of water into placers in and around town. Samual Seabough, California's first feature writer of note commenced his journalistic career on this weekly. Henry George, for a brief time in 1858, was a writer for the Independent. That year the Independent and most of its staff removed to Stockton. In that city about twelve years ago it folded, leaving deserted, behind it, one of the most valuable newspaper files in California.

OUT OF THE ASHES A TOWN RISES

During the winter of 1856 a fire swept away many businesses. In this fire the Bella Union Saloon, San Andreas Hotel and many of the first frame buildings were destroyed. Once the ashes of the great blaze of 1856 had cooled, the men and women of the "village" of San Andreas, looked back upon the past. The town was lacking efficient equipment for fighting fire. The citizens realizing the necessity of safeguarding property not only procured a fire engine but also constructed three large cisterns under the streets, in which water was stored. The old fire engine was operated by hand-power. It was built in New York and after its installation in 1857, it on more than one occasion, saved San Andreas from the ravages of fire. Then pitching in together, they got rid of the wreckage and built for themselves larger and more substantial houses.

The Metropolitan Hotel opened March 19, 1859 in San Andreas on the corner of Main and Court streets. Here the Stockton-Murphys stage arrives. Sadly it burned down in 1926. Photo circa 1895.

Courtesy of Calaveras County Historical Society

Saint Andrews Catholic Church in San Andreas, built in 1857
Courtesy of Calaveras County Historical Society

On a Southwestern hillside stood the Church of Saint Andrew, erected in 1857. Shortly after its dedication, it was gifted bronze bells each bearing the name of the King of Spain. Silvery-toned, the little bells called men and women of the Roman Catholic faith to worship in the hillside ediface. One day, St. Andrew's Church fell a victim to flames, when the steeple tottered, the bells blackened and cracked, dropped with a discordant jangle, into a near-by gulch. Several years later, according to the late John Scieffard of San Andreas, the bells were recovered but were sold to some antique snooper of the Mother Lode in search of pioneer relics.

The Metropolitan Hotel[11], a two-story brick structure, at the corner of Main and Court, was the property of James Oliphant. Erected during the winter of 1858-1859 it was under the management of J. W. Willard who opened its doors to the public with a grand ball on the night of March 24th, 1859. The Metropolitan was one of the finest hotels in the interior of California. Mr. Oliphant sold his hostelry to James Sharp who, a few years later, sold to James Caven[12]. The latter in 1879 disposed of his hotel to Benjamin F. Hawes, who reached San Andreas from his home in Kentucky in 1852. The Metropolitan, a famous landmark, was completely destroyed by fire in 1926.

A rich strike was made at the Dunning claim in 1859[13] in a buried channel of an ancient riverbed. A miner came upon a pocket of gold that weighed 43 pounds. At once, thirty mining companies began sinking shafts to the old channel. The geological formation, which crosses the western end

San Andreas Elementry School. c.1890
Courtesy of Calaveras County Historical Society

of San Andreas, was identical with that of the more fully developed portions of the Mother Lode. A short time after the discovery in the Dunning claim, the Lightowler, Jones & Company, working directly under Main Street, washed up tailings containing gold. This company, from their drift or tunnel averaged two ounces of dust a day to the man. The four miners, working the claim found many chispas each worth from $10 to $24.

San Andreas established Public Schools early. The town was not without a Reading Room, Protestant Church, Sunday school, dramatic society and other cultural activities. All in all, it was a pleasure-loving place and a dressy one too, especially on circus days and evenings.

Lee & Marshall's was the first circus to give performances on the flat near where the Coulter, Friedberger, Osborne and other pioneer homes stood. Credoni, the clown and stiltvaulter, amused the children and astonished the grown-ups of San Andreas. Madame Credoni was a famous and popular equestrienne. Her husband was an equally sensational performer. This circus, noted for its large number of trained monkeys and dogs, toured the Southern Mines' towns each year.

Horse racing was the favorite Sunday and holiday sport of the Mexicans. The caballeros [horseman], rigged-out in the best Mexican style, permitted no drabness to enter a fiesta day. Usually the vaqueros [cowboys] from the near-by ranches gave exhibitions of steer roping. The Americans, on the other hand, encouraged foot-racing, boxing, bowling contests, prizefights, ball games, target practice, and turkey "shoots." Women, the good women, organized singing societies, church bazaars, sewing bees, quilting parties, candy pulls, and charades. Dancing of course was a pastime that was generally enjoyed by everyone.

The large Chinese population celebrated only on "Chinee" New Year. On that day, bursting red papers filled the air with odor of black powder. In the Chinee Joss House[14] [Chinese temple or shrine] on the north side of San Andreas Gulch, near the squatty cross-legged idol, the joss sticks [incense stick] were always burning. A Chinese divinity scattered the "Chinee" devils while the pungent incense sent up wreaths of blue-gray smoke to dim the gorgeous banners overhead.

Long after the Mexicans had thinned out their number, the Chinese were rocking the cradles in both Main and San Andreas Gulches.

People living in the middle and southern part of Calaveras County, were of the opinion that San Andreas, being more centrally located than Mokelumne Hill, was the logical place for the Seat of Justice. So, on May 4, 1863, the qualified voters went to the polls to cast ballots for or against, the removal of their courthouse. In December an election was held. A few weeks previously, S. B. Stevens of San Andreas, acting for the dissenting citizens went to San Francisco where, with the banking house of Donohue, Ralston & Company, he placed on deposit $15,000 for a courthouse, should San Andreas win the election.

Since the election went in favor of San Andreas, the question of the removal of the county records was soon occupying the attention of John Curry, Chief Justice of the Supreme Court of California, of which William D. Harrison was the clerk.

The Mokelumne Hillians, angry as a nest of disturbed hornets, kept up a noisy hubbub and clung doggedly to the county seat. A bitter contro versy was being waged between the two factions. Finally, Justice Sawyer, on October 12, 1866, awarded an Alias Peremptory Writ of Mandate [a written Court Order demanding that addressee do or stop doing whatever is specified] to be served on Judge Silas Brockway and other County Officers of Calaveras. They were required by law, to hold their offices at the county seat, the writ commanded them to move at once, to San Andreas. William (Deacon) P. Peek, of Mokelumne Hill, a member of the Board of Supervisors of Calaveras County, had in his possessions the writ that Justice Sawyer had previously issued, but being no little disgruntled, Mr. Peek had failed to serve it. To those persons who had voted for a removal of the courthouse, his negligence brought down upon his head a storm of protest. The San Andreas "Register," October 16, 1866, printed:

THE MANDAMUS ISSUED

"The Writ of Mandamus[15] for the removal of the county seat to San Andreas has been issued, and is in the possession of Mr. Peek one of the Board of Supervisors, who says he will serve it whenever it suits his convenience. Measures have been taken to compel him to carry out the mandate of the court. If Mr. Peek or any other man supposes that he can set up his will against the operations of the Supreme Court and by his acts prevent the commands of that court from being executed, he will find himself sorrowfully mistaken."

When the teams for the removal of the records, left San Andreas and arrived in Mokelumne Hill, neither the records nor the officers were ready to go to San Andreas. Mr. Peek explained that the Board of Supervisors as yet had not accepted the buildings in the latter town because the San Andreas politicians hadn't whitewashed their courthouse. Until this was done, the county records were going to remain in Mokelumne Hill.

No sooner had the empty wagons rumbled out of Mokelumne Hill then Ben K. Thorn and Jeff Gatewood returned to San Andreas from Sacramento. They had procured a second writ. Their traveling companion Mr. W. Byrnes, a bailiff of the Supreme Court, would serve the writ. A lively span of horses furnished by Richard Russell, were hastily snapped into traces and three determined men climbed into a buckboard and went thundering off to Mokelumne Hill. Near the outskirts of the once greatest gold rush town in California, they met the returning wagons. Ben Thorn, a deputy sheriff, stopped the teams and told the drivers to turn around and return to Mokelumne Hill. An hour later, the Supreme Court's representative Mr. Byrnes served the writ and the county officers made an unconditional surrender. William Peek, the landlord of the popular Golden Eagle Hotel, frowned darkly as he watched the old books being loaded onto the wagons from San Andreas, the removal of which spelled ruin for Mokelumne Hill.

Until midnight, the rumble of wheels was heard, as wagons bearing Old Calaveras' documents rolled southward to the new Seat of Justice.

The following night, a memorable one in the history of San Andreas, a general celebration took place. The old town, gaily decorated, presented a scene of great mirth, hilariousness, and feverish excitement. The Light Artillery, San Andreas' crack military organization, under command of the Rev. M. B. Starr was rigged out to kill, in gilt trimmed uniforms and glistening swords, caused the over-enthusiastic to yell:

"Come on, Boys,
Let's make San Andreas
The pride town
Of the Southern Mines!"

That night, while the noisy, joyous crowd milled through the streets, skyrockets lighted the heavens. Old muskets, "Kentuck" rifles and long-barreled shotguns that had protected the immigrants while crossing the plains were fired at intervals. It was a time for merry-making, especially for the children who in their Sunday best, together with their mothers took an active part in the festivities.

When the brasses of the San Andreas and Angel's Camp bands stopped making martial music, speeches were make by "Buck" Lewis, Rienza Hopkins, Ira Hill Reed, William O. Swenson, William L. Dudley, and Jeff Gatewood.

All night long, liquor flowed, toasts were proposed and general good cheer prevailed. Then, when the cocks began to crow, the music-makers marched away to serenade:
William Irvine,
Major Gorman,

Joaquin Mirando y Wina

And other citizens whose efforts to further San Andreas' cause were untiring. The big hurrah was kept up until after sunrise. Some were dead drunk, others only slightly tipsy. Homeward bound, wobbly-of-leg men, attempted to keep pace with the silver feet of the first October rain.

In April 1867, Calaveras County received bids calling for the erection of a courthouse and jail. In the meantime the Pittman building, on St. Charles Street, served as a courthouse and sheriff's office and the old stone building known as Friedberger's store, took care of the county clerk, treasurer, assessor and other county officers. W. D. Morrell, architect and builder, was awarded the $15,000 contract. A two-story red brick structure was under way. The courthouse, when completed, was a dignified and commodious building, one that reflected credit not only to the county, but also to its designer and builder.

In January 1867, Marshall & Showalter's claim[16], near San Andreas, gave promise of becoming rich diggings. Here, in an ancient riverbed, at a depth of 100 feet, a lump of gold weighing more than a pound was found.

Michael Callahan's hotel and saloon, the Kinderhook Exchange, a two-story frame building, corner of Main and St. Charles streets, was purchased in 1867 by Gordon Sloss and Edwin Burgess who changed the hostelry's name to the Accidental. Callahan, a 'forty-niner' whose daughter Jane, was the wife of William Irvine, returned with his wife and their young grandson "Tommy" Irvine, to his former home in the East.

In April 1867 Judge of the Superior Court, Silas Brockway, meted out to John B. Ferguson a sentence condemning him to death by way of steps and the rope. During the previous year Ferguson a mulatto, Jesus Miranda a Mexican and a few others of their own lawless stamp, entered the trading post of Charles R. Johnson on Calaveras River just below Greasertown and after robbing and plundering it they murdered Johnson.

Corsican by birth, Johnson was a most estimable citizen. The offenders were apprehended and each in his turn brought to justice. Ferguson was the first to suffer for their crime. He was hanged in the San Andreas jail-yard.

A short distance from San Andreas the R. N. Cloyd's Ranch was famous for choice fruits, berries, and sweet apple cider that were produced there. Cloyd's orchard and garden for many seasons supplied the mining district of Washoe in Nevada, with fruits and vegetables.

Charles Whitlock purchased the site of the "Old French Garden" located on the north side of Court Street. He was a merchant and the Wells Fargo & Company's agent in San Andreas. Here Mr. Whitlock built a dwelling house and instead of grapevines, he surrounded it with lilac and rosebushes.

East of San Andreas, a short mile, was a piece of fertile land to which Joseph Kern held a squatter's right and on which he planted an orchard and vegetable garden. Known as Kern's "peddling" garden, it was later sold to the widow of George Leonard of San Andreas. After Mrs. Leonard married Peter Moro, of "Moro's Castle," on San Andreas Gulch, the latter assumed the management of the garden and orchard[17]. No longer a "peddling" garden, nevertheless, the old pear and apple trees of Peter Moro's planting are still producing fruit.

The Chinese merchants, Joss House Priests, and "coolie" gold diggers brought with them from Old Cathay [Old China] rice kettles, ivory chopsticks, peacock feathers, flashy silk queue cords, incense, writing-sticks and vermilion paper. They, with their wide pants flapping around their wooden sabots [wooden shoes] are no longer to be seen. But the ailanthus trees, "Tree of heaven", sacred to the Chinese and the white vestal lilies that Celestials planted in the dooryards of their humble homes are flourishing in San Andreas.

The dwelling house that Joseph T. Bryan[18], a Mexican War veteran, built is now owned and occupied by a member of the Treat family.

The family home of Ben Thorn[19], one of the bravest of California's

Sheriff Ben Thorn's house, The Thorn Mansion, Saint Charles Street in San Andreas.

Courtesy Mr. and Mrs. Rurik Kallis

professional sheriffs now stands surrounded by oak trees, as a reminder of a time when San Andreas enjoyed no small degree of elegance. Dr. S. M. Oviatt, the town's first dentist and his little white cottage, opposite Richard Russell's house, near the bridge, has fallen into ruins. The old homes of Jeff Gatewood, Gallagher, Ira Hill Reed, John Dasso, James Tiscornia, Javier Salcido, John Early, Greenwood, Washburn, and other pioneer dwelling houses are still weathering the blasts of winter.

Dr. Elisha B. Robertson, who in order to save a man's life, in a remote mining camp near San Andreas, using a common meat-saw he performed a successful amputation of a miner's leg. One of the most skillful of the early day surgeons, Dr. Robertson's last days were spent in Jackson, Amador County.

P. Masterson, whose livery teams, like those of Richard Russell's, and later Frank Washburn's were among the best that ever trotted from a public livery stable. These teamsters no longer answer to the roll call of the Sons of Temperance.

Dr. Amereux has ceased to solicit funds for the French Society of Calaveras County and Charles Faville, and his songful regalings have been forgotten.

T. W. Taliaferro, while his memory was still fresh, related in detail to Nathaniel Pitt Langford, his exciting experiences of the days in San Andreas.

The Odd Fellow and Masonic Building at the corner of Highway 49 and Church Street. Calaveras High School was on the ground floor. Circa 1900.
Courtesy of Wally Motloch

Together with Jonathan Hall, P. Davis, and Jeff Gatewood, who could draw a bead as skillfully as he could draw a brief, shot it out one day on Murray Creek, with a group of Murrieta's mounted bandits and on this occasion the Americans again came out best.

THE JUMPING FROG STORY

The old Abyssinian [Ethiopian] fairy tale about weighting frogs with small pebbles may not have reached San Andreas in the fifties, but the Negros from the South had. The miners of this race may have told their white brethren that, while living on the banks of the Mississippi River, they had captured the long-legged amphibians and entered them in frog-jumping contests. Anyhow, in San Andreas, as early as Don Andres Pico's time, games of chance seemed naturally a part of the every day existence. Gambling, in all its phases, was indulged in. For instance, wagering their gold on their ability to wing an eagle at long range, "barking" a squirrel, the number of blue-jays shot at the annual jay hunt, the number of coyote and cougar scalps that would be brought in that season and the number of bears the hunters were likely to trap. Often they gambled for loaves of Mexican bread rather than gold.

Among the sports that resulted in exchanges of gold dust was a frog-jumping contest. It furnished the occasion for the loudest laughter and the greatest amount of fun. Jim Smiley, a Calaveritas gold washer, captured and attempted to train a frog to jump but "Dan'l Webster," failed to win a wager. This is because Pete Stag, a New York Bowery boy, surreptitiously loaded Smiley's amphibian with buckshot. The loading took place while the unsuspecting gold washer was "up street" at the town pump. Smiley was helping Johnny Ludrun fish out one of the yellow-bellied jumpers that made the pump their headquarters.

Lieutenant Benjamin Ross Coon, of the Home Guards of Angel's Camp, was a visitor in San Andreas that morning. Later, Ross Coon, whose flair for a good joke was known all the way from the Cosumnes to the Mariposa Rivers, was openly accused with having furnished Pete Stag with both the idea and the buckshot. Smiley's frog, instead of leaping forward, flopped over and died. The scene of Dan'l Webster's or should we say Jim Smiley's humiliation was the middle of Main Street, directly in front of Knickbocker Hall.

Edwin Booth, Kate Hayes, Madame Anna Bishop, Caroline Chapman, William B. Chapman, Rowena Granice and other famous entertainers of the gold rush days had treaded the boards of that Hall.

Sam Seabough of the Independent, getting wind of the sly betting plot, hastened out of the newspaper office to the middle of the street and joined Victor Gottschalk, Hosea Allen, William Swenson, George Washburn, Jonathan Hall, Arnold Friedberger, Martin Bowan, Wm. Jeff Gatewood, Captain Robert Pope, Chauncey Lloyd, Ben Hawes, Major James Corman, Rienza Hopkins, Oliver and Alexander Wyllie, Richard Russell, Adolphus Coulter, and Ned Roweth and other sport-minded men.

Judge Victor Gottschalk, c.1882

Courtesy of C.C.H.S.

Years later, in his home in San Andreas, Judge Victor Gottschalk told about the defeat of the frog, the "Dan'l Webster" and buckshot that anchored the amphibian to the hard-packed dirt of Main Street. But in spite of its inglorious performance, several years later, the deceased Dan'l's tragedy was capitalized on by Samuel Clemens, whose story "The Celebrated Jumping Frog of Calaveras County," brought him both fame and riches. Once his book was put into circulation "Sam"

William M. Denig called "Pony" operated an express delivery service to the foothills from San Andreas. Locally it was refered to it as "Pony Express"

Courtesy of Calaveras County Historical Society.

Daily Express!

From San Andreas to
CALAVERITAS AND OLD GULCH!
AND
WEEKLY EXPRESS
TO CAVE CITY!

Lumber! Lumber! Lumber!

EL DORADO STEAM SAW MILL,
Eight miles from San Andreas, between Cave City and Mountain Ranch.

WILLIAM IRVINE,......Proprietor.

THE UNDERSIGNED has always on hand, a large supply of all qualities of Lumber, and is prepared to fill all orders on the shortest notice, at the lowest market rates. His YARD is situated in the rear of the Kinderhook Exchange, in the town of San Andreas.

I have also established a Lumber Yard at Campo Seco, with Boyle & O'Neil as his agents.

N. B.—A good supply of long and short shingles always on hand.

dec 20, '56-6m* WILLIAM IRVINE.

LIVERY STABLE.

Main st., West side, between Jordan Bridge and Knickerbocker Saloon, SAN ANDREAS.

A LARGE AND CHOICE STOCK OF SADdle and Carriage Horses, Buggies, and Sulkies, among which may be found the best appointed equipages in the State, kept always on hand, and in the best condition.

☞Private Horses Boarded and Groomed by the day or week. Charges moderate.

R. W. RUSSELL,
W. H. MILLER, } Proprietors.

San Andreas, Sept. 26, '57. sp 26:tf:13

Courtesy of C. C. Archives

Clemens became known to the wide world as the celebrated Mark Twain.

The genial merchants Meyer Rothschild, M. Kaiser, R. Davis, Moses Cohen, Ned Roweth and Lewis Seldner and others no longer open and close iron doors on brick buildings. The cheery voice of the saloonkeeper William Casey has been silent for many years. The painted sign bearing the words, "John Steel, Shoemaker," no longer swings above a Main Street sidewalk. Gone too is the old mahala Mary, who for many years, picked up her living from door to door. Gone is the good, kind Mexican Rafino, whose deeds of mercy were countless. Gone is the Old Kinko of the lame knee, one of Joaquin's bold bandits, who after his release from San Quentin penitentiary returned to San Andreas and a life of usefulness. Tomascito and Mulacho odd Mexican characters that snaked logs from the hills and sold them to the settlers, had no need for burros.

Gone too, is Herman Bode the tinsmith, he is not in his shop on St. Charles Street, soldering leaky coffee pots and dishpans.

Gone is Peter Woodbeck, a man of worth and prominence, who at the edge of San Andreas, was cruelly murdered by Three-fingered-Jack. The E Clampus Vitus, like the Knights of the Golden Circle have folded but the Masons, Odd Fellows and other organizations are still carrying on.

San Andreas is a town of endurance; its pioneer buildings give mute testimony to the skill and patience of their constructors. The walls of many buildings though slightly defaced, still stand upright. The iron doors are in use just as they were in olden days. From these doors the leather mail pouch was handed to the pony express man. Each day "Red" or "Pony," [William M. Denig], astride a fleet pony, clattered out of San Andreas with letters and newspapers for the gold diggers of Calaveritas, Old Gulch, Chee Chee Flat, El Dorado Town, Irvine's Mill, O'Neil's Bar, Tunnel Hill, Broderick Flat, San Antonio Camp, and Colton Flat.

Footnotes

1 It is very likely that the town named San Andreas is associated with Andres [Andreas] Pico. His company was first to mine gold here and at that time, he believed that he was the legal landowner of these lands.

2 Emmet Joy in Chronicles of San Andreas "Father John Bohard, a Frenchman was sent to San Andreas in May 1851"

3 Rather unlikely number for a distance of roughly 400 miles.

4 Sometimes called the Schrack Peak, Schrack Mountain or Butte of Calaveras as opposed to Butte of Amador near Jackson. It is located on the west side of highway 49 about 3 miles out of San Andreas going to Mokelumne Hill.

5 Emmet P. Joy in Chronicles of San Andreas says, "Jean Banq, a Frenchman in 1851 constructed what became the Agostini Building" The bricks came from Doak's brickyard in Stockton.

6 In 2005 this building houses the Calaveras County Archives. The County's downtown Museum in now located two doors up on Main St. while the Mining and Farming Museum (Red Barn Museum) in located on Mountain Ranch Road next to the Government Center.

7 Destroyed by fire on July 25, 1926

8 An article in San Joaquin Republican, May 7,1853 states that Joaquin's real name is Joaquin Muriati. The act of State Legislature May 17, 1853, authorizing Captain Harry Love to raise a company of Rangers, stated that his purpose was to capture five Joaquins- Murieta, Ocomorenia, Botellier, Valenzuela and Carrillo.

9 This building was torn down in 1956 when the highway 49 was realigned.

10 The lower story of this building is the office of the Calaveras County Arts Council in 2005.

11 Emmet Joy in Chronicles of San Andreas states "opened March 13, 1859" No mention of James Oliphant. Oliphant was a resident of Copperopolis and moved to the Met in 1865 after being elected Sheriff.

12 Caven was Mrs. Oliphant's brother-in-law.

13 San Andreas Independent March 27, 1858 reports the strike.

14 The Joss House was located where the Calaveras High School track is located now.

15 A legal order to compel a person to do something.

16 Marshall & Showalter's claim was located near where the Highway Patrol Offices are located today.

17 Located just off the Gold Strike Road.

18 Bryan family house, home of Mrs. Edna Bryan Buckbee the author of this book.

19 This building located on St. Charles Street is a wonderful example of early architecture. In 2005, it is owned and occupied by Mr. & Mrs. Rurik Kallis and they are carefully restoring it to its former glory.

8

THE DUEL AT MOONLIGHT FLAT

When the question of slavery became a pertinent issue in San Andreas, the old landmarks that had served the political organizations as guideposts crashed, some never again to rise. Men, anchored to the Whig or Democratic doctrines soon found themselves without soundings. Politicians accustomed to weighing public opinion and moving accordingly were no longer able to tell where the troubled waters were. They were floundering and were not permitted to find another safe port. Usually, when affairs were in a muddle in this town, a commanding voice was sometimes able to clear the confusion and turn a wavering crowd in the right direction. Wm. Jeff Gatewood, of San Andreas, was probably the most fluent, able and convincing orator on the Mother Lode. Whenever and wherever he spoke men listened to what he had to say.

Jeff Gatewood was a lawyer specialized in land cases. He was one of the most brilliant legal lights in California.

So when in 1853, Andres Pico[1] said:
"Somewhere in that vast space of this country, bounded on the north by the Consumnes River, on the east by the Sierras, on the south by the Mokelumne River, and on the west by the old Sacramento and Stockton Trail, I claim eleven leagues of land,"

Jeff Gatewood, was the first lawyer, to rise up in court and ask the question:
"Where, Don[2] Andres,
Is the old Sacramento and Stockton Trail?"

As it was, no one alive knew of such trail and Mr. Pico lost his case.

In Calaveras County in 1859 the old friendships were being steadily disrupted. The number of sympathizers with the confederate cause was easily noticeable. Evincing no fear of consequences, the Southern faction made the prospect of separating the State from the Union seemed quite possible. This sentiment prevailed mostly amongst the politicians, editors, sidewalk wags, bench sitters and other street loafers who squatted on the drumheads of empty whisky barrels. They also freely and openly discussed the Negro equality and drew vivid word pictures such as:

"Nigger in the bed, with your sister wed."

During the summer of 1859 meetings of the organization, known as the Knights of the Golden Circle, were quietly held in different parts of the county. The primary object of this secret society was known only to a very few of its members. Whether or not it intended to aid the Rebellion in event of a conflict between the North and South, no person was able to definitely state. One thing however is certain and that is, the Knights of the Golden Circle had a powerful group with which to contend. The members of the "Loyal League" kept a sharp watch on the activities of the opposing organization. In those days the citizens were divided; strife, hatred and bitterness resulted. Finally, padlocks were put on front gates, locking out old and once cherished friends and neighbors. The Southerners and there were many living in and around San Andreas, were branded by the Loyal Leaguers, as Copperheads [a person in the northern states who sympathized with the South during the Civil War] demagogues.

Dr. P. Goodwyn was denouncing the Democratic party of Calaveras County[3]. The same doctor who in Volcano had once taken an active part in a "necktie party". He denounced the party as being the

> "most disgraceful, hellish, diabolical, deep-dyed villainous scheme to commit a crime upon the body politic that ever stained the criminal calendars of the entire world."

And, what was even worse, he publicly stated:

> "Daily, I walk the streets of San Andreas with an adder, ready to sting".

The irascible doctor may, or may not, have had in mind Wm. Jeff Gatewood. But in those tragic days leading up to the Civil War, every hair on the heads of men, like the hair of Eumenides [avenging hairy deities in Greek mythology who tormented criminals and inflicted plaques] was regarded as a serpent by one faction or the other. And while men wrangled and separated themselves from each other, the women of San Andreas did their level best to keep their men at home and out of harm's way. Even so, on Friday morning, September 16, 1859, despair hung over the town like a funeral pall. Several days previously, rumors were set afloat about a serious argument that had taken place between Dr. Goodwin and Jeff Gatewood.

The people were without awareness that a duel was in contemplation. The northern doctor, it appears, spat out some ugly words about Copperheads. The southern lawyer resented his erstwhile friend's tirade of abuse. But little of this altercation that resulted in a challenge being sent by Goodwin to Gatewood was ever made known by the public.

The citizens of San Andreas always believed, and no doubt rightly so,

In the backround is Moonlight Flat (near Fourth Crossing), location of the Gatewood-Goodwin duel in September 1859. People from left; Fred Cuneo, Bill Wells, Ernest Bernasconi, Earnest Long and George Poore

Courtesy of Calaveras County Historical Society

that the seconds [supporters, helpers or assistants] for Dr. Goodwin, William (Buck) T. Lewis, and Major Glynn, and for Jeff Gatewood, Captain Robert Pope, and Martin Rowan, had made honorable efforts to establish peace between the "Knight of the Golden Circle" and the "Loyal Leaguer" but had failed to bring about a reconciliation.

In the haze of early morning the duelist's seconds, surgeons and a few intimate friends, left San Andreas for the Kentucky House at the Third Crossing, where the duel was scheduled to take place on the Alabama Trail at six o'clock. Instead, they traveled onward to an open field near Foreman's Ranch at the Fourth Crossing[4]. Here, where the September dust burdened every leaf, every blade of dry grass, a stop was made. Then, after the "field of honor" was reached, the ground was measured off. The agreement was to shoot it out with rifles at a distance of fifty paces. Attorney Lewis, acting for Dr. Goodwin, won the "word" and Captain Pope, a Gatewood second, the "choice of ground". At precisely seven o'clock, the men who had disagreed about the abolition of slavery were ready for position. Calm and self-possessed, they exchanged courtesies with each other before taking positions assigned to them by their seconds.

All in readiness-
At the word 'three'
Each man sprung the trigger of his rifle.
Dr. Goodwin's hung fire and missed his shot.
Lawyer Gatewood, a dead shot,
Fired and struck his opponent in the abdomen,
Inflicting a mortal wound.
Gatewood hastened to Goodwin's side, saying:
"Doctor, I am very sorry for this, very sorry, indeed."

"I'm glad to know that you've acted like a gentleman,"
- was, the injured man's reply.

Mr. Gatewood's carriage, being roomy enough to accommodate the unfortunate duelist, was left for that purpose. With his surgeon Dr. Ford and a tragic look on his face, Jeff Gatewood left the blighted field. Together they returned to San Andreas in the latter's buggy.

That morning the iron doors of all buildings on St. Charles and Main streets remained closed and a deathlike silence pervaded San Andreas, especially when Dr. Goodwin was brought into town and taken to his bedroom in the Metropolitan Hotel. At eleven o'clock on the following morning, he died. Thereafter, the disagreeable word 'Copperhead,' was seldom heard here in San Andreas.

Public opinion exonerated Jeff Gatewood from all blame in the tragic affair. He had done all that was humanly possible to adjust matters between himself and his antagonist but the doctor, hostile, was bent on a duel. No person more than Jeff Gatewood himself regretted the doctor's untimely end. The very thought of having shot and killed a fellow being, darkened and saddened Gatewood's subsequent life.

> The San Andreas "Independent," on September 17, 1859, Chronicled: "We might here, with much appropriateness indulge in a moral essay upon the general evil of the duello [rules and practice of dueling] and prove for the thousandth time its utter incompatibility with the faith of a Christian but, when the Supreme Judge can lay aside his ermine to fight a duel; when a United States Senator does not think it so terrible to face the shot of an experienced marksman, at ten paces. To look public opinion in the eye and incur its scorn by refusing to accept a challenge; when society and the people lavish their favors and caresses upon those who have fought duels and honor them- we see no recognized crime or violence to the commonwealth in the act just perpetrated. If the people desire to put an end to the "Code" let

them say so in some unmistakable manner. But so long as the records stand as they do and the people are more eager to scorn him who refuses, than to punish him who accepts a challenge, we cannot hold dueling as a very obnoxious exception to our public morality, whatever may be said and written under the impulse which some great or good man's fall gives to our sympathies."

William Jeff Gatewood & Friends circa 1865. From right sitting: Rienzi Hoplins, Gatewood, Ned Bushyhead. Standing: J.A. Foster and H.G. Allen the Postmaster.

Courtesy of C.C. H. S.

Jeff Gatewood, after that black Friday morning, was seldom seen to smile, he now moved at a slower gait. His intimate friends and colleagues missed his mirthful laughter. The edge of his quick wit and good humor was not so keen as formerly. Finally, he withdrew from those friends with whom he had always been closely associated and devoted himself to the study of classic literature. He, for a time, was the publisher of the San Andreas "Register," a weekly newspaper, for which he wrote editorials and occasionally verse. He was twice elected District Attorney of Calaveras County. Shortly after the removal of the county seat from Mokelumne Hill to San Andreas, Mr. Gatewood together with Edward (Ned) W. Bushyhead, of El Dorado Town, and Narcisco Bresino (Little Corporal), Gatewood's "man Friday," left San Andreas for San Diego. There, in the Southland, he became one of the foremost lawyers in San Diego County. His services were invaluable as he was an authority in legal cases involving land grants. Among those young men who studied law in Jeff Gatewood's law office in San Diego was late William J. Hunsaker who afterwards became a distinguished lawyer of Los Angeles.

On March 17, 1888, in San Diego Bay, Wm. Jeff Gatewood[5] a native of Virginia died aboard the schooner "Rosita". When the news of his death reached Calaveras County, Victor Gottschalk himself a lawyer of San Andreas, was heard to say:

"Jeff Gatewood was a truly generous, large-souled man.
He commanded the confidence and affection of those
Who knew him."

Unfortunately, over the years Gatewood had become addicted to liquor, the nepenthe, to drown the memory of a hearse. The black plumed Goodwin hearse that in San Andreas was followed by a long line of villagers, moving slowly along a dusty hillside road to the People's Cemetery.

Reddick Hotel or Fourth Crossing Roadhouse or Foreman's Ranch. Hotel was located near the Duel site.

Courtesy of Calaveras County Historical Society

Footnotes

1 Robert Senkewicz in his annotations to Bayard Taylor's book *ELDORADO* states Andres Pico (1810-1876) was born in San Diego. He served in the Mexican military and defeated Stephen W. Kearny at San Pasqual in 1846. After the war, he served in the California state assembly in 1851 and the state senate in 1860-1861"

2 "Don" is a Spanish title similar to an English "Sir".

3 Goodwyn or Goodwin

4 Fourth Crossing was also know as the "Moonlight Flat"

5 A street in San Andreas still bears his name. Gatewood Avenue is located south of Saint Charles Street and one block east of Church Hill Rd.

9

SHEEP RANCH

The Fabulous East Lode

Thirteen miles east of the Mother Lode is a notable system of gold bearing, quartz veins, which runs from Collierville, near the Stanislaus River, to a point close to the Mokelumne River. The Sheep Ranch, Chavanne, Washington[1], Right Bower, Petticoat[2], Horse Thief, and Ritter[3] mines have proved, conclusively, that the East Lode in standpoint of importance, is second only to the Mother Lode and is credited with having produced in excess of $40,000,000[4] worth of gold of purest quality.

Chavanne Mine in 1885 - Sheep Ranch, Calaveras Co. California

Courtesy of Calaveras County Archives

Although considerable prospecting has been done, the East Lode remains virtually unexplored. The country rock is slate and schist, with a width of from one to three miles, and can be traced the entire length of the Lode. All the veins have a varying strike and dip. The general trend is west of north; the dip however tends toward the east. The Lode is distinguished by the branching character of the fissures, the inclusion of slate material in the quartz and by a banded structure of the veins. Unlike those of the Mother Lode, East Lode veins as a rule are narrow and of high grade. Heavy gauge rock, carrying much galena[5] and tellurium[6] is frequently found in the different veins.

On the East Lode is situated the renowned Sheep Ranch mine. The principal ore veins of this valuable property are as follow: Strike, south of east, dip 72 degrees to northeast, average width, 18 inches. Ore, quartz with free gold and a small percentage of unchanged auriferous pyrites. Country rock is the Calaveras slate, dark schist tending to massive argillite. Other near-by claims were the William E. Bean, Washington, Lodi, Fenian, Mountain Quail, Comet, Ferguson and Wallace, Salamander Quartz, Roscoe, Franklin, Toon Q.M., Jim Smiley and Pioche.

Charles Henry Schroebel

Courtesy of C.C.H.S.

Of two versions of the discovery of the Sheep Ranch Mine, the first follows: William E. Bean, a Washington Flat prospector, made daily searches for the yellow metal in the tributaries of the San Antone, San Domingo, and Indian Creeks and despite long hours of brow-sweat labor, seldom found any gold worth mentioning but luck changed in Bill Bean's favor on the morning of September 8th, 1866. That morning, with a pick and pan, he toiled up a narrow ledge trail leading from Washington Flat to Henry Schroebel's camp where sheep were grazing. Here, he found a quartz vein nosing up from the ground and liking the appearance of the rock, stepped off his claim. Then, on paper borrowed from a sheepherder, he jotted down his notice of location and with wooden pegs of his own whittling, fastened it to a pine tree, the "witness" tree. At early candlelight that day, Bill Bean foot sore and weary returned to his home and told his wife Nancy about his discovery. He all but convinced her that poverty for the Bean family was on its way out. And it might well have been except that, during his absence a gust of wind had blown away his location notice. No sooner had the paper fluttered off than two men arrived at Hay Press Flat[7] and filed on his, Bill Bean's promising claim.

The second version runs thus: Captain Amsa Ferguson[8] and Tom Smith, both of San Andreas, equipped with the necessary articles for prospecting and camping, left San Andreas for Yaqui Camp to search for the "color" in Paradise Gulch. The year being 1866, the gulch was no longer rich, accordingly the two-man expedition pressed on to San Antone camp. Amsa Ferguson, a pint-sized, grey haired gentleman did not always enjoy good health and was without muscular strength for a full day's work so he remained in camp to rest. While Amsa was resting, Tom Smith, a raw-boned young Goliath with brawn enough for a half dozen men, poked around in the hills looking for a quartz ledge. That morning, Tom shouldered his rifle and struck off for Red Hill on the San Antone ridge. In his wanderings that day he reached Schroebel's[9] sheep ranch comprising of a log cabin, log corral and a crude hay press. While passing, back of the cabin, Tom found a piece of gold-bearing quartz. After his return to the camp, he showed it to Captain Ferguson, who beamed his approval of Tom's find.

Captain (Cap) Amsa Ferguson

Courtesy of C.C.H.S.

The next day Amsa and Tom went together to Hay Press Flat, so called by reason of the hay press there and since the ground was a free domain, they located a claim, destined for fame as the Sheep Ranch mine. That same day, 300 feet west of his location, Tom found quartz cropping. Although rich, the cropping was without depth and before the day's end had petered out. For the next ten days, Amsa held down the camp and Tom took to the hills to bag a cougar that had been preying on Schroebel's sheep.

Sheep Ranch Mine. The mine office at right in front of waste or tailing piles. Head frame is at left. In the foreground is wood stacked to heat three steam boilers and a double-drawn steam hoist. Photo circa 1890

Courtesy of Jane Canavera

This building was moved from Chee Chee Flat near Mountain Ranch and was used as a General Store and living quarters. In 1904 it was used to construct the Pioneer Hotel. (see below)

Courtesy of Calaveras County Historical Society

Pioneer or Anderson Hotel, Sheep Ranch. The two story hotel was constructed by raising the single story building (upper photo) and building the ground floor under it. In 1904 the new building had eighteen bedrooms upstairs and downstairs were bedrooms, dining room, kitchen and a bar.

Courtesy of Jane Canavera

One crisp morning, Bill Bean came back prepared to work the near-by William E. Bean claim, which as a second choice, he had recently located. In a sense the second choice, made up to him for the loss of his first location.

Ferguson and Smith commenced work on a shaft near Bean's boundary line and this time they found the true lead. The shaft, sunk to a depth of 15 feet, hadn't cost its owners a red penny, for the Sheep Ranch claim yielded gold from the grass roots down.

Tom Smith, cocky as a Mexican horned lark, took the first gold from this Sheep Ranch mine to El Dorado Town[10], seven miles west of the sheep camp and placed it, for safe keeping, in the rock vault of Giovanni Rodesino's store[11]

Tom's reputed wealth so excited the citizens of Chee Chee Flat, Mountain Ranch, Colton Flat, McKinney's Humbug and El Dorado, that complete depopulation was threatened in each of these settlements. When the news of Amsa and Tom's rich strike reached San Andreas a rush to the East Lode was commenced.

Charley Mauritson later called Anderson moved the hotel from Chee Chee Flat.
Courtesy of Jane Canavera

A few weeks later, Tom Smith was felling pine with which to build a log cabin on the site afterwards occupied by Charley Anderson's livery and feed stable. While making the chips fly, he discovered a quartz ledge, which he named Lodi. This claim yielded $16,000 worth of gold. To Tom Smith having cash on hand was something he had never experienced before. Bent on enjoying himself, he quit all work at his Sheep Ranch claim for more than a year. His partners in the Lodi claim were his father and brother Horace but they continued to work the mine.

Tom was still jamboreeing when a big haul was made in the Sheep Ranch claim. At this very time Horace and his father were cooking up a plan by which they might obtain full possession of the above property. As a step in that direction Horace purchased Tom's interest in the Sheep Ranch mine. Amsa Ferguson, strong of will, refused to permit the mine to be worked. The feud continued until midnight in the Smith's cabin while a friendly game of stud poker was played by Horace Smith and Dollard Young. The former lambasted "Cap" Ferguson and the latter while resenting his vicious attack upon his friend's reputation, was stabbed to the heart with a dirk-knife. There being no eyewitness present in the cabin, a coroner's jury exonerated Horace Smith and at that time ordered him to leave the county. A short time later Horace Smith was shot and killed in a Virginia City barroom by H. W. F. Johnston of Nevada.

The affluent Ferguson urged William A. Wallace, County Clerk of Calaveras County, to purchase Smith's interest in the mine. Wallace agreed to do so but conditionally, that Ferguson remains his partner. With Horace dead, his heirs however were only too willing to part with their stock in the Sheep Ranch claim.

Mr. Wallace's first act was to deed his one half interest in the mine to his nephew, John Early of San Andreas. Rebel Early had worn the grey in the Civil War and for his loyalty to the South; his uncle in appreciation relieved him of financial worries.

For the next five years Ferguson, Wallace and Early operated the mine with excellent results. In April 1872, they cleaned up gold to the amount of $60,000. The following June these partners sold their property to James B. Haggin, Lloyd Tevis, and George Hearst of San Francisco.

Under the new management a 65-foot gallows frame was erected, new air compressors were installed and a 20-stamp quartz mill was built. William H. Clary became the superintendent, Asa Tuttle the top ground boss, John Champion was mine foreman, William Dorrah and Adam Poe, engineers, Milton Stephens, boss of the quartz mill, Frank Howard, machinist, James Champion, blacksmith and drill sharpener, Richard Spence, timber gang boss, James Malloy and Bertrand Dilharreguy (Bert Delray) shift bosses. Walter Knight was the timekeeper and Patrick Egan the checker.

The partners, Joseph T. Bryan[12] and William Larkin, from their logging camp near McNair's ranch, supplied the mine with timber, logging and four foot wood. William Armstrong from his sawmill on San Antone Creek, furnished lumber for the quartz mill and other buildings.

The Washington claim, near the Sheep Ranch mine was located in 1867 by Delmont V. McNair[13], a native of the Cherokee nation. A year later McNair sold his promising ore ledge to Andre Chavanne and Jules Fricot of Grass Valley, Nevada County, California. These partners in 1880 sold the Washington claim to Haggin, Tevis and Hearst. Known as the Chavanne mine, now it was worked in connection with the Sheep Ranch deep diggings.

Bill Bean and Tom Martin after taking eight tons of ore from their claim, Oraminta, crushed it in their arrastra and were enriched to the tune of eight pounds of gold. Experience quartz miners thought that the Oraminta located just west of the Sheep Ranch mine, with an ore vein 14 feet wide was worthy of development.

Four miles from the town of Sheep Ranch was the Right Bower mine, the most easterly of all known quartz bearing ledges in Calaveras County. The brothers Samuel and James Woods located this claim in 1867 and with no capital other than their strong arms and stronger faith they sunk their shaft to a depth of 125 feet. They have developed the mine and in time reaped fair-sized fortunes.

Edie and Dick Raggio
Courtesy of John MacPherson

The irregular Right Bower ore shoot varied from 2 to 6 feet in width, and each ton of ore mined yielded from $60 to $80 worth of gold. In December 1872, the San Antone creek froze solid, compelling the brothers to suspend work at their mine. During the shut down the shaft filled with water and the owners lacking the equipment for drainage, never reopened it.

Christmas week of the above year was noiseless in Sheep Ranch. No stamps drummed in the quartz mill. The ice, which covered the silver faced mill plates, had caused the trouble.

On a densely wooded hill, Woods Hill, east of the Right Bower mine was the Rancheria of the several hundred Indians of this region. Each autumn after the acorn crop had been harvested, the bucks and their mahalas and children, from near and far, gathered in Charley Anderson's "cow pasture" in the heart of the town of Sheep Ranch to hold their annual Pow Wow and "big eat".

Semi-circled by conical hills and pine forests, Sheep Ranch is a superbly situated town and in its foundation days was seriously clean and inviting. The dwelling houses were no great shakes but the gardens that surrounded them were objects of beauty. In the best of times there, a day in 1881 the population was about 700, and where Schroebel's sheep had once grazed now stood Arnold Friedberger's general merchandise store. Also the following was there: two church buildings, Protestant and Roman Catholic, Odd Fellows Hall, Swan's drug store, Albert Bader's butcher shop, Dick Raggio's livery stable, Blair's bakery, Silva's barber shop, Ben Stephens' blacksmith shop, Raggio Brothers' store, Joseph Ratto's boarding house, the Egan, Anderson and Forrest hotels, Jim McKay, Bill Smith, and Pat Grennan's saloons. Hubert Ide was in charge of Treat & Wyllie's water ditch. John Hauselt operated a brewery. James Whitesel was the coffin maker and Mme. Anne Javeaux, a native of France[14] owned a berry patch and orchard. Joseph Raggio was the Postmaster, James Stephens was a Wells Fargo agent, Julius Lloyd and Martha Coulter were the first School Teachers here, W. W. Cole was the Justice of the Peace, and Patrick Keen was Constable of the township.

John Hauselt
Courtesy of John McPherson

Frequently from the sawmills and logging camps, east of the town, lumberjacks, intent on a drunken carouse came by horseback to Sheep Ranch "to split the town wide open", with their wild yells and whoops. There weren't any bawdy houses in this strictly moral town. Occasionally, a flashily garbed demimondaine alighted from the stage and after refreshing herself in Forrest's hotel, busied herself with turkey red calico curtains which she hung at the windows of some house in a remote part of the village. But the "fancy woman" after an order from Constable Keen to yank down her curtains, was soon boarding a stage for destinations unknown. Prostitutes were not the only persons excluded from this orderly settlement. Sheep Ranch had early placed a ban against the Mexican, Chilean, Negro and Chinese miners.

Typical dress of Chinese men.
Courtesy of Bank of Stockton Historical Photo Collection

Andre Chavanne, a native of France, tall, elegantly gray, while on a visit to San Francisco he forgot the slogan of the Sheep Ranch miners, "NO PIGTAILS" and engaged a Chinese cook whom he brought to Sheep Ranch.

Chavanne shared a villa with his Parisian wife, Emilie and his business partner, countryman and lifelong friend, Jules Fricot and the latter's son Desire.

On the morning following, the Celestial's arrival at the charming villa adjacent to the Chavanne mine, James Grennan a timber logger, caught sight of a slick braid of ebony hair flapping against the wide sleeve of a black satin tunic. The miners immediately were in conference. That day, while the inoffensive servant was on his way to Bader's butcher shop to select his choice cuts of meat; he was stopped by miners who told him that he must leave Sheep Ranch at once. A half hour later the unlucky "John" was trudging on wooden sabots to O'Neil's Creek under escort of Michael Tischer, Manley Woods, Richard Raggio and Richard Spence who firmly gave directions concerning the road leading from Jacob Zugar's Ranch[15] to El Dorado Town.

On a hill, a short distance east of Bill and Nancy Bean's homestead was the primitive camp of "Old Joe" and his mahala, Jinny. Early in life, members of his own tribe cruelly treated Joe, a Mokelumne Indian, because of his admiration for the white settlers. They in a jealous frenzy, tossed him headlong onto a bed of live coals, and left him there to suffer. Suffer he did indeed; he was rescued and cared for by a comely young Indian maiden from a neighboring tribe. Jinny, after binding Joe's wounds in Mallow leaves, assisted him to reach El Dorado where the Americans gave him protection.

Fifteen years later Joe, badly scarred and faithful Jinny were in Sheep Ranch and here they remained together until each, in his turn, was called by the Great Spirit to the Happy Hunting Ground. Although Sheep Ranch was often the scene of weird ceremonial dances in which hundreds of Indians from hither and yon took part, Joe and Jinny, silent and aloof, preferred the friendship of the white people, rather than the members of their own race. They were content to watch the goings on in Charley Anderson's stubble field from their hilltop camp. Liberally sustained by their friends in Sheep Ranch, they seldom left.

James C. Mauritson[16] (Charley Anderson) reached Sheep Ranch from Chee Chee Flat[17] in the spring of 1867. Better let Charley tell his own story:

"I was living in West Point this county, when in '58, an old Mexican named Chico, who still treasured specimens from a mine that had been worked steadily for hundreds of years in Mexico, came to me and likened one of these specimens to the ore he had picked up over the hills at a spot since known as Sheep Ranch.

The two specimens were identical; each appeared to be sprinkled with stardust. The Mexican impressed me with the earnest manner in which he claimed that wherever this peculiar silvery sprinkled quartz ore existed there also would be found vast quantities of gold deep down in the earth. And this ore according to old Chico is found in but one section of Mexico, where golden treasure has continued to be unearthed for hundreds of years. It is a custom, amounting to a religion with miners, Chico avowed, to worship at the shrine of this uncommon ore.

Old Chico told me that nowhere else in Mexico could this ore be found. That there would never be but one lead found in California and that would be the one somewhere near the spot on which he had picked up the mysterious piece of float rock. Now, when I heard the news of Tom Smith's discovery at Hay Press Flat, I remembered this strange story of Chico's and concluded to locate near the Sheep Ranch mine and here I am to this very day." [February 15, 1902]

"I left Chee Chee Flat and located here for the sole purpose of making a living but as the years slip by I am more firmly convinced that I shall live to see old Mexican Chico's statement come true. I have never conversed with a medium, he went on, nor had I anything to do with spiritualists, yet often at the midnight hour while lying on the ore dump of the Sheep Ranch mine, rolled up in an old army blanket, I have been awakened from a sound sleep by a passing voice, saying; 'Beneath your bed lies gold, millions of dollars worth of gold, it is nearly all below the 2000 foot level'."

Charley Anderson, thereafter, dreamt of a day when signal bells should be ringing on the 2000-foot level. In imagination, he could see kindly Bill Dorrah's hand on the throttle valve of his engine and he could see the steel cable coil as this competent engineer hoisted the huge iron buckets. He could see each bucket bearing the gold-laden blackish quartz being hoisted to the surface.

Charley Anderson's hotel, hall and livery stable were a stone's throw south of the Sheep Ranch mine. Fearful of being laughed at, Charley told only a few of his cronies about his experiences while taking midnight siestas on the East Lode's richest ore dump. Who knows? There may still be fabulous amounts of gold in the underground treasure vaults of the famous Sheep Ranch mine. This mine produced pure, heavy and exquisite gold, large amounts of which were sold direct to goldsmiths East and West for the production of jewelry.

The 2000-foot level in the Sheep Ranch mine is yet to be reached. The phantom voice that awakened Charley Anderson may someday, laugh back a gleeful laughter for having revealed to a trustful dreamer one of Mother Earth's great secrets.

When the Sheep Ranch mine operators stopped blasting the quartz rock, the lowest level was 1,400 feet 18 below the collar of the shaft and although the vein was small, averaging about 8 inches in thickness. It was so uniformly rich as to entirely disprove that "shoe string" ledges did not make "pay diggings". The Sheep Ranch was essentially a "poor man's" mine, having paid its way from top ground to the lowest drift. Under the supervision of Milton Stephens the 20 stamp mill crushed quartz rock for 20 years without exhausting the ore reserves. The ore mined did not contain enough sulphurets to justify the erection of a concentration plant. Sheep Ranch ore carried much free gold and it was superior in fineness to any other mined in Calaveras County.

Sheep Ranch School 1895. Note the teacher with a shotgun on the left.
Courtesy of Jane Canavera

Footnotes

1 Also known at different times as Bullion Hill and McNair mine. Was located between Sheep Ranch and Murphys.

2 Located in Rail Road Flat.

3 Located two miles NE of Mountain Ranch.

4 Undoubtedly, this includes other counties of East Lode, not just Calaveras. Amount converts to $1.2 Billion in today's dollars. Although gold was valued at $20 to the ounce, the miners never received this amount as the quality of gold affected the price. San Andreas Independent May 1, 1858, "the inflated prices of supplies the miner had to buy resulted in his getting $8 to $16 an ounce."

5 Precious Metals are frequently associated with deposits of galena, a bluish gray mineral with metallic luster, consisting of lead sulfide.

6 Tellurium is a semi-metallic, silvery white, brittle crystalline element. Like galena, it is an indicator of possible presence of gold in a deposit.

7 Today, Sheep Ranch.

8 Captain Amsa or Ampsey Parker Ferguson commonly called "Cap"

9 At this point in time, we have no other reference to Schroebel's name that can be connected with Sheep Ranch.

10 Today, Mountain Ranch.

11 Old Rodesino store has been replaced by the Sender's Hardware and Grocery store.

12 Mrs. Buckbee's father.

13 Clement Vann McNair

14 The Javeaux Family came from Belgium not France. Ann Javeaux's daughter May was the Postmistress of Mountain Ranch Post Office for 33 years. From January 1923 to 1956.

15 Located on south side of Sheep Ranch road just west of O'Neil's Creek.

16 Also spelled Mawritson.

17 Chee Chee Flat was an early Gold Rush community. It was located where today is the junction of Whiskey Slide, Ponderosa Way and West Murray Creek roads, and now part of Mountain Ranch. It is reputed that gold was found there at least a year or two before Marshall's official discovery see History of Mountain Ranch-El Dorado, by Phil Alberts.

18 This narrative was written around 1932 and the level reached then was 1400 ft. Later, in 1940s the St. Josephs Lead Co. the new owners of the mine, penetrated the 2000 ft. level and reached down to 2400 ft. As prophesized by Chico, the best gold was below the 2000 ft. level. Prince Andre Poniatowski who ended up leasing 30 gold mines in Calaveras County also predicted this based on his experience in the gold mines of South Africa.

10

OTHER GOLD RUSH CAMPS

Mural in the Red Barn Museum on Mountain Ranch Rd. in San Andreas.
Photo Wally Motloch

YAQUI CAMP

Yaqui Camp on Willow Creek was three miles southeast of San Andreas and was a dangerous place for an honest man to tarry. The Mexicans and Yaqui Indians[1] regarded the ground as being within their sphere of influence and were upheld by Murieta who had found it a safe ground. A Mexican, Ignacio Moreno, the owner of a tiende [store] and a Fonda [small inn, eating place] was a split-tongued renegade. Moreno once assisted Captain Charles Ellis to capture a horse thief and gave this Deputy Sheriff information concerning men against whom he (Morino) held a grudge. He would give Ellis a wrong lead too often and fearing the consequences, left Yaqui Camp for Los Angeles County where he was lynched for cattle rustling.

Here, while the Yaqui Indians dug gold, their Mexican masters plotted and schemed. They robbed sluice-boxes and committed murders. In 1852, within a week's time, eighteen gold washers were murdered between the Calaveras and Stanislaus rivers. Captain Ellis, a Mexican War veteran, was ordered by Wm. Clark, the County Sheriff, to stop banditry in Calaveras County and this he proceeded to do. The Calaveras officers, under Ellis' direction, were determined to break up Murieta's[2] organization and to destroy his several camps, ambushes and hiding places. Wherever possible

Squarehead gold mine at Yaqui Camp near San Andreas
Courtesy of Calaveras County Historical Society

they barred thc cntrances of caves, shallow holes, and discarded mining tunnels, in which the bandits, when horses had been shot from under them, took refuge. In 1852, a posse, led by Ellis, left San Andreas for Yaqui Camp to round up criminals. This foot posse made a house-to-house search, dragged out several lawless ruffians, hung one and sent a bullet into the head of another. Then tore down or set fire to the flimsy buildings of this wicked camp.

From Chaparral Hill, it is said, Murieta and Three Fingered Jack watched their favorite camp being destroyed by fire and in retaliation, galloped their horses down the hill to the Phoenix quartz mine where they murdered two men, one of whom was Peter Woodcock, the mine's principal owner.

Wade H. Johnston reached Yaqui Camp from Placerville in 1854 and dug gold in both Willow Creek and Paradise Gulch. In his home at Paradise Gulch, Mr. Johnston years later, told of once having seen two Frenchmen trundling a wheelbarrow chock full of the precious metal, from Paradise Gulch to San Andreas for shipment to France. Wade Johnston lived and mined at Yaqui Camp longer than any other person. His brother, Charles, was a Yaqui Camp blacksmith and when not busy mending broken wagon spokes and tongues, washed gold alongside his brother in the auriferous [used to describe rock or minerals the contain gold] gulch.

A picturesque campsite, Yaqui, is now but a memory, utterly devoid of Mexican bandits, Yaqui Indians and American gold washers. Its exciting history, however, handed down by word of mouth is more or less intact.

WILLOW CREEK

Willow Creek was located two miles south of San Andreas, was extensively mined by Americans in 1849-1850. It gave promise of becoming a permanent camp but when the near-by Bear Mountain became a strong hold for Mexican bandits, many miners hauled down their tents and departed for more thickly populated regions. Today the site of the Willow Creek encampment is grazing land.

LOWER CALAVERITAS

Lower Calaveritas [Little Skulls], one mile south of Yaqui Camp on O'Neil's Creek [Calaveritas Creek now] this Mexican rendezvous was less prosperous than some of its neighboring camps. It was inhabited by Sonorians in 1848. Senora Gerturdis Cervantes was the first woman to locate claims here. Under her direction, her peon laborers dug gold in her placer claims and after gold petered out, she moved to Upper Calaveritas where she spent the rest of her long and useful life. Senora M. Comeres established a Fonda and fandango in Lower Calaveritas in 1850. In the silver stirrup and sharp dagger days, it was a wild place, filled with reckless men and women. In 1854, Sheriff William Clark ordered his deputies to disarm all Mexicans whom they met on roads, trails and in the camps. The Sheriff's procedure arose from the impossibility of the law, being able to gain any information from a Mexican when one of their numbers committed a crime. Even though he himself had witnessed it, no Mexican due to fear, could be induced to furnish evidence against his countryman. Rather than talk, Senora Comeres went into hiding in Upper Calaveritas where she lived out her leisure days.

After the Mexicans left Lower Calaveritas a large number of Chinamen with "pigtails" streaming down their backs, trudged from Chinese shacks in San Andreas to the Willow Creek mining district. At sundown the long single file of "coolies" returned to San Andreas, poles slung across their necks from both ends of which hung wicker baskets. In this manner, for long years the "Johns" managed to live and if they were lucky, save enough money to pay for the transportation of their bones to China, one dollar each bone.

Benjamin Locke a forty-niner cabined alone, between Paradise Gulch and Lower Calaveritas. He made weekly trips to San Andreas for supplies he obtained these from merchants John Sharp and Joseph Armitage. In 1861 Ben Locke left his claim and cabin to enlist in the California Company A. 2nd Massachusetts Cavalry.

Costa Store in Upper Calaveritas c. 1900

Courtesy of Louise Greenlaw

UPPER CALAVERITAS

Upper Calaveritas, a few miles east of Yaqui Camp, on the San Antone Ridge, commands a splendid view of the surrounding country. Here, in 1849 Alcalde Julian Burdo established a trading post. Orrin Spencer was this camp's first Justice of the Peace. In his courtroom fierce battles between officers and the friends of criminals were frequently waged. The notorious gambler, Sam Brown (Long-haired Brown) when things didn't go his way, would reach for his dirk knife[3]. The blood of more than one man drenched the dirt floor of Upper Calaveritas' gambling saloons.

Upper Calaveritas too, had its lost mine El Arbol, according to legend. Being the richest, this mine was located supposedly, by Mexicans in 1849 and lost by them. Men hoping to stumble upon the lost mine tramped from one ridge to the other but could find no trace of it. The former bandito Kinko of San Andreas, it is said, had knowledge of its location. It was from this treasure pile that he obtained the gold necessary for his livelihood. On nights of storms, Mexicans old and superstitious, believed lights burned above buried gold and in accordance with their belief on stormy nights, they were often seen on San Antone Ridge.

Originally two brothers discovered the El Arbol mine, the youngest of whom was lynched by a mob and his body left to hang from a tree. The hanged man's brother went to the scene for the purpose of cutting the body

Calaveritas School 1896

Courtesy of Louise Greenlaw

down and giving it burial. While digging the grave, he found gold near the base of the tree. He buried his brother's body but in the process, dug out a large amount of gold and departed.

The Upper Calaveritas miners, booted and spurred, straddled cayuses and raced them through the streets, there was never a dull moment here. Sam Brown, Bunty Owens, Alfred Richardson and Lafayette Chioser all professional gamblers, stalked around looking more like traveling arsenals than human beings. Both gold and whiskey were plentiful. Thomas Titcomb, a Calaveritas Creek gold washer, was shot and killed by a man named Bratton. Howard Maupin murdered Thomas Dill[4] a peaceable citizen of Calaveritas. The old stone building where in early fifties, Orrin Spencer the Justice of the Peace held court is still standing along with other pioneer buildings. In this old mining town where the streets and trails are still steep and narrow, the shadows of the past fall upon every flagstone laid there, by the stouthearted ones of the gold stampede days.

OLD GULCH

Old Gulch, a few miles east of the Kentucky House at the Third Crossing, was one of the rich camps of 1849. Among its first settlers were R. Basquez, Victor Bidache, Degno Mariquinne and William Dower.

Emmett Joy at Old Gulch. Circa 1930

Courtesy of Calaveras County Archives

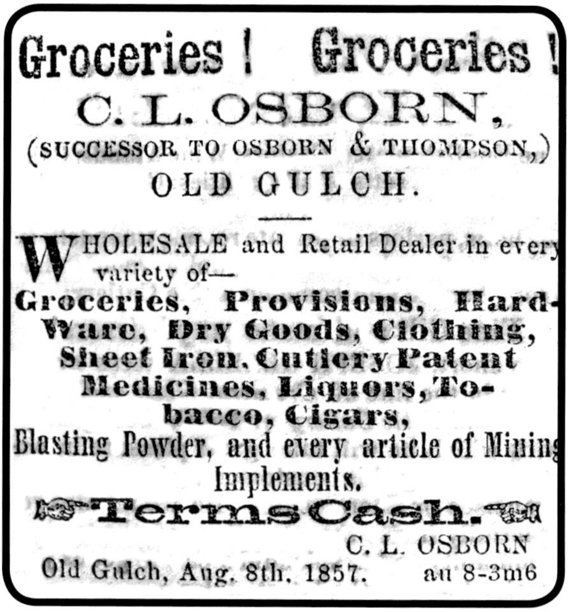
Groceries! Groceries!

C. L. OSBORN,

(SUCCESSOR TO OSBORN & THOMPSON,)

OLD GULCH.

WHOLESALE and Retail Dealer in every variety of—

Groceries, Provisions, Hard-Ware, Dry Goods, Clothing, Sheet Iron, Cutlery Patent Medicines, Liquors, To-bacco, Cigars,

Blasting Powder, and every article of Mining Implements.

Terms Cash.

C. L. OSBORN

Old Gulch, Aug. 8th, 1857. au 8-3m6

Joseph C. Agostini a native of France was the first to erect a stone building here. A good building, it is still in existence. Wm. Thompson, Wm. Tuckerman and John Schunck established the first general mercantile store. Mexican and Chileans first mined the rich placers of Old Gulch.

At the head of Old Gulch was a "hanging" tree over the branches of which ropes were sometimes slung. Criminals by order of relentless "Judge Lynch" were compelled to die with their boots on. Here in 1852, a gambler shot and killed a miner, then turned the smoking weapon on himself. Injured, he vaulted into his saddle and sent his horse galloping from the gulch. His head in a whirl, he wheeled his horse around and returned to the settlement, dismounted and entered the saloon where on the dirt floor his victim's body lay. "Pull off my boots Boys," he gasped to his fellow gamblers. "I don't want to die with my boots on." A moment later, he died with naked feet on the green felt of the only billiard table in Old Gulch.

SAN ANTONE CAMP

Cuneos at San Antone Camp in 1926.

Courtesy of Ray Cuneo

Gold Mining at San Antone Camp in 1896. Note the large overshot water wheel that drove the pumps and the hoist. The Cuneo brothers, Charles, Frank Jr. and Colombo are on the bridge in the center.

Courtesy of Ray Cuneo

On San Antone Creek, at the base of Tunnel Hill, was situated San Antone Camp. It was a wild and reckless Mexican settlement, a strictly masculine camp. A man had to be quick on the draw or his hours were numbered. In 1851 when Benjamin Kent Thorn mined in this rugged and remote diggings the richest placers were in the hands of the Mexicans and Chileans. Thorn's career as a gold miner began on the Yuba River in 1849, but his career as an officer began at San Antone Camp. His life story, if fully narrated, would make a large book chock full of adventure and excitement.

In 1850, John Phipps, an American gold digger, robbed and murdered Pedro Morales a Mexican miner. Phipps skipped camp. Two years later, when Sheriff Clarke appointed young Thorn a Deputy Sheriff, Ben's first act was to ferret out Phipps, arrest and bring him to justice. Here, where pistols barked, cougars shrieked and steel blades dripped human blood, only a few stone buildings and foundations remain. San Antone Camp's story, like that of Tunnel Hill has been forgotten.

INDIAN CREEK

Two miles south of Sheep Ranch, on Indian Creek was the miner's camp. Extensively mined in 1849 the first miner ever to wash gravel in this stream was James P. Whitesel. He took from each panful of dirt between $4 to $20 worth of gold.

John Weaver, a pioneer of 1846 mined at Indian Creek in 1850. In San Francisco, years later he said:

"My luck fluctuated. My best claim was on Indian Creek, about four miles from Murphys. My partner and I used to go to town on a Saturday night with a bag six to eight inches long, brimful of gold. Lay in provisions and other supplies for a week then go home on Monday morning "dead broke" as regularly as clockwork. We rode to town on an old mule, Greaser fashion, one in front and the other behind"

John Weaver, while mining in San Domingo and San Antone creeks, famous for trout as well as gold, may have observed the great marble ledge, which crosses these creeks, however, he made no mention of having seen it. The ledge from 75 to 100 feet in width has frequently been mistaken for a quartz vein. Its pure white surface has lured many a miner to financial ruin.

Stefano Valenti and his wife Angela established on the south bank of Indian Creek, a trading post, a wayside inn and a saloon a rough board building at the roadside. It is still standing with front door wide open, just as it did in Stefano and Angela's time.

In January of 1867 Mr. and Mrs. J. B. K. Church and their three-year-old son while attempting to cross Indian Creek had their buggy overturned by the force of the current. Mr. Church severely injured, succeeded in reaching the shore. Mrs. Church and her little boy were carried down the stream and drowned. The following morning, four miles down stream, their bodies were recovered.

Among the men who located claims in the Indian Creek Mining District at an early date were; Jose Liliana Briseno, Luigi Pescia, Simeon Chase, Juan B. Martini, DeWitt C. Stannard, Angelo Canevaro, Antonio Benoccia, John Otis, Roderick[5] P. Terwilliger and Peter Davis. Some of these men realized fortunes.

CHEROKEE CAMP

This camp's population was mixed with Cherokee Indians predominating. The Cherokee House was a famous wayside tavern around which the camp was built. Situated between Chaparral Hill and John Cottle's ranch, it was looked upon with disfavor by the officers of the law. One day, Officer Charles Ellis picked up a wounded bandit who was hiding in the brush of Chaparral Hill. Upon reaching the Cherokee House he turned him over for safe keeping to the Indian proprietor. Ellis rode on to the Fourth Crossing to make an arrest, he intended, on his return, to relieve the landlord of his charge. The Cherokee, having had a few hair raising experiences with bandits, as soon as Deputy Sheriff Captain Ellis' back was turned, took the wounded desperado outdoors and strung him up to the nearest tree. Nothing remains to mark the site of the Cherokee House.

FOURTH CROSSING

Foreman's Ranch, on the South Branch of the Calaveras River [San Antone Creek], has always been called "Fourth Crossing". The cousins Isaac, Simon and Samuel Foreman, in 1849 took up a large acreage of land six miles south of San Andreas and on it these partners and Captain Moses Thorpe established a trading post and tavern.

Fourth Crossing was not famous for gold until February 12, 1854. A rich discovery was made in the bed of the stream. After the big strike at Red Bar a large number of Chinese flocked to Foreman's Ranch. Here, too, the American gold washers eyed the frugal Mongolians with suspicion. The Chinese miners had no easy time of it either. In September the Americans held a mass meeting and passed resolutions demanding that before the end of that month all Chinese leave Fourth Crossing. If, for any reason, a "Chinese Boy" refused to depart, he was to be expelled by force if necessary. When the day set for the expulsion arrived, the sheriff was on the ground to prevent

Reddick Hotel at Fourth Crossing

Courtesy of Wally Motloch

John B. Reddick was the Lieutenant Governer of California

Courtesy of C.C.H.S

the hostile miners from carrying out their drastic intentions. The skirmish, between the Americans, Chinese and their Mexican and Chilean sympathizers, took place on September 25, 1854. A free-for-all fight, it wound up with two Chileans and one Mexican dead and a dozen or more badly wounded Chinese. Samuel Foreman, sharply aware of the bitterness each faction held against the other, while rocks were being hurled, knives drawn and pistols fired, sent messengers to the neighboring towns for surgeons to bind up wounds and make stitches in battered heads. Dr. Ford of San Andreas, Dr. Wm. Jones of Murphys, Dr. Wm. Kelly of Six Mile Creek and Dr. J. I. Boon, of Angels Camp responded with promptitude.

It was a fast and furious fight in which the Americans were taking the worst of it. Then along came the Jesus Maria Guards, a military organization that had considerable experience in quelling riots. The guardsmen, aided by miners from San Andreas, Willow Creek and Hawkeye managed to save

The Thorpe Gold Mine at Fourth Crossing. In 1897 this mine was leased to Prince Andre Poniatowski (California Exploration Corporation). It became a part of Crocker-Poniatowski empire that included 30 gold mines in Calaveras County, the Electra hydro-electric plant near Mokelumne Hill that started the PG&E. and the Sierra Railroad to Angels Camp.

Courtesy of Calaveras County Historical Society.

the day for their countrymen. That day hundreds of Chinese, Mexicans and Chileans were driven from the Fourth Crossing. Undaunted the Mexicans and Chileans founded Campo Nueve, two miles south west of Foreman's Ranch. Later, many of the Chinese were permitted to return to their claims in which they dug gold, unmolested.

Joaquin Murieta, according to Carlos Noriega and his wife Joaquina, located a claim near Foreman's Ranch in 1849. A year later "Mountain Hounds" leftovers from the rapscallions of Sam Brannan stormed his diggings down stream. These disreputable men, a short time previously, had been driven out of San Francisco. The Hounds, after kicking and cuffing Joaquin into insensibility, raped and murdered his young wife Carmelita Feliz. After regaining consciousness, Joaquin in spite of an injured hand, dug a grave in which he buried Carmelita's body. A rock-bound grave, avowed Joaquina Noriega, was close to the River of the Skulls[6]. In his role of an avenger, for three long and bitter years, Joaquin's banditti terrorized the miners of Old Calaveras. Along the entire length of the Mother Lode, the alarming words "Keep guns loaded and handy" were passed from town to camp.

William Reddick and his wife Elizabeth and their several children, members of the Slab Ranch colony, left Angels Camp for the Fourth Crossing in 1857. Their daughter, Alice Reddick, married M. A. Wells, a Foreman's

Ranch schoolteacher. Anna, another daughter, married John Hill of Slab Ranch. John B. Reddick, their elder son, a San Andreas Lawyer, was once elected to the office of Lieutenant Governor of California. For many years the commodious inn, erected by the Foreman's and sold by them to William Reddick, was a popular place where frequently grand balls were held. A stage and relay station, it eventually became property of M. A. and Alice Wells.

One day at Foreman's Ranch a great excitement prevailed. Three white men made an unsuccessful attempt to kidnap and hold for ransom the beautiful young daughter of a rich Chinese claim owner. A scouting party was at once organized but was unable to capture the guilty ones.

To John Cottle belonged the credit for having raised the funds with which to erect a public schoolhouse at Foreman's Ranch. Mr. Cottle, at his own expense supplied the textbooks, blackboard and chalk. Cottle's ranch house, one of the show places of its district, was early destroyed by fire at which time Mr. Cottle's valuable library went up in smoke.

Later, when the Chinese "cleaned-up" the bed of the south branch, hogs, in large numbers were the main product of Foreman's Ranch. Alfalfa, for the support of the dairy herds was soon attracting the attention of the ranchers of this district. The demand for beef and mutton, cream and butter stimulated the livestock industry. Having for a western background the rugged Bear Mountain Range, large herds of cattle and flocks of sheep were always to be seen inside of the stone corrals that are still in service at Fourth Crossing,

THIRD CROSSING

Situated on O'Neil's Creek[7] was the Alabama House, a wayside hotel, erected by Charles Schroebel at the Third Crossing in 1851. The old Alabama foot trail, leading from San Andreas to Foreman's Ranch at the Fourth Crossing, ran past Schroebel's front door. Schroebel, a native of Alabama not only managed this inn, tilled the land, sheared sheep, built stone corrals, sheds and barns but scoured the surrounding hills for bandits. Indeed, he headed many a posse that successfully rounded up desperate men.

A courageous Deputy Sheriff, Schroebel amassed a fair sized fortune by renting his stone corrals to the outlaw Murieta, whose scalp he was out to get, dead or alive. One day the Alabama House burned to the ground and Schroebel decided to start on a new course. He believed in himself, the land and the sheep. He surrounded himself with capable herdsmen and shearers and with his large family removed to the southwestern part of the county where, shortly his flocks of sheep were as large as any in California.

The Old Kentucky House on Pool Station road in 1920's became part of the Calaveras Cement Plant Complex and served as a rail road station.

Courtesy of Kent Wilson

Opposite the Alabama House stood the equally famous Kentucky House, owned and managed by William Tate, a Kentuckian. Footpaths, from Boston Bar, Red Bar, Limbo Gulch, Lost City, San Domingo Camp[8] and other out of the way places joined the Alabama trail at the Kentucky House[9]. A very dangerous trail was the Alabama. Men trembled with the "shakes" before taking it, always shook hands with Destiny, for along its entire course the gold washers were murdered and the gory hands remained unseen. During Murieta's time on Bear Mountain a strange dread hung over every person in and around the Third Crossing.

Times were liveliest at the Third Crossing when the California Stage Company ran stages between Sonora, Tuolumne County and Sacramento. All stage teams were relayed here. In 1863, Bill Tate sold his popular tavern to John Seiffert of San Andreas. Ten years later it fell victim to flames. Like the famed phoenix, from its ashes another building of the same name arose.

In the flush days at the Third Crossing men did not concern themselves with limestone deposits or adobe bricks, the native stone being the favorite building material of the fifties. If the word "cement" had been mentioned in the presence of an Old Gulch or Third Crossing pioneer, he would have laughed uproariously. But just the same "white cement" has been the means of keeping smoke rising over the Kentucky House.

THE BEAR MOUNTAINS

Rising in the southwesterly end of the county, the Bear Mountain range stretches across Calaveras in northerly direction, but few people are cognizant of the circumstance, which gave name to the rugged hills that form the background of many towns in the county. Before the coming of the Americans the Mexican settlers called this range the "Lomira Hills". A hunter of the old days related the following:

"Back in the days before the miner's pick defaced the shady gulches and wooded hillsides, before the broad-axe of the pioneer had made its remorseless crusade against the green tenants of the woods, the Bear Mountain section was the ranging place for bear and deer. A hunter in those days could fetch down a buck in an hour's hunt. Those men who had the taste and the nerve for such sports could bring a grizzly to bay by simply bearing on the chaparral at the base of this range.

A Petersburg hunter, after one of his morning rambles through the brush, dropped down on a bank of moss to rest. Casting his cycs towards a clump of oaks that shaded a level spot, he saw two grizzly cubs amusing themselves with a pine burr. Soon, all ages and sizes to the number of twenty joined in the frolic. The hunter had an old and trusty "Pike County" rifle with which he was about to change the nature of the sport. But having awareness of the pluck of the grizzly, he looked around for a place of retreat before opening fire. There being no large tree within 200 yards and thinking that he'd better be safe than chewed and clawed, without firing a single shot, he decamped from the perfect grizzly riot. Thereafter, this wild mountain range was called the "Bear Mountains".

BUND'S RANCH

Bund's Ranch and stage station, between Foreman's Ranch and Hawkeye, was located on the south side of San Domingo Creek. Simon Thaddeus Bund born in Baden, Germany was a member of Stevenson's Regiment. In 1849 at his San Domingo diggings, he assumed his nickname, "Johnny Bund" which the soldiers of his regiment had bestowed upon him. In 1850, John Bund built an adobe dwelling house within view of San Domingo Creek and here at his productive ranch he spent the rest of his useful and long life.

HAWKEYE or Hawk Eye

Hawkeye, between Cherokee Flat and Fourth Crossing, was extensively mined in 1849-1850, and though no family fortunes were ever dug here, nevertheless, it was not just bread and butter ground. Among Hawkeye's first settlers was Captain Moses Thorpe, who like many another seaman, left his vessel in San Francisco Bay and struck out for the mines winding up in Hawkeye. After trying his hand at mining he became a farmer. Calaveras Lodge F.A.M. NO. 78 was organized in 1855 in Moses Thorpe's dwelling house at Hawkeye. A few years later, Moses Thorpe's daughter Melissa, married Milton Stephens a Kentuckian and with him removed from Hawkeye to Paradise Gulch.

James Snow, born in Massachusetts, sailed from Boston for California in December 1849. He was on the high seas 203 days without ever touching a port. After a blustery voyage around the Horn his vessel reached San Francisco in June 1850. He went at once to Hawkeye to dig a fortune but the fertility of the fields drew his attention away from his placer claim. After his marriage to Miss Margarte Kold, "Jim" Snow laid aside the pick and pan went for the plow and spade. Snow's Ranch near Hawkeye, responded to cultivation. Fruit, grain, vegetables, livestock and poultry all flourished under Pioneer[10] Snow's direction.

David Maloney was another pioneer rancher of the Hawkeye district. Maloney's Ranch was an active center and was a relay station for the California Stage Company. At the Maloney Ranch the dwelling house that "Dave" built at an early date stands intact and inside of the fenced fields, the sheep and cattle graze.

DOGTOWN

Dogtown, through which chatters the Dogtown Creek is two miles north-east of Cherokee Flat [Altaville]. It received its name from a prospector, who while tramping from Upper Calaveritas in a southwesterly direction, heard the dismal howls of a dog. Realizing the animal's plight, he made a search and found a half-starved little mongrel. The lost and hungry dog proved to be a faithful companion and a vigilant protector. That day while beating the brush, this prospector observed some promising looking gravel and located a placer claim. Later, he discovered that the channel of a dead river existed in this locality and this ancient riverbed was heavily laden with gold. At one time or another, hundreds of miners have worked in the Dogtown gravel claims.

The Jupiter, one of the richest gravel mines in the county, was the property of Windsor A. Keefer. His strange disappearance from Dogtown has remained another one of Calaveras County's unfathomable mysteries. Rumor had it that one of his numerous enemies "bumped" him off and then buried his body in one of his own gravel pits. Keefer, while living in the Palace Hotel in San Francisco, spent considerable time in this famous

..SUPERINTENDENT'S OFFICE..

San Domingo Gold Mining Company

CALAVERAS COUNTY, CAL. 10/28/98

This mine used large quantities of water that was brought from the Stanislaus River. At various times this hydraulic mine was called Jupiter or San Domingo. Photo circa 1907.

Courtesy of Calaveras County Historical Society

marble court. His was a sharp eye for spotting rich widows. It is said that he induced many a "crepe-bonneted one" to invest her inheritance in his Dogtown mine, the Jupiter. Handsome, gifted, blandly courteous, Windsor Keefer entertained numerous rich widows and titled Europeans at his attractive residence in Dogtown.

Both Jack Rabbit and Monarch an early day diggings, still contain inexhaustible amounts of rich gravel. The San Domingo gravel mine was bonded by its owners, Charles C. Robedee and to F. K. Bechtel who tunneled it to a length of 150 feet and found gold every foot of the way.

The miners of Dogtown have laid aside their tin dinner pails. Milo Terry of the Old Guard, no longer tells quaint stories at which his Dogtown comrades laughed in ready chorus. The padlocks on the cabin doors have rusted but the gravel bed of the ancient river is still there.

San Domingo School in 1893
Courtesy of Calaveras County Historical Society

Dogtown, the first camp in Calaveras County to be artificially lighted, may someday throw off its grave habiliments and again take its place as one of the gold producing camps of the Southern Mines.

CHEROKEE FLAT [Altaville]

Cherokee Flat, later called Forks-of-the-Road and still later Altaville, is one mile north of Angels Camp. Clement V. McNair, William E. Bean, William Jones and Harvey Childers were among the first men to mine on this flat. At first, a Mexican rendezvous, it was the scene of no few lynchings. In 1852, the above men together with their wives removed from Cherokee Flat to the Washington Flat [on Old Gulch Road near Mountain Ranch] mining district of which they became permanent settlers.

David Durie Demarest. With his son Clarence he operated the Angels Iron Works
Courtesy of C.C.H.S.

David D. Demarest born in Bergen, New Jersey reached California in 1849. A pioneer of Cherokee Flat, during the famine period of 1851-1852 he paid $100 for a fifty pound sack of flour, which

Demarest's Calaveras Iron and Steel Works in Altaville, 1916.
Courtesy of Calaveras County Historical Society

he carried on his back from Pound Gulch, a distance of two miles. Mr. Demarest was one of the twelve charter members of Calaveras Lodge F.A.M. No. 78, which was organized in the ranch house of Moses Thorpe in 1853. Pioneer Demarest's mining career ended in 1859, when he established a foundry in Altaville[11]. In 1861 he married Salina, a daughter of John and Elizabeth Ward, pioneers of Cherokee Flat. The foundry and machine shop that Mr. Demarest put into action more than ninety years ago, is still going, full blast.

Bartholomew R. Prince, born and educated in Italy, came early to Cherokee Flat. A talented and highly trained sculptor in marble, before leaving Boston, Massachusetts for California, he manufactured astronomical instruments. Upon reaching the flat in 1852, he formed a partnership with G. Garabaldi and established a general merchandise store[12]. Later, he erected a hotel, livery stable and undertaking parlor. A lover of trees and plants, Mr. Prince successfully demonstrated to his townsmen that the silk culture could be developed in Calaveras County. In the field back of his hotel, he planted a hundred or more mulberry trees. In time, the raw silk of his production took the first prize in each county fair in which it was exhibited.

Mr. Prince remained Altaville's foremost businessman for thirty-seven years. He located and developed the Cherokee quartz mine, on Cherokee Creek and in 1883 was rewarded with $60,000 in cold cash.

Thomas Frazier, a 'forty-niner' who arrived on the flat in 1850, located

Altaville School in 1893. This school is now located near the intersection of highway 49 and 4. Presently this school is cared for by the Calaveras County Historical Society and can be visited and enjoyed.

Courtesy of Calaveras County Historical Society

many acres of ground in and around Cherokee Flat. Civic-minded, he donated the land on which the little red brick schoolhouse was built in 1856. The schoolyard with its stately oaks and unexcelled view of the Sierra Nevada and Bear Mountain ranges is a lasting memorial to this pioneer. He also gave to the community the first parcel of ground for the Protestant Cemetery. A beautiful hilltop site it commands a superb view of the distant snow-capped Sierra peaks. Pioneer Frazier and his wife Mary were lowered to rest, in this quiet foothill cemetery in Altaville.

John Calvin Starr reached California in 1849 by way of the emigrant trail. He located in Vallecito and mined in Coyote Creek. In 1853 he married Miss Angeline Isbel, a niece of Dr. Isaac C. and James Isbel who were members of the Carson-Robinson mining expedition. After their marriage Mr. and Mrs. Starr removed to Forks-of-the-Road (Altaville) where, in partnership with Jacob Hartman, John Starr established a blacksmith and wheelwright shop.

Among the first settlers of Cherokee Flat and its immediate vicinity were B. R. and Mary Prince, George and Phoebe Ross, Thomas and Mary Drury, Philip Demartini, J. B. Massone, Andrea Garibaldi, Michael and Margaret Cosgrave, Stephen and Elizabeth Davis, Henry and Helen Nuninger, John, Frank and Joseph Lee (Letora), John and Elizabeth Becker, Franco and Rose Monte Verde, John and Catherine Marchal[13], Dr. L. and Mary Lichau, John and Mary Blackburn and Louis Johnson.

BALD HILL

This mound-like knoll, one half mile east of Altaville, is about 100 feet high. It quickly attracted the attention of the first placer miners. Underneath its mass of lava lies a prehistoric river. James McElroy in 1858, sunk a shaft on this lava hill to the ancient channel, conceded to be rich in gold. The hill soon attracted to itself a large number of miners, among others, Michael Brown, James Matteson[14], James Watson, Jacob Caster, James Bennet, William Laird and Norman Smith.

Bald Hill was destined for prominence principally by a reason of the so-called Pliocene Skull that James Matteson planted in James McElroy's shaft. This shaft not only produced gold but the most baffling hoax of the age. The Pliocene Skull not only caused a furor amongst scientists but writers and poets. For instance, Bret Harte, who added considerable fame to the skill-fully executed hoax.

The story of the hoax, according to the late George Stickle of Angels Camp, went like this:

Dr. Wm. A. Kelly, while on a professional visit to Salt Spring Valley was shown some human bones which placer miners had washed up at Jacob Tower's Ranch. The doctor, taking a fancy to a certain skull took it to Angels Camp for presentation to Philip Scribner, the town druggist. "Phil" in turn gave it to Captain Henry Matthews, his brother and John Scribner's business partner. "Cap" remembering Dr. Jones' interest in anthropology decided to send it to him as a joke but for some reason, he wasn't able to keep up with his good intention. In the meantime, the town's chief prankster took one look at the eyeless sockets of this weather-beaten skull with no small claim to antiquity and at once began cooking up another one of his practical jokes. This time the joke was on Professor Josiah D. Whitney of the State Geological Survey. Whitney was scheduled to visit Angels Camp in the near future. Possession of the skull was gained through Phil Scribner. Jim Matteson, sworn to secrecy, carried the skull to McElroy's mine and planted it underground.

Professor Whitney together with Dr. Jones rode from Murphys to Angels Camp one evening. At Ross Coon's suggestion they paid a visit to Jim McElroy's deep diggings. They found themselves descending a shaft in a large iron bucket. The shaft was dripping water, down under in a drift they found Jim Matteson digging in a "pay" streak and while the professor and the doctor stood by watching, Jim's pick brought to light a badly discol-ored old skull. At once, the professor evincing surprise and pleasure froze, while Doctor Jones overjoyed, commented knowingly on the rareness of the specimen. Fitting, thought Dr. Jones, that it should be found in the bed of an archaic river. Professor Whitney must have been of the same opinion, for shortly, the skull that the placer miner had washed up, was on its way to the Smithsonian Institute in Washington, D. C. and there it created something of a sensation. The burying place where, before the coming of the white man to Salt Spring Valley, the Indians of the region had buried their dead, it was regarded as a scientific discovery of the highest importance.

Today, geologists and writers, in their search for new material are attracted to the Bald Hill, for just as in the plush days, the gravel miners find "nuggets" in Jim McElroy's old shaft.

GOLD HILL

One mile northwest of Altaville is Gold Hill. Gold Hill's first miners were Mexicans, who after the Foreign Miners' Tax went in effect, left for the land of their birth, their burros laden with gold.

George Osborne together with his wife and children reached Gold Hill in 1857 and established a homestead. A pocket miner, he was lucky from the start, for in two days' time, he dug up from his "dry" diggings $10,000 worth of gold.

The Osborne's trip across the plains in a covered wagon was fraught with danger. The wagon train of which George Osborne and his family were members left Arkansas for Angels Camp during the above year. Only by the skin of their teeth, they escaped the Mountain Meadow Massacre, in which so many of their traveling companions were slain.

Gold Hill has authentically yielded in excess of $300,000 worth of precious metal. Occasionally even at this late date, a rich pocket is found there. The stages running between Angels Camp and Milton passed through these diggings and onward past Smith's Flat, Poole's Station, Mathews Ranch, Nassau Valley Station and Carmen City. "Road-knights" eager to lay hands on strong boxes with gold bullion, weren't above robbing passengers as well. On this route at Robbers' Rock one day, Bill Hendricks a shotgun messenger in the employ of Wells Fargo & Co. shot and killed a highwayman. Today, along the old stage road all the way from Gold Hill to Milton, sheep and cattle may be seen grazing.

SALT SPRING VALLEY

In Salt Spring Valley, about six miles west of Gold Hill, all four seasons of the year, present a scene of rare loveliness. The Bear Mountain Range looks down upon it from the East. The floor of this valley with the great

Spring Valley Reservoir is seen through the foliage of the majestic oaks as it shimmers like the waters of some inland sea. This reservoir not only supplied water to the diggings in this valley but also, to those of Lower Rich Gulch, North Hill, South Gulch and Lower Jenny Lind gravel mines.

Lifelong friends and business partners, Jacob Tower and William Bisbee, located ranches in this valley in 1853. In the days when horsemen were the bosses of the roads, their ranch was a lively place, having a population of several hundred people. A relay station for various stage lines, Tower & Bisbee wayside tavern is one of the few houses in the Siberia Mining District. It has refused to experience decay or ruin. Here, Tower and Bisbee besides their tavern, conducted a trading post, blacksmith and wheelwright shop, engaged in the livestock business and raised fine crops of hay and barley.

Though agriculture was the main feature of this productive and beautiful valley, mining received its share of attention. Once water became plentiful here Thompson's Flat, Big Bear Gulch, Slate Gulch and Manados Gulch were extensively mined.

Emmett Joy at Lost City in 1935

Courtesy of Calaveras County Archives

Of course, in the old days, Salt Spring Valley had its shooting scrapes and lynchings were not unknown but, all in all, it was and still is an ideal spot on which each Springtime, an endless variety of wild flowers spill brilliant colors. In this valley, in the sixties [1860's] was located Garcelon's Horticultural Nursery, which was second to none in California.

LOST CITY

Shrouded in mystery, the Lost City[15] is located in the northeastern part of the Salt Spring Valley, a short distance from the salt spring from which the valley took its name. Called by the Mexicans and Yaqui Indians, "Campo Feliz," it was a primitive outpost when California was still under rule of the Mexican government. On Rock Creek, the Lost City's history dates back to the days when Ricca and Castro's vaqueros rode their fine horses over the ranges of Rancho Del Rio Estanislao of which the fertile Salt Spring Valley formed a part.

There is no other place in California where the stone remade [hut] system is better exemplified than in this interesting place. The stone structures are fast falling into ruins but the walls of several of the buildings however are still standing, roofless but erect. Here and there on the hill slope may be seen rudely built outdoor fireplaces, around which are still growing the little "live forever" plants (hen and chickens) without which no

Lost City in 1971

Courtesy of Calaveras County Historical Society

Mexican's dooryard was complete.

The Antelope Trail, leading from Stockton to Murphys and later a stage road skirted the western side of this campo. Here is evidence of flagging native stone. It bespeaks of the industry of the blanked-sheathed Yaqui Indians, who no doubt, paved the footpaths and roadway that can be seen along with stone tables, benches and potholes in rocks where, maybe the corn and sweet acorns were ground for food. The grapevines, planted by the campo's founding fathers are still growing and producing fruit on the banks of Rock Creek.

In 1850, Rock Creek drew to itself a large number of placer miners and as late as 1880, French and Mexican miners were digging gold from its treasure-laden bed. Stone Creek, near-by, was also rich and extensively mined. A short distance from the Lost City was the Caledonia hard rock mine; this mine is no longer in operation.

A few hundred yards east of Lost City is a stone building in which, tradition has it, Joaquin Murieta often took refuge and from its gun holes on occasion, fired his terrible revolver. A steep and twisty trail led from this structure to Carmen Peak the highest pinnacle of the Bear Mountain Range. From a "crow's nest" in a tall pine, Chaparrita, the Mexican chief's faithful spy, kept a watchful eye on pursuing posses.

The Lost City is situated in a forest of rocks, isolated and deserted, but few people know of its existence, nonetheless it exists. Mostly in ruins, a typical Mexican campo of the days before the 'Gringo" invaded this beautiful valley of the salt spring.

FELIX STATION

This wayside station in the southeastern part of Salt Spring Valley was a convenient stopping place for teamsters, herdsmen and prospectors when bells jangled on the leaders of jerk line teams. Its owner, L. Felix, a native of France and his only son, in the rough weather of 1861 while attempting to ford the Calaveras River at Fisher's Crossing (Bellota) had their wagons carried down the stream in the angry current. They met death, together with their horses and mules.

In 1869 Felix Station[16] was robbed and plundered by Tiburcio Vasquez and his destructive bandits. Dissatisfied with the swag obtained they set fire to the frame building. Madame Felix now the sole owner of the station, while attempting to rescue some valuable documents, soon found herself surrounded by flame. Later, her charred body was found among the ruins of the famous old station[17].

It was here that the motion picture "County Chairman," of which the late Will Rogers [1879-1935] was the principal actor, was filmed. Felix Station, now known as the Thomas McCarty Ranch, like all other portions of this delightful section, has untold photographic possibilities.

COPPEROPOLIS

Copperopolis is located near the southern end of Salt Springs Valley, thirteen miles southwest of Angels Camp. As if touched by some magic wand, it sprung into existence shortly after the discovery by Thomas McCarthy and Wm. R. Reed, of a vein of copper ore. Known as the Reed Lode, hundreds of men were soon locating claims along it. The copper ore at this place contained neither gold nor silver, while at the Campo Seco mines are ore with these minerals was common. Ground was broken for Copperopolis' first buildings on July 4, 1861.

A series of shafts were sunk, the deepest being about two hundred feet. The processing of the ores was done in the usual way and then sacked for shipment. Daily, long lines of mules with packsaddles bulging with copper left Copperopolis for Stockton. From Port of Stockton the metal was shipped to Swansea, Wales for manufacturing purposes. At the Reed mine in 1863

Steam traction engines delivered the copper concentrate at Milton. Copper ore from Telegraph City, probably the Napoleon Mine. Photo 1907.

Courtesy of Calaveras County Historical Society

Union Hotel at Copperopolis

Courtesy of Fritzi and Michael Dorroh

three shifts were in operation with 120 miners on the payroll. The shares in this property were sold by the foot and among the original stockholders were Wm. A. Dana, Wm. Jones, Wm C. Ralston, Thomas Hardy and Peder Sather. Discoverer Reed in 1862 sold five and one-half feet of ledge in his mine to Meader, Lolor & Co. of Boston, Massachusetts for the tidy sum of $35,000. The following year, one share alone was purchased for $25,000. Though the shares were never in the market, the estimated value was $300,000 or $2,000 a foot. The dividends were large and were never made known to the public.

Andrew Fontana born in Italy, debarked in San Diego Bay in 1849. A short time later, he was mining in Black Gulch, near Campo Seco. During the copper boom, he went to Copperopolis and established a general merchandise store. When, in 1884, he died at his home in that town, his widow, Anunciada Fontana, successfully carried on in his stead.

The Copperopolis Hotel, built by Luke Kelly, was destroyed by fire on a September night in 1867. In this blaze George McAllister of San Francisco, lost his life.

Captain Thomas B. Meader, a native of Nantucket, Massachusetts, erected Meader's Resort. A seaman, Meader set sail for San Francisco from New Bedford in the ship "Mayflower" under command of Captain George Randall. He made his pile on the American River before removing to Calaveras County, where in Copperopolis he became a copper baron. Meader's Resort was surrounded by farmlands, orchards and vineyards. Among the many

Smelter from the Union Copper Mine in Copperopolis- circa 1890.
Courtesy of Calaveras County Historical Society

pleasant features of this spacious resort were its broad verandas from which magnificent views of the distant country were obtained.

It was in Copperopolis that "Brown of Calaveras" spent his last days. Brown, a miner of Brown's Bar on the Stanislaus River, thanks to Bret Harte, became a famous Mother Lode character. At the time of his death, Brown was a cook at Meader's Resort. His old friend, Andrew Fontana, Copperopolis' leading merchant, selected not only his grave site but also his gravestone. Both are to be found in one of the little rock-walled cemeteries at Copperopolis.

Thomas Hardy cleaned-up a neat fortune in the Copperopolis mines. Mr. Hardy's career is an interesting one. After a rough voyage around the Horn, during which sixteen of his fellow travelers died from cholera, the "Colonel Stanton" hauled into San Francisco Bay in the summer of 1849. Mr. Hardy after a few days at the Fremont House paid $40 for steamer passage to Sacramento. Fourteen days were required to make the trip up the river. In Sacramento he spent $60 for a rocker, $16 for a shovel and $30 for a pair of rubber boots. In 1851 he mined on Graveyard Hill in Volcano. There for five consecutive months, he averaged $1,100. His quickly made fortunes were quickly lost however, but he was never discouraged nor depressed. The Empire Mine in Grass Valley, Nevada County was once Thomas Hardy's property. He sold it to Mr. Williams Bourne of San Francisco for $15,000. A famous quartz mine, the Empire is one of the richest and certainly the deepest sunk in California.

In Calaveras County at an early date, Mr. Hardy located claims at Carson Hill, Marble Springs, and Long Gulch. From 1851 to 1856 inclusive he assumed full charge of the Mountain Lake Water Company in San Francisco. He returned to Calaveras County in 1857 purchased a ranch and engaged in the livestock industry. This enterprise together with his placer claims made him a $20,000 profit in less than three years. This tidy sum he promptly invested in the copper mines at Copperopolis. In 1864 he realized $375,000 on his several hundred feet of copper ore. He was elected four times to represent Calaveras County in the State Senate. Later, he contracted to build a dry dock at Hunter's Point in San Francisco but lost heavily in the enterprise. Thomas Hardy's last days were spent in Angels Camp, where he was attended to the last, by a host of warm personal friends.

Charles E. Bolton [Black Bart the stage robber] prior to November 1883, which year he committed, at Funk Hill near Reynolds Ferry, his last stage robbery, was often seen in Copperopolis. There he was exchanging greetings with Dr. Case, Wells Fargo's express agent and other prominent citizens of that town.

The highway leading from Copperopolis to Eugene in a southwesterly direction is extremely picturesque. Up and down grass-blown hills, across fields are rock fences, one of which is thirty miles long. A full hundred miles of these rock walls were built under the supervision of Billy Sykes. His was the knack and the skill of placing rocks that time has not been able to dislodge.

At its zenith, Copperopolis' population was about 5,000. It supported several hotels and a large number of stores, saloons, gambling halls a schoolhouse and a beautiful little red brick church, erected by Presbyterians. The buildings here were among the best in the county and after the decline of copper mining many of the dwelling and business houses were moved away. Even so, there still remained in Copperopolis gigantic work sheds, gallows frames and machine shop buildings. The population finally dwindled to less than 150 and when this happened it was classed among the ghost towns of Calaveras County.

TELEGRAPH CITY

A short distance west of Copperopolis is Telegraph City. During the copper boom it was a bustling settlement. The Star, Excelsior, and Napoleon copper mines were only a short distance from the town. The life of these mines, though rich in ore values, was of a short duration. When the whistles tooted for the last time at the Napoleon mine, copper miners familiar with the property said that thousands of tons of copper ore, gold and silver remained down under in this mine which has been idle for more than eighty years.

Remains of Telegraph City. Notice the many miles of rock wall.
Courtesy of Calaveras County Historical Society

In February 1867, William H. Clary and John A. Steinberger sold their copper claim on Quartz Hill, near Telegraph City for $80,000.

Near Telegraph City, Edward Parks a Mexican War veteran purchased two thousand acres of grazing land and married a Scotch widow, Mrs. Breckenridge. Here he built a house and barns. In his latter years this prosperous rancher had the satisfaction of watching his flocks and herds multiply. Their daughter, Ella, married Antone Caminetti, a prominent lawyer of Jackson, Amador County, who for many years represented his Congressional District in the Congress of the United States. Today but little remains at Telegraph City except for a few palm trees and stone chimneys.

MILTON

Milton, twenty-eight miles east of Stockton, was the terminus of the Stockton and Copperopolis Division of the Southern Pacific Railroad. In the midst of farming and grazing lands, it was the starting point for all stages running from Milton to Sonora, Angel's Camp, Murphys, Vallecito, Big Trees in Calaveras County and the Yosemite Valley in Mariposa County.

Milton, fourteen miles west of Copperopolis was once the scene of a tornado and in memory of the twister, Pioneer Robinson named his brand new frame hotel, the Tornado. Lillian Lampson, who, as Nance O'Neil became a famous Shakespearean actress, was born and reared in this town. A short distance from Milton is the Schroebel, Langford, Robie, and several

Milton scene near the rail road depot.
Courtesy of Calaveras County Historical Society

other pioneer ranches on some of which gold, has been found.

Once a busy railroad terminus, the passing of the iron horse did not thrust Milton back into the category of a ghost town, for in the production of livestock, it is still a front ranking community.

PINE LOG

Founded by Major William Gerrard, a Kentuckian, Pine Log is now called Hodson and is three miles northeast of Copperopolis. Major Gerrard reached California the hard way, over land. He was a member of George Washington Trahern's wagon train. In company with the Duckwall wagons they battled the rough western slope of the Sierras and were the first wagons to rumble down Relief Peak and onward into the foothills below. Major Gerrard, bent on digging a fortune, settled in Calaveras County at Pine Log. He owned and operated the Winnemucca quartz mine. Moses Cohen established a trading post and prospered. There is nothing left at Pine Log except the old buildings of the Hodson Mining Company.

BYRNE'S FERRY [O'Byrnes Ferry today]

In the lingo of the gold washers "a man to ride the river with was a handy man in a pinch." Peter O. Byrne was just such a man. He was as courageous a young ferry master as ever steered a boat across the Stanislaus River. On more that one occasion, say the records, he risked his life to rescue men who came bobbing down the angry current on the roofs of cabins or desperately clinging to the sides of sluice-boxes. His story, dating back to the days when life was an unbroken series of thrills, is an unwritten one.

The amazing experiences of this pioneer hero are yet to be ferreted out of the old records of the Southern Mines. However, the settlement he founded in 1850 achieved renown. Byrne's Ferry is located a short distance from Copperopolis. It was a rich "wet" diggings in 1850 with a population of 300. Byrne, who arrived on the river to dig gold in 1849 established a trading post and built a log cabin and ferryboat.

POKER FLAT

A stone's throw from Byrne's Ferry was Poker Flat. Here, when the river meant gold, the "Old man" Folinsbee a pocket miner, searched for the "color". Folinsbee's daughter, Josephine (Jo), is said to have been the belle of this river settlement.

Joseph Pardee, a native of France had a little grocery and liquor store at Poker Flat in 1851. In July 1869 Pardee's store was entered, robbed and plundered by Tiburcio Vasquez and his desperadoes. When Joe Pardee died, Pierre Camon, his nephew, carried on the grocery and liquor business at the old stand.

The rude rock walls of Pardee's old store are still standing as a mute reminder of the Stanislaus River's grim history making days. John Oakhurst, Bret Harte's fictional gambler, with a derringer blasted his way, not into oblivion but like Byrne's Ferry itself, is here to endure the fame.

ANTELOPE TRAIL

The Antelope Trail that once marked the way from Weber's Embarcadero to Murphy Diggings is now a legend. Indeed, it is doubtful if today, any person has ever heard of the Antelope Trail but in 1849 it was well traveled. Many a gold hunters on foot, horseback and in covered wagons came this way. On November 18, 1849 Benjamin F. Marshall, who the following year at Murphys New Diggings, was appointed to the office of High Sheriff of Calaveras County penned for public benefit, a description of this trail. Let us quote "Ben" Marshall:

"Old Antelope Trail led from Stockton To Murphys New Diggings and vicinity. Take Antelope Trail to Antelope Ranch, Rock Creek and Salt Spring Valley. Connect with Bear Trap Trail and over the Bear Mountain to Yaqui Camp and Foreman's Ranch on San Antone Creek. Here you will find all kinds of supplies and good whiskey. Right hand trail leads past Steve Maxwell's tent at Hawkeye. Thence past French Dog Town to French Gulch on to Murphys New Diggings. Here you will find supplies. Also at McDougal's Flat and Viacotes [Vallecito] and Kiota (Coyote) Creek are very promising placer mining sections. For some reason, entirely on his own, Mr. Marshall added,

> "Four colored men of Murphys New Diggings are John Smith and one Jenkins, Nigger Lige and Nigger Mage and one Yaqui Indian, Joaquin Romero."

The landmarks mentioned by Mr. Marshall as well as the Old Trail with Rancherias strung along its course should not be difficult to find again. The Trail, which no doubt for long centuries was printed by the bare feet of Indians, should be brushed out and marked appropriately.

Footnotes

1 Not local Indians, the Yaqui Indians came with the Mexican miners from Sonora state in Mexico. Like the Mexicans they were experienced gold miners and frequently found gold bearing spots ahead of the other inexperienced newcomers.

2 The name Murieta was also spelled, Murrietta or Marieta. There were other bandits named Joaquin that operated in Calaveras County. There was Joaquin Carrillo and Joaquin Valenzuela who were bandits at this time. They may have been the same as Murieta, or they may have been different leaders. Coke Wood, Calaveras, the Land of Skulls.

3 Dirk knife is a straight-bladed dagger

4 See Las Calaveras, January 1970

5 Earlier called Lorenzo.

6 River of Skulls is the Calaveras River

7 Today, this part of the creek is called Calaveritas Creek. O'Neil's Creek ends at the confluence with the McKinney's Creek.

8 Originally called "Santo Domingo" meaning Easter Sunday. This suggests that the South American miners reached it on Easter Sunday of 1849.

9 Kentucky House was located just north of the bridge where the Calaveras Cement Plant was on Pool Station Rd. in San Andreas.

10 "Pioneer" is used here as an honorific title, hence it is capitalized here.

11 Now the location of the Save Mart

12 The building is still in use in 2005 but not the general merchandise store.

13 Marchal or Marchall or Marshall

14 Mrs. Buckbee spelled it Matson but Ms. Judith Marvin suggested that it should be Matteson.

15 This story of Lost City is not supported by history.

16 Felix Station story is not supported by history.

17 Named for Silvester Felix.

11

WHITE GOLD

Water flumes and ditches

The winter of 1850 was not a rainless one but few showers fell. However in April '51, severe storms were experienced. That season the miners were short of water for mining purposes. As a result, it soon became necessary for them to turn their attention towards the streams of the Upper Hills in which flowed the waters that miners of that day regarded as "white gold". If they were to continue to work their claims without the loss of time they would have to devise ways and means to bring this water to the various diggings in the foothills below.

Murphys water ditch, typical of the gold rush era water courses. Circa 1905
Courtesy of Calaveras County Historical Society

The members of the Johnson family lived near Jackson Gate [Amador today] and in the month of May 1851, Mr. Johnson and his sons constructed a ditch. One mile long, it ran from the North Fork of Jackson Creek to the gulch below the Kennedy mill and at the time it was built, it was the longest mining ditch in the county.

In the immediate vicinity of Jackson, Horace Kilham and his business associates built the first ditch for the conveyance of water to the placers of Hunt's Gulch, Murphy's Gulch, Murphy's Ridge and Butte City. The two Watkins brothers made the survey for the Kilham Ditch in the fall of '51. Heading on to the South Fork of Jackson Creek, three and a half miles from the town of Jackson, the construction work on this waterway was commenced in the spring of '52. Its owners, Horace Kilham, William Lewis, Thomas Campbell and Merril, purchased the Watkins' interest to the right of way as well as the right to divert the waters of the South Fork of Jackson Creek for the supply of the ditch.

The four partners themselves shouldered picks and shovels and went to work on the project. They were obliged to labor diligently in order to get water to Scottsville by November 20 of that year. This seven mile long watercourse, owing to the industrious partners' hard labor, cost but $3,000. The greater part of this money was expended on the building of flumes.

Mining in Kentuck and Rich gulches during the winter of '52, Kilham, Lewis and Merrill made excellent use of their share of water. Campbell, on the other hand, sold his portion to the gold washers of Scottsville and Butte City. In the springtime of '53, these four men had a branch ditch dug to Murphy's Gulch and Murphy's Ridge, where owners of promising claims were very much in need of water. About this time, Campbell and Lewis, having had quite enough of pioneer life in Calaveras County, sold out their interests in the ditch to Kilham and Merrill. The latter men, during the water supply season of eight months, divided each month six thousand dollars. This lasted for two years. Merrill after making his "pile" shook the dust of the ditch trail from his boots and accompanied by Braxton Davenport with whom he had shared a cabin, returned to his former home in Wisconsin.

In March '53, Major Cunningham, W. V. Clark[1] and Munson realizing, that another ditch was needed, soon had a third one under course of construction. With its head on the South Fork of Jackson Creek, a mile and a half above the Kilham Ditch and miles above Jackson, this project was completed in May of that year. At the Alpi Ranch, east of Tunnel Hill, these same men built a reservoir. After the completion of storage pond, water was sold to the miners at the rate of seventy-five cents for each miner's inch[2].

Emanuel Wise and the brothers, Lyman, Jerome, and Martin Howard surveyed the Amador City and Sutter Creek Ditch Company's watercourse, in the spring of '53. The water was taken from Jackson Creek, four miles below Volcano and was conveyed to the above towns successfully. This waterway built at a cost of $22,000, proved an unprofitable undertaking and its owners sold it to a company of Italians for $6,000. The frugal miners from Italy, in the first run of six months, got back their entire investment.

Of all the pioneer water projects ever undertaken in Old Calaveras, the famous Ham Ditch was the most extensive, costly and unprofitable. Alonzo Platt and James F. Hubbard in '52 surveyed the route for this canal. The purpose of which was to supply the middle and western part of the county with an abundance of pure, clear, wholesome water throughout the four seasons. This canal was intended to be used as a water source and a flume in which lumber could be rafted down from the Upper Hills to the diggings below. Having a width of four feet at the bottom and five at the top, this canal was three feet deep. With gradients and curves, which were supposed, to permit the floating of lumber of any dimensions that was apt to be required in the diggings. Mr. Ham's layout included the erection of several sawmills to be located at the various branches of the North Fork of the Mokelumne River. On Mill Creek, the first sawmill was completed in the spring of '54. An excellent piece of mechanism, it was operated by water power. Two hundred and fifty strokes a minute was the speed of the sash-saw that cut twenty three thousand feet of lumber a day.

J. C. Ham, in '53, contracted to build eleven and one half miles of flume at the following rates:

"Earth grading, 50 cents a yard.
Hard-pan, $2.00 a yard
Rock, $5.00 a yard
Lumber, $80.00 a thousand foot.
Nails, $25.00 per hundred weight."

The sawmill furnishing the lumber for this undertaking contained both an edger and mortising saw. By these appliances, eleven thousand feet of lumber could be put into the flume each day, in five and a half hours. The entire work, except the laying of the flume itself, was accomplished with machinery.

J. C. Ham, born in Kentucky on the Licking River, reached California in '49. Original, inventive, progressive, Mr. Ham while the flume was being constructed, conceived of the idea for a "novel passenger boat". Yes, he proposed to carry passengers both up and down the waters of his flume. Of course, the passengers could come sailing down in a boat, but in order to get them back up stream again, well to a less ingenuous man that Pioneer Ham, the problem might have become a serious one. After pondering upon the subject, Pioneer Ham suggested a car that was to run along a track to be laid along both sides of the flume. Paddle wheels were to be placed at each end of the car and these when turned by the water, would also turn the car's wheels thus propelling the "novel" boat up the stream.

Charles Boynton, a writer whose non-de-plume was "Logan," scribbled breezily about this undertaking.

"Mokelumne's waters will be made to come
And go at their command,
Led round to wash their ore
Or fertilize the land.
And even here in Jackson town
We are expecting soon
To see Cap Ham and all his men
Come sailing down the flume.
Reader, if Logan had the time
He would extend the song,
But, like his liquor bill up street
'Tis even now too long."

Captain Ham's dream of a serviceable boat soon vanished into cool atmosphere. Not only had he put too much of his mental and physical energy into his enterprise, but $25,000 of his hard-earned gold. Later, J. Mora Moss & Company of San Francisco took over the Ham Ditch at a cost of $50,000. In the end, this famous watercourse passed into the hands of Pioche, Bayurque & Company, who as the American agents for Louis Napoleon added it to the French Emperor's long list of American assets.

In the summer of '52, N. W. Spaulding & Company whipsawed thirteen thousand feet of lumber with which to flume the Mokelumne River in the vicinity of Rich Gulch and Murphy's Gulch. There the gravel was spotted with heavy gold nuggets. A traveler passing the rugged banks of the Mokelumne today, can scarcely realize that the stillness broken only by the clatter of the water and the wild songs of warblers, was ever otherwise. On the hillsides may yet be seen the relic of some stone chimney, before the hearthstone of which, a lonely gold washers fried salt pork and flapjacks. These rude chimneys are all that now remain to remind us of the ditch-builders, who in those hazardous days hung wooden flumes to the formidable rock walls of the Mokelumne River canyon.

The survey for the Willow Spring Ditch was commenced in '51. The first ground was broken in January '52. The original owners were A. Wood, J. Riddle, John Cursner, Joseph Jackson and Fitzgerald. Since they themselves were intending to do a large portion of the construction work, they had expected to spend $40,000. But before the ditch was completed its cost had mounted to $80,000 and upwards. Filled with water taken from the South Fork of the Cosumnes River, the ditch ran through the north-western part of the county to furnish with water Forest Home, Puckerville (Plymouth), Arkansas Diggings and several other towns and camps. Porter was the first superintendent; he was murdered while engaged in his duties as collector. Later, in order to work the gravel beds on the Arroyo Seco Grant, this water race was extended in a westerly direction to Irish Hill. In the spring of '54, William Ritter and John O'Brien purchased the Willow Springs ditch for $20,000. The new owners, at a further outlay, enlarged the canal and extended it to the Middle Fork of the Cosumnes River. With grades and curves arranged to float lumber and timbers for mining purposes, it was three feet wide at the bottom, five at the top, and three deep. Even to these men, it continued to be a losing proposition; they finally sold it to Alvinza Hayward for $18,000.

The Lancha Plana Ditch Company, taking water from Jackson Creek carried it across the dividing ridge near Water's Ranch. It supplied water to Camp Opera, China Gulch, Quincy and Steven's Gulch. Walker, Proctor and Lancaster, the owners, expended $30,000 in this thirty-mile water enterprise. Footing in the hills of the Putt's Bar region, it was one of the most profitable ditches in the mines.

A black rag picker was the next ditch owner. He spent several thousand dollars on the construction of Nigger Ditch. He had earned it by gathering cast off clothing and other useless articles, which he resold with considerable profit for himself. Nigger Ditch was eight miles long, carried water from Stony Creek to the Buena Vista placers. It was soon abandoned, the reason being; the Negro found rag picking to be a more profitable business.

The Poverty Bar Ditch, owned and built by McNeely, Davis, Morrow and McCarty was on the south side of the Mokelumne River. A branch of this ditch, by means of a suspension flume, ninety feet high, carried water across that stream. This branch on the north side, coming into competition with Proctor & Walker's ditch, caused a drastic reduction in the price of water. The original cost for building this ditch was $90,000.

Samuel Loree organized a company comprising of twenty men to bring water into Fiddletown in '53. This ditch was forty-five miles long at a cost of $45,000. The ground was favorable for the construction of such an enterprise but this did not prevent some bad management, on the part of Loree, from involving his company in debts. The lumber used for the flumes was sawed at Yeomet[3]. This was very far from the scene of action and the cost of hauling it was $200 a thousand foot. Later, this watercourse was sold to C. A. Purinton, the owner of the Eagle Ditch. Through Purinton's ditch the water was conveyed from Dry Creek to Quartz Mountain and the close-by Glover mines.

One glance around the town and Captain Robert Pope who had reached San Andreas in the spring of '51, realized that this settlement was mightily

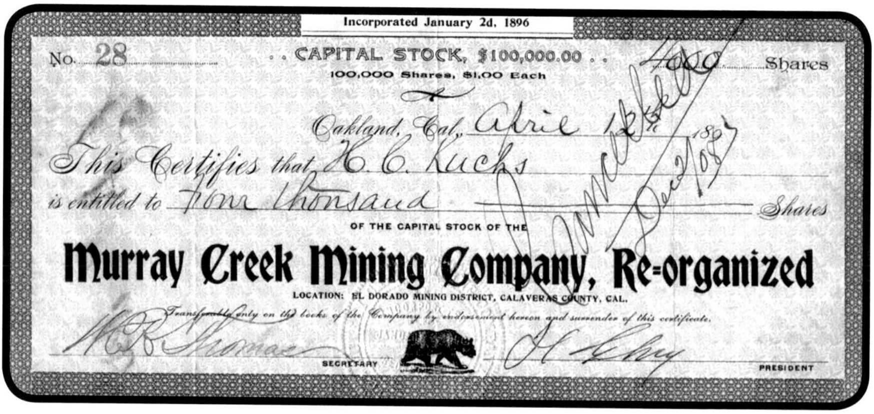
Incorporated January 2d, 1896

No. 28 . . CAPITAL STOCK, $100,000.00 . . 4000 Shares

100,000 Shares, $1.00 Each

Oakland, Cal., April 12th 189

This Certifies that H. C. Kucks

is entitled to Four thousand Shares

OF THE CAPITAL STOCK OF THE

Murray Creek Mining Company, Re-organized

LOCATION: EL DORADO MINING DISTRICT, CALAVERAS COUNTY, CAL.

Transferable only on the books of the Company by endorsement hereon and surrender of this certificate.

SECRETARY PRESIDENT

Courtesy of Wally Motloch

in need of a water ditch. Therefore, his first acts were to locate and survey the right of way of a watercourse, which was to lead from Willow Creek in the foothills, to the town. There was a competing concern known as the Miners' Ditch Company that commenced work on a canal along the same route. When finished in the spring of '52, the Miners' Ditch carried a larger amount of water. Captain Pope lost no time in bringing about a lawsuit against the Miners' Ditch Company and in '52, after a hotly contested tussle in the courts; a decision was rendered in favor to the former.

James Murray, a pioneer of San Andreas, during the winter of '51, organized a company for the purpose of bringing in the water from Murray Creek. Completed in '52, Mr. Murray's water project was a highly successful undertaking. Murray Creek miners' ditch was a factor in developing the placers in the immediate vicinity of San Andreas.

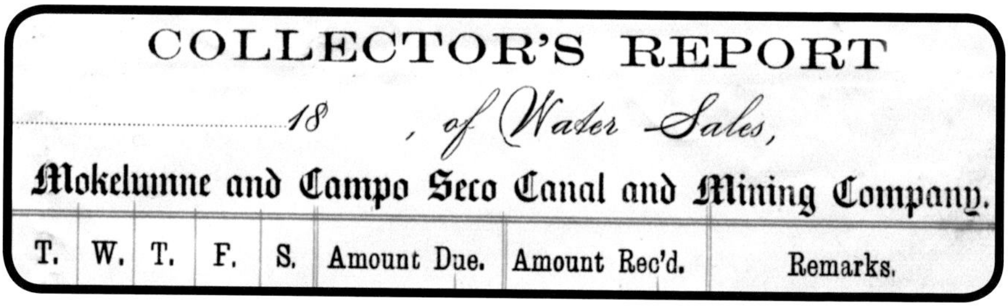
COLLECTOR'S REPORT

18 , of Water Sales,

Mokelumne and Campo Seco Canal and Mining Company.

T.	W.	T.	F.	S.	Amount Due.	Amount Rec'd.	Remarks.

Courtesy of Irene (Gourley) Craik

By far the most valuable and important enterprises ever undertaken in the old county was the construction of the Mokelumne Hill and Campo Seco Canal. The watercourse when completed reached the town of Mokelumne Hill in '52. It had a carrying capacity of one thousand miners' inches of water. This system included canals, reservoirs and distribution ditches. It

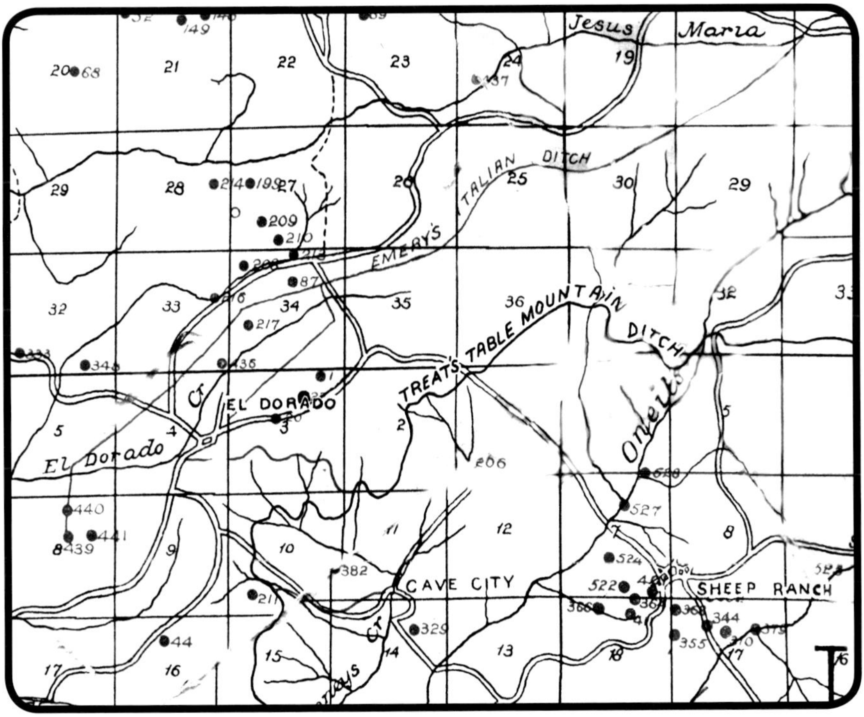

Map of the two larger water ditches near Mountain Ranch, El Dorado and Cave City. Table Mountain (Treat's) Ditch and Emery's Italian Ditch. Note the road from Cave City to Sheep Ranch.

Courtesy of Calaveras County Archives

was the means of developing many of the outlying "dry diggings" in the section through which it was routed. The water, obtained from the Middle Fork, Licking Fork and South Fork of the Mokelumne and from the North Fork of the Calaveras River, was pure, clear and cool.

In order to store and distribute the water successfully, a large capital was required and for the reservoir, a hundred acres of ground was needed. When copper was discovered in the region of Campo Seco, in order that the copper mines might have an abundant supply of water a second reservoir of sixty acres, was established above that place. The towns and camps in this section receiving water from this canal were, Catt Camp, Chili Camp, Campo Seco, Camanche, Benson's Camp, and Valley Springs. Finally, the canal was extended to some more remote ranches in the northwestern part of the county, from the dam at the head a total distance of 65 miles. The enterprise supplied water for washing out the gold from the placers of other rich mineral lands. The original construction work consisted of a wooden flume on the ground and carried across the depressions on high trestles. Owing to the enormous expense for repairs caused by the rapid decay of wooden structures and the extremes of heat and cold, this method was soon changed and

Table Mountain Water Company's Warrant.

T. M. W. CO.'S WARRANT.

No. 493

Company's Office,

McKinnie's Humbug, Calaveras County, California,

$50

November 18th 1854

Treasurer will Pay John Baker or order, Fifty dollars in Water, or Cash, so soon as the same shall be collected from the sales of water, without interest, as per Account now on file in the Secretary's office.

B. H. Evans Secretary.

Robt. McCall President.

Water Warrant, note that the location of the Head Office for Table Mountain Water Co. is McKinnie's Humbug.

Courtesy of Calaveras County Archives

Table Mountain Ditch Company are preparing to bring the water in through their ditch, and as this supplies Cave City, El Dorado Diggings, Old Gulch, French Gulch, and a large portion of the mining section about this place, it will furnish water for a very large number of miners. A portion of Capt. Pope's dam, at the head of his ditch, on Willow Creek, was washed away on Thursday. The Union Ditch, leading from Murray Creek, has been cleaned out and put in proper repair lately, and will, no doubt, bring in water next week. We understand that large quantities of dirt, carted out of the bed of the North Calaveras, and piled up, have been washed away. Mr. Stephenson, near the North Branch, has lost his entire summer's work. C. Tomey & Co.'s dam, on the South Fork, which was not quite finished, was swept away. The Main Calaveras was not fordable at Greasertown on Thursday, and is said to have been within eighteen inches as high as at any time during last winter.

Circa 1853 Courtesy of Calaveras County Archives

a gravel ditch and iron pipes substituted. In addition to the two reservoirs in the foothills, the canal company had a large storage reservoir in the high Sierras. This line of ditches supplied the town of Mokelumne Hill with water for all purposes, likewise for, La Paloma, Pine Peak, Central Hill, Poverty Ridge and Poverty Bar. Since irrigation was no longer a problem, the soil was profitably cultivated. The very thought of enough water to operate their claims successfully, as well as water for household uses, brought a smile to the faces of the gold washers.

The Lockwood Ditch, coming into existence in '53, carried

Jonathan Treat, an argonaut and a San Andreas business man.
Courtesy of C.C.H.S

water to West Point and Rail Road Flat. The twenty-three miles of main ditch and an equal length of distributing ditches derived their water supply from O'Neil's and San Antone creeks.

Warren Clark, a pioneer who recently celebrated his 100th birthday, established a miners' ditch for the benefit of Rail Road Flat's placer operators in '54.

El Dorado town, Mountain Ranch, Chee Chee Flat and several other towns were furnished with water from the Table Mountain[4] and San Andreas Water Company, known as Treat & Wyllie's ditch, which was surveyed and dug in '55. A resident of San Andreas, Jonathan F. Treat was the president of the company, and Alexander Wyllie was the superintendent. They were also the principal owners of this concern.

The Union Water Company owed its immediate success to its originators, Captain Levi Handford, John Kimball and Ephriam Cutting. Planning excellently and purposefully these men from the beginning proved the soundness of their financial investment. Organized in '52, it was first called the "Murphys Canal," and its water supply received from the North Fork of the Stanislaus River. Its waters, fresh, pure and crystal clear came from the melting snows of the Sierra summit. The entire length of the main canal had an average width of seven feet on the bottom and ten on the top. Twenty-five miles long it was constructed on a grade varying from eighteen to twenty feet to the mile and had a carrying capacity of two thousand five hundred miners' inches of water. The banks of this superb watercourse were flanked with alders, sugar pines, cottonwoods, willows, evergreens and also wild grape vines. This made the roadway between the Big Trees and the picturesque town of Murphy's, one of the most scenic in California.

Once the problem of a sufficient water supply was settled, Murphys was able to carry out many community enterprises and important improvements. Possibly, the greatest achievement was the completion of the Union Water Company's suspension flume. Finally, a new drainage canal was accomplished by blasting out an enormous amount of rock in order to make an outlet in a neighboring ravine. The water that was constantly collecting in the placer mines now had a way to drain.

Desire Fricot (back, center) with his ranch gang at Fricot City. Circa 1915
Courtesy of Calavearas County Historical Society

At first reservoirs in the high Sierras that belonged to this company were made by damming up low places between two neighboring hills. However, this method proved unsatisfactory for the storage of water. In the end Levi Handford, one of the most efficient and practical of pioneers, over-coming all obstacles, built a wooden reservoir of two and a half miles in circumference. In order to accomplish this amazing feat, a sawmill was erected a short distance east of Murphys. As the work progressed, in order to furnish the necessary lumber, the sawmill was removed fifteen miles higher up into the mountains. A railway, three miles long, which for the greater part ran over a trestle, hauled down the logs and trees, which had been felled in the higher ranges. The original cost for the building of this canal was $200,000. This amount was increased to $250,000 by the time it was finished. Besides the main canal, this company owned some fifty miles of lateral or branch ditches. The branches conveyed water for mining, irrigation and domestic purposes to the towns of Douglas Flat, Vallecito, Angel's Camp, Carson Hill, Altaville, Dogtown, and Smith's Flat. In 1888, Alvinza Hayward, Walter Hobart and Charles D. Lane, purchased the Union Water Company's rights and equipment for the purpose of supplying water to produce electricity needed to operate their quartz mines, situated in and above town of Angels Camp.

Hydraulicking the Bush Claim near Mountain Ranch. (Cave City and Michel Roads) Season 1895-96. Note the heavy use of water.

Courtesy of Alberts Family

Another of the noteworthy water ditches was the one belonging to Hubert Ide and Lorenzo P. Terwilliger. This canal carried water to the Sheep Ranch mine and the town of Sheep Ranch as well as to Calaveritas and several other camps along the San Antone ridges. Years later the rights of this pioneer water course were purchased by Mr. Desire Fricot, son of Jules Fricot, who replaced the old wooden trestles with steel forms and now instead of the water flowing over a graveled bed, it traveled down a concrete flume[5]. Now privately owned, scientifically managed, it supplies the residents of Fricot City (Tunnel Hill) with good water.

Turning the waters of a river or creek to mine the bed of the same stream was one thing but to carry it a mile or two in a ditch or flume was quite a different matter.

It was now the opinion of many of the pioneers that, at some future date, the water rights held by individuals were likely to become a source for litigation. And with the men of '49 it had always been an open question whether or not the old Riparian [relating to river's natural watercourse] customs should not be restored and the right to divert a stream from its natural course for a temporary necessities, brought about by mining interests, should be relegated to the domain from which it was wrested. The conservative men contended; the water monopoly was quite as detrimental to the county as the land monopoly, especially in a climate without rain for several months each year. Water, they argued, should be regarded by all the settlers in California, as white gold and as precious to the foothill counties as the yellow gold itself.

Footnotes

1 According to Bill Fuller, this dam still holds water in 2005.

2 A "Miner's Inch" of water is a measurement of rate of flow. Unless otherwise stated, in Southern Mines, it is equivalent to flow of 1.5 cu. Ft. per minute. The actual value of a "Miner's Inch" varied widely depending on location.

3 Place in Amador County where the North, South and Middle fork of Cosumnes River join. A this place in 1846, Sutter's Indians were falling trees and hand sawing these into lumber. To the Indians the word means a waterfall.

4 Originally there were two ditches in the Mountain Ranch area, the Table Mountain ditch and the older Table Mountain Flat ditch. These were acquired and incorporated into the larger Treat's ditch system that was over 65 miles long. In his book *A History of Mountain Ranch/ El Dorado*, Phil Alberts includes a more extensive description of the Table Mountain Ditch.

5 Fragments of this concrete canal can still be seen along the roadside, between Sheep Ranch and Fricot City.

12

MURPHYS

The brothers John and Daniel Murphy of San Jose first mined Murphy's Diggings, eight miles east of Angels Camp. With their father, Martin Murphy, Sr. they were members of the first wagon train ever to cross the Sierra summit in 1844. In May 1848 they joined the Carson-Robinson party in Monterey and were soon in the Calaveras locale digging for gold. They gave their family name to a singularly beautiful flat and in return it yielded gold to the ambitious brothers to the tune of $1,500,000.

This is a typical Miwok Indian Roundhouse. There were many of these in Murphys Rancheria. This particular photo shows a roundhouse in Mountain Ranch reputed to be located close to Joses Ranch on Whisky Slide Road.

Courtesy of Kent Wilson.

In and around Murphy's Diggings were numerous Rancherias with several thousand Indians. One of the Murphy brothers was married, Indian fashion to a young mahala [Indian woman]. By arrangement with her brother the chief, the Indians were induced to dig gold for the enterprising exploiter of this primitive labor force. He paid his laborers bright colored glass beads, cotton bandanas and a few yards of calico for the mahala's Mother Hubbard and a bag of "hard rock" candy for a week's work. By this method of exchanging virgin gold for a few sweet nothings, the Murphy brothers grew affluent and prominent.

While traveling through Old Calaveras an early day writer named W. D. Ryan wrote in 1850:

"At the upper crossing of the Stanislaus River, I met a large party of

Americans encamped near an Indian village, consisting of about 600 warriors, of whom an Irish ranchero named Murphy is the head, he having married the sister of the principal chief. He keeps a trading post and furnishes the Indians with clothing and other necessaries in return for their services in digging gold for him. I saw a very fine specimen of the ore weighing about five pounds, which one of the Indian miners picked out with a common sheath knife."

The Murphy brothers established a trading post on Murphy's Creek and did a thriving business. The owners of other trading posts were Doctors Brown, Wilson, Connell, Major Richard Roman and the Daly brothers.

Thomas Matteson, a forty-niner, established the first stage line between Murphy's and Angels Camp. The line known as the "Wingdam" followed Six Mile Creek to Campo de los Muertos and northward, a short mile to Angels Camp.

In 1849-1850 Mexican desperadoes made frequent raids in this settlement. The gold yield during those years was enormous. But on June 1, 1850 when the Foreign Miners' Tax went into effect, hundreds of disgruntled foreigners threw down their picks and crowbars and crunched across the summit into Nevada. That year American gold washers, fearful of losing their gold and possibly their lives to bandits, removed themselves and their treasure out of harm's way. As a result the settlement was soon threatened with depopulation. Regulations in force at this period made it impossible for a man to hold more than an eight by eight foot square of ground and the addition of a partner merely enlarged a claim to eight by twelve feet. For a season's work the claims averaged about $3,000 if the season happened to be a wet one. A French miner in a single season took out $7000.

Gold in and around Murphy's Diggings was found at a depth of from four to ten feet. Only pans were used for washing until late in the fall of 1850 when rockers or cradles, a new invention, were introduced from Woods Creek of Tuolumne County.

Some interesting information regarding the early day activities in Murphys is recorded in a letter written by a resident of the community.

A portion of the letter follows:

"When, in August 1849, I came to this camp, the method of mining was with the pick, shovel and pan. Myself with four others were engaged in mining on the flat and we had from 6 to 8 feet of surface to strip off before we could commence to wash. It was one man's business to carry the dirt in a sack 450 or 500 yards and wash it in a pan of very riley water. Three would sit in the hole with knives and pick out all the gold they could see. When a man would return from

Matteson's "Wingdam" Stage Line and Livery Stables Main Street, Murphys circa 1880's

Courtesy of Kent Wilson

panning, they would give him about three pans of this dirt that had been picked over. His average washing was about eight sacks per day. The fifth man was engaged clearing off the surface. We washed five inches of gravel above tough clay, which we thought was clay ledge, but since have proved to be good paying dirt. I think this mode of mining was generally adopted on the flat. On the 4th day of October '49 we came upon a large quartz boulder, too large to move. We dug a hole underneath it and let it drop in. Immediately behind where it lay, we took out a pan of dirt and took it up to our brush tent at noon. When washed, it had 42 ounces of dust; 63 ounces were our proceeds on that day. If we could have had the facilities for mining then, that we now (1858) have, we could have had 50 pounds of gold in a day".

"The first rocker that was used in these placers was brought from Sacramento. Smith, Hayes and myself purchased it in July '49 for $30. It weighed 20 pounds; we took it to the North Branch of the American River to Horse Shoe Bar. We paid 20 cents a pound for hauling it and worked with it about three weeks. We then returned to Sacramento where we met a gentleman from Stockton buying mule teams. From there we got the rocker taken to Stockton and in this place, I presume when we got it here, it had cost us near $50.

We could not use it to any advantage for the want of water. Until the rainy season set in on the first day of November our only washing place was a small spring at the lower end of the flat. Mr. Vandling, one of our partners, being a blacksmith gave us an advantage over other miners in keeping our picks in order. He brought the hammer he used at home with him and he would dress our picks on a large rock for an anvil. I went to Stockton in November '49 and purchased 1200 pounds of provisions. Then I engaged an ox-team to haul them, for which we paid $600 in dust, at $16 per ounce. Later in the season five bits were paid. We were nine days from Stockton to this place. On the 22nd of January 1850 snow fell, two feet deep. Captain Bell and Dr. Moore were out hunting two miles from camp, the latter becoming fatigued, lay down and perished. The day following three men went out to hunt for Dr. Moore, got benighted a quarter mile from camp and lay down in the top of a fallen tree. In the morning one of them was frozen to death.

In the fall of 1850, when the Secret Diggings[1] and McKinney's Humbug was discovered, A. Vandling and his partners went from this camp and not having lumber to make long toms, dug one out of a tree. In a few weeks they discovered that the diggings would not pay, so they engaged a Mexican with mules to bring them back. The long tom, being unhandy to pack, the Mexican declined to haul it. Vandling took it upon his back and only laid it down once until he reached this camp, a distance of 15 miles over the worst roads in the Southern Mines. He carried it within four miles of the camp before he laid it down, on the summit of a mountain.

In December '49, one partner and myself went to prospect Pennsylvania Gulch near this place. Being the first Americans to work there, it took its name from us, being called the Pennsylvania Company. On going down the gulch we came to a precipice of rocks with the water running over. We noticed several pieces of gold on the rocks. Washing a few pans and picking up what we saw, we had about half an ounce. So we started to go home intending to try a few pans further up the gulch. We put our dust on a small flat rock for my partner to carry. When we came to look at our gold, while walking he had turned the rock upside down and our prospects were gone, nothing to show for our success to the other partners.

While mining on Central Hill in the morning, one of the hands went down into a sixty feet deep shaft. After entering the drift a few feet, the first thing he met was a large Buck [Indian man] I supposed he had gone down in the night to prospect. He appeared to be uninjured and in perfectly good health.

Two men have been lynched in the camp and I think two were

shot dead, and two lashed. Murphys has a population of over one thousand now. There were numerous stores, Hotels, Express and Banking Houses, a Church, Masonic Hall, Division of the Sons of Temperance and others. The Union Ditch Company had their headquarters here and from their extension canal they supply the miners with water for this place and Douglas Flat, Vallecito, Angels Camp, Cherokee Flat and a number of other camps. Among the many good and substantial buildings under contract or in process of erection was James H. Sperry's Hotel; the largest in Murphys and its cost when finished was some $18,000. Mr. S. is induced to go to this heavy outlay in order to accommodate the increased travel through Murphys since the discovery of the Big Trees".

Murphys, in spite of the bandits and the Foreign Miners' Tax, remained a prosperous settlement. At first, the surest means of transporting commodities from Stockton the "Mart of the Southern Mines" to the placers eastward was the lone miner acting as his own packer. Next, followed the mule train. In 1849-1850 capable loaders and cinchers were in demand. During the rainy season prodders of pack animals waded through sticky knee-deep mud. After several weary days of travel, in the face of wind and rain, they would reach their destination. Whenever pack animals were anchored, belly deep in black adobe, the deck loads were removed and the mules "dug out" before the mud dried. The old Antelope Trail and likewise the River Trail were marked with the bones of pack animals that had fallen by the wayside and left there for the summer winds to chant dirges through their sun-bleached skeletons. The delay caused by the loss of the pack animals added to the freight rate. It brought home to the pioneer the fact that he had to plunge down more gold or else bring his own provisions into the diggings. Many a miner paid $100 for a 50 pound sack of Chilean flour and $1.00 for each pound of sugar and coffee purchased.

As a mark of progress, the freighters soon took the place of the mule trains. More than one pioneer, with only a small capital, watched his fortune grow into huge piles from his profits as a teamster. The freight business in some instances brought greater wealth than mining. Men of different stations in life, when they could scrape enough "jack" to buy wagons and teams, commenced hauling goods from Stockton to the mining towns and camps. For several months Professor Shepherd of Yale University swallowed dust kicked up by the hooves of yoked oxen. This erstwhile savant did no grumbling about his daily wage of $60. Another knight of the blacksnake [whip] was J. D. Peters, who began his career in California as a teamster. Peters, whenever he could get a load of freight, hauled it from Stockton to Murphys. He soon had two teams on the road and sufficient capital to engage in Stockton in the steamship business. The freighters, as common carriers were successful. Andrew Blossom and Milton Kruse of Stockton hauled into Murphys in a single load more provisions and sundries than had here-to-fore been dreamed of. To accomplish this a team of fourteen powerful horses would tow wagon and a trailer. In those days team bells meant music to the pioneers, for they helped to consign the bean pot and flapjack griddle to a back lid of the stove.

John K. Doak reached California in 1847. In the spring of 1850 erected a sawmill on Murphys Flat. Before then a hand-sawed lumber for sluice boxes was brought from Sawmill Flat in Tuolumne County to Murphys. However, lumber could now be obtained at Mr. Doak's sawmill for $75 to $100 a thousand feet. The Utica Hotel, a large canvas tent in 1850, was replaced a year later by a two-story building erected from lumber sawed at Doak's mill.

To keep their hostelry in operation, David Shepherd and his wife Jane, owners of the Utica Hotel were dependent upon the regularity of the pack trains from Stockton for the supplies needed. Meals at the Utica Hotel were sometimes butter less and milk less, and often minus tea and sugar. Usually a man was able to get a square meal in David Shepherd's tavern, the first to be established in Murphys. Among the Utica's first regular boarders were Tom Matteston, Sam Barringer, Ben Marshall, P. L. Traver, Charlie Curtis, Peter Kinsilide, Todd Robinson, Alex H. Putney, Riley Senter, Isaac P. Hitchcock, Ephraim Cutting, John Kimball and Dr. Wm. A. Kelly, Murphys' first alcalde. In the dining room, these men frequently discussed together the progress made by the rapidly advancing City of Stockton.

"Only a short time back it took ten days for a launch to make the run from San Francisco to Stockton – cost me $50 for passage, too" Sam Barringer said between gulps of black coffee.

"In '49 retorted Todd Robinson, "cost me $30 for passage in an old leaky boat. We fought mosquitoes as large as grasshoppers all the way up the river."

"I paid $400 a ton to get my freight hauled from San Francisco to this camp in '49", reflected John Kimball.

"I don't guess, I'm so bad off after all" broke in a new comer. "My fare only cost me $5 and my freight $10 a ton".

"Yes, and the boat of today will be replaced by a better one tomorrow", chimed in Judge Putney. "Six months ago the 'Pride of the Slough' was emblematic of the progressive spirit of the age. Now take a look at her. She's as old and primitive as Noah's Ark".

"Well, in my opinion, the Kate Kearny is the nearest to a floating palace on the San Joaquin River", commented Riley Senter, Adams Express Company's agent in Murphy's Diggings.

Next in the march of events were the gaily-painted stagecoaches. Over the heads of swift hoofed horses, the best stage horses obtainable, Tom Matteson, John Olive, Daniel Alma, John Steinbower, and Colonel D. F. Loveless from time to time pulled reins. The fare from Lauren Barada's Lafayette Hotel in Stockton to Murphys was seven dollars. Tom Matteson, a top reins man, when leaving the Lafayette Hotel on South Center Street, always swung around his coach and six horses. He was practically on two wheels in the narrow street then headed his team toward Linden at a whirl-wind pace. In 1850 after Thompson and Whitehead's discovery of the Mammoth Grove of Big Trees, the compass only guided horseback riders from Murphys to the great forest.

Early in 1851 the Murphy brothers rolled their blankets, shouldered their rifles and shook the dust of Murphy's New Diggings off their cowhide boots and headed for their rancho Ojo de Agua do la Coche in the Santa Clara Valley. Their ranch house on the Monterey road south of San Jose was the first really good frame house in California and was afterwards known as the "Twenty-one Mile House". The lumber for the Murphy house was cut and framed in Boston according to Martin Murphy Jr.'s plans and specifications shipped around the Horn to California in "knock-down" form.

Generally when miners left a location it was a signal that it was "washed up" but the mining boom that Jack, Dan and Jim Murphy had started was still on and on it remained for many a long years. The beautiful town the brothers founded has never actually been a ghost town and probably never will be. Nature lovers will see that no grass ever grows in its main street.

The large consignments of dry goods and imports of "wet" goods into Murphys was the reason so many of the "boys" began putting on airs and relegated the XXX patch to oblivion. Suddenly, down went the freight rates and up went the high-toned notions of the miners. Rigged out in Spanish heeled calfskin boots and a square of Chinese silk knotted around their necks they celebrated. A supply of cheroots for "fuming" and three sheets in the wind from too much St. Croix rum, they celebrated and attempted to prove their fitness for society by singing the latest song hits. They were singing while doing a buck and wing in their favorite dance hall.

Murphys had barely reached high peak when a squabble arose between the American, Mexican, and Chilean miners. At first it was just a dispute, but soon resulted in open warfare. The uproar at Six Mile Creek between Central Hill and Los Muertos Campo, though stubbornly contested, it was not exactly a bloody battle. Few men were seriously wounded that day, but many eyes were blackened and noses broken.

James Shannon and Charles A. Curtis, forty-niners who owned claims on Six Mile creek, arrived on the scene in time to help rout the enemy. Prior to the fight the Mexicans were in full control of the rich stream and were desirous of gaining possession of all diggings along its banks. Along the entire length of Six Mile Creek were the arrastras of the foreign miners, always in action. Once the Americans gained the supremacy of these diggings, they constructed a wing dam, which helped to change the methods of placer mining.

In 1852 Charles Curtis, John Kimball, and Ephraim Cutting organized the Union Water Company of Murphys. For many years Superintendent Curtis supplied water to wash the placers in the various near-by towns and camps. Their water project is still in existence. Under the banner of the Pacific Gas and Electric Company of San Francisco, the old watercourse now carries water, if not to the placer miners, then to the ranchers.

P. S. Stephens born in Rome, New York, was a pony rider for Brown's Express and was known in the mines as the "fast express man". Upon leaving the employ of Brown and Company's Express and Banking House in San Francisco, he returned to Murphys where he served as a Justice of the Peace for eight years.

In Murphys in 1851 the cheery words "Merry Christmas" were not spoken. That holiday season a dark shadow hovered over the entire community. Sorrowing ones, shed bitter tears over lonely graves, for small pox had carried away many of the first settlers and was still rampant. Indeed it soon reached such alarming conditions that the citizens of Murphys erected a hospital for the benefit of the afflicted. Under heavy odds the people strove as best they could to wipe out the dreaded disease. The physicians in attendance established for themselves a good record for cures. Under the supervision of Dr. William A. Kelly the hospital was filled with smallpox patients for many months.

Ben Marshall the Sheriff
Courtesy of C.C.H.S.

Ben Marshall, the Sheriff of Calaveras County, received a note, which he carefully preserved along with letters and papers pertaining to his office. The note now on display in the museum at

San Andreas is as follows:

"Murphys Mines, February 11, 1852

Dear friend: I take the opportunity of writing these few lines to you hoping to find you in good health, me and Charley is sentence to be hung at five o'clock for a robbery so goodbye to you, and my best respects to Frank and Sam and Church.

(Signed) John Bancroft"

TWO MEN HUNG --On Wednesday last, great excitement prevailed at Murphy's. Two tents had been broken into at that camp, from one of which four hundred dollars had been taken--and from the other but twenty five. Sheriff Marshall, we learn, arrested the persons who had commit'ed the crimes, and they proved to be an Englishman and an Irishman, whose names we were unable to learn. The people were infuriated beyond control, showing by their excited actions that nothing but the lives of the criminals would be allowed to expiate their guilt. Accordingly, they seized them from the sheriff, and with shouts of passionate exultation, launched the unfortunate culprits into eternity.

Calaveras Chronicle Dec. 20, 1851

Courtesy of C.C.Archives

When lynchings became less frequent, the mingling together of the races became more firmly established resulting in the forming of enduring friendships. The adaptation of the customs and habits of the Americans proved harmful to the local Indian, who as a distinct type of mortal, soon disappeared. The men of the forest, depending upon the wild products of the forest for a livelihood, when changing to a system of living for which they were utterly unsuited, quickly followed their ancestors to the Happy Hunting Grounds.

Lancisco and Santiago, chiefs of the Siyakumna tribe in a conversation with Alcalde Kelly said:

> "When white men despoiled the Indians, they took from them, their heritage of land. They also took their liberty and happiness."

Chief Lancisco, stoical and silent, gave way to Chief Santiago, who grumbled:

> "The invaders of our territory seemed appeased in decimating our numbers by cruel and inhuman treatment. They will be satisfied only when the last Indian has been driven into the sea. The Americans are unjust. Since their arrival here the Indians have at all

Blind Indian from Murphys named "Yellow Jacket"
Courtesy of C.C. Archives

times been peaceable, even friendly disposed toward the whites, therefore, we should have received better treatment than has been accorded to us."

Prize fighting was a distinct feature of Murphys gold harvest. Boxing and bare-knuckle contests were held between E. Hopkins and "Yankee" Sullivan, with the notorious Billy Mulligan acting as promoter and referee. The fight took place outdoors on Murphys Flat. Hopkins, a dapper young blade, was a faro dealer as well as a prizefighter. In the sawdust ring he was no match for the hard-cuffing Sullivan, however it was always Mulligan who left the flat with the long sack of gold.

Murphy's was a politically minded town. Elections were always bitterly and savagely contested, especially where the Whig [Democratic] and Know Nothing parties were concerned. Almost any man could vote, neither registration nor any proviso being necessary. John M. Shepherd born in his parents' Utica hotel on May 16, 1852, was the first child of American parents to see the light of day in Murphys. Years later while serving as a Justice of the Peace of Murphys Township, Judge Shepherd, recalling to mind scenes of his boyhood, he had this to say about an election:

> "The room where the ballot box was kept during voting days was filled to suffocation with men, many of whom had their hands on a six-shooter, dirk or Bowie knife, ready to blaze away or stab at a moments notice on behalf of some favorite candidate. In the streets the miners and others surged to and fro or else stood in a solid phalanx eager to cast their 750 votes. Numerous toughs, either in a feeling of bravado or for the purpose of intimidation, pointed their weapons above the heads of the crowd. A click of a gun was merely a suggestion for others to do the same. Benjamin Marshall, the Constable of the Township and his fearless Deputies entreated all to be thoughtful and discreet, for once a Colt hissed, serious trouble was apt to ensue."

In Murphys in 1855 there were other ways to gamble besides betting on the outcome of elections, there was the Monte tables and taking a turn at the roulette wheel.

A losing venture[2] on the part of the miners was when they spent $80,000 to blast out a cut in the flat for drainage purposes. When the work was

Known as Deep Cut, this 37 feet deep channel in the rock was necessary to drain the swamp just south of town. Draining allowed for mining activity.

Courtesy of Old Timers Museum

completed a celebration was held with a large high-spirited crowd in attendance. The drum corps of the Calaveras Light Guards marched across the flat, all decked out in gilt trimmed uniforms. At the same time the bulkhead was torn away accompanied by the gold washers' yells, which were loud enough to be heard in nearby Owlsburg. That evening "home brew" and the more rapid convincer the "fire water" were freely indulged in. The following morning blackened eyes and bandaged heads galore were in evidence at the celebration in which the Irish and Cornish miners tangled with the Mexican and Chilean gold washers. In such fracases nothing short of a free for all fight could settle matters. The mixed population, let alone the intoxication of so many men, was quite enough to cause judicious men to return to their homes and permit the noisy crowd to run the celebration according to its own fancy, which say the records, was done in regular "whoopa-mula" fashion.

A large amount of dirt was scooped out of the gravel to a considerable depth for the drainage system. The water being pumped to the drainage cut from which a lively stream rushed down the flat. The project took the name of the Murphys Flat Fluming Company. Off to a good start at first, the enterprise soon threatened to ruin those miners who had put down the gold.

Ladies posing at a water flume over the Vallecito road, circa 1890.
Courtesy of Old Timers Museum.

When a short time later a suspension flume constructed from one mountain to another was completed, another "big time" was held on the flat. The flume carried water to the Central Hill miners. Here the Bisbee & Thomas Mining Company was operating in the ancient river channel with no small degree of success.

James L. Sperry in 1855 left off driving for the California Stage Company and went to Murphys, where in partnership with John Perry he purchased the Utica Hotel. One of the most fearless of men, he was a brother of Simon Willard Sperry who in 1852 established the Sperry Flour Company in Stockton.

Stragglers from the numerous bands of marauders would ride into Murphys, leap from their saddles, tie their horses to some handy hitching post and strike off for the barroom of Sperry & Perry's Hotel. As bold as any thieving crows, they would demand that the barkeeper pass out liquors and cigars. If anything was said about payment for the goods consumed, the intruders whipped out their revolvers and began peppering the room with lead, ridding the barroom of both customers and glassware.

One day when the outlaws entered the barroom, the owner Jim Sperry was standing back of the bar. They demand free drinks and smokes, Sperry set out glass tumblers, brandy and whisky and boxes of his choicest cigars. While there was a look of determination in their dark deep-set eyes, the desperadoes drained the liquor bottles dry, emptied the cigar boxes and as usual started to leave without so much as a "thank you". They reckoned

Sperry and Perry Hotel, later it became the Mitchlers Hotel. Circa 1885
Courtesy of Old Timers Museum

ill that day, for before they had time to reach the front door, Jim Sperry, a revolver in each hand, jumped up on the bar. Covering the would-be thieves, Jim ordered them to pay their bill not only for that particular day but for several other days as well. That was the last time ever that the bandits attempted to make a raid on a barroom in Murphys.

Sperry & Perry's Hotel, built entirely of stone, was commenced in 1855 but not completed until three years later. This hotel has entertained more prominent people from all four corners of the world than any other hotel of its size in the West. Its only rival was the Sperry & Perry's hostelry in the Mammoth Grove at Big Trees. The old register of the Murphys Hotel carries the names of world famous people and occasionally, infamous ones. Scanning the pages now yellowish and brittle, one finds the names of John Jacob Astor, U. S. Grant, Baron Lionel de Rothschild of Paris France, Count Lichtenstein of Vienna Austria, Henry Ward Beecher, "Jack" Hays Hammond, Master Jimmie Phelan, Mr. and Mrs. George Hearst, Master Willie Hearst, Horatio Alger, Jr., John Muir, Charles Warren Stoddard, Mr. and Mrs. Leland Stanford and other notables, all for whom were on their way to the Big Trees. Men not concerned with scenery who signed the register were: Charles E. Bolton (Black Bart), Andy Keegan (Snapping Andy), Bunty Owen the pal of the notorious Sam Brown and Bill Holt.

When not in lonely ravines holding up Chinese miners, Bill Holt, Dave Parks, and Andy Keegan, experts with blades and pistols were frequently seen creating a disturbance in William Crispin's saloon in Murphys. Dave Parks an exconvict was shot and killed in a drunken brawl with a fellow rowdy in Virginia City. Owen Bunty of Bunty's Gulch wound up in San Quentin Prison, and along with him to the "big house" went Bill Holt and Andy Keegan.

Chinese men conduct business.
Courtesy of Calaveras County Archives

While on his way home from his saloon one night, Garrett Rooney a "gentleman" gambler, faro dealer and saloon owner in the middle fifties, was shot and killed from an ambush. As far as anyone knew he was without an enemy. Had his slayer been apprehended many believed a lynching would have resulted. Rooney's death has remained one of Murphys' unsolved mysteries. Some years later, quite a stir was created in Murphys, when his friends recognized this "high quality" gambler, this time in fiction. Bret Harte, his imagination fired, evolved the character of John Oakhurst (the Unknown) and with magic pen painted a splendid prose portrait of Murphys' dignified and chivalrous gambler Garrett Rooney (the Unfortunate).

Victorie Compere, a native of France, came early to Murphys, built a large stone building and established himself as a general merchant and importer. Indeed, his importations, mostly from France, made his store one of the most popular in the Southern Mines. A picturesque pioneer building, Compere's old store and outdoor baking oven are still in an excellent state of preservation.

In the old days Murphys supported a first class bookstore, where American and English publications could be obtained at reasonable prices. As late as 1896 copies of the London Quarterly, British Review, Westminster Review, Macmillan's Magazine, Harper's Weekly, Graham's Magazine, and

Godey's Ladies Book were to be seen on the shelves of Fiske's old book and Yankee Notion store.

Mary Anne Conway was Murphys' first private school teacher. Mary Anne's mother, a young Irish widow, married Philip Kelly, a member of Stevenson's Regiment of New York Volunteers. When the vessel "Susan Drew" set sail from New York for California in 1846, among the passengers were Mr. and Mrs. Philip Kelly with the golden haired young girl, Mary Anne Conway. There being no school in Yerba Buena [San Francisco] Mary Anne was placed in a convent in Monterey, California. There she learned to speak Spanish fluently. At the close of the Mexican War, Philip Kelly along with his family went to Murphys and established a home. Mary Anne opened a private school and by so doing earned for herself the distinction of having been Murphys first schoolteacher. In 1864 Mary Anne Conway married George Frederick Wesson of Mokelumne Hill. Four years later Mr. and Mrs. Wesson moved from Mokelumne Hill to San Andreas where they spent the rest of their lives.

Mary Ann Conway, the first school teacher in Murphys

Courtesy of C.C. H. S.

Murphys' first cemetery was near the brewery of the brothers, John and Conrad Hauselt. In the limestone belt where so many smallpox victims were lowered to rest, no head stones mark their forgotten graves. Buried there is Eddie Duffy, the first man to meet a violent death in the town. In Crispin's Saloon a dispute over a poker game arose between Sam Barringer and Eddie Duffy and ended by Sam shooting Eddie to death.

Murphys was a great old town for celebrations with July Fourth and February twenty-second the Americans' favorite days. The Mexicans never forgot their national holidays either. The sons and daughters of Montezuma, observed Good Friday and Easter Sunday. The Irish settlers always wound up their St. Patrick Day festival with a Grand Ball and the French orated and picnicked on Bastille Day.

Whenever a political event of importance loomed, tallow candles in tin containers were lighted and placed at intervals along both sides of Main Street. For further illumination red powder was used to light the way for US Senator David C. Broderick. When he spoke to the people of Murphys in August 1859. Senator Broderick's campaign speech brought out a large number of people who listened attentively. Prior to the speech-making, four abreast, hundreds of miners carrying flaming pitch pine torches marched down the street. The "torchlight" procession headed by the Calaveras Light Guards, the Local Militia under the command of Captain C.W. Smith, added a warlike aspect to the festivities.

The legal fraternity had lively "confabs" in the old days. Court was usually held in the saloon of William C. Crispin who sold his whiskey for "two bits" a drink and cigars for "one bit" each. Here where the dingy walls were pierced with bullet holes, the brothers William and Allen Dudley of Mokelumne Hill locked horns with the able lawyers such as Edwin Galvin and James Coffroth of Columbia, Calab Dorsey and Colonel Benjamin Moor of Sonora, William Jeff Gatewood and Rienza Hopkins of San Andreas. These legal lights observed the best traditions of justice in the courts of this state. During a court session Ben Marshall, the Constable for Murphys Township, kept the reckless element well under control.

When court days arrived the Indians of the nearby Rancheria donned feathers and wampum and were followed to Murphys by their draggle tailed dogs. During the annual Pow-Wow the Indians from far and near gathered at the edge of town to feast, dance, and chant, if not musically but weirdly. It was quite a spectacle to see the Braves with their flaming red head bands stuck full of eagle feathers, dressed in beaded buckskin tunics and carrying spotted wildcat pelt quivers filled with jasper tipped arrows. The mahalas were rigged out in bright sprigged calico and glass beads with their faces smeared with indigo blue and carmine. Hand in hand they formed a large circle and danced the hours away.

Philip Burrows[3] and his wife Sarah, and his brother Edward, reached Murphys in 1854. Philip and Sarah found employment at the Utica Hotel and Edward settled in San Andreas where for several years he served as a Justice of the Peace.

In 1859 when the business section of Murphys was destroyed by fire, James Sperry and John Perry generously offered the protection of their supposedly fireproof hotel. One half of the town brought their worldly possessions there for safekeeping, but due to a crack in an outside wall the flames ravished the dining room and kitchen. For the most part, all dwelling houses were in of the path of the fire and those persons who had removed their belongings retrieved them, though water soaked. A new culinary department of stone the hotel soon replaced the frame kitchen.

A funeral service was being performed in the Protestant Church when the fire broke out in Crispen's Saloon. Philip and Sarah Burrows' daughter,

Mary Louise aged two, was lying there before an altar, in her little white coffin when the cry of fire startled the mourners and friends. So great was the panic when the flames came through the windows and were spreading out in all directions, that everyone rushed out of the building to help stay the blaze. The grief stricken mother found herself alone with her dead child, for her husband too, had rushed away to join the fire fighters. When fiery tongues began to lick the walls of adjacent buildings, unnoticed by others, Sarah Burrows took the little coffin in her arms and in the crimson glare carried it to Murphys Creek for safety. Later she was found keeping a lonely vigil there. That night with lanterns to light the way to the hilltop cemetery, Mary Louise was lowered to rest in the soil of Murphys, her birthplace.

The year of 1859 brought to Murphys the noted writer and lecturer, Bayard Taylor of New York. Popular with the people, Mr. Taylor's lectures packed the Armory Hall to the doors.

Freeman Dunbar, a native of New Hampshire, reached Murphys in 1850 and engaged in the lumber business. His son Willis, who was born in 1838 in Sullivan County, New Hampshire, joined his father in 1856 and remained in Murphys for ten years. Then, returning to his native state, he entered the Manchester Business College. After graduation from that institution, he headed west to establish himself as a man of business. When John Kimball, the principal owner of the Union Water Company died in Murphys in 1878, Willis Dunbar was appointed administrator of his large estate. The Superintendent of the Union Water Company was a title, Willis Dunbar held for the remainder of his life.

Harvey H. Blood, a native of New Hampshire, purchased the Murphys Hotel. In 1882 he sold the famous hostelry to Mrs. Elizabeth Mitchler who came to California from Bavaria in 1851. A Mexican who was handy with a blade murdered her husband George Mitchler, who had been working in the Mariposa mines. Under Mrs. Mitchler's management the hotel continued to prosper. Today with its appearance little changed, the Hotel continues to serve the public and flourish.

John Moran who was born in Roscommon, Ireland, was mining on Murphys Flat in 1852. A few years later he married Miss Theresa Curren of Murphys. Attracted to the upper hills he purchased eleven hundred acres of land, four miles southwest of Big Trees Grove. His stand of yellow pine, silver fir, cedar and sugar pine made John Moran's ranch one of the most valuable in the mountains. Michael Moran, John's brother and mining partner was a prizefighter of local fame.

Armory Hall perched on top of a hill that looked down upon the town from the north was the scene of great activity during the Civil War days. Daily the sound of flutes, fifes and drums played by members of the Light Guards, echoed around the hills. The Guards commanded by Captain Smith, had in their front range, Page Cutting who was six feet tall and Peter Pope Avery who, unshod, stood just a little better than four feet high. Back of these, eighty muskets, issued by the military company by the State of California, were 80 would-be soldiers. Captain Smith was ordered to Arizona to wage a war against Apache Indians and incidentally, to check on men who were constantly leaving California to aid the cause of the Confederacy. William Crispin was given the command of the Militia, which he retained until the close of the war. Among the soldiers who crossed the Sierras with Captain Smith were John Weston, John Pray, and Joseph Wade of Wade's Flat.

John Manuel and Adolph Keilbar, partners at an early date, established

Early logging methods where oxen were the primary source of power.

Courtesy of Old Timer Museum

a general mercantile store. The trade was not confined to the immediate locality but reached over a large territory. In later years on his own John Manuel, engaged in the lumber business. Adolph Keilbar established a wholesale butcher shop. Both men were successful. Manuel's sawmill, which was a short distance east of Murphys, was in operation for many years. John Manuel figured prominently in the development of Murphys and in the timber resources of Calaveras County.

After the discovery of silver ledges in the high Sierra, miners began packing out of Murphys to help populate Alpine County. M. J. Dooley, a pioneer stage owner, ran a line of stages from Stockton to Silver Mountain, in the newly created county of Alpine. This line stopped at Murphys, Half-Way House [Avery], Big Trees, and Cold Spring Ranch.

Steam powered traction engines replaced the oxen and horses as a hauling power. Unfortunately these heavy machines destroyed the roads and caused great panic amoung horses.

Courtesy of Old Timer Museum

About this time, work commenced on the Big Trees and Carson Valley Turnpike Toll Road. Volney E. Shearer of Murphys was in charge of construction on the road. It required a force of 140 men to build the roadway, which was completed on June 1, 1864.

On the Big Trees Road, a short distance east of Murphys, A. Tanner, a forty-niner, began his career as a rancher and orchardist. Many of the trees and vines that he planted are to be seen growing near the old ranch house. The Tanner Ranch has been productive since 1851. Under the direction of his son, the ranch was known from one end of California to the other for the excellent quality of "blue ribbon" apples and other fruit.

Table Mountain Ranch, one mile southeast of Murphys, this ranch has had many owners. Established in 1852 by Samuel Perkhiser, James B. Smith and Jabel Terhune, it was first called the Bachelor's Ranch. In 1860 it was sold to George and Alfred Brown and thereafter was known as Browns Ranch. It was admirably situated in the vicinity of Pennsylvania and Missouri gulches. The new owners planted 2000 apple trees, 200 pear trees, 1000 foreign grape vines and 300 other fruit bearing trees. In 1862 these farmers planted an additional 5000 apple trees and 12,000 foreign grape cuttings. Well fenced and equipped, Table Mountain Ranch contained two orchards, a dwelling house and a small lake. The lake located at the foot

Ethel Willard Adams with the forman of the Table Mountain Ranch
Mr. George Hinkston. Circa 1905

Courtesy of Calaveras County Historical Society

of a knoll supplied water for livestock and recreation. Two large springs of pure water furnished abundance of water for household purposes, irrigation, gardens and reservoirs. This ranch of vast acreage is surrounded by rugged hills the highest of which is the Table Mountain. A glorious stand of oak and pine, green fields and meadows dotted with fruit and ornamental trees, made the ranch the most beautiful and interesting of all foothill ranches.

Under the ownership of Zabdiel A. Willard of Boston Massachusetts and later of Mrs. Ethel Adams, Mr. Willard's daughter, this ranch featured true-blooded Jersey, Durham and other breeds of dairy cattle. When Mr. Fred Kenny was the owner of the Table Mountain Ranch, it was one of the most extensive dairy projects in this section of California.

John Garland's Ranch was southward near Central Hill. A short distance north of this ranch the miners had cut an enormous gash in the earth in their search for gold. The stark grey boulders seen in their excavation gave mute evidence of the determination and industry of the men of the blazing fifties.

Dan Pillsbury at the Table Mountain Ranch. Circa 1923
Courtesy of Old Timers Museum

In April 1865 P. L. Traver, a public spirited progressive merchant, applied for a charter for a toll road from Murphys to Altaville, there to connect with a similar enterprise from Altaville to Copperopolis. The "grade" road as it was known, followed Angel's creek to Washington Flat and thence direct to Altaville. Along this picturesque highway are the Richards, Massone, Johnson, and other early day ranches. Near the toll house in the west end of Murphys were the dwelling houses of a few of the first settlers, including those of John Heinsdorff, J. Snyder, and Louis Schwoerer.

Painted signboards along Main Street called attention to the various business enterprises, for instance: "Samuel Parsons Fashionable hair dressing saloon, next door to Wells Fargo." And from another we learn that Alex H. Putney was a lawyer and notary public and still others tell us that Armand Rolland was a general merchant since 1850. That A. Henry Stevens was the owner of the Post Office Saloon, that Matteson & Hughes kept a livery stable that was second to none in California, that the partners J.J. Worden and J.W. Harker were in the dry goods business, that Allan Rhodes was Murphys first telegraph operator, that Dr. Jones' Apothecary shop "for sale, just received, cheap 300 Hungarian leeches".

Among those camps that poured gold into the coffers of the professional and businessmen of Murphys were Owlsburg, Yeaho, Colliersville, Starvetown, French Gulch, and Grapevine.

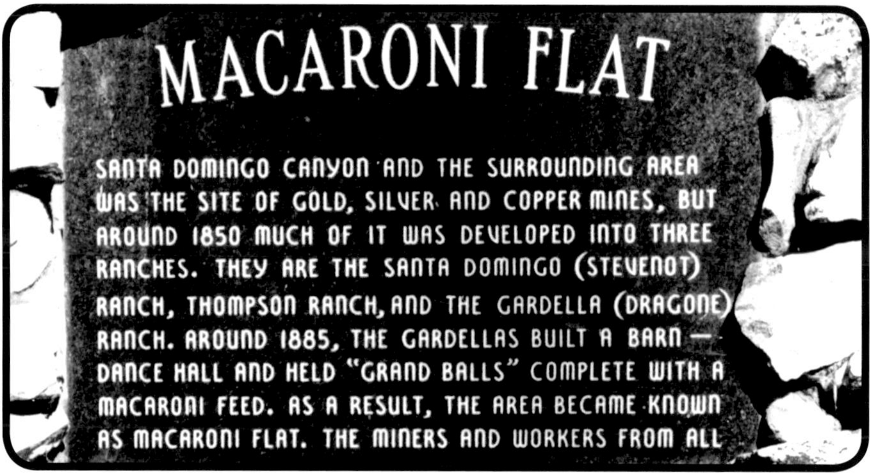

Part of Historical Monument near Stevenot Winery on San Domingo Creek.

Photo by Wally Motloch

Northwest of Murphys a short five miles, on the old Cape Horn Road[4] leading past Shaws' Ranch into wild country, was the Macaroni Flat[5] where gold was plentiful and halcyon days but few. Virgin forests threaded their way to the tops of lofty hills surrounding the flat, making it one of great natural beauty. Augustine Gardella, born in Italy, came early to Macaroni Flat where he mined and became a permanent settler.

The good angel of the flat was a Frenchman named Perishon. A man to whose cabin door, the lonely and homesick gold washers beat a path. Another miner there was simply called "French Hookey" by reason of having a wooden right forearm ending with an iron hook for grappling. During his time on the flat the French Hookey became as rich as King Midas but had earned no respect for himself. There was the petite and fluttery French prostitute known merely as Mariquita whose "fancy" house, built of rocks and mud, stood high on a bluff, below which in a sunless ravine the miners dug fortunes. One day in her primitive house Mariquita was found with a hole in her head. All that was ever found out about her murderer was, that someone left-handed fired the shot. Since French Hookey's name had been coupled with hers and since he was often seen going and coming along the trail that led to Mariquita's mud hut, the gold washers, looked at the wooden stump and iron hook that served for a right arm, then they looked at each other, and winked.

The narrow and winding Cape Horn Road presents attractive vistas as it winds its way in a westerly direction to Esmerelda and Dogtown. At the present time at Macaroni Flat, there is but one family left, the members of which raise turkeys for sale to the countryside.

One half mile north of Murphys on the Sheep Ranch Road is the Ora Plata quartz mine. In 1852 the Chilean miners took vast amounts of gold out of these deep diggings. A short distance from the Ora Plata was Page Cutting's claim and log cabin. Pioneer Cutting's placer diggings, were in regard to scenic loveliness, appropriately named "God's Own" by Page himself.

Walter Mercer Jr. of Murphys, son of the discoverer of the Mercer Cave.

Courtesy of Old Timers Museum

Mercer's Cave, one and one-quarter miles north of Murphys was chanced upon in a strange way. While out prospecting one day near San Domingo, Walter Mercer of Murphys became tired and sat down to rest close to a large limestone boulder. Nearby he noticed a small opening in the ground with the surrounding grasses waving as though agitated by a strong draft of air from below. Curious he got up and poked the ramrod of his shotgun into the hole and decided he'd made a discovery. More accurately, he had rediscovered what another miner had experienced in 1852. Now, more than thirty-five years later, Walter laid his gun aside and did some further investigation. With the assistance of a follow prospector and a lighted candle that afternoon, Walter wormed his way into what is now called the Gothic Chamber but did not make much progress that day. In the following days with the use of ropes, more of the chamber was explored. Ladders soon took the place of ropes and then stairways with reliable railings replaced the wooden cleats, lessening the hazards of the descent. The distance of the cave from the entrance to the exit is 930 feet and the depth is 150 feet. The dripping of water created the limestone formations. Its seven huge chambers are filled with fantastic stone giants and strange formations resembling animals, angels' wings, musical instruments, and other oddities. Half buried in the debris of the ages were found the bones of hundreds of Indians, which added to the mystery of the ancient hole.

Footnotes

1 The location of McKinney's Secret Diggings was not near Cave City where the McKinney's Humbug was located. The Secret Diggings was located at the spring near headwaters of Murray Creek. In 2005, this location is just east of Railroad Flat Road and Sheep Ranch Road.

2 Known as "Deep Cut" it is located not far from Murphys Hotel.

3 Burrows or Barrows "E.W. Barrows, Justice of the Peace of San Andreas, was found dead on Thursday morning under the bridge that crosses the gulch on Main street in that place. He is supposed to have fell off the bridge while going home the night previous." Alpine Chronicle, Sat. Dec. 16, 1876

4 Now San Domingo Road. Shaw's' Ranch is now the Stevenot Vineyards.

5 Not far from Stevenot Vineyards is a historical marker for Macaroni Flat and Santo Domingo [Easter Sunday] mining camp. Suggesting that the Spanish speaking argonauts arrived there Easter Sunday of 1849.

13

MURPHYS FAMOUS RESIDENTS

Kitty O'Donnell

The meadow lark, the earliest of songsters was sending notes like darts to the April air when a covered wagon bearing John O'Donnell and his wife Mary and their daughter Catherine aged two, came to a halt on Algiers Street in Murphys. The travel weary O'Donnells located that day on Pennsylvania Flat, one mile southwest of the town. Here in Pennsylvania Gulch, John O'Donnell began his career as a miner. Table Mountain looked down in a cold sublimity upon their log house, humble and comfortless. Cathleen, a robust little girl, romped, played and sang in the dooryard of her parent's home. Later she attended the public school in Murphys. Kitty O'Donnell (she was always called Kitty by her friends on the flat) was not only gracious and cheerful but beautiful and studious as well.

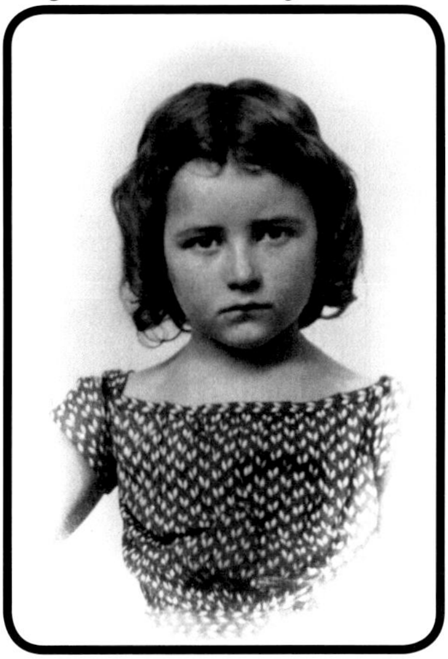

Cathleen (Kitty) O'Donnell circa 1854

Courtesy of Dominican Sisters of San Rafael

A young boy destined for fame named Albert Michelson was Kitty's classmate. Albert always stood at the head of the class. Being anxious to keep up with Albert, a close application of studies was necessary for Kitty. But Kitty O'Donnell was like that. She wanted to excel in whatever she undertook and better still, she did.

Early in life, Kitty decided not to waste precious hours in needless sleep. Up at the crack of dawn she was soon flying around in the kitchen helping her mother prepare breakfast and caring for the younger children. Even the childhood life meant something other to Kitty O'Donnell than mere luxuriant ease. Reared in the tumult of a restless mining camp where the iron banded chests and seamen's trunks were always going or coming, her sensitive ears had often been startled by the sharp barking of six shooters. In the tender years of childhood, she knew all about stern old "Judge Lynch" and his high-handed methods, which no doubt troubled her generous mind. The tragedies and heart breaks that she must have witnessed while living on Pennsylvania Flat may have served to elevate her spirit, until finally, she passed into the realm of true nobility.

Mother Mary Louis O'Donnell 1852-1931. Born in New York lived in Murphys, Benicia and San Rafael. Was elected Mother Provincial of the Sisters of St. Dominic in 1887. She was a major force in the Catholic Education System of Northern California.
Courtesy of Sisters of St. Dominic of San Rafael

There was never a moment in Kitty O'Donnell's life when she did not despise the despicable. She honored only the honorable. Truth, devotion and constancy had free rein in her vigorous mind. Her schoolmates in Murphys chose her from among other gifted children. They chose wisely, for Kitty O'Donnell was never known to desert a friend in poverty, misfortune, sickness or disgrace. The coolness of the purse proud, the frowns of the affluent meant nothing at all to her. Kitty's thoughts were heavenward bent. With gracious presence she moved joyously and freely among the youth of Murphys. Whenever there was a sting to be removed, she helped to do it and by her courage, service and intellect, strengthened those whose spirits and endurance appeared to lack the mettle necessary for a successful life.

Catherine O'Donnell while still in her teens entered the novitiate of the Sisters of St. Dominic at St. Catherine's Convent at Benicia in May 1868. Upon hearing this news her friends in Murphys recalled that Kitty like her chosen guide, St. Dominic, was preeminently a girl of prayer. Only yesterday it seemed to them that Kitty O'Donnell, wearing a snowy muslin dress and filmy veil, had walked up the hill to the little red brick church of St. Patrick wherein, with other children of Murphys she was confirmed. Her religious profession was made in August 1870. Seven years later as Sister Mary Louis she was elected Mother Provincial of the Sisters of St. Dominic and in 1889 she founded the Dominican Convent at San Rafael, Marin County, California.

Cast in a heroic mould, Mother Louis was admirably fitted by nature and by grace for the work of Christian education that was the mission in her life. With the same fortitude and devotion she had displayed while living on Pennsylvania Flat, she established on the Pacific Coast an educational institution whose reputation was not only statewide but nation wide.

Mother Louis' outstanding virtues were charity, kindliness and humility. In the annals of the Murphys Public School the name of Kitty O'Donnell, who studied her lessons cheerfully is inscribed. The records of the Roman Catholic Church tell us that Mother Mary Louis, born in New York City on February 22, 1852, died at the Mother House in San Rafael on Friday, March 6, 1931, after sixty-one years of religious life. Like a happy child falls asleep, Mother Louis went out of life, leaving behind her a hallowed and treasured name.

John and Mary O'Donnell's second daughter, following in the footsteps of her sister Kitty, became Sister Mary Rosalie, O.P.A. A woman of marked ability, she too became a teacher of renown in California.

German immigrants Samuel Michelson[1] and his wife Rozalia (Przylubski) and their young son Albert arrived in Murphys in the spring of 1855. Before starting for America, Mr. Michelson shipped merchandise around the Horn, his intention being to locate in San Francisco, but upon reaching the city and finding it over-flowing with stores of all kinds, he decided to try his luck in Murphys diggings. Competition in Murphys at that date was keen, especially in imported goods but of this fact Sam Michelson was unaware.

Albert Michelson

In a stone store a few doors west of Sperry & Perry's hotel Mr. Michelson opened his doors to the public. In his business venture he was assisted by his wife and a few years later by Albert.

Albert Mickelson 1852-1931
Photo of monument by Wally Motloch

Albert was born in Strelno, Poland[2] on December 19, 1852. As a youth in California he fished for trout in Murphys Creek and flew his kite along the wooded slopes north of town. Young Michelson's boyhood was contemporaneous with the times and personages described by Bret Harte. He may have vaguely remembered hearing of the old Wingdam stage

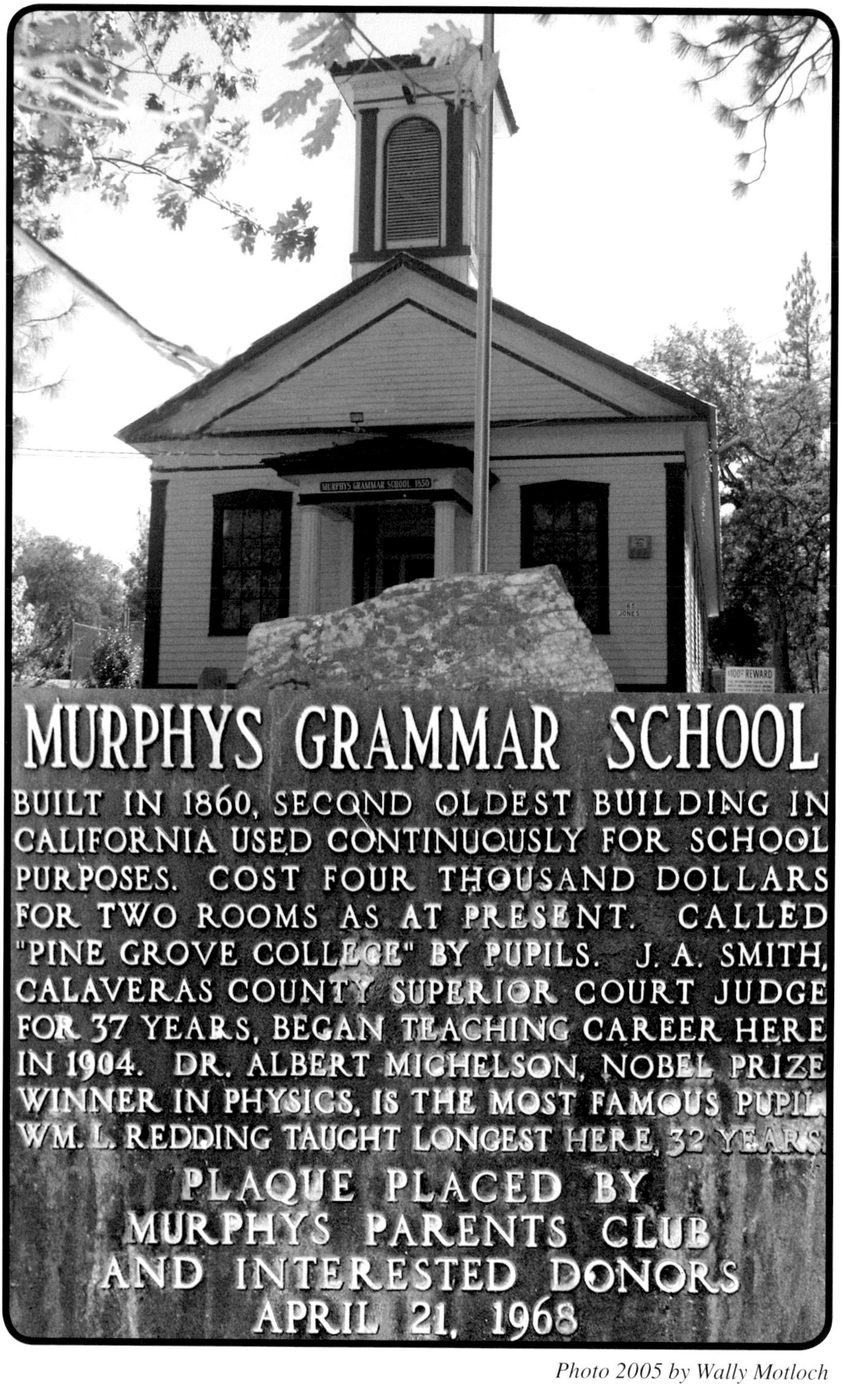

Photo 2005 by Wally Motloch

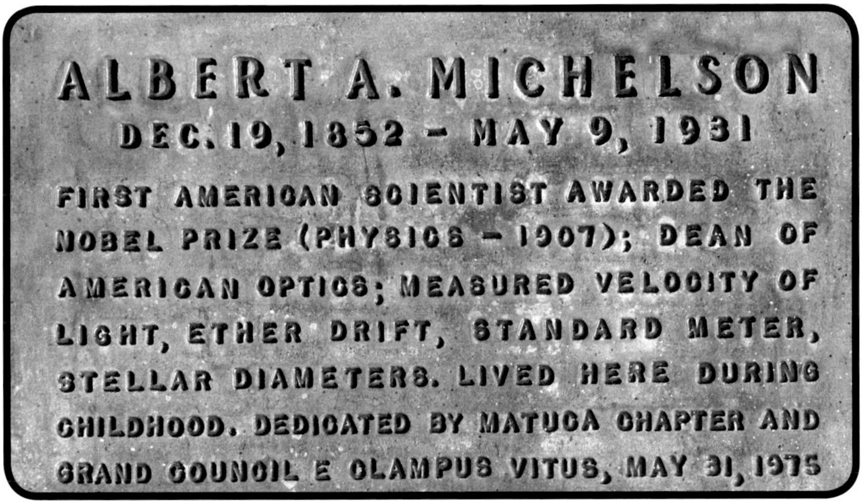

Plaque in front of Michelson's home in Murphys. This plaque is part of E. Clampus Vitus monument.

Photo by Wally Motloch

that rumbled daily from Murphys to Angels Camp, Wade's Flat, Sandy Bar, Grapevine, Roaring Camp, Gooseberry and French Camp were all lively places when Albert was old enough to sweep the flagstones in front of his father's iron-shuttered store. His next job was to carry groceries to some gold washer's cabin. When his duties allowed he would sit in a quiet location in the store and study French. His education in the languages and classics was wholly under the direction of his mother. Mrs. Michelson had the advantage of a sound training in languages and literature.

In later years when speaking of his mother to one of his old friends he said:

"I recall how anxious she was for me to master the French language, but I made a poor job of it and I'm afraid she was most discouraged with the dullness of her pupil."

However dull Albert may have thought himself, the fact remains that when he was an exchange professor at the Sorbonne in Paris, he delivered a series of scientific lectures in the French language.

In Murphys he learned to read and write English in the old schoolhouse on the flat. It was Volney E. Shearer who went among the citizens and collected the moneys with which to erect that public school. Later the building was moved to a pine-clad hilltop and there it still stands, the educational center for the youths of Murphys. Built in 1861 the old schoolhouse with its classic portico and long rows of green shuttered windows bespeaks of the dignity of days now past.

At the age of thirteen Albert was sent to San Francisco to enter high school. While in the city he resided at the home of relatives, but each vacation period he spent in Murphys with his parents and his sisters[3], Bess and Pauline and his brother Charles, who became a famous newspaper writer and publicist in Washington DC.

In 1869 Albert graduated from Boy's High School in San Francisco, the youngest member of his class. About this time the gold petered out around Murphys. Business slacked off and Samuel Michelson, his wife and children, and a large stock of merchandise moved to Virginia City, Nevada.

Albert was encouraged by his father to go to the Virginia City courthouse and take an examination for admission to the US Naval Academy at Annapolis. He took the test and came out first. In 1873 Midshipman Michelson was graduated and promptly ordered to sea duty. While at sea he was asked by Captain Sampson, who later became admiral and a hero in the Spanish American War, to give a lecture to the midshipmen on the velocity of light. Midshipman Michelson later said, "I didn't know a thing about it, but I saluted smartly and said, 'Aye, aye, Sir!'"

As the Dean of American Scientists, Albert Michelson gained fame for his discoveries regarding the velocity of light, upsetting all previous calculations and computations. He was known throughout the world of science as a great physicist and still later as the "Wizard of Light"[4].

The town of Murphys has great natural beauty. The alder and willow flank the creeks like a streak of white light through the flat. Many of the old stone and adobe buildings still stand, their iron doors closed. On the eastern end of the town on ground that once was part of Conrad Hauselt's ranch is the Bret Harte Preventorium[5], property of San Joaquin County. Here in the pure dry mountain air, spiced with pine and cedar, hundreds of ailing children each year were nursed back to health and happiness.

Footnotes

1 Las Calaveras, April 2003 "The Michelsons left New York to join their relatives in California, choosing to travel by the Panama Isthmus route"

2 The town of Strzelno (Strelno) is located in central Poland. In 1800's, when Michelsons lived there, this area was called East Prussia (Provinz Posen, Kingdom of Prussia) and was at that time, a part of Germany.

3 Las Calaveras, April 2003 "Born to them in next few years in Murphys were Julia, Benjamin, Bessie and Miriam" Charles was born in Nevada in 1869.

4 Michelson received the Nobel Prize in Physics in 1907. The first American to be so honored by this prestigious award.

5 Later called Bret Hart Sanatorium for children and adults with tuberculosis.

14

A SYLVAN LAND YIELDS ITS GOLD

DOUGLAS FLAT [The New Diggings]

One and one half miles west of Murphys is the town of Douglas Flat, once a settlement of great activity. The records shed no light on its founder or the origin of its name. John and Daniel Murphy, Dr. Isaac C. Isbel and his brother James first mined it. They were members of the Carson-Robinson mining expedition, which reached the Calaveras locale from Monterey in the summer of 1848. Douglas Flat became a permanent settlement because of the agriculture and the convenience of irrigation, rather than for gold. Nevertheless, the mines here were rich and extensive. Many of the first miners were Welsh, Italian and French with a goodly sprinkling of Americans. Among the latter were Moses H. Harper, Ben Lewis, J. R. Coe, J. P. Hitchcock, J. B. Burgess and J. Wells. These men along with hundreds of others worked in the Central Hill channel, an ancient river deposit from which were taken vast quantities of gold. One of the oldest landmarks in Douglas Flat is the Dinkelspiel store[1], which dates back to 1852. Close by ruins is all that remains of the Wells Fargo office. A tiny cottage draped with vines that once served as a post office stands close to the highway. The most interesting relic to be seen there is the old Galleado building, a combination bank and store. Constructed of stone and adobe with iron doors and shutters, it still stands. The shotgun window was cut into a rear wall so the guard who was stationed inside the store, close to the back door, could more easily protect the gold on deposit in the safe.

Owing to the great quantity of water seeping through the main lead it became necessary to cut drains from the claims to Coyote Creek in order to mine the channel. One "open cut" was 1300 feet long and 18 feet deep. Working since 1851, the South Western Tunnel Company realized more that $500,000 three years later. The surface diggings too, gave up gold to their owners.

At this writing, in Douglas Flat only a few of the old-time dwelling houses are to be seen. Occupied by the descendants of the first settlers, they are in no danger of destruction, at least not by wind or rain. The miners' cabins that once dotted that flat have long since disappeared from the landscape. Time has healed the gouges and gashes that the bewhiskered young giants made in the earth with their picks and shovels.

VALLECITO

Founded by James Murphy, Vallecito was first called "Shooter's Town". American, Mexican, Chilean and Italian miners recklessly handled their weapons in those days when gold flowed as freely as water. Situated between Angels Camp and Murphys, the rich placers in and around Vallecito were first mined by John and Daniel Murphy. In 1848 Coyote Creek, which flows through the flat was extensively mined. The first miners, after reaching the little sun scorched valley, found a Rancheria swarming with braves, mahalas, and children living together peacefully and contentedly. The foreigners' way of life which was baffling to the Indian mind created unrest among them. They were on the move again, this time to Murphys and onward to Grapevine. Even so, the settlement was not without campfires, for where wickiups had once stood the town of Vallecito sprung into quick action. It was no mere touch and go Mexican campo but a firmly established village with a population of 1500.

Luke Sanguinetti's General Merchandise Store in Vallecito with Mining Suppies and Post Office. Dave Batten standing in front. Circa 1912

Courtesy of Calaveras County Historical Society

Running between Sonora and Sacramento the California Stage Company changed teams in Vallecito. It was reported that in 1852 for two months there was a murder committed every week. The first two-story frame building named the Wingdam Hotel was erected here. Tradition has it that Bret Harte glorified the hotel and stage station in his story "Brown of Calaveras".

In Vallecito several stone and adobe buildings were constructed each having iron door and window shutters, which served three purposes, protection against fire, burglars and wild cattle. More than one savage bull had thundered into these stores and smashed crockery, ripped open salt, sugar and flour sacks and destroyed the contents. So, whenever herds of cattle were driven through the streets, the merchants closed and barred their iron doors.

In its flush days Vallecito boasted a church, schoolhouse, town hall, saloons, a fandango, gambling hall, reading room, choral society, butcher shop, several stores and a post office. Among the many attractive dwelling houses were those of the families, Batten, Gerlach, Isbel, Starr, Joy, Lewis, Kruze, Mitchell, Blossom, Slaten, Copeland and Sanguinetti.

Vallecito's Bell came from a ship on San Francisco bay.
Bell was cast in Troy New York in 1853.
Courtesy of Calaveras County Historical Society

The town being in need of a bell the miners, as miners would, chipped in together and raised funds. They sent a man to San Francisco for the sole purpose of procuring a bell. He found one in a deserted ship, which had been cast in 1853 in a foundry of Jones & Hitchcock in Troy, New York. The bell was bought and shipped to Vallecito. Upon its arrival it was mounted in the wide spreading branches of a canyon oak. Today, just as in the days of gold, the silvery toned bell rings out fire alarms. It also calls the reverent to prayer meetings and mournfully tolls while caskets are being borne to Vallecito's pioneer cemetery.

Sunday was always Vallecito's busiest day. One Sunday in 1859 until a late hour, the streets were crowded with people from the gulches and ravines. The merchants were busy receiving orders to be delivered on Monday. On

View of the Moaning Cave entrance in 1920's. Today this cave has been adapted to visitors needs and is open to public.

Courtesy of Calaveras County Historical Society

that particular Sunday Cohen & Levy, purchased 1067 ounces of gold and other merchants bought about half that amount, making 1600 ounces for the week. Pioneer Isbel, an uncle of Dr. I.C. and James Isbel, had a streak of good fortune in his quartz ledge in August 1859. In less than two days he took out $15,000 worth of gold. Joseph Wade's claim at Wade's Flat, one of the richest in the vicinity of Vallecito, coughed up $9,000 worth of dust in a single day. Humbug Hill close by proved that it was no humbug, for in a week's time five men working together took 65 ounces of gold from their claim. The claims of Murphy & Company and Peter King & Company also produced handsomely.

A short distance south of Vallecito is the awe-inspiring Moaning Cave. Any motorists who want to speed through Vallecito on the way to the State

Park in Columbia, in Tuolumne County may do so. If he misses seeing this gigantic underground cavern, well, that's his hard luck.

Gooseberry, a short distance south of the Moaning Cave, was cradled between the granite walls of the Stanislaus River gorge. In 1849-1850 hundreds of French miners wielded picks and shovels and grew rich there. When each man had made his pile, he would take his gold and sailed back to his native land. One of the richest of the Stanislaus River camps, Gooseberry's stone buildings have fallen into ruins. Once the Frenchmen had departed, their old camp was occupied by Chinese miners. They were content to mine the ground that all other gold washers had abandoned as being "worked out".

THE NATURAL BRIDGES

Group of visitors at Natural Bridges.
Note Old Batch sitting between two men, front row. Circa 1893
Courtesy of Calaveras County Historical Society

Located on the Coyote Creek, three miles south of Vallecito and 500 yards from the old stage road that led from the Big Trees to Yosemite Valley is the Natural Bridges site. It is best visited in the springtime when there is an abundance of water in the stream. After leaving the road, the hill trail takes a half-mile downward course to the first bridge. Near the bottom of

Coyote Canyon, one can walk to the top of the first bridge. At the left, where Coyote Creek winds through a dense chaparral brush, the trail continued downward to the southern entrance of this massive span of stone. The length of this bridge is 240 feet with a height of from 8 to 47 feet and a width of from 12 to 76 feet.

During the months of April and May the scene at this marvelous limestone bridge is entrancing. The hills in a northerly direction are stark and bleak while southerly; they are clad with oak and pine. Maidenhair ferns and wild flowers growing and blooming above the entrance of the first bridge add to its interest and beauty. When in 1850 the miners of Vallecito attempted to explore the interior of this bridge, the water of Coyote Creek, which flows through it, stopped them. Finally entrance was gained by means of a raft, on which they steered through the dark tunnel, to the imposing cathedral like northern entrance. People bent on reaching the northern entrance on foot were obliged to pick their way gingerly, especially when the descent was over a limestone formation. None except the most experienced mountain climbers attempted to descend this newly blazed trail. Ferns and flowers wreathed the loftier, more impressive northern entrance. Adorning the nearby glades and ravines were Mariposa Lilies, lupines, Indian paint brush, Johnny-jump-ups, harvest brodiaea and miner cloth of gold, all blooming in wildest profusion. Unlike the southern entrance, this spectacular northern opening had no secrets to reveal. It left the explorers to ponder in solitude upon Nature's master bridge builders and heroic stone squarers.

One hundred yards down stream was another stone bridge, equally wonderful. This second bridge was and still is a sort of sanctuary for wild birds, including the secretive water ouzel, cliff swallow and other varieties of feathered tribes. Here, the birdsong was loudest, nests were built and fledglings taught to fly from the rocky projectors of this bridge's titanic archway. In the autumn, when the toyon bushes turned red as fire and the black oaks threw shawls of amber and brown upon the ground, the region of the second bridge is breathtaking. On the hillsides above the two prehistoric bridges now and again may be found traces of the road that once connected Murphys with New Diggings, Old Diggings, Pennsylvania Flat, Douglas' Flat, and Vallecito. This road also connected with one or the other of the several ferries on the Stanislaus River. For instance the Abbey's, McLean's, Hughes', Robinson's, Bradbury's and Reynolds'.

A. L. Barnes by right of discovery was the custodian of the natural bridges. Known far and near as the "Old Batch" or "Greaser Barnes", he was an American without tinge of Hispanic blood. On May 2, 1850 he started on foot from Chicago, Illinois, for the gold fields in California. On his strong back he carried a rifle, roll of blankets, coffee pot, fry pan, and provisions. A stouthearted young man, he dared to travel on his own through the Indian country. While trudging westward, Barnes overtook and passed two emigrant trains and reached Sutter's Fort none the worse for his long and toilsome journey on August 26, 1850. September found him in Vallecito, mining in Coyote Creek. It was while following this stream in a southerly direction that Barnes discovered the two bridges. Amazed at the perfection of Nature's handiwork, he laid claim to the limestone bridges. Close by he built a cabin, the rock foundation of which is still to be seen at the southern entrance of the first bridge. Here, Old Batch, for long years, lived alone in peace and happiness.

The Old Batch quickly discovered, that the Indians at the nearby Rancheria got along all right without hats. So he tossed aside the old woolly one he had worn while crossing the plains and went about bare headed. On frosty days he wore, Davy Crockett fashion, a coonskin cap with long tail dangling. Old Batch when visiting his Vallecito friends never risked losing his coonskin cap to a dog but kept it tucked under his arm. During the warm dry weather he laid it carefully away in the spicy leaves of the Yerba Santa plant (Miners' tobacco), a shrub highly prized by the first miners.

Old Batch of Natural Bridges.
Courtesy of C.C.H.S.

Old Batch when visiting Angels Camp where he was well and favorably known, wore faded blue cotton jeans, patched with flour sacks bearing such brands as Austin and Simon Willard Sperry's Stockton City Mills or Tulloch's of Knights Ferry. It all depended upon which company had presented him with his last sack of flour. This eccentric lover of mysterious solitary places exacted no fee for admission to the bridges. Instead he threw out a hint that one could hardly ignore. On the outside of his cabin in plain view, he tacked a crudely painted sign, which read:

"Old Batch can't live on nothing"

Returning one day from a trip to Murphys, Old Batch found that during his absence he had a distinguished caller, who when leaving had left gratuitously, a bit of advice:

"I say, Old Batch, why don't you match
With some Calaveras maiden fair?

The life you lead must be sad indeed:
Compelled to sleep by yourself alone.
No, don't think twice, but take my advice
And ask some maiden to your home."
(Signed) Joaquin Miller

Old Batch's answer to the poet of the Sierra follows:
"But Maidens now are hard to find,
And what is worser still,
Money is what these maidens seek
And that void is hard to fill.
But show me the maid with cash in bank
And plenty there for two;
Then I will jump for such a trump
And not make much ado."

Each springtime, the flaming japonica, purple lilac and white bridal wreath planted there by the keeper of the wondrous bridges, still blooms around the Pioneer Barnes' deserted dooryard.

The old stage road that connected Calaveras with Tuolumne County was steep and narrow. It ran past the head of the trail that led to Old Batch's wonderland and then dropped down to Abbey's Ferry, where the grey slate walls of the Stanislaus River gorge were enlivened by the rush of water that flowed westward to mingle with that of the San Joaquin River.

Nature lovers, while plodding along the old hill trail blazoned by A. L. Barnes, like the local poet Harry Noyes Pratt, may say to themselves;
"Wonder who has passed here
In the long ago,
Laughing, weeping, sighing
I shall never know.
Only know the hill trails
As they are today
The makers of the hill trails
Have lone since passed away."

Footnotes

1 Dinkelspiel store was located in Vallecito

15

THE MAMMOTH GROVE

Ten years after David Douglas, the botanist and explorer, saw what he had termed "the mammoth trees in California" John Bidwell, while making his way on foot down the western slope of the Sierra, may have stumbled upon a fallen tree (Sequoia Gigantia) which ever since 1852

Place of great wonder and festivities, the Big Trees attracted visitors from all over the world. This stump provided room for 32 couples to dance. The stump is still there and one can dance on it today.

Courtesy of Calaveras County Historical Society

has been known as the Father of the Forest. Later, in his book "Echoes of the Past" John Bidwell wrote, "We went on traveling as near west as we could. When we killed our last ox we shot and ate crows or anything we could kill and one man shot a wildcat. We could eat anything. One day in the morning I went ahead, on foot of course, to see if I could kill something, it being understood that the company would keep on as near west as possible and find a practical road. I followed an old Indian trail down into the canyon, meeting many Indians on the way up. They did not molest me but I did not quite like their looks. I went about ten miles down the canyon and then

STAGES,

FROM

Stockton to Murphys, via San Andreas Angel's and Vallecito.

The above Line leaves the Company's Office, corner of Centre street and Levee, Stockton, every morning at 4 o'clock, or on the arrival of the boat from San Francisco.

Returning, leaves Sperry's Hotel, Murphy's, passing through the above places, and arriving at Stockton in season to connect with the steamer for San Francisco same day.

N. B.—This is the only direct route to Cave City and the Big Trees. feb 28-tf

Trasportation from San Francisco and Bay area to the Big Trees, San Antone Falls and Cave City was provided by Matteson Stages.

Courtesy of Calaveras County Archives

began to think it time to strike north to intersect the trail of the company going west. A most difficult time I had scaling the precipice. Once I threw my gun ahead of me, being unable to hold it and climb and then was in despair least I could not get up where it was but finally I did manage to do so and make my way north. Just at dark, I came to an immense fallen tree and tried to go around the top but the place was too brushy, so I went around the butt, which seemed to me to be about twenty or twenty-five feet above my head. This I suppose to have been one of the fallen trees in the Calaveras Grove of Sequoia Gigantia or Mammoth trees, as I have since been there and to my own satisfaction identified the lay of the land and the tree."

The Father of the Forest, one of the largest trees that ever graced the floor of any forest, had been lying on the ground for many years before the arrival of John Bidwell in California in November 1841. The "Father" with head buried in dirt, measured 112 feet in circumference, at the base and its bole could be traced 300 feet to where it had been broken off by falling against another tree. At this point it was 16 feet in diameter and when standing, this tree had a height of about 450 feet. A burnt cavity, large enough for a horse and rider to pass through, extended through the trunk for a distance of 200 feet. Near its base, was a never failing spring of water. Walking on top of the great log and looking downward from its uprooted base, its prodigious dimensions are scarcely conceivable.

J. Marshall Wooster on April 1, 1850, left Jackson for the "Cabins" at Independence Flat, where he attempted to join a mining company that was preparing to start in an easterly direction but was told by a man named Whitehead who was the organizer, that the company was already too large. Wooster, intent to stake second choice claims then rounded up three companions and followed the Whitehead party up into the hills. After waiting six weeks to catch a glimpse of Whitehead digging and shoveling in some gully, Wooster discovered that Whitehead and his men had secretly decamped, each man taking a different trail.

Falls on San Antone creek, two miles west of Arnold.
Photo 1919 by Paul Lewis, Courtesy of Wally Motloch

The ground being soggy, no difficulty was experienced in tracking the prospectors and to Wooster's surprise he found that all the trails came together three miles from Whitehead's former encampment. From this point they trudged onward until stopped by snow. While passing through a small valley they saw a large number of blue cranes, so Wooster named the spot "Crane Valley". That night they camped on the north bank of the Stanislaus River and while waiting there for the Whitehead party; they washed the black sand in icy cold water.

Whitehead and James Thompson instead of trying to find a quartz ledge went bear hunting and on May 20, 1850, accidentally stumbled upon a grove of big trees. Two years later, A. C. Dowd, a hunter and ditch tender in the employ of the Union Water Company of Murphys, in a search for wild game for his company's mess, chanced to find this same grove of Sequoia Gigantia.

Two days after Whitehead and Thompson's discovery, Wooster and his

Lillian Doran and her friend Ann Buckley visiting the Big Trees Park in 2003. The tree shown here is named the "Pioneer".

Photo Wally Motloch

companions made their way into the Mammoth Grove of Big Trees and each man cut or burnt his name into one or the other of the trees.

The Calaveras Big Trees, the first grove to become widely known, grew in a small valley, near the headwaters of San Antone Creek, a stream once famous for both trout and gold. The Mammoth Grove was found to contain 10 trees, each 30 feet in diameter and over 300 feet in height. Growing close by were 70 other trees of the same species, size and height. Many of the trees bear the names of distinguished men; George Washington, Thomas Jefferson, Abraham Lincoln, Henry Clay, Sir John Franklin, Henry Longfellow, U. S. Grant, Andrew Johnson, W. T. Sherman and Philip Sheridan. Other trees include the Father of the Forest, Three Graces, Hercules, Salem Witch, Leaning Tower, Mother of the Forest and the Sentinels.

The altitude here is 4730 feet above sea level and contains hundreds of yellow pine, sugar pine and other trees of enormous proportions, all having a diameter of from 10 to 12 feet and a height of not less than 250 feet. Near the Mammoth Grove is the beautiful waterfall of San Antone Creek and westward a short distance is Woods Hill. A habitat for the Indians of the several tribes that gathered there each summer to crunch acorns, dry fish and venison and store away food against the winter to come.

For many years the most pathetic sight in the Upper Hills was a Sequoia without its green vesture or heavy brown bark. The calamity that befell the Mother of the Forest was not because of any forest fire, lightning bolt nor the relentless hand of Time, but as usually happens, it was due to the vandalism of man. Under the supervision of George Gale, the life-preserving coat of a tree, the bark, was stripped off with girding irons for cxhibition purposes in the East and Europe.

The bark of one of the Redwood trees. It was shipped in sections to Washington D.C. Reasembled there and at various other cities to show the size of the original tree.
Courtesy of Calaveras County Historical Society

The story of the debarking of the Mother of the Forest is thus: In the summer of 1854, L. Trask, Michael Burns and other men were hired to strip off its bark to a height of 116 feet from the ground. Its circumference at the base, including the bark was 93 feet and without bark was 84 feet. The thickness of the bark ranged from 11 inches to 2 feet. The height of this tree was 327 feet and it is said to have contained about 537000 feet of lumber. The distance from its base to its first branch was 137 feet. The bark, removed in sections, was eventually taken to England where it was riveted and bolted together to resemble the original tree. At the crystal Palace in which it was on exhibition, Mr. Trask glibly related its history. After the London sensation that the patched together bark created, it

"Mother of the Forest" tree after its bark was shipped off, the tree died.
Courtesy of Old Timers Museum

was finely ground and made into pincushions to ornament Victorian sewing tables and so it was that a superb tree was wantonly destroyed.

For long years the debarked bole stood, like a ghostly white column of some ancient temple, stark and alone in the midst of living green. At last, blackened and burnt to the very heart by a forest fire that threatened to destroy the entire Mammoth Grove some years ago, it is now a sorry spectacle. It was again ravaged by fire that destroyed its last remaining claim to beauty.

The Mother of the Forest was not the only tree to meet a tragic end. In 1853 one of the most magnificent trees in the virgin forest was felled by the use of pump augers. It took five men twenty-two days to do the boring. It was no easy task to bring this tree to the ground. This great Sequoia was 96 feet in circumference and over 300 feet high. For over three thousand years had battled against the storms of winter, possibly weighed one thousand ton. Even after the stem was severed from the bole, it was still standing. Its extreme straightness together with the breadth of its base enabled it to maintain its perfect balance. Two days were spent inserting wedges, driven into the hole with the butts of other trees without success. In despair the workmen went away and when there was no person present to see it fall, the wind howling down from the Sierras, lowered it to the forest's floor with a mighty crash.

The perpetrators of this outrage felled this tree for the sole purpose of converting it into a bowling alley. Upon this log, side-by-side were two "ten pin" alleys, each 81 feet long. The stump was reserved for pleasure. A roof was built over it and the floor smoothed for dancing and theatrical performances. In James Sperry's time at the Big Trees thirty-two couples danced on this stump and yet there was ample room for the spectators. It was on this stump that John Heckendorn printed his semi-weekly newspaper "the Big Tree Bulletin and Murphys Advertiser". The first edition of which was pulled off the press in the spring of 1858.

Pluto's Chimney, hollowed out on one side by fire, is 20 feet in diameter and about 300 feet in height.

The Quartette cluster the highest of which is more that 220 feet, grew close to the Pioneer's Cabin tree. Through Pioneer's Cabin tree an opening was cut, it was large enough to admit a stage loaded with passengers. The stage could pass through, without injury to the tree, which is still waving its green top skyward.

The Big Trees Ranch, including the trees, was the property of James Palache and A. S. Haynes, who built the first hotel in the Mammoth Grove. In May 1858, these partners sold their land and buildings to Sperry and Perry, owners of the Murphys Hotel. These well-known and popular partners enlarged the Big Trees Hotel to accommodate 100 guests. The new setup had a laundry, barber shop, hot and cold baths, parlors, ballroom, barroom, billiard table, spacious verandas and light airy sleeping apartments. The table was supplied with the best food that could be purchased. Many notable people visited the Big Trees during the 'sixties, among others were: Clarence King, John Muir, Ralph Waldo Emerson, Mr. and Mrs. J. Pierpont Morgan of New York, Marquis and Marchioness E. de Briges, Le Count Avon Rothschild, Marquis de Sourbel of Paris France, Josh Billings, G.H. Derby (Squibob), Ulysses S. Grant, George and Phoebe Hearst and their son "'Willie" Leland and Jane Stanford and others.

The South Grove, a few miles south of the Mammoth Grove, is nearly two miles in extent and contains more than 1300 Sequoia trees. A ledge trail only led to this grove and its route was through wild and heavily timbered country. Upon reaching the ridge between Big Tree Creek and the Stanislaus River the snow covered pinnacles of the Sierra can to be seen. After twisting around a mountainside, a big tree was glimpsed and in another moment the plunge into the great forest was made. Here any tree less than 18 feet in circumference was not regarded as being large.

Trapper Smith lived in "Old Goliath" tree

Courtesy of C.C.H.S.

Surpassing all other trees in size and grandeur was the one named in honor of the State of New York. This stately tree is 400 feet high, 104 feet in circumference, and 34 feet in diameter.

Having lived in its burnt out base for many years, Smith's Cabin, so called by reason of Andrew Jackson Smith. He was a hunter, trapper and mountain guide. This tree, in spite of injury is still vigorous. Trapper Smith's quarters of this Sequoia was 16 by 20.5 feet.

In the terrible winter of 1862 a terrific gale toppled the majestic tree "Old Goliath". Trapper Smith later told Horace Davis of San Francisco, that the crashing to earth of this gigantic tree was like an earthquake, for the entire forest trembled and groaned. Another enormous tree, its foliage still green has a base, excavated by fire, large enough to contain sixteen men on horseback. In the hollow in the base of the tree "Grand Hotel" forty persons once clustered. In another, "The Tree of Refuge" sixteen head of cattle sheltered during the rough weather of 1862.

From Virginia City Nevada the Arabian camels plodded down the rocky western slope of the Sierra, weary and hoof battered they paused for rest near the Big Trees Hotel. There was considerable excitement and laughter amongst the horsemen assembled here. When the "ships of the desert" headed for Murphys' Jim Sperry Stable, the hands no doubt wondered how it was that Jefferson Davis had been persuaded by Edward Beale to sponsor such a "wildcat" scheme.

The "Ships of the Desert" as the camels were refered to are paraded at the Big Trees in 1863? Detail from a larged poster by Edward Vischer.

Courtesy of Calaveras County Historical Society

The road over which the strange beasts traveled from Silver Mountain, Alpine County to the Mammoth Grove, was constructed under the personal supervision of Volney Shearer of Murphys. This highway, known as the Big Tree and Carson Valley Turnpike Company's Toll Road, was not only an excellent example of road building, but widely publicized and traveled.

On June 6, 1868, the Board of Supervisors of Calaveras County established rates for each tollgate, which read thus:

For loaded wagon, with two horses or oxen	$2.00
Each additional animal	.50
Empty wagons, half rates	$1.00
Any pleasure carriage, buggy or other vehicle drawn by one animal	$1.50
Each additional animal	.50
Man and horse	.50
Each empty pack animal	.25
Loose horse, mules or meat cattle	.25
Loose sheep, goats or swine, each	.05

Eastward from the Big Trees Hotel which unfortunately burned to the ground some years ago was John Gardner's Cold Spring Ranch, beyond which lie numerous lakes and lush green valleys such as Onion, Pacific, Bear and Hermit. The most beautiful of these valleys is situated under the granite walls of peaks, which in several instances, rise to heights of nine thousand feet.

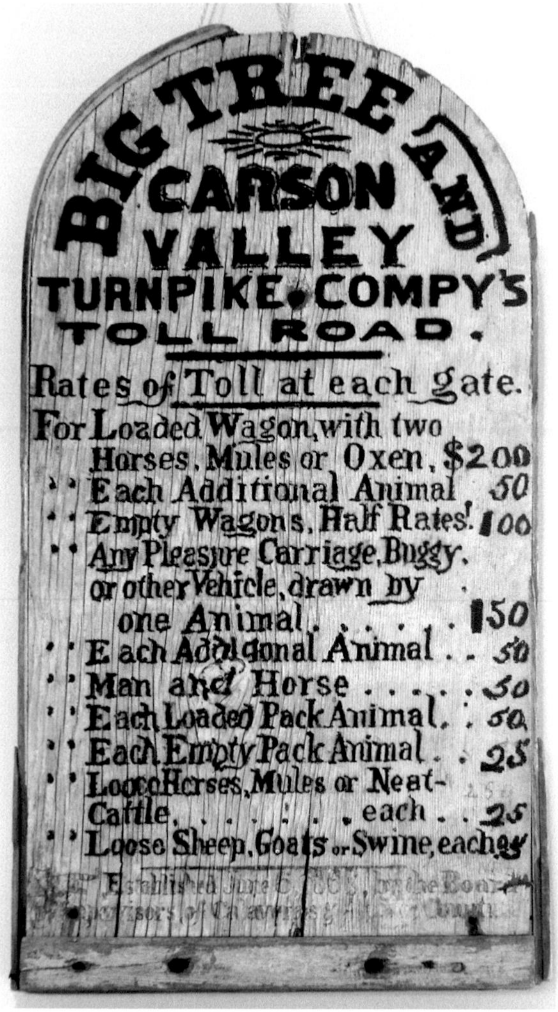

This sign and many other treasures and historical artifacts can be seen at the Calaveras County Museums in San Andreas. The Downtown Museum at 30 Main St. covers the Gold Rush, Miwok Indians and Geology while the Red Barn Musem on Mountain Ranch Road, covers Mining, Farming and Local industry. All are invited!

Courtesy of Calaveras County Archives.

Westward, ten miles from the Mammoth Grove was George Avery's Half-Way House. A little farther along were the wayside stopping places of the Forrester Ranches where teamsters, herdsmen and tourist alike received a hearty welcome and the best of food...Editor's note- the rest of this story was not found.

16

ANGEL'S CAMP

Henry P. Angel's golden ground.

It was summer 1848 and the streams had lost their vigor. Henry (Hank) P. Angel and his boon companion Henry K. O'Dell and a few other members of the Carson & Robinson mining expedition, lighted a campfire on the north bank of a creek. Ever since that day, this creek has been called "Angel's Creek." In the creek, gold glistened and over its slow current, the tendrils of wild grapevines trailed downward from the cottonwood trees that lined the banks.

Henry or George Angel
Courtesy of Old Timer Museum

Where the Dry Creek, flowing from the north, mouthed into the larger stream, Henry Angel established a trading post. In 1850 and again in 1851 it was entered, robbed and plundered by bandits. In fact, they carried off most of Trader Angel's valuable stock of merchandise, liquor and tobacco. Of Henry Angel's antecedents nothing is known. The records of Calaveras County tell us that he was born in Rhode Island in 1824 and died in San Andreas on March 17, 1897. According to the War Department in Washington, D. C. neither the name of Henry P. Angel or George Angel is listed on the muster role of Stevenson's Regiment. Mr. Angel for that matter was not listed on any other military company of the United States Army. Whether Angel[1] was a beaver trapper, sailor or a guide, well one guess is as good as another. One thing however is certain, in the middle sixties; he left Angels Camp with his mining partner Henry O'Dell to dig gold on Indian Creek. Later, say in 1870, they were in Calaveritas building a cabin in which they batched for the next twenty-seven years. The founder of Angels Camp, Henry P. Angel, avowed by his friends among who were, David Selkirk, Myron Hill Reed, Michael Cosgrove, John Gardner, and Andrew J. Crooks, they claimed that he was an honest, generous-hearted and worthy man. His grave in a San Andreas cemetery is unknown[2] and in Angels Camp, the stone marker that is standing at the corner of Main Street and Chinatown Roads, which was erected to the memory of the founder of that town, sports a wrong name. Owing to a mistake somewhere along the line, it bears the name of George Angel, instead of that of Henry P. Angel.

Angels Camp located some fourteen miles south of San Andreas was one of the few towns in the Southern Mines that was not over-run with Yaqui Indians, Mexicans, Chileans and Peruvians. From the beginning, it attracted to itself a desirable population, which in November 1850, the smallpox threatened to exterminate. Angels Camp, in the spring of 1849 had a population of 300 exclusive of Indians. The family fortunes that were founded here soon became the mainsprings of commerce and industry in various parts of the world.

During the above year, Angels was strictly a man's camp. The town's first hotel, constructed by C. C. Lake, was a one-story frame building and stood at the northwest corner of Main Street and what became the Chinatown Road.

J. D. Borthwick, in his book, "Three Years in California," told of the hospitable manner in which these miners lived. Mr. Borthwick had the following to say after attending a "ball" in Lake's Hotel:

"At Lake's hotel, though there were no women in the camp, a ball was given. The dancers depended for music on two amateurs, a fiddler and flutist. The fiddler shouted out the various figures of the quadrille and the merry-making was kept up for several hours. After each dance had come to an end the fiddler, remembering the dancers' thirst and the welfare of Mr. Lake's barroom, called out in tones louder than usual, Promenade all to the bar and treat your partner! The absence of women in the camp was a difficulty easily conquered for it was arranged that any man wearing a square patch on the seat of his jeans, was to be treated as a "lady" at least, for the time being. It was a strange sight to see a party of long-bearded men in heavy boots and flannel shirts going through all the steps and figures of the dance with so much spirit and often with a great deal of grace."

At this time cloth tents dotted the hillsides, there were no frame houses only brush and hide shanties. This condition changed for the better in 1851, when the wives of some of the American miners arrived to establish family homes. Cooks were now earning $20.00 a day and dishwashers $10.00 including board and room. The miners too, were more prosperous.

In the spring of 1851, the brothers Isaac and Thomas McCauley went to John Scribner's tent store on Main Street where they exchanged gold dust for groceries. These brothers who in 1850, had located claims on Angels Creek, were now preparing to mine on a flat, three miles west of the town. A few weeks previously, in a fight on Angels Creek between American and Mexican miners, a Mexican was slain by a member of the McCauley's company. Upon returning to camp, they found it surrounded with Mexicans, heavily armed and warlike. The brothers were captured and taken before the authorities in Angels Camp. The enraged Mexicans then ordered a group of men who were mining in a gulch to join in the line of marchers and since the Mexicans were armed, they obeyed. News of the rumpus reached the ears of some prospectors living in cabins close-by and these men scattered in all directions. Shortly 300 men armed with guns and knives were hastening to the support of their countrymen. When the captors caught sight of the small, determined army, they set their prisoners free and fled. The Americans gave chase and captured three of the Mexicans and brought them into town to stand trial, in the Justice of the Peace's court. Investigation, however proved that the Mexican miners were not altogether in the wrong and after much talk about "freezing" foreigners out of their claims, the three captured Mexicans were taken to the whipping post and given the usual number of lashes with a black snake. The squabble of the flat ended and both factions were at work in their claims on the following day.

Andrew Schollars, a Mexican War veteran, reached Angels Camp from his home in New Albany, Indiana in February 1851. He spent the next ten years mining unsuccessfully in Angels Creek. In 1852 he wrote to his wife Margaret, as follows:

> "I have now found me a good gold claim and I am at work in it and am doing better than most any man in this region. I expect to get plenty of gold out of it if we get plenty of rain this spring. I think there are thousands of dollars in my claim, I have been working alone with a common miner's cradle and some days I make more and some days less, but my average is about $8 to $10 per day. I expect to stick to mining until I make my pile. How long that will be I don't know but you need not look for me until I do make it, for I am never coming back without it, to spend my days at the bench [harness bench]. Tell all who talk of coming to California to stay where they are, with all the chances in my favor the clouds have hung heavily over my pathway, for the few that are successful there are tens of thousands poor and miserable."

On May 15,1856, he wrote to Margaret, thus:

> "I wrote you a letter on the last mail, and sent in the letter $25 in coin, this time I send you a draft for $50 payable in Louisville.

I think it is safest to send drafts on good banks than to send gold coin, but it is hard to tell who are good bankers. I will now give you the result of the last two weeks, which you will see is more encouraging than usual, but if I had been fortunate enough to have got water to work with I could have made a great amount of money before this time. The result of those last two weeks' work was $224.75, out of which, besides having to pay for two streams of water, he had wages to pay his five Chinese employees.

Even so, he vowed, in writing:

"I want to see it out, and I think I will come off victorious yet.

Gold washing," wrote Schollars a year later, "is a very uncertain business because it often occurs in little spots, it may pay good wages one day and the next not pay board, and perhaps you may never make wages in the claim afterwards. Some few cases in many thousands occur where a fortunate man may hit a rich claim that he may make thousands of dollars per day until he makes a pile of thousands of dollars, but these cases are extremely rare indeed. Expenses are high in this country and eats up a great deal of money. I have been in California since February 2, 1851 and my regular board bill has been $10 per week. Every day a man travels about in the mines prospecting, looking for other diggings, his meals and expenses for his lodging it costs him $3.50 per day. I have paid out for board since I have been in this country a goodly sum of money and I have not traveled around much either. I have never seen a particle of snow since I have been in the country, nor seen ice thicker than an ice-blade, but I can any day I choose to go and take a look at the distant mountains that tower high above the frost line, white and glistening they stretch out as far as the eye can see. In the eternal snow depth, the white reigns supreme. The hottest summer sunshine has no power to clothe the mountain tops in living green."

This gold-hunter, with misfortune still dogging his footsteps, left Angels Camp for other diggings and at Coloma, El Dorado County, on November 2, 1862, he wrote a letter to one of his three sons:

"My son Aaron, I embrace this occasion, to partly at least, come up to my promise with you, which was to send you my likeness and some gold-dust. My son, I have not got the gold-dust to send you. Notwithstanding I have no gold dust, I send you a daguerreotype which looks as I looked six weeks ago. At that time I was in good health. I then left Angels Camp and went to Sacramento County on the American River and commenced mining hoping that I might make some money, but misfortune attended me. I was stricken with a violent fever, which came near losing time with me forever. When the fever broke I left this sickly region and came here where it is healthy and as soon as I am able to work I shall go mining again."

Andrew Schollars, whose name is to be found on the muster roll of Stevenson's Regiment, was never able to strike a rich gold pocket in California, on Angels Creek or elsewhere. At last, in 1868, he turned homeward to his wife Margaret and their sons, but before they could be reached, Andrew Schollars 57, died in Kansas City, Missouri.

This is an example of the type of photographs miners would send home from California. The earliest cased images were called Daguerreotypes.
Courtesy of Wally Motloch

The oft-repeated words, "halcyon days," did not always dawn for the gold washers. Many an honest and hopeful young man who, like Andrew Schollars, had sacrificed family and home for the elusive metal, met with but small success in the mines of California. Sometimes banks of caving dirt, smallpox, scurvy, revolvers, daggers and dirk knives threatened their security and in more than one instance, brought lives to an untimely end.

William Maltman, Charles C. Robedee, John Fritz first developed the quartz ledges in Angels Camp, the brothers E. and A. Winter, Cameron, Lightner & Company and Joseph Hill & Company. In 1851, William Maltman discovered a rich quartz ledge a short distance south of the Blue Wing saloon. This ledge, afterwards known as the Lightner mine, was one of the richest hard rock diggings in Angels Camp. During the years 1851-1852 over-shot and flutter wheels were to be seen in Angels Creek, and in 1853, the sound of iron stamps, drumming in quartz mills was to be heard too.

The year 1852 did not favor this town. During the winter of that year smallpox reared its ugly head a second time and for miles around people were stricken with the dreaded disease. Famine too stalked the land, to such an alarming extent that all unmarried men, who were physically able, left Angels Camp so that married men might be able to sustain their wives and children.

But in spite of smallpox and a shortage of food the brothers E. and A. Winters, after two hours work in their quartz claim took out $9,000 worth of gold. Then, sinking a shaft, they struck limestone containing gold mixed with sulphurets which when crushed and milled yielded from $150 to $200 a ton. This claim in 1854 was known as the Marshall mine was extraordinarily rich diggings. The "glory hole" of this quartz mine, on Democrat Hill, enriched the Winters brothers to the tune of $100,000. One of the first frame dwelling houses in the camp was erected by E. and A. Winters, a good example of a pioneer dwelling, it is still standing near the public highway, untenanted, but in no danger of falling into ruins.

John Peirano, in 1852, pitched his tent on the south bank of Angels Creek and started on his career as a general merchant. In the fall of 1854, he broke ground for the erection of a stone building at the southeast corner of Main Street and Chinatown road.

Chinatown Road took its name from the Chinese miners whose shacks were scattered along Angels Creek. Peirano's new store quickly became a household word. John's wife, Julia, was a daughter of Joseph and Nettie Podesto, pioneer hotel owners from Columbia, Tuolumne County. Julia Peirano, one of the most beautiful women in the Southern Mines, proved to be a successful businesswoman.

Peirano Store in Angels Camp

Courtesy of Calaveras County Hisstorical Society

Myron Hill Reed, born in Portsmouth, Ohio, reached Angels Camp on September 9, 1852, by profession a writer, he mined at Slab Ranch, however, the attention of the reading public of America was soon called to Angels Camp. In the spring of 1853, Myron Reed's articles began appearing in Harper's Magazine of New York, the Golden Era of San Francisco, San

Julia Podesto, considered one of the most beautiful woman in the Southeran Mines.
Courtesy of C.C.H.S.

Joaquin Republican of Stockton, Record Union of Sacramento, Evening Bulletin of San Francisco, The Chronicle of Mokelumne Hill, and the Trumpet of Angels Camp. Fearless, aggressive and caustic, Reed in 1861, left Angels Camp for Virginia City, Nevada, where, for the next several years he was employed as a writer on the Territorial Enterprise. Upon his return to Angels Camp, he established the "Mountain Echo," a weekly newspaper, the first edition of which was circulated on May 5, 1879.

In autumn of 1879, a group of 150 Chinese miners swarmed into Angels Camp and set up camps on a spot that has since been known as Chinatown. Owing to the large number of "Johns" in the locality, wages were lowered from $10 a day to $4 and $5 a day. One sixth of the population was now Chinese. Money was plentiful and want unknown. That year, due to the advance made in the quartz mining industry, the population reached 4500, a number it has never exceeded.

William Reddick, a native of Richmond, Virginia, was well and favorably known to all Californians of the gold rush period. He commenced his business career by outfitting emigrants and personally conducting them across the plains. The first of his three trips was made in 1849. This plainsman in 1853, accompanied by his wife, Elizabeth and son John B. and daughters, Anne and Alice, after reaching the Isthmus of Panama, embarked for San Francisco on the steamship "Golden Gate". After a few days spent in San Francisco, the Reddick family journeyed to the mines at Slab Ranch. The young children arrived at Slab Ranch in the spring of 1854. Thereafter, "Joe" Hill the gold-digger, was obliged to give considerable thought to the civic betterment of his community. The heat of summer spent, he rented a room in a building belonging to Benager Rasberry and here at the corner of Main Street and Rasberry Lane, in Angels Camp, was organized the first public school in the southern part of the county. The teacher, Charles Bricknell, was given free board and room in the Hill household in return for piloting the children of the Slab Ranch colony to the schoolroom and return. Bricknell, in order to guard his charges from wild cattle, was obliged to go to school each day, heavily armed.

Until a Protestant Church was built in Angels Camp sermons were preached at the home of Joseph Hill, by a minister named McGowan, of Murphys Diggings. Late in the autumn of 1854, due to the efforts of Joseph Hill, the erection of a Protestant Church and Sunday School building was commenced and at this same time, Mr. Hill was instrumental in having a branch of the Sons of Temperance organized in this town. This was accomplished in September 1854, with Henry K. O'Dell acting as the recording secretary and the names of many prominent men were enrolled.

About this time Michael Cosgrove donated a site on which was erected the Roman Catholic Church, Saint Colombo, a beautiful little edifice. Upon completion of the building, the Right Reverend Joseph Sadoc Alemany, Archbishop of San Francisco, dedicated it. The little church, in a havoc of green, was surrounded by the graves of some of the first settlers. Saint Colombo stood almost directly in front of the quartz claim, "Invincible". Two gold candlesticks graced this church's altar. The name of the donor at this late date is unknown, however, traditions has it that they were presented to the church by Mrs. James G. Fair. Their home in Angels Camp was a stone's throw from the church in which three of her children were baptized. Years later when the fabulous Utica mine began sinking shafts thousands of feet into the earth the buildings in its immediate locality became unsafe. Finally, when the church of Saint Colombo was no longer steady on its foundation, James V. Coleman, owner of the Angels Deep Quartz mine, gave the land for a new edifice and at this same time, permission to change the name of Saint Colombo to Saint Patrick was granted.

Frederick Gerstacker visited Angels Camp in April 1854 to gather material for a book. His traveling companion, "a white-haired, odd sort of old tyke," brought with him a quicksilver machine to carry on, as he explained to the boys, the gold washing business on a larger scale. Later, Mr. Gerstacker had this to say about Angels Camp:

"It seemed to be or to have been a very important gold field. A number of tents were pitched between the hills and the soil of the broad bed of the river (creek) was everywhere turned up and the lights shining down from the hills afforded proof of the crowds of diggers who were trying their fortunes here."

Natives of Boston, Massachusetts, Thomas L. Lindsay and his wife Mary sailed around the Horn and reached San Francisco on August 10, 1849. Removing to Angels Camp in 1855, he erected the Revere House, the site of which hotel was later occupied by the Calaveras Hotel which about 15 years ago, was destroyed by fire.

The Revere House was famous for the excellency of its cuisine. Travelers on their way to the Natural Bridges and Mammoth Grove made a point of stopping at this hostelry to partake of the delectable food that Thomas and Mary (Miller) Lindsay prepared for their guests. To Angels Camp, in 1859, came a sorry-eyed English gentlewoman. Lady Franklin, wife of Sir John Franklin, while waiting in California to receive news of her husband, she spent several weeks at the Revere House. In 1845 Sir John Franklin had set sail for northern waters. When Captain McClintock and his rescuing party, after a long search, returned to California with indisputable proof of the navigator's death on June 11, 1847, Lady Franklin knowing the worst bade goodbye to the Lindsays and other sympathizers in Angels Camp and returned to her home in England.

On June 24, 1855, Angels Camp was almost totally destroyed by fire. The buildings at this date were for the most part, of flimsy construction. With true pioneer spirit, while the coals were still glowing, those businessmen who had lost all began preparations for the erection of larger and more substantial structures. Shortly, sign-boards swinging from metal hinges, bore the firm names of Handford & Downs; lumber; J. I. Boon, surgeon; C. W. Ostranger, Livery and feed stable; C. E. Young, lawyer, Alexander Love, lumber and dairy products; George Nuninger, bakery; Michael Cosgrove, hotel, livery stable, hall, lumber and pack animals; Ackerman & Company, butchers; Philip Scribner, druggist; William Spellner, cobbler; J. T. Fletcher, undertaker; J. Barkhorn, billiard parlor and saloon; C. C. Lake, agent for Wells, Fargo & Company's express, office, Angels Hotel. The general merchants were: B. Strauss, Ackerman & Company, John Peirano, Norman Smith, Andrew J. Crooks, Joseph Peirano, Matthews & Scribner, and Edwin and George Stickle.

James Wayne, formerly of Wayne's Bar on the Stanislaus River, was a heavy loser in the blaze that swept through Main Street. He not only lost his cabin, but also treasured keepsakes and gold coins. This gold washer, instead of lamenting his loss, began sluicing the ground where his home had stood and was amply repaid with his gold coins, which were soon, back in his pocket. Wayne, it seems, was what the gold washers termed a "lucky cuss," for he washed out of the scorched ground that day enough nuggets to pay for the erection of a new cabin, furnishings and replacement of clothing.

Allen Taylor sailed from Boston, Massachusetts for California on the bark "Velasco" and reached San Francisco on October 6, 1849. Next, we find him in Stockton, wading in water up to his knees. Owing to the rain, he was obliged to go aboard a riverboat, anchored in the slough. When the weather cleared, he chipped in with a companion and purchased two yoke of oxen and a wagon and off they started for Vallecito where they mined in Coyote Creek. Later, Allen Taylor was in Angels Camp squaring limestone blocks for John Scribner's store. A stonecutter and monument maker, Allen

Stickle's Hotel in Angels Camp. On the balcony is Mrs. Buckbee.
Courtesy of Calaveras County Historical Society

Taylor's only peer in the Southern Mines was Hugh Coyle, Sonora's master craftsman. Examples of both Coyle and Taylor's skill in marble cutting may be seen today in the cemeteries of the several foothill counties. Shortly after the blaze that razed Angels Camp's business section, Allen Taylor commenced to hew stone taken from Lava Hill for the construction of C. C. Lake's new hotel. Lake's Hotel, completed in December 1856 was opened to the public on New Year's Day following. A high time was had; it ended with a grand ball, attended by people from all four corners of the county.

The brothers George and Edward Stickle left their home in Milan, Duchess County, New York, on January 31, 1849 and after an eight months' sail around the Horn landed in San Francisco. They were in Stockton two months later, conducting a grocery store. In 1852 they removed to Angels Camp and engaged in the general mercantile business. The frame building that these brothers erected that year was destined for a long life. Here, in a side room, used by the brothers as a tin shop, homeless citizens gathered after the disastrous fire of 1855. By a strange twist of fate, this building was the only one on Main Street that the flames hadn't licked up. Thirty years later to the day, fiery tongues leaped hither and yon along both sides of this

Detail from the photo on page 188. Shows Mrs. Edna Bryan Buckbee, the author of the narrative in this book, and her sister Mrs. Colon is peeking from the doorway.

Courtesy of Calaveras County Historical Society

same street and carried every thing except Stickles' old frame building in their wake, the people who had been burned-out took refuge in it again. That evening each and all ate supper in the tin shop and some few spent the night there.

In 1854 George and "Ed" Stickle built a theatre on Circus Hill, a short distance east of Main Street, out of the fire zones. The stage, drops and other equipment were as modern and handsome as could be found in any playhouse of its day. In this hillside theatre the brooding-eyed young Edwin Booth, utterly unconscious of the fact that, only little further on an unsurpassed fame awaited him. He gave a spirit-rousing performance of Hamlet that not only brought down the house, but chunks of gold out of buckskin pokes. Edwin Booth's histrionic ability was at once recognized by the Angelites. Indeed, this actor's name was associated with that of the old clapboard theatre, until Circus Hill became the center of the quartz mining industry. The historic theatre was converted into a stable for horses and mules and the latter contributed mule-power towards its final demolition. Among the thespians who trod the boards of Stickles' Theatre were Mr. and Mrs. J. B. Booth, Edwin Booth, Mathilda Heron, Fanny Morgan, Wesley Venua, George Ryer, Christopher Bachus (One-eyed Kit), Mrs. Judah, William B. Chapman and his sister Caroline.

In 1856 the Stickle brothers erected a two story fireproof building. The stone for this building was quarried out of Lava Hill and was dressed under the direction of Allen Taylor. Today this building stands on the east side of Main Street, probably the soundest structure in Angels Camp.

Michael Cosgrove a native of Dublin, Ireland, in 1851 built a sawmill on Angels Creek and before the year drew to a close Mr. Cosgrove had several dwelling houses under course of construction. A year later, he established the town's first livery and feed stable. In 1853 he built a large frame hotel and the Cosgrove's Hall, later known as Armory Hall. Among the world-renowned singers who gave concerts in this hall were Kate Hayes (Swan of Erin), Madame Anne Thillon, and Madame Anna Bishop. Cosgrove's Hotel and Concert Hall went up in smoke in 1855, were rebuilt, only to be swept away by fire in 1885. With mining as his objective, Dr. William A. Kelly reached Murphys Diggings in 1849, which year he served the community as Alcalde. Dr. Kelly received his literary education at Meadville, Pennsylvania and medical training at the University of Pennsylvania, graduating from that institution in 1844. He was doing all right for himself in his placer claim, when the need for a physician became so great that he laid aside the pick and pan and court obligations for a scalpel and medicine case. His great skill as a surgeon and general practitioner coupled with his kindly and genial nature, made Dr. Kelly one of the most deservedly popular men in the county. In the towns and camps all the way from the Stanislaus to the Calaveras River his name was a revered one. Long after the gold rush had slowed down, he straddled his horse and with medicine-case strapped to his saddle, jog-trotted up and down lonely roads and trails, through the heat of summer or the snows of winter, to serve alike the affluent merchant and the down on his luck prospector. He willingly tended the gold digger who had been injured by caving dirt, the Chinee boy who had been stabbed by marauding Mexican or the utterly wretched half-starved Indians. In fact, this understanding pioneer doctor aided all the unfortunate ones in various ways. Dr. Kelly, unfailing friend of humanity, practiced medicine in Angels Camp for forty-nine years, during which time he was never known to mail a statement for services rendered. Instead, when funds seemed to be getting low, the following notice appeared in the newspaper (Mountain Echo):

> "All persons knowing themselves indebted to the undersigned will please call and settle at least a portion of their indebtedness, as I am very much in need of money.
> (Signed) William A. Kelly"

Dr. William A. Kelly
Courtesy of C.C.H.S.

In 1849 John Gardner, left his home in West Scotland and was soon on the high seas bound for America. The next two years were spent in New York City. Lured by tall tales of treasure, he embarked for California and after a stormy five months' voyage around the Horn, reached San Francisco. Variously occupied, he remained there until 1853, which year he went to Angels Camp. John Gardner's wife Rebecca accompanied her husband from Scotland to New York but not to California. Once he was permanently located, she followed by the Isthmus route without a mishap. She arrived in Angels Camp together with her young daughter Elizabeth, who eighteen years later, married Harvey S. Blood, of Murphys. The Gardner family home was at Slab Ranch where, in partnership with William Gibson for the next fourteen years, John Gardner mined. Later, he purchased the Cold Springs Ranch, three miles east of Big Trees. It is now called Dorrington, so-named in honor of this pioneer's wife Rebecca (Dorrington) Gardner. Mr. and Mrs. Gardner's last days were spent in their home in Angels Camp.

Benager R. Rasberry, a 'forty-niner, while hunting for gray squirrels on Gold Hill, near Cherokee Flat, found a gold mine in a strange way. He aimed at a squirrel and fired a shot that loosened his ramrod from its moorings. The ramrod took an upward, sidelong flight and struck at the base of a manzanita bush, about twenty feet from where the bushy-tailed rodent was nibbling on a pine nut. Benager, agile as a bobcat, plunged into the manzanita thicket and emerged with his ramrod and a lump of gold. An experienced prospector, he soon located a quartz vein. That day when he returned home, squirrel-less, he had nevertheless seven hundred dollars worth of gold to show to his wife Maria. On the following day he dug out $2,000 worth of precious metal and the third day treated him even better, for by nightfall he was the possessor of $7,000 worth of gold. A rich pocket mine, it kept the proverbial wolf from Benager's door for many a year to come. Rasberry Lane leading from the east side of Main Street to Dead Horse Hill is named in honor of Benager Rasberry. On a rocky steep was situated Rasberry's orchard and dwelling house. Later, on this hill Angels Camp's first schoolhouse was built and Silas Brockway was the teacher.

Benager Rasberry
Courtesy of C.C.H.S.

On the afternoon of a September day in 1856, James Colbrook stood in front of Ackerman & Strauss' store on Main Street, talking to a fellow rancher when John Armstrong emerged from Barkhorn's billiard saloon and took a long, hard look at Colbrook, who left his companion and walked towards Lake's Hotel.

"There goes the man who claims I stole old man Harrison's hogs,"

Yelled Armstrong, loud enough for Colbrook to hear.

Colbrook, giving no indication of having heard a word, continued on to the hotel, then changed his mind, turned around and went to Barkhorn's saloon.

Once inside, Armstrong made a lunge at Colbrook, saying:

"Don't you dare call me a hog thief!"

They grappled and struggled. Armstrong, the stronger of the two, broke away and struck his opponent in the face. Colbrook reeled but stood his ground.

"You'll not call me a thief again,"

Stormed the other, preparing to follow up the attack. Again they clashed. This time Colbrook unsheathed his Bowie knife and plunged it into Armstrong's left side, near the heart.

"He's killed me,"

Gasped the man, who a moment later, was dead.

Colbrook made a desperate effort to escape but was tracked, arrested and turned over to the officers Rodgers and Abbott. Great excitement at once prevailed. It was the intention of the officers to take the prisoner to the county jail in Mokelumne Hill after the uproar had subsided.

The people however, were unwilling that the prisoner should be removed from the town. In the meantime runners were sent to the neighboring camps and at eight o'clock, when the examination was to take place, the prospect of a lynching was freely discussed. A peremptory notice was sent to the Justice that he must at once commence an examination of the prisoner. Of course he had to hear and to obey. Accordingly the doors of the prison house were opened and the populace entered pell-mell, a heterogeneous mass, Scotch, English, Dutch, Italian, French and American. They all mingled with one another "in delightful sociality." Before the examination of the third witness was completed the cry of "Bring him out! Bring him out!" was yelled outdoors and in rushed a body of men, mischief bent. The officers made no resistance, other than verbal. They perhaps, knew too well the spirit of the mob. The prisoner was heavily chained to the floor. Even so, a rope was put around his neck and those who had hold of it started off, nearly dragging the unfortunate young man through his chains. The humanity of one man however, conceived the plan of bursting the manacles from the floor, which was done and the men holding the rope then started a second time, dragging the prisoner along with them. Some one proposed that the prisoner should have a fair trial, that it should take place at the schoolhouse, that the prisoner should be allowed time to make his peace with God and settle his worldly affairs and to this, all agreed. The evening was drawing to a swift close when James Colbrook was taken to the school house, where he hurriedly wrote a few lines to his brother concluding with the hope that "father might never know of his terrible fate." After reiterating that he had used his weapon in defense of his life, he was taken outdoors and "hung like a dog" from a limb of a tree. James Colbrook's rock-bound grave on Dead Horse Hill, except during vacation periods, was never without a bouquet of fresh flowers as the school children of Angels Camp took care of that detail.

At the time of the murder, Mary E. Hill, a daughter of Joseph Hill of Slab Ranch, was a schoolgirl. In a letter, written to this writer in 1931, she, Mrs. Mary (Hill) Arnold related the following:

> "Mrs. John A. Jackson, my Sunday School teacher died in childbirth. Seeing my teacher in her coffin with her little dead baby on her breast and what happened afterwards made an impression on my mind that I have never been able to forget. As we wended our way up Main Street to the Protestant Cemetery to bury her, the line

of marchers was broken by men running and screaming: "Catch the murderer! Catch the murderer!" The men carrying the coffin set it down in the middle of the street and hastened off to join the chase. The pursuers soon caught the assassin and shortly after they had buried Mrs. Jackson, they lynched him. The next morning as us children came over the hill trail on our way to school, there was a newly made grave under a pine tree which make us all feel very sad."

The first known foot messenger in the southern part of Calaveras County was Gerome, an Indian of the Miwok tribe. He was young and tough-muscled when the men of '48 reached Coyote Creek. Friendly and trustworthy, the gold-hunters soon discovered that he was a great Indian for walking, so they hired him to carry their raw gold from Vallecito to Angels Camp and onward down the Antelope Trail to Stockton. And even after the Adams Express and Banking Company was acting as a common carrier in the Southern Mines, Gerome was still a foot messenger, his strong back on the "down trip" weighted with dust and nuggets and on the "up trip" with letters, medicine and a bottle of sour pickles. Gerome quickly discovered, that the gold diggers were pickle eaters.

On a spring day in 1852, Gerome strode into Vallecito, shook his shaggy head, around which was a twisted scarlet headband with an eagle's feather sticking up out of the folds. Every miner for miles around knew Gerome; the hero of many grizzly bear exploits and each one knew what a head shake from him meant. On this particular day it seemed to say louder than words,

"Let somebody else tote your gold. I'm through with work,
at least, for today."

Gerome turned his back on Morris Cohen's store, and headed for his camp where his mahala should have acorn soup brewing over a lazy campfire. Always for Gerome, the big event of the "up trip" was to surprise Manuela, his Mahala; it pleased him to shower her with gifts. Two weeks before he had given her glass beads and sprigged pink calico for a dress. Now, in the pocket of his deerskin tunic, a bright cotton bandana, large enough to cover her coal-black hair, was wrapped in paper, ready for bestowal.

Upon reaching his camp, Gerome had another job staring him in the face. He didn't bother to ask any questions. Being a direct actionist, his victory over his rival was but a matter of a few moments. In the clash between them, Gerome received a head wound. Then, when his white victim's body lay dead upon the trampled ground, the enraged Indian turned his wrath upon his Mahala; she fled in terror, in the direction of Angels Camp. Manuela terrified, took refuge in a shallow prospect hole and there trapped and defenseless, Gerome put her to death with stones. No spade was needed to prepare the earth to receive her body. Gold miners had dug the grave that Gerome, in his fury had filled with rocks. One after another he hurled stones until, at last, he built a mound above the grave of his erring mahala.

Thereafter, that no person might see the scar left by the wound inflicted by his antagonist, Gerome discarded his flaming headpiece, for a broad-rimmed felt hat, pulled low over his scarred forehead. This foot messenger after that dark day dwelt apart from his own people. In 1854 he left Vallecito for Angels Camp where, on a hilltop opposite William Coddington's encampment, he set up a wickiup for himself. In it, glum-visaged and alone, he lived in the best way he could. In Angels Camp, Gerome confided in but one man, Dr. William A. Kelly. At the bier of this beloved physician, at whose home for over forty years Gerome had eaten a hearty breakfast, this aged old gold-totter stood, bowed with grief and the memory of years gone-by.

The pioneers of Angels Camp supported Gerome for many years previous to his death. He made occasional visits among them since time mellowed him. As a mark of respect and esteem, when this Indian of the old regime, was laid to rest in the Indian burial ground at Albany Flat, a scarlet flannel head-band was wrapped around his venerable hoary head. Gerome died in Angels Camp on February 25, 1900. He was 98 years old.

Benjamin Ross Coon, called by his friends "Sly Coon," was as full of pranks as a porcupine's hide is full of spines. He was a dressy young blade, tall, lithe of limb and a living fountain of fun and quick wit. A bartender in C. C. Lake's hotel, he was Angels Camp's champion chess player. Taking Jim Fair's advice, he located a quartz claim near the Crystal claim. Out of the Crystal, recently its owner Jim Fair had scooped in excess of 300 ounces of gold. Ross, besides being a claim owner, was now a lieutenant in the Angels Camp Home Guards, a military organization of which Philip Scribner was the Captain.

Ross Coon of Angels Camp had the "two bit" habit, which is to say, that to him a nickel was worthless, not even a "chicken feed". He carried this off on the grounds that it would be destructive to his high standard of living to be otherwise. Ross Coon was called "High Old Coon" because; he refused to recognize the lowly nickel as legal tender. Be this as it may, he was a raconteur of the first order, a sort of bugle-horn for Angels Hotel.

The Bear Mountain Range was wearing a mantle of snow on the 24th day of December, 1863, when a buckboard drawn by a span of blood bays rumbled down Hanselman's Hill to Campo de los Muertos and onward to Angels Camp. The occupants, Jim Gillis, Dick Stoker and their guest, Sam Clemens, they had a long and cold ride that day. The tramp from Jackass

Courtesy of Holt-Atherton Special Collection, University of the Pacific Library.

Hill to Tuttletown hadn't been any too easy either. The buckboard ride from Tuttletown, Tuolumne County, down the steep, crooked slumgullion road to Robinson's Ferry, thence up the rocky, rutted hill to Carson Creek and onward to Lake's Hotel in Angels Camp was anything but soothing. Small wonder that these friends, out to spend a pleasant holiday, were alighted stiff of knee and chilled to the bone.

Upon entering Lake's Barroom they saw hanging near the large iron stove, water-soaked woolen caps and felt hats. In the room the odor of rubber and elk skin mingled freely with that of tobacco, Old Bourbon and other equally well-known brands. At the card tables, in friendly games sat William Coddington, George Tryon, Jacob Caster, Ben Strauss, Jim Anderson, Bob Patterson, Phil Scribner, Jim Fair, Jack Crooks, John Gardner and Doctor Kelly. Evergreen wreaths hung from the inside of windows, Tom and Jerry flowed freely and in fact the barroom was filled with Christmas cheer.

After the storm-coated trio had refreshed themselves at the bar, Ross Coon, who was off duty that afternoon, stopped in the middle of a chess game with Bill Finnegan, got up, straightened his velvet vest and gave the guests from the south side of the Stanislaus River, a right royal greeting.

Old Alex, the town-crier, dozing near the stove awakened and blinked red-rimmed eyes when Sam Clemens and his companions seated themselves in hickory chairs, lighted their pipes and prepared to enjoy a peaceful smoke. Old Alex, perceiving their desire for quiet, left the scene for the street. No sooner had his back been turned, than Ross Coon drew a chair close to the visitors and by way of entertainment related the story of a frog, named Dan'l Webster. This frog had failed to win a wager for its trainer, Jim Smiley of Calaveritas because while its owner was at the town pump, a couple of smart alecks loaded the yellow-bellied jumper with buckshot.

The droll, inimitable way that Ross' voice drifted through the yarn and his apparent complete approval of the way in which Sam Seabough had written it, was of interest to Sam Clemens, who thought the story of a jumping frog, however well related was absurd. A moment later, Old Alex returned to the barroom with news of a lunar rainbow, a rare sight in Angels Camp. His curiosity whetted, Sam Clemens went outdoors and looked skyward at the Gossamer band of light, a sort of promise of good fortune.

A short time later, when Sam Clemens picked up a billiard cue to send ivory balls over green felt in a game of pool with Jim Gillis, he kept hearing, in his imagination, Ross Coon mimic Pete Stagg, one of the buckshot artists:

"I ain't got no frog, but if I had a frog I'd bet you."

Ross Coon's narration of a newspaper story, at the time seemed unimportant, but later it proved to be the nucleus around which an unsurpassed fame was built. Other treasure piles in Calaveras County have yielded golden nuggets, but none so sparkling as the one creviced out of a news sheet in the barroom of Lake's Hotel on Christmas Eve in 1863. No sooner was the great literary nugget published, under the title "The Celebrated Jumping Frog of Calaveras County" than Sam Clemens, became to the wide world, the celebrated Mark Twain.

The pranks concocted and executed by Ross Coon, if recorded, would fill a small-sized book. He knew everybody for miles around and everybody had a good word for him. Among his bosom friends were Bill Coddington, Jim Fair, George Stickle, Phil Scribner, and Dr. Kelly.

Mark Twain display.
Courtesy of Carl Heller

Ebenezer Love, a local dairyman, was once accused by one of his best "pay" customers of having "watered" the milk that was left at his cabin door.

Ebenezer stoutly denied the accusation. Ross Coon, over-hearing the dispute between the dairyman and the miner, that took place at the watering trough in front of Waterman's blacksmith shop, decided to do something about it. Reaching down into the wooden trough, he pulled out a few tadpoles, not yet ready to turn into frogs. When the disputants weren't looking, he dropped them into the bottle of milk in question and stood-by, sober-faced as an owl, listening to Ebenezer, in defense of his product, say:

"No such thing, Hiram.
The milk ain't watered.
Ain't no purer milk in the whole darned town."
"Ed, your milk, besides being blue as indigo,
ain't got no cream on it," grumbled the customer.
At this point, Ross broke in, saying:
"Boys, why not let Phil Scribner settle the matter.
After he has made an analysis of the milk, you'll both be satisfied."

A few moments later, at the drug store, the laughter that the tadpoles occasioned told each and all present that "Sly Coon" had taken a hand in the affair. Anyhow, the matter of "watered" milk was dropped, at least, for that day.

William Coddington, whose droves of cattle were the largest in Calaveras County was the principal owner of the Miners' Ditch, a profitable watercourse. Having plenty of mazuma, he was able to stow away food, while others in this community were obliged to live from hand to mouth. That is exactly what happened during the wet, blustery winter of 1859. When, at last, Angels Camp became storm-bound and the rivers, creeks, and roads impassable, there were left only six sacks of flour and those six were in the storeroom of Bill Coddington's brand new "mansion" in the south end of Main Street, and were not for sale to any person, at any price.

Coddington was offered by a prosperous mine owner of Angels Camp a large amount of gold for a single fifty pound sack of flour, product of a Knight's Ferry milling company, but gold being of no inducement to the town's richest citizen, the would-be purchaser was obliged to turn away empty-handed. Ross Coon, hearing that his friend Bill had refused to sell to his friend Jim a measly fifty pounds of 'flap-jack' ingredient, decided that he himself, would made a try for it. So sure was he of his ability to wrest flour from Bill Coddington and at the same time do the town a good turn, that he looked up "Cap" Matthews and offered a $100 wager that he would be successful. Matthews, as canny a man as Angels Camp was ever to know, took up the wager. At this time, Bill Coddington had several prize shoats, imported from China, running at large in Main Street. Just the ticket, concluded Ross, while chasing the handsomest of the "Chinee" shoats into a corner where he captured it and placed it, squealing, in a gunnysack.

Then smeared its pinkish snout and sides with flour from Mr. Lake's fast diminishing barrel. He secured the sack, which he hoisted to his back and struck off for the Coddington house. Once across the wooden footbridge spanning Angels Creek, it was a mere matter of seconds when he would be able to drop the heavy sack, filled with a squirming shoat at the front door. A Peruvian woman servant told him that the Senor was busy in his private office and did not wish to be disturbed. Ross feigned anger, raised his voice, and brought out Bill, who queried:

"What's the trouble, Ross?"

He opened the sack, saying:

"This your pig, Bill?"

Bill took a look, and said:

"Why, yes, it's my pig."

"Well, I'll have to send it to the slaughter house.

The golblasted nuisance ripped open my last sack of flour, ruined it, too." Ross lied, in a worthy cause.

"Ross - Hogs, Chinese hogs, are valuable.

Better let me give you a sack of flour to replace the one it messed up".

Suggested Bill, who was ever ready to right a wrong.

All right, providing you agree to get your shoats in a pen and keep them there",

Assented Ross, who ten minutes later was collecting $100 from "Cap" Matthews, with whom he divided a 50-pound sack of flour.

In 1866 James G. Fair was quite certain that, for him hard times would not come again. He supplied the cash with which his friend Ross Coon, after leaving Angels Camp for San Francisco, established a saloon, round the corner from Montgomery Street. For many years, Ross Coon's saloon was the favorite gathering place for mining men of the famous lodes, Mother Lode of California and Comstock Lode of Nevada.

James Graham Fair began his career as a miner at Caldwell's Garden in the northern end of Shaw's Flat in Tuolumne County. Tarlton Caldwell's auriferous ground was frequently called "Whimtown," and here in the richest orchard and vegetable garden in the whole of California Jim Fair dug gold during the years 1851-1852.

One day in the Mississippi House, Shaw Flat's leading hotel, Jim Fair struck up an acquaintance with Juan Madrid of Fiddletown. Juan liked nothing better than to spin tall yarns about hidden treasure. Of all the many tales he had listened to since coming to California in 1850, the one that Juan Madrid had related that day, in Jim Fair's opinion, was the most intriguing.

North of the Stanislaus River, the yellow 'chunks,' Juan avowed, were plentiful at Carson Hill, he knew that because he explained, while waiting there to have his mule's shoes reset, he had seen lying on the ground, a large canvas square piled high with dust and chispas.

Jim Fair
Courtesy of Nevada Historical Society.

There and then, Jim Fair decided that the time had come when he should shake the dust of Shaw's Flat off his cowhide boots. He traveled light in those days, for it was his ambition to go far. Anyhow, in his brief span of twenty-six years, he had learned that life is life wherever a man goes and all he really has is what he carries with him. Jim Fair, being big, strong, able and chock full of ideas, was certain that Carson Hill was the right place for him. There he would, not only grow rich but powerful as well.

A few days later Jim Fair while crunching down a steep declivity, he may have recalled Brigham Young's advice to the Mormons, which was:

"Raise vegetables and feed the miners and you will all grow rich,
But most of you will die in poverty."

Upon reaching John Robinson's ferry house on the Stanislaus River, he was told that the Miners Cottage, at the Cow Ranch on Carson Hill, was noted for good food and comfortable beds. Jim Fair reached Carson Hill just in time to see 500 miners leave these diggings for San Francisco where a majority intended to embark for Australia. It wasn't because Carson Hill lacked gold-bearing ore that her hard-rock miners had gone elsewhere, but to save their bodies from being hacked into pieces by the blades of Mexican bandits.

Remembering what he had heard about the Miners' Cottage, Jim decided to give it a try. Dogged tired and hungry as a bear, he reached the Cow Ranch, as Thomas and Alice Rooney's place was most often called. At the white picket gate he stopped and stared, not at the flower beds in front of the long, rambling two-story house, but at young Theresa Rooney, lovely as a luscious flower. Tom and Alice Rooney's only daughter Theresa, a mere child, gave Jim Fair another idea to ponder upon. Three years later Theresa left Carson Hill to attend a convent in Benicia. In 1860 when she returned to her home, she was a beautiful, gracious and well-educated young woman.

During Theresa's absence, Jim Fair continued to live at the Miners' Cottage. He made daily horseback trips to Angels Camp and while there, he never passed a piece of float rock without examining it. As a result of his acquisitiveness and attention to detail, he discovered a rich claim, Crystal by name.

At Carson Hill one day, Jim Fair, as though woolgathering, listened to Henry Thomas Paige Comstock (Old Pancake) brag about the ore ledge that he had accidentally stumbled upon in 1850 which over night had turned into a full-blown mine called the "Morgan," in honor of its chief owner, Captain Alfred Morgan. Jim Fair, for many days afterward, held in mind the words uttered by Old Pancake:

"Reckon we're lucky dogs, us boys,
For our gold pit up on yonder hill
has got mor filthy lucre in it
than all the other gold pits
In California put together."

The old Comstock, it appears, worked when he felt like it but mostly, he didn't feel like it. He was filled with wanderlust. To throw down his pick and shovel and ascend a mud-bespatter ladder, without excuse or reason, was for him a very natural thing to do. Comstock neither lost his inclination to wander nor his garrulity, from both of which Jim Fair was to benefit.

About this time William Irvine of El Dorado Town, who said his friends and enemies alike, was a "hard nut to crack," came horseback to Carson Hill. Taking squints at other men's diggings had become a habit with Bill. Bill Irvine of the cold blue eyes and fiery red hair at once began to connive in every way imaginable to gain possession of the astonishingly rich Morgan Mine. But, Jim Fair, square of jaw, blunt of nose, lynx-eyed and with a physique not unlike that of the biblical Samson, wasn't paying for board and room at the Miners' Cottage to be out-witted by Bill Irvine or any other man. Jim Fair soon proved his adroitness for, after taking out of his Crystal claim 450 ounces of gold, he acquired an interest in the mine, which was still "Old Pancake's" loudest boast.

Bill Irvine was the type of man who would act quickly or not at all. In this instance, he was just a little in advance of Jim Fair, that is, in the purchase of Morgan Mine stock. These Carson Hill gladiators, in trying to pick the same plum out of the same pudding, got into a squabble with each other. For a short time, Bill Irvine was "whipped out." The Calaveras County's two most covetous, relentless, and grasping miners soon became bitter enemies. With grim determination they took their grievances into court, first in the Superior Court, then in the Appellate, and United States Supreme Court. There they fought out one legal bout after another. But no decision ever meted out, no settlement ever offered, was entirely satisfactory to these gold-greedy, ambitious men.

Each year the feud between them grew more intense. One day, Bill Irvine, his red hair standing straight as the hair on a timber wolf's back, swore a mighty oath;

> "The Morgan Mine, he declared, Would never be opened by Jim Fair or any member of Fair's family during his, Irvine's life time".

Bill Irvine, possessing bulldog tenacity, made good his oath.

William (Bill) Irvine in his Carson Hill mine in 1892.
Courtesy of C.C.H.S.

Jim Fair, debonair and confident of success, in 1861 married brown-haired, lupine-blue eyed, gentle mannered Theresa Rooney. The marriage ceremony was performed in the parlor of the Miners' Cottage and was witnessed by the "first families" and of course, few of the so-called "second families," of the immediate locality, including Angels Camp. On this occasion, Miss Jeanette Tarbat, of Campo de los Muertos, was Theresa's friend and a bridesmaid. The wedding festivities over, the bride and groom went to Angels Camp. A few nights later, the noisiest charivari ever heard in that town, sent the whole community scurrying to Theresa and Jim Fair's newly completed cottage where the people were given a warm welcome.

On February 12, 1853 in Angels Camp, Jim Fair, while meandering in the neighborhood of his Crystal claim, discovered a vein of sulphurets about seven feet wide, and this claim he named the "Invincible."

Several years passed. The mine was eventually leased to a prospector who suddenly disappeared and so did the lease and by common unexpressed consent the Utica mine was considered abandoned. In due time it was acquired through that mysterious process known as "claim-jumping," by Robert Leeper, Alexander Love, and William Keyes of Angels Camp. They were experienced miners and keeping a long line of arrastras in constant operation along Dry Creek, they were never able to strike the gold-bearing ore vein. In 1880 these partners bonded the mine to David Hunt for $3,000. He, too, worked without results.

Four years later Hunt's lease was taken over by Charles David Lane who, alone, struggled for the next three years. "Charley" Lane was a spiritualist, classified by some of his Angels Camp friends as a specific sort of fool. Even so, he kept right on consulting the medium in whose psychic power he had complete confidence. The Utica was no "poor man's" mine, and Charley Lane had no capital to draw upon, other than the advice of his spirit friends. One day, in debt to his eyes, he said to Joseph Low, a mining engineer:

"Everybody says no, but my ghost says yes,
So I'll have to work a while longer."

Later, Charley Lane formed a partnership with Alvinza Hayward and Walter Hobart, San Francisco capitalists and commenced work in the one hundred foot shaft in dead earnest. With Hayward and Hobart owing two-thirds of the property and the mine's name changed again to Utica, the old diggings that Jim Fair had so painstakingly applied the "shotgun" method to its hanging walls, quickly gained prominence as a gold producer. The Utica mine is credited with having yielded approximately $333,000,000[3] worth of gold to its owners, Lane, Hayward and Hobart.

The news of Old Pancake's discovery 1859 of a rich ore ledge east of the Sierra summit reached Angels Camp, Jim Fair, having fallen desperately in love with Theresa Rooney, could not be induced to leave Carson Hill. Now, in 1866, circumstances were entirely different. That year Jim Fair accompanied by his wife and their children, Katie Quiggs, housekeeper and her brother Michael, coachman and general handy man, left Angels Camp for Virginia City, Nevada. At least for Jim Fair, a wise removal, his rise to fortune on the celebrated Comstock Lode was instantaneous and spectacular.

Shortly, Jim Fair, in need of a bodyguard, engaged Jack Tarbat of Carson Hill to serve him in that capacity. Along with Jack Tarbat to Virginia City went Owen Kelly. He became general superintendent of the Consolidated Virginia Mine of which John W. Mackay, James Flood, William O'Brien, and James G. Fair were the principal owners. Owen Kelly, who reached California in the vessel "Susan Drew" in 1846, was in Angels Camp in 1849. Here he proved to be as good a miner as he had been a soldier.

At last, when opulence stuck out all over James G. Fair, he separated himself from his family and removed to San Francisco, principally for the purpose of watching over his large personal holdings. The holdings were intended to support his political aspiration; a seat in the United States Senate and this was eventually realized.

Years later, in her palatial home in San Francisco, Mrs. Fair recalled the years spent in a vine-clad cottage in Angels Camp in which, she once told a friend, she had lived peaceably and happily with her husband. But, so far as money was concerned, they were the leanest years she was ever to know.

Though a kindly, indulgent parent, Jim Fair after attaining riches became an indifferent husband whose chief interest in life was gold, plenty of it and he got it at the expense of honor, wife, children and home.

The wooden troughs, overflowing with clear water from a near-by spring, into which fagged-out horses plunged their heads and blew bubbles and snorted in unmistakable satisfaction, no longer stand on Main Street. The hitching posts and town pump too, are gone. The kerosene lanterns that served for light in the "gold pits" deep down in the ground and that hung as signals when the streets were dark or under repair have gone the way of the root cellars. The wheelbarrow in which its owner, tired of digging and shoveling in his claim, rested and smoked is gone also. The ailanthus bearing evil-scented greenish flowers, that sprung up in Angels Camp, from seeds planted by the Chinese miners are everywhere in evidence. The ailanthus Tree of Heaven is a sort of memorial to the Chinese miners, who like their shacks that were strung along Angels Creek, have disappeared from the scene.

Angels Camp, firm-based and strong against adversity, has never been classified as a ghost town and probably never will be, for the mettle of its endurance has been tested and not found wanting.

Footnotes

1 Angel constructed a hotel in Cave City see copy of Deed in the appendix.

2 According to local historians, Judy Marvin and Dr. Julia Costello, Henry P. Angel is buried in an unmarked grave in the "Potters Field" also known as the County Hospital Cemetery near the County Government Center in San Andreas.

3 Mr. Bill Fuller, a local mining engineer says that this is a great exaggeration. He stated that "even 10% of this would be too high".

17

CAMPS NEAR ANGELS

CAMPO DE LOS MUERTOS

This campo [camp of the dead], situated on Arroyo de los Muertos, was one mile south of Angels Camp. In the first period of its history it was an unsafe place for any man other than a Mexican or Chilean. A large number of murders were committed on this shallow stream in which men were washing gold as early as 1848. Along its banks the bodies of a large number of men were buried in bloody graves, hence the name, Creek of the Dead.

Alexander Tarbat and his wife Catherine reached Los Muertos from Paisley, Scotland, in the autumn if 1852. Their daughter Jeannette, born in New York City was the first fair-complexioned child to arrive in these rich diggings. Her playmates, being the children of Mexican settlers, she soon learned to speak Spanish fluently. A few years later it was no unusual sight in Los Muertos to see a Mexican miner, flaunting a bright serape, swoop down from his saddle, pick up the little Tarbat girl and ride away with her to some Justice of the Peace, before whom she would act as an interpreter for the Mexican and the Court. Alexander Tarbat erected the Tarbat dwelling house, the oldest building in the vicinity of Angels Camp. He was a plasterer, he hung paper and he mined. The little house by the roadside still stands to give mute testimony to the skill of its builder.

Montecello, a Chilean miner, went among the Indians and picked out a wife for himself, built an adobe house that looked down upon the Creek of the Dead and with the Indian girl Sally, moved into it. Together they spent the rest of their lives, not always in peace either. Sally, while serving the Dent family in Knights Ferry, had met and talked to U. S. Grant[1], Mrs. Dent's kinsman and this honor coupled with her association with Montecello gave her a feeling of importance. Around Sally's front doorstep no mahalas and their bright-eyed papooses ever clustered, for Sally held herself aloof from the members of her tribe. Tall poplar trees now grow where their picturesque adobe once stood. Each autumn the poplars spill pale gold leaves upon the humble graves of Campo de los Muertos' oldest miner, Montecello and his haughty mate, Sally of the Miwok.

MARBLE SPRINGS

A short distance south of the Camp of the Dead was Marble Springs, so-called by reason of pure water gushing up out of a vein of marble. Between these springs and Hanselman's Hill was a Rancheria, where swarmed more than a thousand Indians. The braves made an impressive picture for those travelers who enjoyed a few moments of rest at Jacob Hanselman's stage and relay station. In 1884 a local newspaper chronicled:

> "A half-breed returning to the Rancheria near Hanselman's Hill,
> After filling his stomach with 'tarantula juice' set fire to his wickiup.
> He died in great agony a few hours afterwards,
> His legs and arms being badly burned."

In 1849 Robert Leeper at sixteen left Galesburg, Illinois to drive cattle to New Mexico. He set out with a government train for California and assisted in driving one hundred head of cattle to Sacramento. A year later, he was at Marble Springs, digging gold. In 1860, Robert married Susan, only daughter of Samuel and Susan Bolitho. The wedding took place in the Marble Springs Hotel, one of the best-equipped wayside taverns in the mines. Near-by Samuel Bolitho owned and operated a quartz mine. A "grass roots" mine, the gold petered out where the roots ended.

Today nothing remains at Marble Springs, even the founts have gone dry and the foundation of the old tavern has rotted away. But near-by, at springtime, the laughter of thousands of different voices is heard as frogs jump to win wagers for their trainers.

HANSELMAN'S HILL

Hanselman's Hill, on the road between Marble Springs and Albany Flat, was a rich "dry diggings" in the colorful fifties. Its first settlers were Gwin Raymond, Louis Graham, Jacob Hanselman, Henry B. Miller and his wife Sarah, Antone Figgaro and his wife Rose and William Spellner.

Today chaparral brush covers Hanselman's Hill. Not a single foundation stone remains as a reminder of Jacob Hanselman's two-story tavern and stage station. There Concord coaches once rumbled and drivers brought their teams to a full stop with the words: "Easy, hoss, easy."

James Romaggi Tavern at Albany Flat. Presently, this building is in great need of preservation and can be seen in a delapidated state on the west side of highway 49, between Angels Camp and Carson Hill.

Courtesy of Calaveras County Historical Society

ALBANY FLAT

Albany Flat is located two miles south of Angels Camp. After the Indians had discarded their bows and arrows and settled down to mining, the Flat was a lively place where fortunes were dug up over night. Its first miners were Chileans and Mexicans who arrived on the scene in 1848. A year later Thomas Hardy was prospecting and locating quartz claims in this locality but it was not until after the arrival of James Romaggi in 1850 that these diggings took on the appearance of a settlement. Romaggi, a native of Genoa, Italy built a stone and adobe house at the roadside and opened a boarding house, second to none in the Southern Mines. Murrieta and his terrible outlaws, on more than one occasion, watered their horses at the wooden trough across the road from Romaggi's Tavern. If in need of food and a drink, they went indoors to eat spaghetti and moistened their throats with red wine. Paying their bill, they vaulted into their saddles and thundered off without leaving the customary trail of blood back of them. The pocket miners of the close-by Chaparral Hill spent their spare time and gold at Romaggi's where dances were frequently held. The Chaparral Hill gold diggers were prosperous, for the ore ledges there were extremely rich. This area had two trading posts, a fandango and a Fonda, several gambling tents, saloons, blacksmith shops and other business enterprises.

There came a day at Albany Flat when Mary Dixie "Old Dixie" was its only inhabitant. Mary of the Miwok tribe, when she was a snowy-haired

Mahala, often recalled the day that changed the life for the members of her tribe. The sight of a mining expedition moving in a southerly direction had, for a time, frightened her. However, since it was a harmless expedition, she took pride in telling that the explorers had reached this spot, afterwards called Albany Flat, under the guidance of Chief Jose Jesus, of the Siyakumna tribe of Indians. Mary, widow of Bill Dixie who was a full-blooded Indian, was a woman of worth and character whose friends were numberless. Whenever there was illness, death or trouble of any kind in the home of a white friend, Mary trudged off from her home on the flat, to Angels Camp to offer sympathy and if necessary, render service. When Mary Dixie was 99, she died at Albany Flat on February 5, 1932. At Albany Flat where Indians once Pow-Wowed and made "heap big noise" and prospectors searched the hills for quartz ledges, nothing remains except the ruins of Romaggi's stone and adobe tavern.

CAMPO de NULONES

This Mexican campo was one mile, as the crow flies, west of Albany Flat and was occupied for the most part by renegades of all nationalities. In the days of gold, it has been recorded that life in this campo moved fiercely, wickedly and suddenly. Lawless rascals who had been driven from El Tiger - Sonora's Mexican quarter, crossed the Stanislaus River and took refuge in Campo de Nulones, into which settlement no honest man dared to enter unless he was armed with a six-shooter and Bowie-knife. Hard-knuckled roughs and toughs, many of whom had been driven out of San Francisco by the Vigilantes of 1849, belonged to an organized gang of hoodlums called the "Mountain Hounds," and of these Campo de Nulones had excess. Reckless vagabonds, they raced their horses up and down the main street of the campo. In fact they terrorized the whole Albany Flat mining district, kept the days full of roar and nights full of agonized shrieks.

If at that day, the newspapers reported correctly, then this campo, in standpoint of wickedness was without a peer in California. A touch-and-go campo, built on the remada[2] and bullock hide system; it was a cache for stolen gold. In years after, no erstwhile renegade could be induced to admit that he had ever been in Campo de Nulones, much less lived there. Bloody ground, Campo de Nulones its history no doubt bitter, is unknown.

Footnotes

1 General Ulysses S. Grant and later the President of U.S

2 Remada is a hut or shack made out of straw, place to eat, a sort of a rest stop.

18

CARSON'S TREASURE PILE

James H. Carson a native of Virginia, the leader of the Carson & Robinson Mining and Exploring Expedition into the hills was a quartermaster of war sloop the Lexington. After a sail of 181 days on board the Lexington, he reached Monterey from New York on January 23, 1847. Under command of Lieutenant Wm. Bailey, the Lexington brought to California the soldiers of Company F, 3rd Artillery.

The men of the Carson & Robinson Mining and Exploring Expedition, who made this great trek for gold, were inured to toil and hardships. They were all young, hardy, fearless and daring. Their hearts had grown big with love of freedom, adventure and desire to live and let live. Among those whose concepts of life had grown extra broad were, James Carson, John Robinson, Stephen Mead, the brothers John, Daniel, and James Murphy, William Bailey, James K. Casement, Henry K. O'Dell, Henry P. Angel, John Hance, Captain Alfred Morgan, Brander Curtis, James Duncan, James Lovelock, Henry Perkins, Henry Thomas Paige Comstock and the brothers Dr. Isaac C. and James Isbel. The expedition comprising of 92 men, left Monterey on May 4, 1848, chronicled Carson, "at high pressure mule speed."

Each man was well equipped for the journey into the foothills and their pack mules were heavily laden with provisions and ammunition. No steamboats whistle as yet had tooted on the San Joaquin River to startle antelopes grazing by the thousands on Captain Charles M. Weber's vast acreage. There was no well defined trail leading from the French Camp ranch into the unexplored country eastward, nor were there any ferry boats to carry the gold-hunters across the swift, deep and dangerous streams. Guided by the sun and distant mountain peaks the explorers finally reached the foothills where the Mariposa River entered the plain. Pushing northward, they examined all river and creek beds for gold. Somewhere along the line they took on as a guide, Jose Jesus, a Siyakumna chief and he perhaps led the Murphys brothers to Coyote Creek and beyond. It was Carson's report of the finding of gold in the beds of the various rivers and creeks that caused the territory, later known as the Southern Mines, to become populated prior to 1849.

Three miles north of the Stanislaus River, Carson encamped at the base of one of the richest hills in the whole of California.

"The gold washers at Carson Creek", Carson chronicled,
"In 1848, worked their claims quietly."
We have James Carson's written word for it:
"Honesty was the ruling passion amongst the men of 1848. Old debts were paid up, heavy bags of gold dust were left carelessly lying in their homes, miners' tools though scarce were left in their places of work for days at a time and not one theft or robbery was committed".
Miners, he went on, "Made no division of the ground into claims. Witness trees were unnecessary. Four or five men frequently dug gold within a circle of six feet in diameter. Later, to prevent disputes arising from a division of the ground, it was measured off with exactitude under the direction of the Alcalde. The different diggings had different rules and allotments of ground. But this fact seldom, if ever, caused a serious disturbance. Whenever disputes arose over the ownership of ground or the boundary lines of a claim those miners, working nearest, were called upon to settle matters, thus misunderstandings were satisfactorily adjusted without cost to the wranglers. Peaceful days, the days of 1848, were the best that Carson Creek was ever to experience. Carson himself was the first man to strike the "color" in the creek, which was to bear his name. For weeks later, eight men including Carson divided equally 800 ounces of dust and nuggets. The name of the handy man that fashioned the scales on which the treasure was weighed will never be known. These were community gold scales; they consisted of a piece of pine wood for the beam, sardine cans for the scales and silver dollars for the weights. Gold dust, plentiful in the winter of 1848, brought only $4 to $6 an ounce. Even so, according to Jim Carson, the men camping at Carson Creek during the above winter were the "Happiest men on earth."

The great ore ledge that was soon called the "Mother Lode" was discovered, say the records, on Carson Hill by John Hance however, Henry Thomas Paige Comstock (Old Pancake) is frequently credited with having made the discovery. On a September afternoon in 1849 he struck out to hunt quail. With a jack-knife and cow horn shot-flask fastened to his leather belt and shot gun slung across his shoulder, he broke a trail from his camp to the top of the conical hill. The North Slope of which was called Carson Hill and the south slope was given the name, by Mexicans of course, of El Cerro del Melones [hill of the melons]. All the way up the steep hill through dense brush he had patiently followed a long line of black feathers, turned backwards. Suddenly, when the "old trusty" spat fire, there was a noisy whir of gray wings as mountain quail rose from a manzanita thicket to seek

View of Carson Hill, the note at the top say "Morgan" on the left and "Bonanza" on the right. These two mines were the best producers.

Courtesy of Calaveras County Historical Society

safety in the upper air. "Old Pancake," hungry for quail pie, had shot one of the birds, he could see its reddish-chestnut breast half hidden on a clump of horehound. While climbing on his knees after his quarry he came abreast of a quartz vein that jutted up out of the ground. The keen-eyed hunter closely inspected this outcropping; his joy had no bounds when he saw running through it, bands and threads containing gold.

That night in a rude cabin at the base of Carson Hill a mining company was formed with Alfred Morgan as president and Henry Perkins as secretary. Working together in dim candlelight these pioneers made plans for developing Comstock's recently found vein. This location is since then known to mining engineers world over as the Morgan-Melones quartz mine.

The bliss of the Carson Creek gold washers was of short duration. Once a word of Comstock's discovery was voiced their days of easy living came to an abrupt end. The great swarm of human rovers that soon came buzzing to Carson Hill, like the raiding wasps, laid cold the bright calculation of the first gold hunters. Having found the precious metal at every step, they had come to regard the supply as inexhaustible.

James Carson and his boon companions were among those men who had reckoned on having both the creek and hill to themselves for long years to come, because few emigrants, in their opinion, a very few would ever reach the Stanislaus River. Therefore, the treasure they had so avidly sought

Miners at the Irvine Mine, Carson Hill, circa 1900
Courtesy of Jim Irvine

and eventually found would not have to be shared with strangers, only with each other who had dug it out of the creek bed.

The town of Carson Hill sprung up over night. The summer of 1850 came to find 100 flags flying over the business houses, which flanked both sides of a long street curving southward. Prominent among the buildings was a Roman Catholic Church, which tradition has it, was the first to be established in the mines of California. This log church was undermined and ruined by miners' picks in the early 'fifties. The gold washers, quick to respond to guitars and fiddles, paid nightly visits to fandangos, hurdy-gurdy

Inside one of the Carson Hill mines.
Courtesy of C.C.H.S.

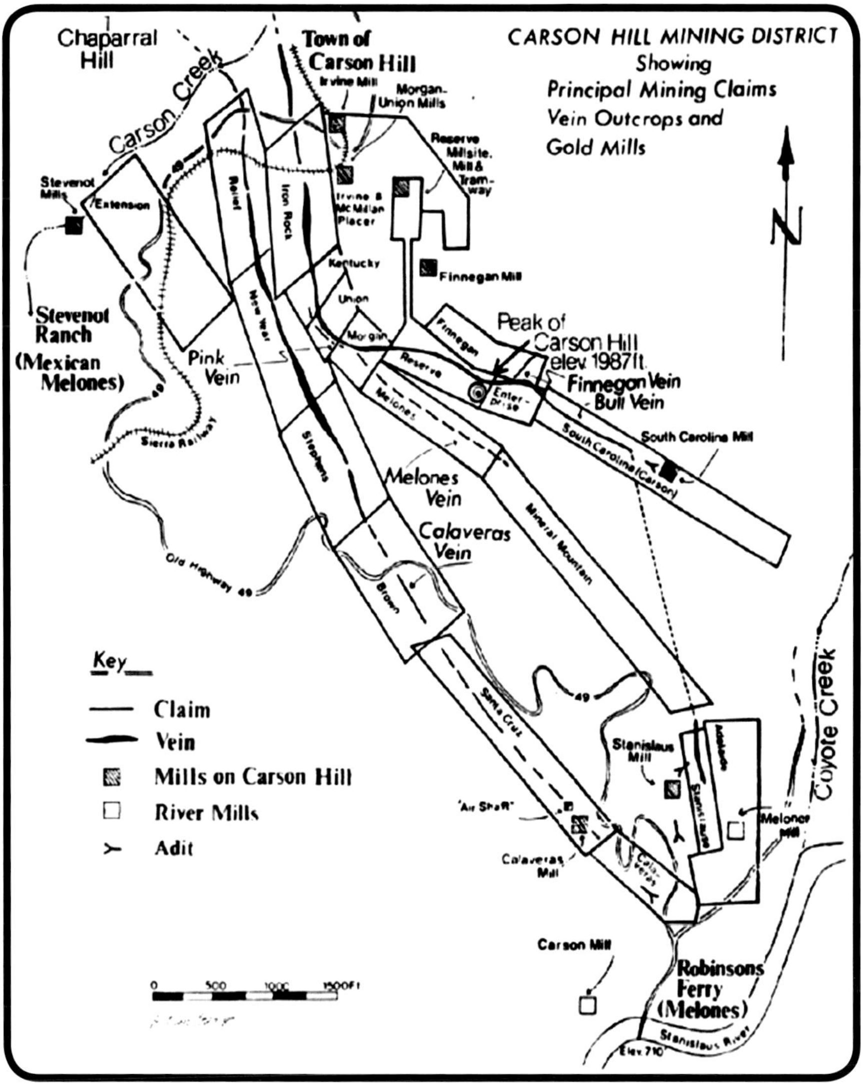

Gold mines of Carson Hill.

Courtesy of Calaveras County Historical Society

houses and gambling halls. It was not an unusual sight at Carson Hill to see an elegantly rigged out Spaniard go to a Monte table, bet an arroba [Old Spanish unit of weight equal to 25 pounds, in Portugal it equals 32 pounds] of gold "win or lose" as coolly as if it had been a mere bag of Indian coveted seashells. At first, there were no ministers of the Gospel here that took time off to preach sermons. Each Lord's Day, instead of pointing the way to heaven, they relegated religion to the background and went gold hunting.

One day in 1850 when the leaves lay in drifts upon the ground, the miners dug a grave in which to lay the body of one of their comrades, whose life had been snuffed out by caving dirt. His friends were determined to give him a funeral befitting his worth and refinement. Living in a tent was a man known simply as Parson. He, according to his own say so, had once occupied a pulpit "back East". Since coming west, gold in its abundance had a corroding effect on him; in fact, he took a drink of whisky now and then. But in spite of his tarnished gospel habiliments, he was invited to officiate at this funeral. A decent funeral, to the miners at least, meant digging a six foot deep grave, lining it with pine boughs, wrapping the body in a blanket or canvas sheet, tying it securely, Egyptian mummy fashion, lowering it into the ground and covering it with evergreen branches. The grave was filled and that wild animals might not molest it, a rock mound was built over it.

When Parson, donned in broad cloth, tall silk hat and "boiled" shirt, arrived at the cabin of the deceased, tin cups were being freely passed amongst the gold washers. Parson after taking brandy, solemnly said:
"To the peace of the soul of our comrade."

Parson, it seems, was not one to miss a round of drinks, so when the hour for the service arrived, his mind was not only befuddled but his legs were wobbly. At the grave side, miners, their hats doffed, encircled the grave into which the body was reverently lowered. After reading a chapter from the Bible, Parson asked the men to sing a hymn but no one present, except himself, had ever memorized a hymn, so he sang one, to the tune of "Old Hundred." There was no stumbling over the words of the first verse, but his tongue thickening, he was unable to go on to the second verse. Stuck, a former British seaman came to his rescue and sang a song, popular with John Bull's jolly Neptunes. Two verses rendered and his memory deserted him. The words as sung by the former seaman follow, more or less correctly:

"A ship's crew of sailors I will soon let you know
To a voyage from Old Liverpool
And to California were to go.
There was one laddie mongst them I wish that I knew
He's a bonny, bonny sailor lad
In a jacket so blue.
As I walked out one morning down by the ship's side
To view those young sailors
And to hear what they said,
My love he passed by me and aloft then he flew,
And my heart it went along
In his jacket so blue."

Parson next informed the group that he would go on to a prayer. A few of the miners fidgeted, wrinkled their noses and stood with arrow straightness, while others knelt around the open grave. One bearded young blade

Newspaper clipping, unidentified but appears to be circa 1880's

Courtesy of Calaveras County Archives

sat down on a rock, saying:

"When the Parson gets his steam up,
He's hell on a prayer."

During the long and meaningless prayer the kneeling miners commenced, through a force of habit, to examine the dirt, which had been shoveled up and nudging each others, whispered:

"Gold, boys,
By gosh, Gold"

Warmed up, Parson prayed until, glancing downward, he exclaimed:

"Holy smoke!
Gold!"

The discovery made that day proved to be a rich sort of diggings. A windlass soon marked the site of the first grave. A marble headstone was placed over the second grave, over which quail whistled and coyotes barked.

……………. Rest of this story, was not found.

But his honesty, so universal in 1848, was not to be found in the crowds that daily thickened around Carson's encampment a year later. In 1849, hordes of pickpockets, robbers, swindlers, gunmen, and knife-wielders were mingling with men whose intentions were honest.

"These rascals," grumbled 'Jim' Carson,
"had lived all their lives by the sleight o'hand and
it was evident that they had not come to California
with gold rings on their soft white hands for the purpose
of using a pick and shovel."

During the later years, many petty thefts, heavy robberies and murders were committed at Carson Hill. But there were men there who had ridden the Elephant of this world all their lives and knew well the course they had to pursue under the new order of affairs. Whipping, cutting off ears and hangings, soon became daily happenings.

James Carson was one of those pioneers who believed in the efficacy of "Judge Lynch's Court." In his Book "Recollections of the Mines," Stockton, 1852, he stated:

> "The civilized world may cry down the court and concise code of Judge Lynch, but I feel confident that every man in California has hailed it as a God-blessed evil to them. A depredation was committed, the long rifles of the honest boys were slung across their shoulders and the depredator was soon ferreted out and brought to prove him innocent. If he was found guilty, his sentence and punishment were immediately put into execution. Petty thefts and frauds were punished by inflicting on the bare back of the culprit from fifty to two hundred lashes; laid on according to the directions in the code. If the offense was stealing horses, mules, oxen or large amounts of gold dust, death was always awarded. Hundreds of the bodies of these rascals, who came to California to steal, because we had no law, are now rotting in felons' graves. We were not blessed that day with statutes as unintelligible as a Chinese Bible or with hordes of lawyers who, for a mere pittance, would screen villains from just punishment, under plea of informalities in indictments of proceedings. There were no jails or prison ships but if the culprit was taken he never escaped. Money or influence availed him nothing. If he attempted to escape, the unerring rifle brought him to a sudden halt."

................Rest of this story not found.

[This loose page, it may or may not belong to this chapter.]

During the fiercely contested tussle that followed some one in the milling crowd yelled a warning:
"If a single shot is fired,
There will be fifty dead men in less that five minutes!"

Twice a rope was placed around the Mexican's neck, and twice the resolute Sheriff cut it as he hissed defiance.

At this point of the fracas, Pierre Sompayrac, a prosperous French merchant of Jackson, was asked to say a few words, few quieting words to his furious countrymen.

Seizing this opportunity to give voice to his feelings.

He shouted out:
"Lift the Greaser!"
And the mob,
According to the Code of Mobsters,
Lifted the "Greaser."

...................Rest of this story not found

James Carson, the Odysseus[1] of the Southern Mines, firmly believed in the Miners' Courts in 1849 and in the various vigilance committees in 1850-1851. He was sure that these had a purifying influence in California.
"These institutions," he defended,
"And their steadfast devotion to the cause of right,
Saved California from becoming the theatre of
strife and bloodshed,
Unknown before in the history of the world."

Illustrative of how the law was dispensed at Carson Hill in 1850, was a trial in which two Hebrew merchants opposed each other. One of the partners, wanting to go a different way, asked for a final settlement and was offered $2,200. A quarrel ensued, making it impossible for the former partners to reach an agreement so the matter was turned over to Alcalde Carlow for a decision. A jury was summoned. The jurymen miners were not without awareness that the merchants had obtained their pile at the expense of the gold washers, so they brought in a verdict ordering the litigants to pay the expenses of the trial and the remainder of the money to be equally divided between them. This order might have been carried out to the letter except that a barroom was directly back of the courtroom.

The lawmakers were thirsty so they invited all by-standers to have a drink. At last, after $1,800 worth of liquor had been consumed and a bill for the drinks presented to the court, the Jews raised a rumpus and flatly refused to pay. But the verdict of the jury and the money being in the hands of the Alcalde, William Carlow, he informed the Jews that the oath of his office compelled him to execute the jury's decision which included in court costs, the drinks. He then produced from a gold sack the amount due the court, the saloon and divided the remainder between the erstwhile partners. Each of them struck off in different directions, uttering Hebrew curses portending no good to the lawmakers.

Footnotes

1 Odysseus was a king of Ithaca and a Greek leader in the Trojan War. After the war he wandered for ten years before reaching home.

19

EL CERRO DEL MELONES

In 1848, Mexicans first mined the hill El Cerro Del Melones [The hill of the Melons], six miles east of Angels Camp. But it was Charles M. Weber's Stockton Mining Company it is said, that took the first coarse gold from the bed of Stanislaus at this point. Legend has it that gold was first discovered on the hill by a young senorita who, on a trail found little chispas, smooth, flat and oblong, resembling melon seeds and from these the southern slope of the hill took its name.

This photo shows the size and shape of the characteristic "melon seed" gold nuggets the were found at Melones.

Courtesy of Jack Burns

On a long, narrow strip of level land straggled the settlement called Robinson's Ferry[1], in honor of its founder, John W. Robinson. Here, on the slope of this hill, was developed one of the first two hard rock, deep diggings in California. Word of the abundance of gold the Melones mine yielded to its owners traveled with the rapidity of a brush fire. Morgan, Perkins, Comstock, Hance, and a Swiss partner were the owners. At once, men eager to make their pile and then say goodbye to California, flocked to Melones Hill, the most majestic of all the many hills to be seen along the westerly course of the Stanislaus River.

Robinson's Ferry on the Stanislaus River

Courtesy of Calavaras County Historical Society

These men first operated Robinson & Mead's "foot" ferryboat in December 1849. It soon was replaced by a larger craft. Their Stanislaus River transportation venture proved highly successful. In six weeks time, say the records, the new craft earned for ferriage $10,000 and their trading post close-by also showed an immense profit.

Samuel W. Prichard, born in Petersburgh, Virginia, was one of Stockton's first commission merchants. Since his references bore the names of James King of Wm., Arrington & Company, William T. Coleman & Company, H. Berton, A. Topping and Randolph & Lipman of San Francisco, Prichard was engaged by Robinson & Mead to purchase merchandise and forward it, by mule train, to their trading post on the north bank of the Stanislaus.

Robinson and Mead were not the sort of traders who, when the Indians went on a shopping spree en masse, boosted the price of calico from $1 to $20 a yard, blankets from two to six ounces of dust, serapes from $20 to $30 and everything else the Indians needed, or thought that they needed. Prior to 1848, the Stanislaus River had been the favorite gathering place for the Indians of the Siyakumna tribe but after the discovery of gold in its eddies, it was popular as a "heap big eating place." The braves soon looked upon it as a bewitched stream, no longer a desirable region to hold a Pow-Wow in honor of the benevolent spirit that according to the belief of the Indians, dwelt beneath the surface of its waters. This river took its head far up in the Sierra and from December to July was a wide, deep and swiftly running stream. In its boon days Robinson's Ferry boasted a population of 3,000, it all depended upon the season of the year. The first houses, small, were made of brush, mud, stone and adobe, roofed with hides. In thc month of January, when the rock-bound Stanislaus canyon was bitterly cold and from across the deep gulches could be heard the wild shriek of cougars, the gold washers, their boots wrapped in gunny sacks, were then doggedly plodding to add to Robinson Ferry's mixed population.

Don Gabriel Stevenot

Courtesy of C.C.H.S.

Gabriel Stevenot, a native of France, reached Robinson's Ferry in 1849. He located a claim, which soon enriched him to the tune of $60,000. Stevenot, called Don Gabriel by the Mexican settlers, took up land between Carson Hill and Robinson's Ferry and engaged in the livestock business, secondary to his mining activities. The old ranch house, once occupied by

Monica Motsko and Lillian Doran with a roadside monument on highway 49
This monument marks the location of Stevenot Ranch and Winery.

Photo May 19, 2005 by Wally Motloch

Don Gabriel his wife and their children, still stands a short distance west of the State highway, intact and occupied[2].

Among the first American miners to reach Robinson's Ferry were John Whittaker, Frank Hazleton, Frank Bradbury, the brothers John and William Palache, Dr. William Jones and Samuel E. Newlands to whom belongs the credit of having been this settlement's first public school teacher.

The first bridge to span the Stanislaus was built by W. W. Stewart in 1850. Between Robinson's and McLean's Ferries and it served the traveling public for many years.

John L. Brown and Joseph E. Critchfield, on August 8, 1850 while working together at Brown's Bar on the Stanislaus, near Robinson's Ferry, unearthed a huge lump of pure gold. J. W. French, digging and shoveling close-by, took out of the stream enough yellow metal to establish a trading post and ferry a short distance west of Abbey's Ferry.

The first marriage ceremony ever performed at Robinson's Ferry united John Palache and Cerelia, a beautiful daughter of one of the first Mexican miners to reach the river.

The richness of the Melones quartz mine was too great to be witnessed in peace. One day in 1851, under the violent leadership of Billy Mulligan, more than a hundred ruffians armed with bludgeon irons, bricks, rocks, knives and guns, stormed the mine and drove away its owners. Mulligan, a New York bruiser, before coming to California, had been a Texan Ranger with a good record for bravery and daring. Mulligan's rapscallions, a motley gang of hoodlums, were mostly convicts from Botany Bay and Van Dieman's land, (Tasmania) which were Great Britain's penal colonies in Australia. They were known in California as "Sydney Ducks." Others willing to further Mulligan's cause were Mexicans, Chileans, Negroes, Irishmen and a few renegade Americans. Despite the strong resistance, the mine was seized and worked by Mulligan's unskilled followers for nine long months, during which time this famous deep diggings was virtually ruined. Under Billy's incompetent supervision the drafts were "rawhided" and the long tunnel, which Morgan and his partners had driven into the hillside was looted in a shameful fashion of its gold-banded quartz rock. At the end of ten months, the dapper little dude Billy Mulligan, whose chief ambition now, was to become a San Francisco politician, was still in command of the valuable property. Finally, Morgan & Company tired of carrying on brutal fights against trained thugs, engaged three of Calaveras County's ablest lawyers, namely Wm. Jeff Gatewood and the brothers Wm. L. and Allen P. Dudley, to institute a lawsuit. Their petition urged that Mulligan and his lawless gang be ejected from the Melones Mine by the authorities of Calaveras County.

Benjamin Marshall, the High Sheriff of the county, was on the ground sounding the death knell of the infamous mine wrecker's hope, to retain possession of the property. Late in 1852, Mulligan left Robinson's Ferry for San Francisco, in which city he cut quite a dash in saloons and gambling halls. Backed up by a large amount of gold stolen from the Melones Mine, he soon realized his ambition to become the political boss of San Francisco's underworld.

In the spring of 1855, Alfred Morgan and Henry Perkins went together to London, England, to dispose of both the Morgan and Melones mines. During their absence Mulligan again interfered and again lawyers were hired to defend these excessively rich ore ledges, the former on the north side of the hill, the latter of the south side. Morgan & Company unfortunately did not have a clear title to the Melones and there was no final judgment rendered until many years later. In the meantime the mine remained idle for thirteen years. It was reopened for a brief period in 1867. In 1899, William C. Ralston, whose father had once washed gold in the Tuolumne River, became the General Superintendent of this mine and under the standard of the Melones Consolidated Gold Mining Company, it again became one of the great gold producers of the Mother Lode. Under Mr. Ralston's management the Melones yielded in excess of $19,000,000 worth of gold of the purest quality.

Thomas Deare, a Robinson's Ferry miner of 1849, was thoroughly familiar with the discovery and development of these deep diggings. He once told J. Ross Brone who, later, made a United States government report under the title "Mineral Resources of the United States for 1868," that, from February 1850 to December 1, 1851, the production of gold at the Melones mine continued uninterrupted and with very little decline. During the above years, Mr. Deare said, $2,800,000 worth of gold was extracted from the ore shoots of the Melones. When the mine was first operated, he went on to say, immense amounts of gold were stolen from it by the "high-graders." One day in 1851, a Mexican stole $1,500 from the arrastra Tom Deare was tending and the next day he bought a horse for a like amount. All the rock taken from the mine was too poor for hand mortars so it was ground in arrastras and Chilean mills, of which fifty were often in operation at the same time. The opportunities for stealing gold at the Melones mine were very great and the inclination strong.

Morgan and his partners having better fish to fry failed to develop the ore ledges, which contained a valuable "ribbon" rock located on the South Carolina claim. The original owners thought the ore vein, since it was only from six to ten feet wide and paid for each pound of rock mined but $1 to $6, was hardly worth bothering with. In 1851 the South Carolina was sold to James Connor, E. Hunter, P. Devlin, Emanuel Linoberg and Captain de la Rey of Sonora, Tuolumne County. The Sonora Company, with Linoberg as president, comprised of 17 shareholders, each of whom paid from $2,000 to $3,000 for one share of stock. During the summer and fall of 1851 the gold yield was $2,000 a week to each arrastra or Chilean mill in operation. The Arkansas and Texan mines situated on nearby Coyote Flat were owned and managed by Captain de la Rey and E. Hunter.

In 1852 the South Carolina mine was bonded to Senora Elisa Martinez, the boldest, bravest, most colorful bit of femininity to ever to reach the Southern Mines. Elisa and her forty peon laborers, whom she brought with her from Mexico in 1849, founded the town of Martinez in Tuolumne County. Her settlement, once the barking place for timber wolves was situated in the midst of rich mineral deposits and was thickly populated with Mexican and Chileans. Senora Elisa of Hidalgo class was a young, beautiful, educated and ambitious woman, with only a slight sense of honor. Tradition has it that she was an heiress in her own right. She left Hermosillo, Mexico, together with her peons that she might be near her lover, Juan Claudio. He is said to have been the handsomest young Sonoran in Murrieta's gang of terrorists. California's first woman quartz mine operator worked the mine on a large scale. In 1854 she found herself an exceedingly rich woman. In two years the South Carolina had poured into her coffers $2,500,000 and was far from being worked out. That year, the lease on the South Carolina expired; she left Robinson's Ferry and never returned. Hard-bitten and selfish, she left behind her faithful peons to fend for themselves. The same peons that toiled each day lugging rawhide buckets filled with ore from the mine to the arrastras and Chilean mills.

In Stockton, she was a guest in the Chicard home. The late Mrs. Jules Pache, a member of the Chicard family, years later in Angels Camp told

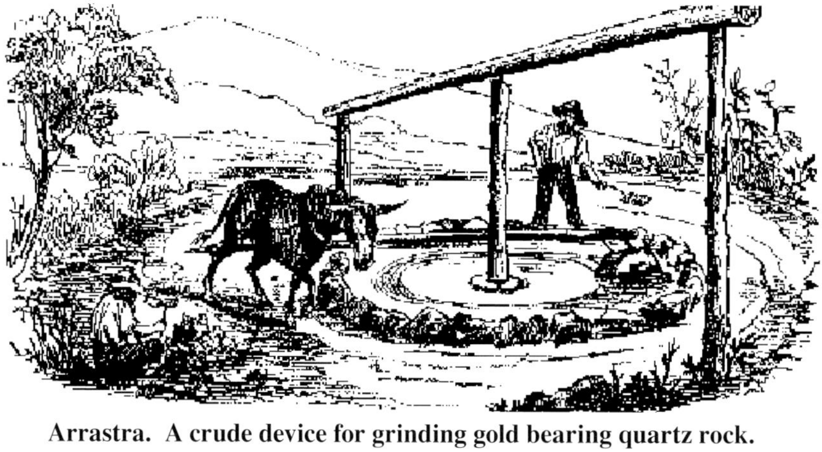

Arrastra. A crude device for grinding gold bearing quartz rock.
Courtesy of Calaveras County Historical Society

her neighbors that the Senora Elisa had arrived at the Chicard home from Robinson's Ferry weighted down with valuable jewelry and virgin gold. She was so bulky that her friends were obliged to assist her into the house. On occasion, one sometimes hears Senora Elisa Martinez' name spoken, but it is always in connection with the South Carolina mine.

John P. Jones, desiring to be near his friend, John L. Brown, located in Robinson's Ferry. Partners, these staunch friends staked a few claims, one of which in the middle 'fifties' coughed up $12,000. Mr. Jones, at this particular time, was living in Virginia City, Nevada but distance was no obstacle to Mr. Brown who, taking Mr. Jones' share of the treasure with him, set out for Nevada. He knew full well that news of a lucky strike in Calaveras would mean little or nothing to his friend. Only recently Mr. Jones had made a large fortune for himself on the Comstock Lode. When Mr. Jones' office boy asked the stranger to jot his name down on a card for delivery to his employer, the miner from Brown's Bar on the Stanislaus, tore a page from his notebook and scribbled thereon:

"Brown of Calaveras,"

Ever after that day, by such name he was known.

John P. Jones' ambition and wealth alike increased and in time, he became a United States Senator from Nevada. While on the other hand, Brown back in Calaveras County, down to his last dollar, found work as a cook in Meader's Resort in Copperopolis. After the publication of Bret Harte's story "Brown of Calaveras" many amusing incidents were recalled by pioneers at Robinson's Ferry concerning Brown's misguided generosity, droll sense of humor and inability to hang onto his gold.

In 1850, John Robinson the ferry master towed Joseph Merritt across the Stanislaus River. Fresh from the sea he recently arrived here to try his luck. His feet firmly planted on the north bank of the stream, he pitched a tent near the mouth of Indian Gulch, located a claim and worked in it for many long years. Merritt, while a sea rover had touched at every important port in the world, including the Coast of Africa, on which he had engaged in "Black birding". Merritt, said a Robinson Ferry pioneer, knew how to keep his mouth shut as tight as a trap, when sober. When only slightly tipsy he was apt to boast loudly and freely about his "distinguished ancestors." Strong of body, tall, lean, with eyes sharp as a sea eagle, Merritt when all except dead drunk, was remembering about a slave ship loaded with Negroes whom he had bought "on block" on the African Coast and his inhumanity on the homeward run. Off Sandy Hook, he found himself in a peck of trouble when a government boat gave chase to his vessel. In order to save his own skin Captain Merritt ordered his crew to toss the contra-brand human cargo into the Atlantic Ocean.

Harvey and Marinda (Gee) Wood from Robinson Ferry
Courtesy of Calaveras County Historical Society

Out from under the influence of liquor Captain Merritt could not be induced to relate any of his experiences while engaged in the slave traffic along the Coast of Africa. It was evident however, that the memory of his foul deed on the high seas was still pricking his conscience which hard liquor only could soothe.

Harvey Wood, born in New Jersey[3], sailed in the "William B. Travis" from New York on February 13, 1849, he reached California on the day of July 4. A month later, he crossed the Stanislaus River at McLean's Ferry and encamped at the mouth of Indian Gulch, a short distance west of Robinson's Ferry. Mr. Wood's messmates were, Jacob M. Fouse of Baltimore, Charles Ackerly of New York and Abraham Huyler of Keyport, New Jersey. Later, Pioneer Wood, in his book "Personal Recollections of Harvey Wood," stated:

"On looking over our baggage, I found that we like the rest, had a large amount of useless trash. We had a five-story gold washer, that is, five sets of sieves, one above the other graded from very coarse to fine and warranted to catch all the gold, fine or coarse. It had been thoroughly tested in New York to the entire satisfaction of a large crowd, by a bucket of sand and a few scraps of lead thrown in. Not a particle of lead escaped during the washing process. Then we had axes, picks and shovels and even a ten pound crowbar and last but not least of all, a box containing various acids, duly bottled and labeled, so that no bogus gold could be played on us, for with our valuable box of acids we were not to be fooled".

Robinson & Mead, August 15, 1849, had a store in a tent, near the mouth of Indian Gulch. Mr. Mead, a stranger to us all, welcomed us on our arrival, saying:

> "Camp anywhere around here, boys,
> And any provisions you want I will furnish you,
> Money or no money, price fifty cents a pound."
>
> "A fall to fifty cents a pound on Provisions and an increase of 200 per cent in the diggings, was encouraging to us all and we went to work with a will".

After mining until September 1, I took my first trip to San Francisco to look for some goods that were shipped around the Horn to Ackerly, Huyler and myself. Traveling at that time differed so much from the present mode (1878), I will give an account of the trip. Two acquaintances and myself left the Stanislaus River in the afternoon, our blankets packed together with a frying pan and a tin cup for each and a few provisions. No extra clothing was considered necessary. Thus equipped we started for Stockton on foot, driving the mule ahead of us. We took our time, camping out every night. A bush or a tree to spread our blankets under we preferred to any house. The food generally used was hard bread and beefsteak with a cup of coffee, which we drunk out of a tin cup, no vegetables could be had at any price. On arriving at Stockton we camped outside of town and kept our own hotel. Stockton, in September 1849, was not a handsome place, but money was plentiful and the gamblers were reaping a harvest from the miners who had been fortunate in finding good claims, made money fast and spent it still faster. Often bags of gold dust would be staked on the turning of a card with apparent indifference as to the result. No steamboat had as yet been put in between Stockton and San Francisco so we were obliged to take passage on a schooner paying $16 for the passage. We made the trip in six days but tying up in the tules at night at the mercy of millions of mosquitoes was anything but pleasant. On my return to the mines, I found my partners doing very well. The day before I returned, Huyler and Fouse had made some two ounces each and concluded to have a grand supper by themselves. They invested $8 for a small can of preserves, $4 for a tin of sardines and a few extras, making the cost of their supper $16 each. By November 24, the goods that had been shipped to us around Cape Horn arrived, but the storage I had to pay in San Francisco was nearly the value of the goods. The rainy season had commenced and long-legged boots were scarce, the price going up to $100 per pair.

In the autumn of 1849, Mr. Wood and his companions erected a cabin, which he described thus:

> "Sides of logs, with canvas roof and the usual stone chimney of that period (barrel shaped), in putting it up I found the draft was

always the wrong way, all the smoke coming in the cabin instead of passing out, but by tearing it down and rebuilding, we were more successful. We had some very good diggings near us; Jackass Gulch in Tuolumne County and Indian Gulch in Calaveras County, yielded large amounts of gold. El Dorado Bar, between McLean's Ferry and Coyote Creek, was found to be exceedingly rich. The "Independent Twelve Company" had a very good claim on the Bar. The company men had one rocker; they wanted to keep it going till about ten o'clock A.M. with the assistance of four to six bottles of brandy at $4 a bottle. By ten o'clock they would be so much fatigued that to work any more that day was too hard on their systems, therefore, after washing out the rocker and getting from twenty-four to thirty-six ounces of gold and laying in a fresh supply of brandy they would rest the balance of the day by getting gloriously drunk."

Good diggings were struck at Scorpion Gulch in 1850. The amount of gold taken out around Carson Hill was enormous, some quite heavy nuggets were found, but as usual, fortune did not always favor the most deserving. One day a prospector came into camp dead broke in finance, called at the trading post and made known his condition, then he went out to try his luck, in less that an hour he found a seven pound piece of gold. A happier miner I never saw before or since. As for myself I was never very successful at mining. I had some good claims but none of them ranked as first-class.

In the flush year of 1852, hundreds of Chinese miners rocked "cradles" in shallow pools at the river's edge. Also in Coyote Creek, near the mouth of which were pitched their flimsy cloth tents. The "Johns" when not washing gravel tended their vegetable gardens and peddled the products of their industry from door to door in Gooseberry and Robinson's Ferry. In the latter settlement "Chinee" washhouses were numerous. A "washee-man," was spraying linen shirts and coats with water blown from his mouth as this was allowed in the 'fifties.

Of the Ferry's many buildings Armory Hall was the settlement's loudest boast. Within its walls, in the early 'sixties, Yankee men responded to the bugle's call to discuss ways and means for helping to bring an end to the Civil War. John W. Robinson was no longer captain of the Home Guards. The founder of the town, a southerner, when steel began clashing against steel, sold his interests at the Ferry and left the Stanislaus to join the Confederate Army and while fighting under command of General Robert E. Lee, lost his life on a battlefield.

Benito Morales, an 1848 Stanislaus River miner, growing tired of sloshing knee deep in cold water, exchanged his crowbar for a few goats and, one mile north of the ferry, established a goat ranch. The Morales ranch

Today the town of Melones is under the waters of the New Melones Reservoir. Upper photo shows the town of Melones in 1900 and lower photo is here for comparison.

Upper Photo - Courtesy of C.C.H.S.   Lower - Wally Motloch

house, rain-stained and brown as a coffee berry, is still to be seen a short distance west of the State highway.

At Robinson's Ferry in the troubled 'sixties were organized the "Arcadian Shepherds Association," and "Kedron Vine and Fig Tree Growers Association." The Mexican fig trees and Mission grape vines planted at this time by the pioneers Stevenot, Whittle, Pendola, Whittaker, Allison and Riedel are still producing luscious fruit in and around Robinson's Ferry.

In 1856 Harvey Wood purchased Stephen Mead's half interest in Robinson & Mead's ferrying craft and five years later he bought out John Robinson. Here at the old ferry house on the north bank of the Stanislaus River, Harvey Wood and his brother, James, batched together until, in the early 'sixties, Harvey married Miss Adelaide Gee, of Marlowe, New Hampshire. Their old homestead still stands at the river's edge, but the curtains of the two-story white house are drawn and no bluish-gray smoke curls skyward from the red brick chimneys for, with the song of the Stanislaus in his ears, Harvey Wood, able and honest as day is long, died in 1895.

The first pioneers of this region have all handed in their checks. Some, like "John Oakhurst," struck a streak of bad luck, however most of them were able to leave this world without the aid of a derringer.

At sunrise El Cerro del Melones, is flooded with coral and topaz light, but twilight finds it wrapped in a purplish haze and far below winds is the Stanislaus. The long and narrow strip of level land, across which Billy Mulligan's scarlet pageant once swept, no longer is flanked on both sides with business and dwelling houses. The same deep diggings, from first to last, are credited with having yielded in excess of $30,000,000.

Frank Casseretto's stone store[4], erected to withstand the ravages of winter storms, is today a sorry sight. The sod roof, supported by walls three feet thick, has tumbled in and rusty on the ground lay the iron doors and window shutters. On the hillside, near the original site of the Melones claim, is a weather-beaten adobe. Intended for endurance, the small, squatty and almost square bricks that were used to construct it were no doubt made by one who understood the art of fashioning adobe bricks. The evil deeds that were committed here by lawless men are now seldom if ever, referred to, but the exploits of the gold washers of El Cerro del Melones, go sweeping onward to make a truce with time.

Footnotes

1 Now under New Melones Reservoir.

2 Now identified by a monument and a marker on highway 49 by the Melones Bridge.

3 "Melones" a Story of a Stanislaus River town, by Julia G. Costello page 33, "Harvey Wood was born in Bedford, New York in 1828"

4 Julia Costello's "*MELONES*" book page 23, "Ceccenello's store"

20

GOLD CAMPS IN THE TIMBER BELT

RAIL ROAD FLAT

Situated a short distance from Jesus Maria, Rail Road Flat[1] took its name from a pioneer enterprise, a train of homemade wooden cars, drawn by burros over a wooden track. A stranger coming to the flat was surprised to see cars loaded with ore and promptly named the location Rail Road Flat. The Two Dollar Gulch and the close by Alabama Hill, extensively mined in 1849-1850, made a generous contribution to the prosperity of this flat. No evanescent settlement in the midst of placers, this camp was also in the midst of magnificent stand of timber.

A horse drawn cart similar to carts used in Railroad Flat.
Courtesy of Wally Motloch

Henry Seeman and his wife Marianna reached Railroad Flat in 1849. That same year from Boston, Massachusetts, came down Richard McNamara. Somewhere along the trail, McNamara found a cow and brought it with him to the flat. In lean times, when pay dirt was scarce, he sold butter for $2 a pound. Henry Haye in 1849 established this flat's first trading post.

Railroad Flat neighborhood in 1899

Courtesy of Chuck Ellsworth

The gold hunters, Erastus Huston, George Woodbury, Elias Fields, John Paul, the brothers Allen and Ezra Patridge, Andil Keigan, Willard Mead, Daniel McReynolds and William Aoslem arrived on the scene in 1850. Sterling Lancaster reached the flat in 1851, a few hours ahead of Samuel Bunker, who on horseback brought the first mail into the settlement. A year later Felix Brood operated a stage line, maintaining a stage depot in Rail Road Flat. Edward Taylor of London, England established a general merchandise store and his was the honor or annoyance, of becoming the flat's first official Postmaster. Pioneer Taylor's frame store fell a victim to

Eureka School in Railroad Flat, circa 1900

Courtesy of Lillian Browning

Prussian Hill Mine also called the Del Monte, circa 1900

Courtesy of Lane Family

Concentration tables inside of the Del Monte Mine in Railroad Flat.

Courtesy of Lane Family

flames a few years ago. In this blaze, many valuable relics of the settlement's prosperous days went up in smoke.

Rail Road Flat, in its flush days, boasted a population of 1,500. Delray's boarding house, Mrs. Luddy's Miners' Home Cottage and the Irish Hotel, each enjoyed a liberal patronage. The flat supported seven stores in addition to the usual number of business enterprises. The first public school was opened in 1853, which year, two church buildings and a town hall were also erected. A division of the Sons of Temperance was installed and a choral society organized. Everything possible was done that year to advance the civic, social, spiritual and cultural welfare of the community. The flat was not without saloons and gambling halls, but houses of prostitution, hurdy gurdy dance halls and Mexican fandangos where prohibited within the limits of this town.

Several murders motivated by jealousy were committed at the Rancheria close to town, where a "squaw man" sometimes tangled with his rivals over their mahalas. Even so, the history of Rail Road Flat records no lynchings. This town, so far as rowdyism was concerned, had a clean slate.

Near Rail Road Flat, where the hills are more mantled in a rough splendor of rocks, was the homestead of John Dunnington McNoble, a forty-niner. To his sons the late George F. and Hugh McNoble, prominent lawyers of Stockton and to the late Maurice Taylor the son of the flat's first postmaster belongs the credit that is due for the preservation of much of Rail Road Flat's history. Rail Road Flat is pretty much a ghost town now. Little remains there except natural beauty in the way of forest, trees and rocks. Rocks were unearthened by the first miners. There are some ore dumps and perhaps a remnant or two of an old wooden car.

RICH GULCH

Situated a short distance from Rail Road Flat, this gulch was first mined by Stockton Mining Company of which Captain Weber, a pioneer of 1841, was the President. The members of this company included: Captain Charles M. Weber, Major Pierson B. Redding, Victor Portion and Andrew Deles. These men took an active part in the gold rushes of 1848-1849.

The entire length and breadth of Rich Gulch was strewn with gold and adjacent Rich Gulch Flat was just as rich. Small wonder then that the gold fever epidemic increased by leaps and bounds at this place. The discovery of the Dutch Gulch lead, a mile distant, created nothing short of a stampede. No sooner had this gulch's possibilities for quick fortunes been noised, then every foot of ground for miles around was staked off for claims. Many of the men who had driven pine stakes into the ground were soon rejoicing. Years

Rich Gulch Hotel sometimes called Charley Hoeys Hotel.
Courtesy of Calaveras County Historical Society

later, the faces of these same men were still wearing smiles, for Rich Gulch and its immediate vicinity continued to give up its golden hoard for long years after.

Although the miner's pokes were chock full of yellow dust, the living conditions were unsatisfactory and food, especially vegetables, were very scarce. Soon, scurvy, bilious fever, diarrhea, pneumonia and rheumatism reared their ugly heads and went on the rampage. These localities as yet, were without facilities for hospitalization. In the winter of 1849, things took a change for the better, when Dr. A. H. Hoerchner established a community hospital in Rich Gulch. This was the first general hospital in the Southern Mines. It was afterwards known as the "County Hospital."

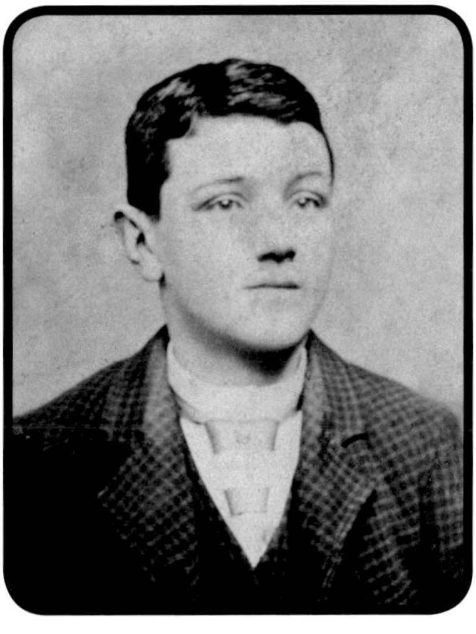

Charles Hoey
Courtesy of C.C.H.S.

When Mexican bandits were riding from camp to camp to murder

San Bruno Mine in Glencoe.

Courtesy of Calaveras County Historical Society

honest men for gold, Beaver's Hotel was the safest place in Rich Gulch. In this rude wooden hostelry, the gold washers set up an arsenal for the protection of their community against lawless men.

B. F. Clerc discovered the ore vein that was later known as the Barney Quartz Mine. Other discoverers of quartz ledges were Dr. Overton, J. B. Sauve, Robert L. Sloan, Calixte Vincent, Alimano Guiseppi, Remanque Pascal, Charles J. Buffum, Kasper and Hans Rathgeb.

Here at Rich Gulch, where once hundreds of shovels in the hands of sturdy men wearing navy blue or gray flannel shirts, bedecked with gilt and silver buttons, brought the "color" to light, no rock chimneys remain. Once gold had petered out at Rich Gulch, the settlement fell upon bad days. After the miners had crunched away to find new diggings their cabins and other flimsy buildings became living places for wild animals. All the buildings are now in ruins, but Rich Gulch filled with rocks, stark and grey, is there to give silent evidence of its invasion a hundred years ago. An invasion by resolute young men, who for gold endured untold hardships. Indeed, many of these men are sleeping there in nameless graves.

MOSQUITO GULCH

This gulch, near Rail Road Flat, was later called Glencoe. Founded by Mexicans in 1848, it was a rich placer ground. A Mexican stronghold, these settlers were able to withstand all the attacks made against them by Indians of a near-by Rancheria.

Mosquito Gulch's chief attraction was a well or spring of pure water. There, the priests, when making annual pilgrimages through the foothills would baptize Mexican and Indian children. This natural fount called by the Mexicans the "Sacred Well" produced ten gallons of water every three minutes after all others had gone bone dry.

In 1848 an aged Indian said:
"This gulch was bloody ground".

According to his story, when the July sun seared the grass and the coyotes, deer, squirrels and rabbits panted from thirst, the Piutes and Washoes Indian of Nevada, stalked down the western Sierra slope to take possession of the sacred well. The Mexicans regarded the fount as belonging to them exclusively. They put up a brave fight in which many of the intruders were slain. The old Chief pointed out the graves of the enemy. These were marked by piles of rock and today are in the Indian burial ground near the head of Valentine Gulch.

Here in 1851, two Frenchmen, with left arms locked together, fought a duel with long, sharp-pointed scissors. Each duelist, horribly lacerated, lost his life. Over their graves near the sacred well, friendly hands planted seeds that sprouted green shoots and in time, two pear trees were scattering petals upon the graves of the too hasty French miners.

McNoble and Hoey were partners and conducted a general merchandise and hardware store in Mosquito Gulch in 1852. Their competitors were Burt, Berry and a few other general merchants. At this time the gulch's population was about 1,500. In 1854, instead of brush shelter huts, cloth tents and log cabins, you would find frame and stone hotels, stores, an express office, business and dwelling houses. The town hall, two church buildings and public school house enhanced Mosquito Gulch's landscape.

Joseph and Mathilda Woodcock came early to Mosquito Gulch. Thomas, their son, was born at the gulch. He was a schoolboy in 1863. That year, as the legend has it, Bret Harte was the master in the gulch's public schoolhouse. But Tom Woodcock, older grown, when asked about his school teachers, just couldn't recall ever having heard the name Bret Harte mentioned in connection with the gulch's school. When William O. Nuner, a classmate of Tom, was questioned as to whether or not Bret Harte had ever placed a dunce cap on his head or stood him in a dark corner of the little schoolhouse, he shrugged and said:

"No, Bret Harte never taught in a public school in Calaveras County"

Bill Nuner, himself a school teacher and for many years a County Superintendent of Public Schools, therefore had at his disposal records, with which to back up his statement.

Valentine Gulch, like the Paradise Gulch ran through a little green valley in which were situated Gus Stotzer's combination tavern, gambling saloon and fandango. Here, where life rolled in and out on wild and dangerous waves, the elegant Spanish man, Rosendo V. Corona, wooed an Indian maiden Jawea of the close-by Rancheria. Jawea, it appears, after the arrival of the Spanish and Mexican men, lost her taste for dried beetles, grasshoppers, jerked venison and acorns.

Stotzer's rude tavern, by reason of its remoteness together with its owner's ability to prepare wholesome food, quickly became a loitering place for desperadoes, who between raids, while resting their mounts, had there a high old time feasting, dancing and gambling. The trail, leading from Mokelumne Hill to the three gulches, Mosquito, Valentine and Paradise, has been opened for more then one hundred years. Along this trail the dreaded Mexican youth Murrieta, frequently galloped his fine buckskin stallion.

Stotzer's nightly fee for a wall bunk in the attic, which was reached by a rickety pine ladder, was a cool $18.00. This was a wall bunk with pine boughs for a mattress and a bag of dry straw for a pillow. A muleteer once grumbled:

"In order to give my pack animals a little salt,
I was obliged to pay old man Stotzer one dollar a pound for it."

Bayard Taylor, the first feature writer ever to visit the California gold mines, was in Mosquito Gulch in 1849. In New York City he later painted a pen picture of a rich claim owner of Valentine Gulch whose nickname was "Buckshot". A queer fish, Buckshot was a black bearded, bald, short, dumpy man from forty to fifty years of age. Let us quote Mr. Taylor:

"He (Buckshot) lived entirely alone, in a small tent and seemed rather to shun than to court the society of others. His tastes were exceedingly luxurious; he always had the best of everything in the market, regardless of cost. The finest hams, at the dollar and a half a pound, preserved oysters, corn and peas, at six dollars a canister, onions and potatoes whenever such articles made their appearance, Chinese sweetmeats and dried fruits were all on his table and his dinner was regularly moistened with a bottle of champagne. He did his own cooking and when particularly lucky in digging, he would take his ease, for a day or two until the dust was exhausted, when he would again shoulder his pick and crowbar and commence burrowing in some lonely corner of the Rich Gulch. He had been in the country since the first discoveries and was reported to have dug between $20,000 and $40,000 all of which he had spent for his subsistence."

Bayard Taylor's word picture of Buckshot differs from those cooked up by other early day writers, who depicted the California gold digger as being lean as a greyhound from lack of nourishing food and sinewy from hard riding and tramping. Buckshot, who was forty, but in Valentine Gulch he was looked upon as an ancient old type.

Joseph Bayles arrived at Mosquito Gulch early in 1852 to find one hundred arrastras[2] in operation in Paradise and Valentine gulches. A miner, he soon dug out enough gold to purchase Stotzer's old tavern in which in 1900 he, Joe Bayles, was brutally murdered and his flimsy, mice ridden tavern was set ablaze by some unknown person. The murderer and "firebug" who destroyed Joe Bayles' life and property was never brought to justice.

The little green valley with the three gulches is now lacking in population and in gold. But the Sacred Well is there, as are the huge grapevines which long ago, where planted by "Old Man" Stotzer. In the springtime, the two ancient and gnarled pear trees shower the graves beneath them with delicate petals.

WEST POINT

This early day settlement, about ten miles east of Mokelumne Hill, lies within the granite or East Belt. In 1844 here, John C. Fremont and his exploring party guided by Kit Carson according to tradition, encamped on a point of this land. Six years later, this point of land was named West Point.

The men of 1849 didn't believe it worthwhile to follow a vein of decayed rock found there in the hard granite, but finding the soft quartz easy to extract, they called their diggings "Poor Man's Camp".

Early logging with oxen teams.

Courtesy of Kent Wilson

West Point soon became a town of importance and quick action. It was surrounded by a fine stand of timber, although not as prosperous as its neighboring towns. Places like Esperito Campo, Skull Flat, Campo de Flores and Mott's Gulch were more prosperous nonetheless, West Point's placers yielded bountifully of pure, heavy gold.

Its first settlers, not too young nor too old but in their best years, feasted, drank, joked, danced, shed blood and rendered deeds of mercy with equal freedom. Michael Schmidt, a pioneer of 1849, began his business career here by erecting a sawmill on Bear Creek. He was soon the owner of four water ditches and a dwelling house on Pine Street in West Point.

Louis Chicard, a Stockton commission merchant, in the summer of 1849, sent a heavily laden mule train to Mokelumne Hill and a few weeks later, Chicard himself, took a long line of pack mules to West Point. Chicard, a native of France was blinded by vermilion dust, which had covered the roadway like a scourge. After reaching his destination with merchandise of all sorts, he sold clay pipes for $2 each and course wool blankets for $40. Gunpowder, medicine, saleratus and vinegar pickles all but brought their weight in gold. Whiskey netted Chicard $2 a drink. But when a tin cupful of hard liquor was requested, the price was boosted to an ounce of dust. When Chicard's pack train filed out of West Point in a westerly direction, his stock of merchandise and liquor was completely exhausted. Many a man during Chicard's brief sojourn in the town became loose of tongue and unsteady of leg. One sober man, seeing a man dead drunk said to another sober man:

" Tain't the gentleman's fault, 'tis the Frenchman's liquor."

Traction engine in 1908. The iron wheeled tractors were not popular, they chewed the roads to ribbons and their noise frightened horses.

Courtesy of Calaveras County Historical Society

Statistics of Chicard & Company's Dispatch and Importing House in Stockton indicate that as late as 1877 their freighters were still hauling goods to West Point. From January 1st to December 31st of the above year, Louis

Superior Court Judge James Alexander Smith, son of Thomas R. Smith. He helped to organize, and was the president for 12 years of the Calaveras County Historical Society.

Courtesy of Calaveras County Historical Society

Transporting logs to the McKay Mill.
Courtesy of Calaveras County Historical Society

Ladies with a child at the McKay Mill.
Courtesy of Calaveras County Archives

Chicard's firm loaded 950,000 pounds of merchandise onto freight wagons drawn by horses and mules and sent them eastward from the Port of Stockton to Calaveras County's mining towns and camps.

Thomas R. Smith, after trying his hand at mining in Lancha Plana, Poverty Bar, Chili Gulch and a few other mining camps, located permanently in West Point. Here, when not panning gravel, he planted fruit trees, mostly apple trees. Pioneer Smith is no longer in West Point but his sons are at the family homestead, busy in the old apple orchard.

To James Alexander Smith, son of Thomas R. Smith belongs the credit for the preservation of the lively story of West Point's flush days. Alex Smith was born, reared and attended public school in West Point. In this school was laid the foundation of his successful career. He was a schoolteacher, lawyer and a Judge of the Superior Court of Calaveras County. One of the ablest jurists in California, Judge Smith enjoyed a wide and favorable reputation.

SANDY GULCH

Sandy Gulch, near West Point, in 1850 was pierced by numerous "coyote" holes, many of which had been sunk to a depth of 20 feet. Four years later in one of these shafts, two miners, one pig-headed so to speak, while working together struck up an argument, resulting in a bitter quarrel in which one of the participants lost his life. The miners quit work earlier than usual that day to form a Miners' Court, assembled to try the offending miner for murder. A jury, comprising of miners, found him guilty of first-degree murder. Then, without fuss or flurry he was hustled off to the scene of his crime where a rope, one end fastened to a windlass, was put around his neck and by means of his own windlass, his body was lowered into the 18-foot deep shaft. Next, the executioners, feeling a need for food, went to a near-by cabin and cooked and ate a hearty supper. Their hunger appeased, they returned together to the shaft, dug a single grave, brought the bodies up from under ground and buried them in the same rude grave.

For many years George Bell faithfully served the West Point Township as its Justice of the Peace. Charles Condgon[3], a gold washer, was the Constable of this locality. Ernest Shuband, a highly skilled cabinetmaker, manufactured billiard tables and had no trouble at all in disposing of them. Addison Flanders, formerly of Massachusetts and David McCarty were prominent both as citizens and sawmill operators.

J. F. Paulk ran a line of stages, which, he boasted:
"Is the best line of coaches in this part of the county."

Harry Greve held down the driver's seat of one of Paulk's gaily painted coaches. Mr. Letanois erected a large adobe building in which he established a dry goods store. L. Pozadoeux's "brand new" fireproof building served him as a grocery store. Mr. Ecklemaur's brewery, capable of brewing 500 gallons of beer a day, was not lacking in patrons. Charley Anderson dispensed liquor in his own saloon, the Elkhorn. The West Pointers who built bridges over the north, south and middle forks of the Mokelumne River were Robinson and Son, Lampson brothers, and Morrill. Before the bridges spanned the three forks the settlers had no means of communication with Volcano, except by foot or horseback.

The Scorpion quartz mine, on the East Lode, was discovered and developed by West Point citizens. Other deep diggings on this lode were Petticoat, Horse Thief, Montezuma, June Bug, Henry, Panhandle and Harris. Prominent among the Superintendents of these and other quartz mines of this district were Elkanah Said, M. D. Henry, W. Jones, M. Ivanvitch, G. Wickham, F. Williams, Thomas Dunstan, George Cook, John Champion, Bertrand Delray, Henry F. Terry, Albion P. Whitney, V. A. Metlo, A. A. Motta, Jose Alcaraz, John Albers, Captain Haight, Abraham Pickering, John Doe and Daniel Caradi.

In one of the lava covered, Ancient River channels in West Point, the first miners traced the "pay" streak for 20 miles and occasionally found nuggets varying in value from $5 to $90. The nuggets led the gold washers to think that they had come from a wash thousand of years old and that this channel alone would furnish gold in large amounts to the West Point miners of the future.

Here, in the scenic West Point region where the pines grow tall and the creeks chatter merrily, there are many reminders of the days of gold when human life was lived in the raw. West Point now is not or never has been a ghost town. It isn't likely to be anything, except what it actually is, a retreat for nature lovers, students of geology and forestry and the descendents of its pioneers.

HAPPY VALLEY

This beautiful little valley, two miles east of Mokelumne Hill, was settled in 1849 by French miners. A congenial group of men, the laughter and songs that fell from their lips while they wielded picks and crowbars were heard by a party of American miners who named the peace-pervaded French settlement "Happy Valley."

Louis Baudin and his wife Jeanne, natives of France, reached Happy Valley in 1851, Jeanne, young and beautiful at the time of her arrival, was the only woman in the settlement. There for several months as a means of personal safety rather than for comfort, she went about dressed as a boy.

Louis Baudin erected a rock and adobe building. Ambitious, he was soon the owner of a trading post, bakery, winery, and a small tavern. In his different enterprises Louis was aided by the thrifty and capable Jeanne. Hers

North Star Gold Mine at Happy Valley.

Courtesy of Kent Wilson

was the satisfaction of knowing that she had helped to make their undertakings profitable. Their daughter Jennie (Mrs. Henry Meyer) was born in her parents adobe home in Happy Valley. Years later, in her home in Mokelumne Hill, Madame Baudin related to this writer a few of her exciting experiences while living in Happy Valley. Some hair-raising tales, for in Madame's day, bandits heavily armed and spurred, while on their way to mining camps to pillage and commit murders, have never failed to stop for food and drink at Baudin's tavern. The food was prepared in the best French manner by the genial host and hostess, Louis and Jeanne Baudin.

INDEPENDENCE FLAT

Situated in wild and mountainous country, this flat was the habitat of many miners who had taken up arms in 1851 against the Chilean miners at Jesus Maria about twelve miles distant. In spite of a lack of water the log cabins were erected here and became the foundations for many family fortunes. A touch-and-go camp, the miners hoisted rolls of blankets to their shoulders and headed for other, less remote diggings. The Indians moved in and made the flat their own. Here and there through the pines, on the trail leading from Independence Flat to Blue Mountain City, a few rocks and mud chimneys are to be seen, defying the elements.

A miner's shack in Whiskey Slide.

Courtesy of Kent Wilson

WHISKY SLIDE

Whisky[4] Slide was an 1849 camp. It reached its peak six years later when its population was at about 200. Just how the name Whiskey Slide came to be tacked onto this only moderately rich diggings one guess is as good as another. Oft repeated is the story about a mule train from Stockton to this little settlement near Jesus Maria. This train brought Old Monongehela, a favorite brand of whiskey in the days of flannel shirts and elk skin boots. No sooner had a halt been made than the miners were dickering with the muleteer for liquor. Their supply obtained, yelling at top voice, they began their general and prolonged spree by sliding down from the top of a steep incline to the mining ground below.

A story carrying a grain of truth about gold buried here in 1852 and a Negro's fidelity has floated around in Whisky Slide for many years. A widowed miner, as the story goes, thought best to take his little boy to San Francisco and leave him there to be cared for by friends. The miner, before leaving with his only child, placed two tin cans filled with gold in the care of his trusted servant. The Negro, fearful of robbers, buried the tins outdoors under a pine tree. On the return trip, desperadoes set upon the miner and to them he lost his life and some gold. The years went slowly for this Negro. One day a young lawyer, anxious to see the log cabin in which he was born and if possible his mother's grave, arrived in Whisky Slide. The cabin had been easy to locate. A white haired Negro opened the door in answer to the stranger's knock. Inside the dingy cabin the lawyer made known his identity. The Negro, at first, slightly suspicious, soon realized that his visitor

Raggio Cabin at Blue Mountain City.

Courtesy of Barbara Kathan

was in fact his slain master's only son. That evening, outdoors, the erstwhile slave dug from the ground two tins filled with dust and nuggets and turned them over intact to the lawyer.

The frame house erected by John Noce in the middle fifties, is still to be seen unoccupied at this settlement. Whisky Slide, once a noisy camp where men tore into pieces the ground with savage ferocity, is now quiet, alone, a mere memory.

BRANDY FLAT

A dry diggings, Brandy Flat most likely derived its name from John Podesta's brandy. John's burro train plodded from Yankee Hill in Tuolumne County to peddle Podesta's newly distilled brandy, called by the miners of both north and south of the Stanislaus River, the "Jackass Brandy." The gold yield here was not heavy but it attracted many American miners to these diggings. Originally a Mexican settlement, it soon became a hideout for bandits. At Brandy Flat many a fierce fight between Sheriffs' Posses and Mexican bandits is said to have taken place. Today it is just another campsite with no strings of scarlet Chili drying in the sun.

BLUE MOUNTAIN CITY

John C. Heckendorn, editor and publisher of the "Big Trees Bulletin and Murphys Advertiser" founded Blue Mountain City on the northern slope of picturesque Blue Mountain. The first edition of this little newssheet was pulled off the press in Heckendorn's printing office, which in this instance, was atop the stump of a fallen giant sequoia gigantia, in the Mammoth Grove of Calaveras County. Heckendorn's discovery of a quartz ledge on Blue Mountain created intense interest, especially to quartz miners.

A miner of 1848, Peter Davis of Central Hill hoisted a roll of blankets to his back and followed his heavily laden burro to Blue Mountain. After reaching Heckendorn's rude settlement, Peter located quartz claims, Good Gunter, Star of the West, Last Chance and Big Hurrah, none of which were worth developing. On the way back from Blue Mountain, Peter Davis traced a well-defined vein of copper ore from Stag Gulch to his San Domingo placer claims on San Antonio Ridge. Blue Mountain's production of gold was small and disappointing to those men who had located claims there.

The streams of Blue Mountain in which the barefoot Indians once fished for quick tempered trout are still visited in the early summer by the devotees of the wicker basket, rod, reel, and fly hook. Blue Mountain's Golden Age was of short duration. The village's loudest boast was the Blue Mountain Hotel and Livery Stable.

This region, long since famous for its magnificent and valuable stand of pine, fir and cedar is now producing lumber, rather than the yellow metal. The buildings at Blue Mountain City were of flimsy construction. All have fallen apart and tumbled into the humus created by centuries of needle fall and its story, never fully recorded has for the most part, been forgotten.

Footnotes

1 Rail Road Flat also spelled Railroad Flat.

2 Arrastra was a crude device for crushing ore. The Mexicans first used it. A large rock was dragged around in a rock-paved and encircled area by a horse or a mule. After the quartz was ground to powder, the ore was worked to free the gold from the debris.

3 Possibly Charles Condon.

4 Whisky Slide is also spelled Whiskey Slide.

21

JESUS MARIA TOWN

The Chilean War

Esteban Niades is credited with having founded Jesus Maria in 1848. But tradition carries this settlement back to 1837 when a Mexican colony[1] was established at this location. Long before the latter date, the Indians of this remote region maintained a Rancheria on the site where Esteban pitched his camp. After the arrival of the American miners, an old grizzle-haired Chief of the Mokelumne tribe told them, that years before the coming of the white man, many terrific battles between the Washoe Indians of Nevada and the Mokelumnes, had been waged at Jesus Maria.

The town of Jesus Maria, locally pronounced "Sus Maria" circa 1900. It was such a picturesque place that artists would come from all over California to paint it.

Courtesy of Calaveras County Historical Society

Jesus Maria, despite its saintly name, was a rude camp, filled with reckless gold-greedy men. All trails seemingly led to it, enabling it to keep in close touch with its neighboring camps. Places like; Soap Root, Upper

Rich Gulch, Black Penny, Alabama Hill, Independence Flat, Rail Road Flat, Mosquito Gulch, West Point, Secreto, Brandy Flat, Whisky Slide, Happy Valley, Esmerelda, Dogtown and Tunnel Hill.

In 1850, due to the continual aggressiveness of the Chilean miners, men who had served their country in the Mexican War formed a military organization, the Jesus Marian Home Guards under the command of A.C. Clark. [Appendix A, page 332 and www.militarymuseum.org/JesusMariaGuard.]

Owing to the richness of the gravel, American miners adopted a resolution to limit the size of a claim, from six to sixteen feet square. The specific size depended upon the richness of the ground. Every time a resolution like this was passed more resentment was created. Chilean hotheads set up a hubbub louder than the roar they had made at Chili Gulch, a short time previously. Chilean miners resentful of the resolution were soon hurling curses at the American miners. Chief amongst the malcontents was Dr. Juan Concha who ignoring the regulation, continued to locate placer claims not only in Jesus Maria but also at Campo Seco, Camanche and Poverty Bar.

Dr. Concha, a soundly schooled physician and surgeon, had reached California with Esteban Naides' expedition, which had brought from South America to the Calaveras locale, a large number of peon laborers to work in the mines. The Americans refused to tolerate bondage of any type in the placers and frowned upon vassalage of this sort. To bring himself into competition with the lowly peon was something no American miner would do. At last, the Americans called a mass meeting to decide whether or not the peons should be permitted to remain in that locality.

The bad blood resulting from the Foreign Miners' Tax[2] of June 1st 1850 was now past the boiling point and it threatened to explode hourly. The fight was not on in dead earnest however until, Concha had attempted to deprive Americans at Jesus Maria of the rights to make new discoveries within certain boundaries, which he had designated as being in his " Sphere of Influence". Now, whenever an American staked a claim in forbidden ground, Concha's favorite bruiser "Tirante" drove him from the scene. Of course, this defiant attitude, on the part of the South Americans, served only to widen the breach between the two peoples.

At a second mass meeting a demand was made to exact punishment and execute vengeance. Ear splitting were the yells of the Americans after a firm declaration not to allow any more placer ground to slip through their fingers was made. The next insolence displayed was when the South Americans drove the members of a New York Mining Company from the forbidden ground. Bristling with indignation, the men from the Empire State reported the details of the attack to their fellow miners.

A third mass meeting was hastily called with Alcalde Collier presiding. At this meeting the Americans, their patience worn to a frazzle, set up the cry,

"All Chileans must go!"

The cry meeting with approval, the miners made free use of bear and burrow's grease on the locks of muskets, rifles and shotguns. Horses and mules were hurriedly saddled up. Men vaulted into saddles and the galloping centaurs rode fast and furiously with the warning:

"Dr. Concha and his peons must leave this section
On the day named in these resolutions"

Dr. Concha was not to be intimidated. He straddled a mule and with the hilt of a dagger showing above the folds of his azurite sash, rode to Stockton. There he managed to wangle a writ of arrest from one of the presiding judges in that city[3]. Returning to Jesus Maria, he served it. His method of serving a legal paper was displeasing to the American miners. At once the New York boys and their sympathizers began to make battle preparation.

In the meantime, the Americans, desperate in their exasperation, sent mounted messengers to the gold camps in the timber belt, to inform their countrymen of Concha's insolence and treachery. The gold diggers were urged to knock off work in their claims, shoulder flintlock rifles and in other ways prepare themselves to take part in the impending fight.

The American miners, as American miners would, made immediate response. On foot, on horseback or on mule back, they came from far and near to add strength to the American force.

When Dr. Concha got wind of the Americans determination to fight, he assembled a large number of peons and other South Americans and as their leader, tramped off to capture the stronghold of the enemy.

At once, the Americans combined their forces and with yells rivaling the whoops of the Indians who probably stood by watching with curious eyes, Americans armed to the teeth, marched across the forbidden ground and there at the edge of Jesus Maria, a halt was made.

Dusk came and with it came Dr. Concha and his armed guerrillas who swooped down upon the claims of the New Yorkers, shot and killed two of their number, seized and bound thirteen and held them as hostages in a Chilean camp.

For the rest of the evening, the fighting men of both armies did nothing but curse, fret and glower at each other's stronghold. In the American camp, each of the bewhiskered parcel of nerve and energy questioned the wisdom of attacking the South Americans under cover of a pitch-black night.

Gnecco House in Jesus Maria. Gnecco Family owned the Winery.
Courtesy of Barbara Kathan

While they waited for dawn to streak the sky with rose and amber, an opportune moment happily arrived for the New Yorkers.

Concha's insurgents, after nightfall, began to show signs of drowsiness. Each and all succumbing to sleep, were snoring loudly when a resourceful Albany boy worked loose the deerskin thongs binding his wrists and ankles. His hands and feet again useful, he moved quietly among his companions, awakened them and set them free. Together they slipped along the lines of sleeping Chileans and disarmed them. Now in possession of all weapons, the New Yorkers were in command of the situation. They seized Dr. Concha and his followers and took them under guard to the American stronghold.

The game was up. Concha realized that the Americans were now in a position to rid the Jesus Maria placers of his cheap labor. On that dreadful night in Jesus Maria there was general chaos. Many Chilean settlers, frightened, fled from their camps in wildest disorder. Others suspected of aiding Concha's cause, were arrested and given a form of trial in Alcalde Collier's court.

The murderers of the two New Yorkers stood trial in a Miners' Court. A jury composed of miners brought in a verdict of guilty. The condemned men, however, escaped being led to some tree and lynched. Instead, they were taken to Mokelumne Hill where they were made to suffer death on that

From John Gnecco's distillery in Jesus Maria, side of a brandy case.
Courtesy of Barbara Kathan

town's permanent gallows. Other Chilean offenders, who had been unnecessarily rough with their prisoners, were taken to the stake and given from 75 to 100 lashes on their naked bodies.

The victor's form of punishment, drastic and painful, had an electrifying effect upon the aggressors. Fear of the rope, blacksnake whip, branding iron and shears, rather than knives and guns, brought peace to Jesus Maria.

The effects of the Chilean War were far reaching and came near causing trouble between the government of the United States and Chile.

Esteban Naides, who had taken no part in the Chilean War, was in Mokelumne Hill on Christmas Day in 1851. While walking on Lafayette Street he was told by a friend that James Campbell of Jesus Maria, was about to leave Mokelumne Hill on his, Esteban's mule. Esteban, a peace loving man, hurried to a certain livery stable and in his usual quiet way remonstrated with Campbell, only to receive a blow to the face followed by a fatal knife thrust to the stomach. The young Peruvian of gentlemanly deportment and good character, while reaching for his dagger, sank slowly to the ground. His brain in a whirl, he rose up and resting on an elbow, hurled the blade at Campbell but missed the mark. The weapon, for a distance of ten yards ripped through the cold December air and struck, quivering, in a wall of the Empire Engine House.

Campbell was hotly pursued while attempting a getaway. Caught up with, he was arrested and given a form of trial in a Miners' Court. Found guilty of first-degree murder, he was about to have a hemp rope put around his neck when, by a vote of the people, he was handed over to the civil authorities. While Ben Marshall the Sheriff, was on his way from the County Seat in Jackson, Campbell strong as an ox, escaped from Mokelumne Hill's calaboso. He left town under cover of darkness and was never again heard from, at least not in Calaveras County.

Those same men who were instrumental in saving Campbell's neck from the mob's rope, became impatient with jail conditions as they then existed and determined to see justice meted out to murderers. They formed a vigilance committee, the first formed in California.

Footnotes

1 In her article "Forgotten Towns of '49" in National Motorist Dec. 1937, Mrs. Buckbee calls this place "Jesus Maria of the Holy Name". Possibly, this is the name of the 1837 colony that she refers to in this writing. Unfortunately she was not in a habit of listing her sources. But if there is any truth to this statement, then this may be the oldest non-Indian community in Calaveras County.

2 Foreign Miners' Tax was an extremely high tax. In "Gold Rush Dollars" this $20.00 per month tax bill would equal to $600 per month or $7200 per year in 2005 in current dollars.

3 Quite a different account of events is presented in the Chilean version of California Gold Rush by Edwin A. Beilharz and Carlos U. Lopez in their book *"We were 49ers!"*

Also see *Las Calaveras* June 6, 1999 by Maud S. Washburn, and

Appendix A page 332 for a copy of a 1850 letter from Chileans at Jesus Maria to then Governor of California Peter Bernett.

22

MOKELUMNE HILL

An old town with a history.

View of Mokelumne Hill 1855. Detail from a poster purchased from Bancroft Library.

Courtesy Bancroft Library

It was due to the extreme richness of the Mokelumne River that the town of Mokelumne Hill was indebted for its rapid rise in population. James P. Martin and his party were taking gold out of this stream at the time of the arrival there of Captain Charles M. Weber in the summer of 1848. Contrary to expectation, the Indians of this region displayed no hostility towards the white men and that included Jim Martin and his eight companions. Captain Weber and members of his large party, in a short space of time took out gold, not in ounces, but in pounds! Soon after, Martin's men became ill with diarrhea and left the river for the Ione Valley. About this same time, Weber and his companions broke camp and pushed northward to the Cosumnes River and onward into El Dorado County where in a little creek Andrew Kelsey, a member of Weber's company, discovered gold.

During the summer of 1848, Colonel J. D. Stevenson together with one hundred men recently mustered out of the army, built campfires on ground whereon soon arose the town of Mokelumne Hill. Colonel Stevenson drew up, for the use of his companions, the first mining laws ever written in California. The soldiers felled pines and built log cabins there. When autumn came, Colonel Stevenson returned to Sutter's Fort. In midwinter, a report that his men were snowed in at Mokelumne Hill reached him. But since the ex-soldiers had provisions and shelter sufficient to withstand any siege of snow, the colonel placed no credence in the report.

Col. J.D. Stevenson (1800-1894) Leader of the Regiment to colonized California. He organized California's first Grand Lodge of Free Masons.
Courtesy of C.C. Archives

Early in the spring of 1849 J. S. Smythe, Michael and John O'Neal, Peter Jacobs, Captain Rogers of the Sandwich Islands [Hawaiian Islands] and the brothers Godey and Perry Lake, dammed the Mokelumne River near Rich Gulch. These men formed a partnership and located claims at this point, but since the riverbed did not yield bucketsful of gold each day, they became discouraged and went elsewhere to seek fortunes. Then along came Colonel James and his partners, the Vanderslice brothers, one a doctor, the other a gambler, to mine at the bar. Afterwards this bar was called "James' Bar". W. Fowle Smith and Haskell became partners and established a trading post at James Bar, presumably the first on the Mokelumne River. Shortly, a thousand men were mining on this stream. That springtime the American gold washers started to discuss ways and means of ridding the Mokelumne region of foreigners. They called mass meetings; the result of these meetings was the Foreign Miners' Tax that became effective in June of the following year.

E. McKim, J. Donnelly, J. D. Davis and Dr. Elliott washed gold at James Bar in 1849. That year McKim and Donnelly each took out seventy-five pounds of gold and both were flat broke a year later. Their gold foolishly spent, they became teamsters and hauled stove wood into Mokelumne Hill.

Men, owning claims in Rich Gulch, Black Gulch and Murphy's Gulch, realized from five to six thousand dollars worth of the yellow metal each day to the man. With so much gold in the hands of the miners, small wonder that Mokelumne Hill went at a terrific pace.

N. W. Spaulding built a sawmill in 1850 and whip sawed thirteen hundred feet of lumber with which to build a water flume and for other purposes as well. The town's mixed population was badly in need of lumber for houses, for as yet none had been erected. The Americans and Europeans lived in tents, the Mexicans and South Americans clustered in brush remadas, the native Californians contented themselves with hide shanties, the Chinese camped outdoors under the shelter of rocks and the Negroes banded together and got along as best they could.

In Mokelumne Hill, in 1850, for seventeen weeks straight running, a death by violence was reported. Dr. Louis Soher, a prominent physician of the Hill, afterwards said:

> "Each week a man was slain between Saturday night and Sunday morning"

But when, within a week's time, five men had been wantonly murdered and the condition of affairs in the town had become unbearable, a sort of "law and order" group was organized. The leaders decided that the surest way to discourage crime was to erect a permanent gallows.

No sooner was the scaffold built than a Mexican, of desperate character and powerful physique, was led to it and hung. Before the rope was put around his neck, he confessed to having committed eight murders between Mokelumne Hill and Sonora, the county seat of Tuolumne County.

In a restaurant oneday two strangers sat quietly talking to each other. A gambler, sitting at a table close by, imagining he heard his name mentioned, whipped out a revolver and fired a shot that mortally wounded one of the innocent strangers. In 1850 the most trivial offense, it seems, furnished an occasion for a shooting or stabbing affray.

During the winter of 1850-1851, the quartz ledges were traced into the hills where, frequently, the yield of gold was enormous. Mokelumne Hill, supposedly, was a continuation of the same "wash" that made Tunnel Hill, north of the river, so rich.

One evening in 1851, a drunken sailor[1], while on his way from a saloon to his cabin, staggered and fell to the ground and slept the night on the trail. The next morning he awakened to find himself in Steep Gulch. Sober, he got on his feet and in his efforts to ascend the rocky trail, disturbed rocks underneath which was gold. Using a clasp knife, he creviced out from between boulders several pounds of gold. Then and there he staked a claim, 14 feet long and 3 feet wide, and in less then two weeks, dug out of it $17,000 worth of the precious metal.

A party of French miners, when news of the sailor's good fortune reached them, hastened to Steep Gulch to dig out fortunes. Sixty Frenchmen, each with a large amount of gold in his possession, left Steep Gulch for France.

Bayard Taylor was the first writer of note to visit the Southern Mines.

With Lieutenant Beale for a companion, Mr. Taylor was in Mokelumne Hill in 1849 gathering material for a book. Let us quote Mr. Bayard Taylor:

> "Alcaldes were elected who had power to decide all disputes, complaints, and to summon juries. The rights of each gold digger were definitely marked out and observed. In a region 500 miles long, inhabited by 100,000 people, who had neither locks, bolts, regular laws of government, military or civil protection, there was as much security to life and property as in any state in the Union. In the evening we sat down to a supper prepared by Baptiste and his partner M. Fisher. I was completely astonished at the resources of this wonderful land. There, in the rough depths of the hills, where three weeks before, there was scarcely a tent and where we expected to live on jerked beef and bread, I saw on the table green corn, green peas and fresh beans, fresh oysters, roast turkey, fine Goshen butter and excellent coffee. I slept soundly that night and went early down to the river."

While visiting the river, the writer and soldier, were entertained by Dr. Gillespie, Colonel James of James Bar, Captain Tracy and other " big guns" of various "wet" diggings. A Frenchmen, known simply as Baptiste and his partner Fisher, erected the first hotel in Mokelumne Hotel. It was a crudely constructed tavern. A few poles stuck into the ground and a roof of cowhides answered the purpose for which it was intended.

One day, while Taylor and Beale were carefully descending a trail, they met a young man astride a donkey, who told them that during the day's ride from Double Springs, beside quail and partridges, he had encountered grizzly bear, timber wolves, deer and a cougar. Upon leaving Baptiste's tavern Mr. Taylor made the following notation: "Bill at hotel $11.00 per day, per man and mule, $4.00 for the man and $7.00 for the mule". This amount did not include lodging. Where his guests slept was of no concern to Batiste, knight of the fry pan and flapjack griddle.

Don Andreas Pico, a Mokelumne River gold washer, was able to display, before the astonished eyes of Bayard Taylor and Edward Beale, a 62-ounce nugget, which he took from his claim near James' Bar.

In 1850, Colonel James J. Ayers paid a visit to Mokelumne Hill where, prosperity was everywhere in evidence. Sundays and holidays the streets were impassable, made so by the "gentlemen" gamblers and gold washers who rode into town from the river settlements. The gamblers, rigged out in fine broadcloth clothes, buff colored grenadine vests, beaver hats and spike-heel boots, were easily distinguishable in the motley crowd that made up Mokelumne Hill's population of 15,000. Serious-minded gold washers were most apt to be found inside of tent churches but the "hoi polloi" flocked into saloons, gambling tents, fandangos, Fondas, rowdy houses and hurdy-gurdy dance halls.

The blockaded streets and the milling throng, striding carelessly along, put an idea into young "Jimmy" Ayres' head. The following year together with Henry Hamilton and H. A. DeCourcey he returned to Mokelumne Hill. A few days after the arrival of this trio a printing press was unloaded from one of Chicard's freighters and on October 18, 1851, the first edition of the "Calaveras Chronicle" was run off the press. This newspaper, the second oldest in the Southern Mines, was well edited, prosperous from the very first and for many years, was widely circulated, principally for its informative and fearless editorials.

Henry Q. Clark was the first man to represent the Adams Banking and Express Company in Mokelumne Hill, and the first to organize a theatrical company and his cultural project was an event of importance in the community. The enterprising agent fully convinced that the young blades of the town, like himself, were in need of mental stimulus, rented a building and transformed it into a little theatre with a stage, drop curtain and scenery. The footlights were candles stuck between three nails and light reflected by pieces of tin. "Richard the Third" was first presented, then the "Box and Cox". One evening, during a rehearsal of "Richard", Clark reminded his audience and players, that Queen Elizabeth permitted no woman, however talented, to tread the boards for the amusement of her court. Also, the queen demanded that her Shakespearean performers render perfect diction. At this time there was a dearth of women at Mokelumne Hill, at least, women able to speak English understandably.

Among the prominent citizens who attended the opening performance of "Richard the Third: were George T. Badgley, William P. Peek, Benjamin F. Langford, H. L. Buchanan, the brothers George and William B. West, George H. Campbell, Williams L. and Allan P. Dudley, Wm. Jeff Gatewood, David Mulford, H. L. Sturgis, Thomas B. Wade, and General Cadwalleder and his son, Charles. "Webfoot" Hanley, "Short-card Red", "Texas Mike" and "Snappy Andy," may or may not have been nudging elbows and chewing wads of tobacco in some far corner of Mr. Clark's little playhouse, but more than likely they were in the Blue Tent Saloon dancing with some satin-haired senorita. For in spite of the dust, this saloon from dusk to sunrise was the liveliest place in Mokelumne Hill.

Peter I. Jewell and Thomas Stevenson erected a stone building, which they rented for a jail to Calaveras County for $150 a month. Now, in 1851, Mokelumne Hill had more than 100 business houses, a goodly number of dwelling homes, a Catholic Church, reading room and a newspaper.

The arrival of a "bill sticker" in Mokelumne Hill meant that an event of importance was about to take place. No sooner had a "bill sticker" arrived with his bucket of paste and brush, than the sides of houses and barns were placarded with boldly printed broadsides or hangers, announcing a bull and bear fight. The "hanger" of the promoter of the grizzly, "General Scott," was worded as follows:

"War! War! War!
The Celebrated
Bull-Killing Bear
General Scott
Will Fight a Bull
On Sunday the 15th.
At 2 p.m.
At Mokelumne Hill.
The bear will be chained in the middle of the Arena.
The Bull will be perfectly wild, young and of Spanish breed,
The best that can be found in the country.
The Bull's horns will be of their natural length and
Not sawed off to prevent accidents.
The Bull will be quite free in the arena and
Not hampered in any way whatever."

A bull and bear fight was a popular sport in Mokelumne Hill, where the enthusiastic owners of Spanish bulls and ferocious grizzlies promoted fights, until the local Vigilance Committee ordered the custom stopped.

On Corral Flat near the arena, was a bullpen near which stood a shake shanty, known as Fash's dried apple pie house. Fash, in 1849, was a mule-prodder who owned his own pack train and also owned a cabin in which was a small sheet iron stove. As a monopolist Fash was second only to Fourcades. When the fall rains came and the packing business slowed down, Fash would go to Mokelumne Hill's grocery stores and in each bought its entire supply of dried apples. A sign on the outside of his cabin door stated, that inside, dried apple pies would be offered for sale to gold diggers.

Fash was his own pie maker and his pie-eaters, in their eagerness to pay him fifty cents and sometimes two dollars for a quarter cut, got in each other's way. The price ranged according to the scarcity of apples. For the modest sum of one dollar, Fash permitted a miner to roast a joint of venison in his oven. One day when his dried apples gave out, he concocted a bean pie and, as a novel and delectable delicacy, imposed it upon his numerous customers. A young man named Todd, a letter express carrier between San Francisco and the Mokelumne River, when in Mokelumne Hill made Fash's pie camp his headquarters and so it soon became known as Fash's Letter

Bull and Bear Fight.
From an unidentified newspaper clipping.
Courtesy of C.C.Archives

Camp. Between the pies and express letters the shake shanty was one of the liveliest spots in the town. Fash could always count on William G. Depew, Conrad Platt, the brothers Charles B. and William Higby, T. S. Louttit, Simon Forman, Phil Piper, M. Gradwohl, L. Weil and "Deacon" Peek to gather in his house every two weeks to the day, to receive from the express rider Todd, letters and newspapers.

Mokelumne Hill's rise was astonishing, both in prosperity and in population. Daily a long file of burros with packsaddles bulging with "high grade" left Adams & Company's express office for Stockton, its final destination being the United States Mint in San Francisco. Guibal & Dharbourne of Stockton ran a line of stages to Mokelumne Hill three times a week and incurred the gratitude of Stockton businessmen. Maintaining communications with the mining towns and camps was an important factor in the development of both Stockton and Sacramento. A Stockton newspaper in 1851 chronicled:

> "In Mokelumne Hill are some of the richest mines
> in the midst of an immense population."

Each Tuesday and Saturday morning, Troy and Concord coaches belonging to Provendie & Paxton, left the Stockton House on the north side of the channel, for Mokelumne Hill.

If, in late October, the leaves were still clinging to twigs, the faces of the miners took on a pained look, for the leaves bespoke a late season when water would be scarce. To the gold washers, not having sufficient water to wash gravel meant cutting down of rations of bacon, salt pork, molasses, pickles, dried beans, sugar, tea, coffee and flour.

Two days of torrential rains in early November brought smiles back to the faces of both the miners and the merchants, for in Mokelumne Hill alone $100,000 was put into circulation and it was inevitable that the gold would sooner or later flow into Stockton's marts of trade. One week's rain in mid-

that was sent out of this booming town. That year Chicard's teams hauled freight to Mokelumne Hill for twelve cents a pound, in contrast to the 50 and 75-cent rate charged by Chicard & Co. in 1849.

Rain, just the right amount of it, and good times were synonymous in the gold era. Too great a rainfall spelled disaster, for when the roads became impassable to all but horsemen; freighters didn't dare venture across the swollen streams. When this condition prevailed, merchandise of every description stacked up in warehouses and as a result, prices fell in Stockton and skyrocketed in the Mokelumne River settlements. When supplies were nearing exhaustion and starvation threatened the people of Mokelumne Hill as well as all neighboring towns and camps, a sack of flour and a bag of dried beans would demand almost any amount of gold dust. During the famine period of the winter of 1851 prices for food were outrageously high. That season, the discouraged and hungry miners grumbled and one man was heard to say:

"The prospects in the claims are excellent,
If us gold washers,
Don't die before food can be sent into town."

During this winter, more than one person in Mokelumne Hill was obliged to face his once abundantly filled cupboard, only to turn stoically away hungry.

The first Protestant Church in Mokelumne Hill was a canvas army tent pitched near Church Street. The Gay residence later occupied the site. Mr. S. Newman donated a log cabin, the first parsonage, to the church. Later this site became widely known, as the Italian Gardens. The Reverend J. B. Fish was the first Protestant minister to preach sermons in this tent church. A member of the Methodist Episcopal Church, Reverend Fish and his wife reached the Hill in August 1852. That year Mrs. Fish opened the town's first school. The daily session in the church tent was three hours, her salary $75.00 a month. Three of Mrs. Fish's five pupils were the children of Negroes.

One Sunday morning a woman, while on her way to church, found a four-ounce nugget, which, upon reaching the church, she placed in the contribution box. The Reverend Fish rose to the occasion with the remark that,

"It is not sinful to look for gold on the Sabbath day,
If what was found,
Is given to the service of the Lord."

Nigger Hill, close to the town, sprung into prominence as the result of a practical joke in the summer of 1852. A young Negro, presumably a deserter from some ship, came footsore and weary to Mokelumne Hill. His cowhide boots, scuffed by rocks were all but sole less. His faded calico shirt was in tatters, and his black woolly hair covered with stickers and burrs. He gave himself a moment of rest before approaching two gold washers who were seated in the shade of a tree, smoking and talking together in a friendly way. The hesitant Negro finally mustered up enough courage to say to one of the men:

"I's lookin' foh a gol' mine, sah."

"Can you dig?"

"All right," said the practical joker grinning from ear to ear.

"Get yourself a pick and shovel and climb to the top of yonder hill and after digging like hell, you may find gold."

The credulous Negro, profuse in his thanks, followed instructions to the letter and was soon making dirt and rocks fly. At sunset, to the great surprise of the town's chief joker, the Negro strode down the hill holding in his arms a chunk of gold worth $13,000. He again thanked the miner and with his treasure well secured, departed for the cooler, breezier region of the bay. Ever since that day, by eminence, this hill has been called Nigger Hill, with the exception of French Hill; it was the richest ground in Mokclumne Hill.

Mountain Ranchers on the Mokelumne River bridge 1915, Maurice Zwinge on the rail, Roy Dale, Paul Lewis and Dave Zwinge behind the wheel.

Paul Lewis photo courtesy of Wally Motloch

Dr. W. Gillespie, while resting near the roadside one day in 1852, aimlessly poked his walking stick into the ground and turned up a two-pound nugget and when the worthy doctor left the spot his pockets were weighted with 14 pounds of virgin gold.

In November 1852, the citizens of Mokelumne Hill decided amongst themselves that they could handle their civic affairs better if county rule was not imposed upon them. Together, they discussed the prospects of a government for a better regulation of their town's activities. A police force was organized and urged to preserve order and prevent rowdyism and killings.

The month of July 1853, so far as gold was concerned, was Mokelumne Hill's banner month, for during that month immense amounts of precious metal were shipped out of this town. At this time the Mokelumne Hill Canal Company increased its capital stock to $200,000 and the original shareholders promptly took up the issue. Now, other than an occasional robbery, Mokelumne Hill had little or nothing to disturb its tranquility. Its newspaper, the Chronicle, on November 27, 1853, printed:

"Our town now contains a population of sixty-five hundred inhabitants within a square mile, three fourths of whom are American citizens. The hammer, plane and saw are in constant use. New buildings are going up every day. We have a new and handsome theatre nearly completed. Every one of our citizens displays spirit, enterprise and liberality."

A few miles southwest of Mokelumne Hill, within view of his stage station, Lewis Schrack of Golden Gate ranch, established a flour mill thereby lessening a famine hazard in event that the coming winter should prove to be a rough one.

In September, 1853, the "Golden Era," a San Francisco weekly newspaper, stated:

"The total production of the California miner, since the diggings commenced in 1848, is a little short of $300,000,000.

And three months later this same newspaper chronicle:

"Calaveras County is now one of the most quiet and peaceable in the state. The strict watch kept by the officers on suspected parties has caused a general clearing out of these troublesome customers and the roads are now traveled with the utmost confidence. Even John Chinaman is relieved of his fears and trudges along with his pack in perfect safety. A year ago such a course would have cost him his pile, if not his life."

To prove the richness of Mokelumne Hill, in 1853 an aged mahala, who lived at nearby Sport Hill, had a curtain in the doorway of her wigwam, and to keep the wind from blowing it, she placed as she supposed, a heavy yellow rock on the bottom of it to hold it down. Some Frenchmen came along and seeing the rock, took a fancy to it. A little dickering and a bargain was struck whereby the mahala received some cheap glass beads in exchange for her yellow rock which, in reality, was a nugget of gold worth several hundreds of dollars.

A certain night in December of 1853 was a long remembered one by the people of Mokelumne Hill. A gala night, full of music and mirthful laughter, it marked the opening of the town's brand new theater, dedicated as the "Calaveras Theater". There was no other place in California where amusements were more liberally patronized than in this town. Generous with their gold, the people not only encouraged and applauded performers, but if need be, overlooked their lack of talents.

Harriet Carpenter, a favorite with Sacramento and Marysville audiences, on opening night, was the star performer in the drama, "The School for Scandal." Miss Carpenter, besides winning "rapturous" applause, was showered with nuggets, bright and heavy. A few weeks later, in Mokelumne Hill, this gifted actress married Ben Moulton, a shotgun messenger in the employ of the Adams Banking and Express Co. Mrs. Moutlon, accustomed to a busy routine, plunged into Mokelumne Hill's civic and social activities, especially those of the theatre, taking up where Henry. Q. Clark had left off.

The Chapman troupe, following Miss Carpenter's company, played a long engagement in the new theatre. Caroline Chapman as Pauline in the "Lady of Lyons," packed the house with an appreciative audience. The highly gifted and popular sister of William B. Chapman, himself a first rate actor, was presented with a poke, chockfull of gold dust, during the farewell performance of this famous theatrical troupe, of which she, Caroline, was the stellar attraction.

Kate Hayes, the "Swan of Erin," a world famous opera and concert singer, was warmly received in Mokelumne Hill. The operatic concerts in the Calaveras Theatre, at Poverty Bar and Winter's Bar, netted this gracious Irish soprano a tidy sum of gold.

Many notable actors and actresses played engagements in the Calaveras Theater, one of the best playhouses of its day, which in the great fire of 1854, was burned clear down to the ground. During its brief existence, among those to appear before its footlights were; Madame Duprez, Edwin Forrest, Mrs. Sinclair, Edwin Booth, Mrs. Judah, Anna Westayer, Alicia Mandeville, George Ryer, Madame Anna Bishop, Mary Provost and the Robinson Family, including little Susan.

When trouping through the mining towns the players experienced but few inconveniences, especially in Mokelumne Hill where William P. Peek's, well equipped, Golden Eagle Hotel was second to none in the Southern Mines.

Madame Anna Thillon, a celebrated French Prima Donna, attempted a season of grand opera in the mining towns. She opened at the Calaveras Theatre, in "La Somnambula", a work that went over the heads of the Mokelumne Hillians. The French Opera Company, headed by Madame

Thillon, met with only small success in this mining town.

"Our rough friends don't sabe" [don't know or don't understand]
Was the comment of the "Owl's" music critic, Charley Boynton.

Charles Boynton, who had helped to snatch the county records from Double Springs, was a capable newspaper writer, employed on the "Chronicle," and had access to Colonel Ayres' press and types. So, he ran off several editions of his "Owl," a small weekly, which delighted his readers living on both sides of the Mokelumne River. Wit fairly dripped from Charley's pen and caused gales of laughter, but his pithy satires on local happenings got more than one "bigwig's" dander up. The "old-timers" at the Hill used to say that, Charley Boynton swam across the Mokelumne River with a weekly edition of the "Owl" tied to the top of his head and when he got back to the Hill from Jackson he always had a couple of fist fights all on account of his "noisy hoots" in the "Owl". Boynton's editorials and comments, flagrant and unshaded, were set forth vauntingly.

At this time the politicians of Jackson did some loud grumbling, going so far as to say that:

"The county seat had not been transferred from their town to Mokelumne Hill as a result of choice.

That the money collected for taxes was not being turned into the State treasury and,

That the county officers were wasting the funds of Old Calaveras on lewd women. The general charge was this:

"Whenever we wish to see a county officer on business,
We must look for him in one of the many fandango houses.
That ornaments and conserves the morals of this high-toned town" [Mokelumne Hill].

The State Legislature of 1853-1854, having abolished the Board of Supervisors in Calaveras County, empowered the Court of Sessions to transact the business of this county. The first act of the Court of Sessions was to levy a tax of 50 cents on each $100 worth of property, of which five per cent was to be devoted to public school purposes.

At the above session of Legislature an Act was passed calling for the vote of the people for a division of Calaveras County. June 17, 1854, was the date fixed for the election. W. L. McKim, E. W. Gemmill, A. G. Sneath, Alexander Boileau, and Alonzo Platt were appointed commissioners, in event the people voted for a division, to organize the new county. State senators, E. D. Sawyer and Charles Leake, drew the Bill. When, on a swelteringly hot August day of that year, word reached Jackson that on the 24th it was again made a county seat, there was great rejoicing amongst the people of the new county. Charley Boynton, highly elated, with wit too lively to be bottled up, penned for his weekly "The Owl" the following:

"There was a sound of revelry by night
And our new county seat had gathered then
Her miners, and her merchants, and the light
Of tallow candles shone on drunken men.
A dozen hats had bricks in them; and when
Some jolly fellow, tighter than the rest,
Invited the whole crowd to drink again,
Not one among them needed to be pressed;
But hush! Hark! A deep sound strikes every guest.
Did ye not hear it? No, 'twas but the wind,
Or some damned jackass braying in the street.
Give us our drinks, let joy be unconfined
Nor part till morn, we've got the County Seat."

After the organization of Amador County, Charley Boynton left the Mother County for Jackson where he established a weekly newspaper. For several months the "Sentinel" was printed in the office of the "Chronicle" and the editions were so small at first that Boynton was able to carry them under his arm from Mokelumne Hill to Jackson where they were distributed. The "Sentinel," one of the oldest of weekly newspapers in California, is still being pulled off the press in Charley Boynton's town, Jackson. Henry George, advocator of the single tax plan, once earned his board and keep in Jackson as a writer for the "Sentinel."

At the time Amador was set off from the Mother County, a provision was made that the new county should assume a just proportion of the common debt. No special method of determining this amount was provided, so the matter was neglected until, on January 27, 1857, Calaveras County brought suit against J. C. Shipman, auditor of Amador County, to recognize the obligation known as the "Calaveras Indebtedness". Commissioners were appointed to determine the exact amount of the debt, which they finally fixed at $26,517.32 A warrant was issued for this amount and as No. 103, it became famous in the history of the two counties as the source of invasions, injunctions, and lawsuits. The interest on the debt had accumulated to $9,281.05, making a total of $35,798.37. Finally, after a series of lawsuits the matter was settled in 1865. The delay eventually cost Amador County $50,000, which sum included the interest paid on the warrant and attorneys' fees.

Calaveras County was in the Third Division of the Third Collection District in California and William F. Colton, a deputy collector of United States Internal Revenue Service, was to be found in his office in the Court House in Mokelumne Hill.

View of Center Street in Mokelumne Hill circa 1909 Building on the left is the Odd Fellows Hall, in the center is delapitated Eagle Hotel.
Courtesy of Kent Wilson

In 1853, Calaveras County made the largest contribution in the State to the Washington monument fund, with Mokelumne Hill leading all other county precincts.

Mokelumne Hill was almost entirely destroyed by fire in 1854. The property loss at this time was terrific, however, her citizens refused to become disheartened, instead they pitched in together and cleaned up the ruins and built for themselves a new and better town. The main street was widened to seventy feet and more than 100 buildings were erected, many of which were of stone quarried from Corral Hill. Water for household and mining purposes, was brought into town that year, and as a result a large number of miners congregated here.

The Odd Fellows Building[2], next door to the Golden Eagle Hotel, constructed of stone, was possibly the first three-story fire proof building erected in California. That old landmark still stands. The large street lamp at its entrance is no longer lighted and across its massive iron doors no bolts are drawn. Its nearest neighbor, a stone structure was once the property of Adams Express Company. Later, it served Wells Fargo & Co. for an express office. This old stone fireproof building, during the flush days, housed millions of dollars worth of dust and nuggets and occasionally it was the scene of intense excitement.

In California, Joseph H. Zumwalt of Mokelumne Hill was the founder

Center Street in Mokelumne Hill in 1901. On the left is Eagle Hotel, center, Peek Store, and on the right is the Post Office. Note the horse and buggy.

Courtesy of Wally Motloch

of the organization labeled E. Campus Vitus. Mr. Zumwalt and W. C. Wright, his boon companion, before boarding an ox-train for California in Missouri in 1849 purchased a copy of the first ritual of the "Ancient and Honorable Order of E. Campus Vitus" which was printed in the office of the "Bowling Green Journal" in Pike County, Missouri.

In Placerville, Joe Zumwalt in 1850, using the ritual, organized a lodge, the first in California. It was No. 1000 and had only a few members. Even those few were disinterested so the lodge was of short duration. Zumwalt became a resident of Mokelumne Hill in 1851, where he again made use of the ritual, this time to organize Lodge No. 1001. The first meetings were held in the Van Pelt building, and later in the old District Court room, in which Judge Charles Creanor had once occupied the Bench. The initiation fee was $5.00. The paraphernalia of the Mokelumne Hill "Clampers" was destroyed in the fire of 1854 and the loss sustained at this time came near wrecking Lodge No. 1001. Its charter members were George Schuler, Billy Burnside, Fred Gall, Martin Bohen, John Hansen, Wm. McFadden, Bob Cardwell, Charley Spires, Charley Clark, and Teat Thompson.

The main spring of the organization left the Hill for Sierra City in 1855, and when, a few years later he returned, the E. Clampus Vitus Lodge in the matter of funds, was down to bedrock. Again, Joe Zumwalt started the ball rolling. In Mokelumne Hill, during the holiday season of 1858, the Clampers now 500 strong, wearing full regalia, headed by the town's brass band, paraded through the streets. Among the new members were

County Judge Silas Brockway, Joe Douglas, Judge W. W. Porter, Napoleon Broughton, Patrick H. Kean, Edward Taylor, Edward Fahey, A. R. Young, H. J. Naman, William Briggs, Colonel Mount, Judge Grant, Dr. Hoerchner, William P. Peek, Ned Patterson, Pink Smith, Joe Vaughn, Wm. Badgley, Bill Carileu, Allan and William Dudley, Mose Ferguson, David Aldrich and William Howell.

Joseph Zumwalt organized the San Andreas Lodge of E. Clampsus Vitus in the town of San Andreas. It was the second oldest in California, being No. 1002.

Jacob Erni, a Mexican War Veteran, dug gold in Mokelumne River in 1848 and quickly made his pile. On the road between Middle Bar and Mokelumne Hill in 1850, he planted grape vines and established a winery. By reason of his warm and generous heart he was known, as the "Good Angel" of the river. "Uncle Erni" as his friends affectionately called him, assisted many a man to regain both his health and fortune and no orphan in his locality was permitted to go to school hungry, shoeless and coatless. Indeed, he made his neighbors' losses and hardships his own. When Jacob Erni, eighty-six, died in Mokelumne Hill in 1899, he bequeathed his fortune to civic and religious enterprises of that town.

W. L. Dudley a lawyer and Benjamin Marshall, a former Sheriff, were all set to meet on the "field of honor" Corral Flat, near Fash's Letter Camp, in 1854, but their seconds, remembering Ben Marshall's skill in drawing a straight bead, were able to make a satisfactory adjustment of the would-be duelists grievances without the resort to the derringers.

In 1854 a rich strike was made in one of William Wells & Company's placer claims; one of the many chunks of gold unearthed at this time weighed 23 ounces. Other companies, at work in near by diggings, were doing equally well. The quartz veins too promised a bountiful yield. That year a large group of men were employed setting poles for a telegraph line between Stockton and Mokelumne Hill.

In the production of gold that year Oregon Hill was well to the front, having 100 ounces of dust to show after a short week's work. After working two weeks in their claim in Steep Gulch, two brothers cleaned-up $80,000 worth of gold. In Mokelumne Hill the Fall River Company took $600 worth of gold out of a single pan of dirt. The String Bean Company at Columbia Bar, on the Mokelumne River, averaged $1,800 worth of gold a day for several weeks.

Mokelumne Hill, the richest, the largest and the wildest mining town of the gold stampede days, in 1855 was on the down grade and not because gold had petered out but simply because the Canal Water Company had raised its

Peek Store in Mokelumne Hill.
Courtesy of Calaveras County Historical Society

price for water too high. Consequently the gold washers left the town for new and less expensive locations. When finally the water company in order to stay in business, reduced its rate from six dollars to four dollars for the first "tom" or sluice-head, conditions changed in Mokelumne Hill. Owing to the reduction, ground that couldn't be worked at the high rate for water again began yielding bountifully.

That year, when Squires Notion Store went out of business, along came Isador Sokolowsky to open a combination store, which is to say, he sold nails, brass tacks, blasting powder, face powder, Florida water, French cologne, and other sundries in his stone store on Center Street near Peek's Livery Stable. Madame Baptista Marx, in her establishment on Main Street, sold harness, saddles, bridles and saddlebags, in fact all equipment necessary to horsemen.

L. Weil, at his Yankee Notion Bazaar kept his shelves stocked with "fancy" autograph and photograph albums, "fancy" sewing-boxes, sheet music, Meershaum pipes, school books, popular novels and such. Meyer Gradwohl, owner of the Emporium, boasted that he always sold flour, the best quality, from "4 to 6 bits" cheaper than any other merchant in the town.

C. Schlund was the owner of a Main Street jewelry store. Schlund, one of the best jewelry craftsmen in existence, bought gold dust and out of it made jewelry to order and his "California" gold jewelry was second to none in the land.

made jewelry to order and his "California" gold jewelry was second to none in the land.

Conrad Platt was an importer, principally of Irish and Bohemian glassware, English pottery and porcelain, French foibles and German knick-knacks. He also sold kitchen and parlor stoves, of which the most popular was the "Franklin". William G. Depew, after leaving Mosquito Gulch for Mokelumne Hill, purchased Conrad Platt's unique store.

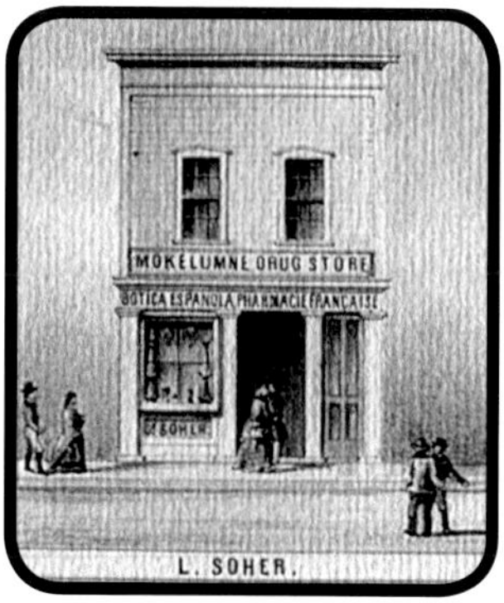

Mokelumne Drug Store
Botica Espanola Pharmacie Francais.
Detail from Bancroft Poster.
Courtesy of Bancroft Libray

Hotel de France, later the Leger Hotel. Detail from Bancroft Library Poster
Courtesy of Bancroft Library

George Leger's Hotel d' Europa, corner of Main and Lafayette streets, was made of native stone. With balconies running along all four sides of the top story, it had light, airy and spacious bedrooms, was handsomely furnished and had the finest ballroom in California. The wonder of its day, this hotel, runs on the European plan. Besides bathrooms, it had a combination barroom and waiting room, the former famous for choice brands of liquors and cigars. Leger's Hotel[3] still stands as the credit to its builders and the town of Mokelumne Hill.

Thomas S. Louttit, drill sharpener, pick manufacturer, wheelwright, horse and mule shoer, was rarely ever absent from his blacksmith shop on Lafayette Street. Meyer Davidson's "one price store" where "merchandise was never shopworn," was in Mr. Adams Main Street building, near Mrs. McFadden's Saloon. Davidson enjoyed an exclusive trade, by reason of his large stock of "elegant" dry goods, fans, shawls, kid slippers and "fancy" combs. E. P. Bruce was the town's foremost boot and shoemaker. Edwin Fahey, Justice of the Peace and Notary Public, was always to be found in his office, which was opposite the Town Hall. Pellaton's store and restaurant on Lafayette Street, was only a stone's throw from John Danz' furniture, coffin and undertaking establishment.

Hemminghofen and Suessdorf Brewery in Mokelumne Hill.
Courtesy of Kent Wilson

P. Bunker ran a line of stages from the Hill to the Gwin Mine at Paloma, and Camanche. Twelve different brands of tobacco were to be found at F. W. Peek's Variety Store. Mrs. Thomas Magee, in her Prospect Hill residence, conducted a millinery store. Her flower and feather bedecked hats and bonnets were the rave of the women for miles around and besides chapeaus, Mrs. Magee carried a full line of artificial flowers, imported ribbons, laces, satin, velvet and all kinds of trimmings dear to the hearts of the lovers of finery. Charles Jacobs' general merchandise store was at No. 333 Main Street. Gebhardt's Brewery, where the first beer in the county was bottled, was located on Church Street. Later, the partners, Hemmifhofen & Suesdorf, purchased this brewery. M. Lamphear built the United States Hotel in 1854. The Hoerchner, another stone structure of the old days, was the property of Dr. A. E. Hoerchner, the county physician. These buildings stood the test of the great fire, resisting the flames when other structures, close by, were completely destroyed. Dr. Hoerchner's daughter, Mrs. Patrick Kean, was the first white child born in Mokelumne Hill.

Mokelumne Hill, like all other gold rush towns, had a Town Hall, Masonic Hall, Odd Fellows building, three churches, Engine House, with fire fighting equipment, and being a county seat, a roomy courthouse which was swallowed up by flames in 1864, at which time Calaveras County lost many of its valuable records. Mokelumne Hill's public schools were among the best in the state, one of the first teachers here being Professor James Garvey, a graduate of Yale University. M. Joseph Grand-Chavin of Paris, France, in addition to the day classes, conducted evening classes for the benefit of "ladies" and "family groups" who were desirous of learning to read and write in the French language. The French school had a large attendance and since the population was pre-dominantly French, M. Grand-Chavin's educational venture proved a successful one.

Dr. H. A. M. de Chesne, physician to the French Society of Mokelumne Hill, resided on Main Street, a short distance south of the Congregational Church.

F. Mayer[4], a native of Germany, reached Mokelumne Hill in 1849. At first a miner and later a vineyardist, he used the products of his 17,000 grapevines to make wine. A vintner of experience, the white wine, claret, and angelica that he distilled and distributed were of excellent quality. For long years, Mayer's winery was a jolly, popular and profitable place.

The Hydraulic Water Works of Mokelumne Hill, a concern that supplied water for use in business and dwelling houses, made it an invariable practice to shut-off the water if non-payment extended longer than one month. Samuel Forman was the owner of the water works and H. C. Hamer, the collector who did the dunning.

At Middle Bar, where the first ferrying craft of importance plied the Mokelumne River, lived George Kelton, a native of Grafton, New Hampshire, who arrived in California in 1849. He located at this Bar in 1850 and engaged in the livestock business. Here, at his livestock ranch, within sight of the famous stream, George Kelton and his wife spent their old age, died and were buried.

Mokelumne Hill, with an elevation of 1350 feet above sea level, possesses all the irregularity of streets and buildings that characterize so many of the old mining towns. No person living there at this date can remember when the old town was lighted with "pitch-pine" gas. Even so, Mokelumne Hill isn't just another colorless little ghost town, for it lies in the center of a district, rich in auriferous deposits, valuable fine timber and agricultural land. Round Mokelumne Hill sleep the little brown camps where, in the gold rush days, the Mexicans and Yaqui Indians, when the day's work was done, puffed cigarillos and talked together about the starry-eyed senoritas and of course, of gold.

Charles Smith, known to the miners as "Shanghai Charley," and to the school boys of the Hill simply as "Old Shang", before coming to Mokelumne Hill in 1850 was a sailor man, handy in a dozen different ways. In his humble sphere, Old Shang, fantastically tattooed, was a good and kind mulatto who had countless friends from all walks of life. His generosity, like his willingness to serve, knew no bounds. As a nurse, unfailing in kindness and patience, his services were in constant demand. Versatile, he could sing songs, strum a banjo, spin tall yarns, do a buck and wing, splice ropes, shake a gold pan, send off rounds of black powder and whitewash houses, barns and fences. With equal skill he could plane pine boards for coffins and furniture. Whenever there was an offensive job to handle, one that nobody cared to approach, Old Shang was just the man to send for. For his was a way of doing obnoxious work in the most approved manner. At bedsides, when black smallpox raged in Mokelumne Hill, there was Old Shang ministering to the afflicted. Finally, Shanghai Charley fell a victim to cancer. One day, so as not to trouble his white friends, he put his cabin in order, brought in some rough boards and arranged a bier, bathed and put on his Sunday best clothes, laid himself down upon the bier, swallowed poison, drew a white sheet over his face and died. His friends, unconscious of his malady or his suffering, buried him near the "Tree of the Stranger" in the hillside cemetery in Mokelumne Hill, where tales of his goodness are still afloat.

Pajes, the miser of Mokelumne Hill, who, rather than disturb his golden hoard, preferred to listen to his empty stomach rattle against his ribs. He wore ragged clothes that any respectable Digger Indian would scorn, now lies in an unknown grave, his name forgotten.

The old pioneer, David R. Nye, no longer rides to the "big" town on his "roll-gaited" strawberry roan from his Revere House hotel in Campo Seco. Andre Charreaux, a French-Canadian, who sharpened the miners' picks in Camanche in 1849, does not crunch into Pellaton's store to dicker with its owner for groceries and tobacco. This doesn't mean that their names are not to be found graved deep in white marble, in the hillside cemeteries near which the Mokelumne flows.

The Congregational Church still stands in Mokelumne Hill. This beautiful little white church, built in 1852, by public subscription solicited by Mrs. Fish and other public-spirited women, is still in use. It stands today, as a sort of memorial to the pioneers of this most generous of towns.

In Mokelumne Hill, each Sunday morning, the bell in the steeple of the little white Protestant Church on Main Street, just as in the old days, tolls to call the faithful to worship.

The descendants of Mokelumne Hill pioneers are not without awareness that;

The Protestant Church of Mokelunme Hill (Congregational Church)
Courtesy of Calaveras County Archives

To every generation,
By the handiwork or generosity of their forbears
Something is given in trust.
That the generations to follow
May profit from or
Be aided by it.

Today, Mokelumne Hill's little white church is something more than a place for worship, weddings and funerals; it is a principal, an ideal and a trust.

Footnotes

1 In "Memoirs of a County Judge" J.A. Smith says "Sailor was named Clark"

2 The Odd Fellows Building is still standing in 2005

3 The first floor constructed in 1854. Second story 1874. The Ledger Hotel is still in business in 2005

4 Frederick Mayer, a Bavarian baker from New York, served baked goods from 1851 to 1853. Then he operated The Monitor and developed his fifty-five acre vineyards to start a wine cellar in 1871 that made him one of the richest men in the town. From Romance of Mokelumne Hill by E.S. Zumwalt p. 49

23

THE "WAR" AT FRENCH HILL

Among the immigrants of various nationalities in Mokelumne Hill were a large number of Frenchmen and not the least of who were the Fourcades brothers. In fact, the French colony here was called "Les Fourcades."

Les Fourcades made history for Mokelumne Hill in the spring of 1851. One day a French miner discovered gold at the foot of a hill and revealed the fact to other Frenchmen, but since they believed that gold existed only in canyons and riverbeds, they laughed at him. He let them poke fun and laugh at him as he went quietly about his work. One day he made the mistake of boasting about his good luck to an Irishman who owned the adjoining claim. These miners used the intervening space between their claims to throw waste dirt and rocks. The Irishman was getting an edge of his ground, so French neighbor made a complaint. A quarrel ensued, in which not only harsh words but also blows were being exchanged between the disputants. It was being noised around in Mokelumne Hill that the Frenchman had actually discovered a fabulously rich quartz ledge. Thereafter, an American company crunched off to the scene of the new discovery and in their mad scramble for claims, these miners too, tangled with the boastful Frenchman. Soon the mix-up was general. The Irish miners sided with their countryman. The French backed the discoverer and the Americans looked after each other in the fight that followed.

The French miners hoisted the French standard over Les Fourcades and prepared themselves to defend their property but the unlawful raising of an alien flag gave the Americans an advantage. With bristling gusto they called attention to Count Raousset di Boulbon who, they avowed, was planning to take possession of California and rename it New France. At that time Boulbon was in the Southern Mines assembling French recruits for his filibustering expedition into the State of Sonora, Mexico and his presence in their midst was emphasized by the Americans.

The Frenchmen, armed with muskets, shot guns and revolvers, marched to the rat-a-tat-tat of a drum from Les Fourcades to the Heights of Andres, afterwards called French Hill. Here, at Don Andres Pico's old camping ground, they formed themselves into companies and selected as their captain M. Villacerque. All in readiness, they set the French tri-color afloat and resolutely waited for the enemy to attack.

View of French Hill in Mokeumne Hill. This is the location of the Franco-California skirmish, hardly a war. Note the remains of a stone fort on top.
Courtesy of Calaveras County Historical Society

The Americans and the Irish hunted up and cleaned old rifles and shotguns and made ready to storm the heights. In the meantime the authorities, unable to cope with the situation, sent a messenger to Benicia with a request that the governor send the State Militia to Mokelumne Hill to quell the riot.

The American force, led by a man named Blankenship, marched to the French stronghold and from then on, the day was full of roar. And though the French fought bravely, they were finally obliged to surrender. That day four men were wounded and M. Bourdon, one of the most aggressive of Frenchmen, killed the Irish claim owner who was fighting with the Americans. Unfortunately, while the fight was in progress, marauders taking advantage of the general confusion, after pillaging the tents of the French settlers, set fire to them.

On May 3, 1851, Butler King, Collector of Customs, Colonel Woodleaf, M. de la Riviere, Consular agent of France and Mr. Dillon1 of San Francisco, arrived on the scene. Housed in a tent, American, Irish, and French miners who called for Mr. King soon surrounded them and he, speaking in English, responded with a plea for moderation. M. De le Riviere, who did his level best to calm his excited countrymen, followed Mr. King. An American, on behalf of his comrades, replied thus:

“We have no hostile feeling against the French. We Americans are proven to cuff one another and to even indulge in the exchange of pistol shots occasionally, but things end there. The wounded man carries his complaint to the Alcalde if he does not feel strong enough to obtain justice by his own means. A controversy having arisen between a French miner and another of ourselves, things should have followed the usual course. Instead of that, at the first sign of trouble, all the French hastened to leave their diggings and fully armed, went to camp upon a hill. Much to our regret we were obliged to answer the French aggression. We would rather quarrel with any other people and although once in a while scamps and rascals slip in among us, the bulk of the American miners who are present will endorse what I have just said.”

A Frenchman, in answer, said that the English convicts from Hobart Town and Botany Bay, alone were responsible for the conflict.

That day order was restored, the French flag was pulled down and Frenchmen without opposition took possession of their claims, which were probably the richest in Mokelumne Hill. In the case of Bourdon an exception was made and his claim was confiscated for the benefit of the wounded. In 1854, Bourdon a member of Bourdon’s second filibustering expedition was shot to death in Mexico.

Near the top of French Hill, from the east, the remainder of what now appears to be the foundation of an old stonewall, extending along the edge of a lava bluff, may be seen. All around below, are piles of rock, gravel, tailings and tumbled down banks of lava, is in fact, the evidence of an abandoned placer claim. This spot, the wall and the remains of the fortification built by them to defend their claims were once the property of the French miners of Les Fourcades colony. It was one of the richest spots in the whole of California.

Example of the water worn nuggets found in and around French Hill in Mokelumne Hill.

Photo Wally Motloch

Footnotes

1 Annals of Mokelumne Hill by Emmett P. Joy p.12 "The French Consul, Patrice Dillon was called from San Francisco"

Also, *OLD 'FRENCH HILL'* A Reminiscences of the Franco-California War at Moke Hill, a first person account of events. Calaveras Prospect January 15, 1898

24

PARSON PETE OF POVERTY BAR

Almost a legend now, after ninety years, the Poverty Bar on the Mokelumne river, in spite of its name, was a rich diggings in the come-easy, go-easy days of the gold harvest. Where the hours sped by with bristling gusto, were situated Mike Regan's Good Cheer House, a combination saloon, dance hall, bunkroom, loafing and eating-place. And here, back in the early spring of 1852, Peter Gracey dropped his roll of blankets, straightened his weary shoulders and jerking off his shabby woolen hat, walked up to Mike Regan, to whom with the utmost politeness, he said:

"Sir, what is your lowest rate for gold washers?"

"Polecats?" the tavern keeper spat out tersely.

"By the week?" laughed Peter, showing his strong white teeth.

"Seeing its room and board that you want,
I'll make the price cheap for you,
Say, twenty-five dollars a week,"

Mike, eyeing the stranger approvingly, countered.

"All right! Money down, I suppose, " questioned Peter.

"Betcha boots. Money down.
But, mind you, I offer the first meal free,
That is to those who pay in gold." Mike induced, purringly.

Peter's jaw tightened. He thrusted his hands into his pants pockets and kept his gaze fixed rigidly on the liquor bottles standing back of the bar. He seemed to be listening for a message from back East, where lived his widowed mother and young brothers and sisters in a humble home.

Watching the far-away look on his face, Mike could easily understand why he was one of the most serious minded gold washers that ever dropped a roll of blankets in this wild camp, especially when he laid upon the bar three coins in bright new gold.

"That is a good beginning,"
Mike said as the coins went tattling into the cash drawer.
"Now," said Peter,
"Where's the washroom?"
"You'll find tin basins, roller towels, bar soap, combs and
The hand pump, out-of-doors near the well,"

Mike said, pointing a stubby finger in a westerly direction. A white-coated Chinee boy wearing wooden sabots clattered past Peter, ringing the dinner bell. An instant later, the wild horses that were recently saddle broke, curveted and pranced up to the hitching post in front of the Good Cheer House. Their riders, following the example set by the newcomer, "washed-up" and stood waiting for the second and final tap of the welcoming bell when the dining room door would be thrown open to Mike Regan's odd assortment of guests.

Peter Gracey, lanky-legged, raw-boned, sandy complexioned, slow-eyed and even slower voiced, came somewhat bashfully into the long and narrow lean-to, which since forty-nine, had served as a dining room. Six feet two inches tall, Peter took a slow glance round the room before sitting down at a pine table where miners, gamblers, thimble-trimmers, freighters, muleteers and wagon-show troupers were about to make a devastating assault on "a mess" of corned beef and cabbage. Iron handled knives and forks were rattling against ironstone plates when Peter lowered his steady blue eyes and said in deep and solemn voice:

"Brothers, let us give thanks!"

A sudden hush fell upon the room. Men, with food half lifted to their lips, bent their unshorn heads and listened attentively. Thereafter, Peter Gracey was called "Parson Pete," that is, in Poverty Bar and other out-lying mining camps.

The fun-loving gold washers not only played pranks, but also told jokes at the expense of Parson Pete. Aimed of course to rile his temper, Parson Pete instead of resenting the gibes and pranks, quoted passages from the bible, in secret and in the open.

One morning, at the breakfast table, a Poverty Bar habitual prankster substituted salt for sugar in the ironstone bowl on Parson Pete's table. Having a sweet tooth, the pious fellow helped himself generously, as he supposed it to be sugar. It required but one swallow of bitter saline fluid to cause him to knit his bushy eyebrows together more closely, and then calmly say:

"How long will ye imagine mischief against a man?
Ye shall be slain,
Every last one of you!"

Fearful that Parson Pete intended to do a little killing on his own, a bewhiskered gold washer turned to him and said:

"Which one of us do you intend to slay first, Parson Pete?"

The man from back east stroked his russet sideburns and replied, cryptically:

"The Lord will attend to that in due time!"

A typical Miner and his outfit on the Mokelumne River
Courtesy of Calaveras County Archives

Once the novelty of the camp life wore off, Parson Pete tramped from the "wet" diggings to the "dry" diggings where, at each claim visited, he stood round observing how panning was done. Deciding that he was just as apt to make his pile in Poverty Bar as in any other mining camp, he located a claim, which promptly ran him into hard luck.

Flat broke, he went to work as a ditch-tender. By practicing strictest economy, he managed some how to save the larger part of his earnings. Later, he resumed mining operations. His second venture too blew up, higher than a kite. A group of humorous gold washers got their heads together and figured out a way to help him out of the fix. An ingenious young fellow whose nickname was "Lippy Luke," went to Stockton and procured from a foundry, two pounds of brass filings and a few brass slugs.

It was Tuesday, the last day of the month. All day long, Parson Pete, without hope or plan had shoveled dirt and sand in silence. At sundown he donned his leather boots, black and shiny, and in them crunched back to

Mike Regan's far-famed hostelry, where alone that night, Poverty Bar for him, became an oppressive and terrible place.

"Well, should a hard-working man with a widowed mother and
a whole household of helpless children to support, be allowed to
make a complete failure of his mining activities?"

He asked himself as he tumbled into bed, his faith in prayers badly shaken.

A full moon was silvering the pines when finally, the boys began gathering at Parson Pete's placer claim to commence that mysterious process known to miners the world over, as the "shotgun," or "salting" method. The following morning as Parson Pete, glum as an oyster, began to dig and shovel dirt in his "wet" diggings a dozen or more bearded young gold washers were hovering near but out of sight, to await the outcome. They didn't have to wait long. Parson Pete, after washing a panful of sand, was grinning from ear to ear. At last, with the pan held high in his hands, he gave a loud and joyous shout:

"Land of Goshen!
I've struck a gold pocket!
Struck a rich one, too!"
"Eureka!"

This was enough to bring the boys out from their hiding places.

"Good work!"

"Hurrah for Parson Pete!"

Shouts went ringing along the brush-covered hills as the joshers ran, single file, to congratulate their duped messmate.

"Ain't none of us but what's willing to
Allow that you, sure 'nough struck it rich,"

Piped up Benny Jones.

And, Billy Skaggs, peering over Parson Pete's shoulder into his iron-pan, truthfully said:

"Why, I never seen anything like that,
Since I been a-minin' in this neck-of-the-woods."

That mid-morning Parson Pete took a few ounces of his gold and offered it to a merchant in trade for groceries. Dan Haskell, Poverty Bar's foremost storekeeper, shrewd and wary, ran the filings through his fingers, gingerly. He squinted, reached back of the counter for a bottle of acid, and said:

"Where in the world did you get this stuff, anyway?"

For a brief second a look of complete bafflement over-spread Parson Pete's honest face.

"Mr. Haskell," he questioned in his hushed voice,

"Is there anything wrong with it?"
"No, my boy, nothing at all," replied the storekeeper, regretfully.
"You've got the best lot of brass filings this side of foundry, where these came from."

As the boys, one-by-one, strolled into the store and idly lolled against the counter, Dan Haskell began to understand what had taken place that morning. Even so, he had a serious time trying to convince the lean and lanky Vermonter that claim salting, was only a practical joke, at least in the Mokelumne river district. When the merchant had set the bottle containing acid back on the shelf, Parson Pete, turning a disappointed face towards his tormenters, said in low and quiet voice:
"The wicked plotteth against the just.
Their sword shall enter into their own heart."

There was no laughing now. The joke had suddenly lost its savor. Like the three-ply carpet in the front parlor of the Good Cheer House, its colors were dim and dingy.

That afternoon Parson Pete, a perplexed look on his ruddy face, packed out of the Good Cheer House. Put up a log cabin at the edge of town, in a frugal and lonely way, he started batching by himself in the best way that he knew how to housekeep. The next morning after he had "trashed-up," he went back to his claim to shovel away all the top dirt, still glistening with foundry gold. He was knocking off work for the day when Lippy Luke, feeling somewhat sheepish and remorseful after the part he had taken in the gold-hoax, went to Parson Pete and urged him to join in with him. Together he explained, they could work his "dry" digging, which, in the past had yielded bountifully. He believed it would continue to be, if rightly managed, a good gold producer for long years to come. Anyway, for the time being, it would pay them both very handsomely.

Parson Pete slowly ran his fingers through his mop of reddish hair and replied unperturbedly:
"No, Lippy Luke,
I began mining here and
Here I shall remain until I've got my pile!"
"Gosh dang it all, Parson Pete!
Why you don't even know how to trace the color.
You'll never strike a gold pocket!
You'll starve to death here!"
The contrite gold washer told him in all honesty.
"I shan't either," protested Parson Pete.
"The Lord is my shepherd.
I shall not want,"

He slowly chanted, turning away.
"Yeah!" grunted Lippy Luke, stalking off down the trail.

Parson Pete, with physical strength equal to his determination, kept right on working his claim for three long weeks without finding a single speck of gold. Finally, he began taking in his leather belt. His food and funds were now utterly exhausted; nevertheless, he toiled on from sun-up until sundown.

In the meantime, a wave of pity, perhaps remorse, swept through each jokers heart. Lippy Luke stung by the gaunt shouldered serious-faced Parson Pete, hastened to Haskell's store and purchased a large supply of groceries, including such delicacies as fresh eggs, maple syrup, white flour, sweet butter, sugar-cured ham and had them carted to Parson Pete's cabin as a surprise. Bearing a box of tea direct from China, Lippy Luke with his peace offering, went whistling to the cabin nestled in a pine grove. There, he found Parson Pete, he found him with both hands chockfull of the yellow metal!

"Well, gol darn my hide if I'm a-seein' wrong,"
Yelled Lippy Luke, tossing his old woolen cap high in the air.
"But, you're not seeing one half of it," Parson Pete told him.
"Why, Lippy Luke," he added serenely,
"I actually struck a rich pay shoot.
You see, those brass fillings edged me on until,
At last, I reached the simon-pure metal."
"Yeah!" retorted Lippy Luke, winking a baffled eye.

"Us boys planted them clean down to bedrock.
That's where gold lies in these diggings."
"Gold is where you find it!"
replied Parson Pete, turning his blue eyes skyward.
"Yeah! Of course!" said Lippy Luke,

handing Parson Pete the gaily-painted box filled with choice tea.

Parson Pete's gold pocket was no mere flash in the pan. He cleaned up in excess of $50,000 after which, he decided to shake the dust of the famous river diggings off his boots and return by way of Cape Horn to help his folks back East.

His parting benediction has been lost in the misty annals of Time,

However his "Lord will provide" system,

Is still serving those gold washers who, at the present time, are digging for the precious metal in and around the historic Poverty Bar.

25

POVERTY BAR

Poverty Bar, [now under the waters of Camanche Reservoir] on the south bank of the Mokelumne, a short distance from Lancha Plana, was a great old place in the days of gold. It was no touch-and-go settlement, either. Its active life was of long duration. At this river bar in 1849, Yankees and Southerners, together with men from all four corners of the world swung picks and shovels, feverishly excited.

A. Luffton, a former lieutenant in the United States Army, came mule-back to Poverty Bar early in 1849. A noisy braggart, ever ready to avenge some imaginary wrong, the sobriquet "Squawman" was soon tacked on him and not without good reason. Luffton, at the least of provocation, unsheathed his Bowie knife, flourished it and then put it back in its scabbard without bloodstain. Usually, the miners took his display of anger or valor, for what it was worth. But, one day, when Luffton held his prowess in too high esteem, he was plastered from head to heel with white flour dough. Angry as a hornet, he ran cursing, down Main Street with the boisterous laughter of pranksters in his ears muffled with dough. Thereafter, loud-mouthed Luffton kept his blade sheathed and talked less about the "Code" and the dueling pistols.

General Stedman, an engineer, who in his native state, had helped to build the Ohio Canal, was employed by the Oregon Bar Mining Company to construct a dam to turn the Mokelumne River as all previous efforts to accomplish this task having failed. Stedman, aided by a competent gang of workmen, build log pens, 12 feet square and floated them down stream to the desired location, where the pens were filled with rocks causing them to sink. After timbers, brush and gravel were heaped on them. The dam when finished gave proof of this engineer's skill and enabled the Oregon Bar Company to operate their gravel claims profitably.

An odd character, Stedman, left the river each evening wearing sopping wet drugged jeans. Barefoot he went to his cabin in Poverty Bar where he spent his evenings playing chess with William and Allen Dudley and other cronies. Stedman, in the manipulation of chessmen was without a peer at Poverty Bar. General Stedman, the first engineer to successfully dam the Mokelumne River was long remembered, not only by devotees of chess, but by those men who had worked under his direction and by the miners there.

Composed entirely of Southerners, the Oregon Bar Company had brought to California in 1850, a large number of Negro slaves, presumably freedom bent. At this time the Mokelumne River miners were hard set against the introduction of slave labor in the mining camps and towns. To this objection, rather than to any moral principle, they owed the prohibitive clause in their constitution.

One day the manager of the Oregon Bar Company sent a dozen Negroes out to round up and return some horses and mules belonging to the company. They were to tether the animals close to the company's encampment. Once the boss' back was turned, the Negroes being swift runners made a dash for liberty and were never seen again.

K. Koon, President of this mining company, made efforts to organize a party of miners to go after the runaways, but not a single gold washer there responded to his appeal.

Newspapers, grown yellow with age, tell us that many famous theatrical troupes, while touring the Southern Mines, played engagements in Poverty Bar's little wooden theatre. They also tell us that this river bar, although a pleasure-loving settlement, leaned towards culture as well as gold.

At Poverty Bar, the yellow dust lay in heaps on card tables and drinking bars were enticing. Each Saturday night a brass band blared and a quartet of Mexican guitarists regaled the visiting miner. At Poverty Bar where the whiskey flowed quite as freely as water, nothing remains, nothing at all.

Prospector at North Branch, Dragomanovich Store in the background.

Courtesy of Calaveras County Archives

26

POVERTY BAR AND ITS SISTER CAMPS

Penn Mine foot bridge across Mokelumne river near Campo Seco.
Courtesy of Calaveras County Historical Society

WINTER'S BAR

A short distance east of Poverty Bar was Winter's Bar, whose founder William Winter reached the Mokelumne River in 1848. A "wet" diggings of the first order, it soon became a hilarious camp with a large population. Due to the richness of the gravel found here, it drew to itself some ambitious gold washers but mostly, it was a rendezvous for gamblers and their "ladies" who lived by the law of chance.

Winter's Bar, like other river diggings, had its full share of "coolie" miners, merchants, and vegetable peddlers. Indeed, the Chinese in this settlement erected and supported a Chinese Theatre employing eight or more actors who had been trained for the boards in the Old Cathay [China].

The early history of Winter's Bar was never recorded. Newspapers printed an item now and then about some unimportant local happening at these once important and prosperous "wet" diggings.

CAMP OPERA

1849 diggings, it probably received its name because of the nightly serenades of the Mexican settlers' burros. At Camp Opera[1] in 1850, a large group of Mexicans were encamped. With horn spoons and wooden bateas the senors and senoras alike mined the gulches and the flats.

Lacking sufficient water for mining purposes the population soon dwindled to the ghost camp stage, but in 1852, when the Lancaster Ditch Company brought in an abundance of water, several hundred people flocked to the place. Reckless and wide open, Camp Opera was a hangout for horse thieves, cutthroats and other lawless men. After committing crimes, they came to this camp to gamble, get drunk, whoop, shoot glassware to smithereens and otherwise have a general rough and tumble time for themselves.

Ike Mansfield and his partner Kemp established Camp Opera's first trading post. Trader Kemp came to a bad end. One day, miners found him stealing a gold specimen, and promptly strung him up to a limb of a tree. Before life was extinct however, his executioners relenting lowered his body and cut the rope from around his neck. Then, on the condition he leaves California forever, he was ordered to leave the camp.

Patrick Sculley too, operated a trading post here. At the time of his arrival the miners were shoveling dirt upon the riverbank for winter washing. The season of 1852 was a dry one and since a goodly supply of gravel could not be washed without water, the miners soon fell upon bad days. Many a man, flat broke, was grubstaked by Pat Sculley. Winter came rainless. Depressed, the miners moved onward to other diggings. Sculley remained and took for remuneration, the piles of dirt which, when washed, proved poor compensation for his valuable stock of merchandise.

At the edge of Camp Opera was a small graveyard wherein, in humble graves, were rude pine coffins containing the bodies of self-indulgent young men who, it is said, had fallen victims to strong drink.

The ground here was rich in spots, however the coarse gold was found in the gravel underlying a coal formation. In many places an over wash had swept the gold towards the valley, out of range of the miners. Of the many rock chimneys, of log and shake cabins once to be seen at Camp Opera not one remains to give hint of the skill of their builders.

FRENCH CAMP

Two miles south of Camp Opera, French Camp derived its name from a party of Frenchmen who mined here in 1849. The gravel beds, rich and extensive, drew to this locality besides miners, traders, a doctor or two, gamblers and a few women of loose morals. Then, as now, but few camps were without gambling dens and bawdy houses. The Chileans and Mexicans in 1850 found coarse gold in the ore veins threading the near-by hills.

In 1853 French Camp was over-filled with Yaqui Indians, a large number having arrived from Mexico that year. Despite Yaqui's savage appearance, he was given to sociability. These Mexican Indians with piercing eyes and coal black hair were soon on friendly terms with their French neighbors. At evening, the Yaqui Indians, wrapped in bright blue blankets, went contentedly to the different saloons where they watched with curious jet black eyes their dust and chispas flow into the pokes of sharp trick gamblers. Joseph Septon, in 1852, traced the gravel flow to a range of hills and found under them many rich deposits. In one of which, in less than a week, he extracted $10,000 worth of the yellow metal. French Camp's days of gold are all in the past. Its site is still there, but its flimsy buildings vanished from the landscape as early as 1855.

PUT'S BAR

This river bar was found to contain gold by a man named Putman, a forty-niner. A year later several hundred miners, including a few Chinese, were encamped here. No rich strikes were made at this point of the stream. Put's[2], seemingly, was never anything better than a "wage" claim proposition. The ground, lacking in "color" proved excellent for the cultivation of melons and vegetables. The "Old man" Borden came early to Put's Bar and on July 4th, 1852, toted a large watermelon, grown at his little ranch to a trading post and sold it to the trader for a high price. The "river melons," at Borden's ranch, ripening earlier than those grown in the Ione Valley, soon monopolized the market.

CATT CAMP

First called Haightville and later Frankfort, Catt Camp[3] in 1851, gave promise of becoming a permanent town with a large population. John A. Lyon, John W. MacKay, and Jackson McNabb were mining here in 1852, but their claims were no great shakes. MacKay, having ambitions to satisfy, shook the gravel off his boots and went questing for something better. He crunched to a flat, which, say the records, was extremely rich, and the spot on which he located............

Town of Campo Seco. In addition to gold, copper was discovered here in 1853.
Courtesy of Calaveras County Historical Society

CAMPO SECO

A dry diggings, a few miles northeast of Valley Springs, Campo Seco was founded in 1848 by Esteban Naides of Lima, Peru. At first, the American miners called this campo Turnersville, but the name refused to stick. The settlers, predominately Hispanic Americans, finding the new name a tongue twister held doggedly to the old appellation. Prospector Blanchard, a native of France, established a trading post in this dry camp in 1850. A year later his customers, for the most part were Mexicans and Yaqui Indians who, in droves had flocked to this region to gather gold. Campo Seco had its full measure of gold. But not until sufficient water had been brought in to wash the placers did it become a first rate town. The water, taken from the Calaveras River, near Double Springs, kept the diggings at Campo Seco, Chile Campo and Red Hill running on an even keel.

When, in 1852, the first child of American parents was born in Campo Seco, each gold washer there did his level best to outdo his neighbor in generosity. Gold nuggets, in profusion were showered upon baby Jack Yarrow, named in honor of his father's mining partner, John (Jack) Branscom.

Campo Seco's streets and lanes in December, 1852 were rocky, muddy and seldom printed by the little feet of children. That year, few children of American parentage were to be seen there. One of these was a fair-haired little girl, laughing happily and playing with her rag doll. She was sitting outdoors in the winter sunshine, in front of her parents' tent, when without warning; a Spanish bull charged down upon her and gored her to death.

Mokelumne-Campo Seco Canal Mining Co. Certificate 1861.

Courtesy of Judy and Frank Brockman

Campo Seco had its full quota of saloons, gamblers, prostitutes, fandangos and hurdy-gurdy dance halls. It boasted four stone buildings with iron shutters and doors. In the town were four hotels, one of which was David Nye's famous Revere House and Charles Hopkins' popular hostelry, a town hall, a church, public schoolhouse, blacksmith shops, livery stables and the usual number of dwelling and business houses. Early in the month of August 1854, this town was almost totally destroyed by fire. The blaze at this time laid low about $107,000 worth of property.

David B. Nye, born and reared in Massachusetts, came early to California. A lover of plant life, in 1849 he poked a few cork tree seeds from Spain into Campo Seco's ground. The seeds sprung up, thrived and although slow to grow, in time became beautiful and interesting trees. Today in Campo Seco, these same cork trees attract attention, for they are probably the only ones growing in California[4].

Dr. Marcel, at an early date established Campo Seco's first hospital. James Creighton was the first American there to engage on a large scale in the livestock industry. His ranch close to Campo Seco was productive, producing besides cattle and sheep, hay and barley.

In 1852 Hiram Ashley Messenger, born in Peru, Berkshire County, Massachusetts started for California in his twentieth year. In St. Joseph, Missouri, he paid seventy-five dollars for the privilege of traveling through the Indian Country with a party of emigrants. When the wagon train reached

Jim Bridger's bullet riddled fort at Green River, he decided to abandon his companions for an opportunity of making a trip to Fort Hall, a British Fur Trading Station two hundred miles distant, with "Old Bill" Williams, a free trapper. By this route the young Messenger hoped to eventually reach the Oregon Country. After a week's travel with this highly eccentric mountain man at whose belt hung dangling a large number of Indian scalps, Hiram had enough, so they parted. Other trappers like California Joe, Jim Bridger, Jim Beckworth and Kit Carson were intensely jealous of Old Bill for so vauntingly displaying his trophies. Later Hiram drove an ox team for a concern engaged in hauling freight between St. Joseph and Salt Lake City. "Cattle punching" was not to this New Englander's liking so he again directed his footsteps in a westerly way and finally reached the summit of the Sierra Nevada Mountains in the fall of 1853. Westward, far below their snowy crests lay Yuba Valley. Hiram, descending to the plain, washed the sands of the Yuba River for several months successfully. The spring of 1854 found him in Lathrop, where he remained for several days to rest his travel weary and blistered feet.

Capt. Hiram Messenger.
Courtesy of C.C.H.S.

Lured by tales of Mokelumne Hill, a few weeks later he moved onwards to that astonishing place. Here he found employment with the water company. The following winter he mined near Jesus Maria but gold was less plentiful than formerly, so he again went to work for the water company.

A party of Campo Seco miners, in 1853 stumbled upon a copper vein[5], but preferring gold rather than copper they did not file on it. So it was, not until Hiram A. Messenger in 1860 discovered possibly this same copper vein and commenced development work on it that Campo Seco gained prominence for the production of copper ore.

Messenger of Revolutionary War ancestry, sold his valuable copper interests in 1863 and at his own expense, organized a military company of which he himself was the Captain. Wm. A. Broad, first Lieutenant and Wm. L. Innes, second. His organization, known as Company E. Seventh Regiment of Infantry, California Volunteers, left Campo Seco for Arizona to wage a war against the Apache Indians. The organization comprising of Calaveras County pioneers, in June 1866, were mustered out of service at the Presidio in San Francisco.

Campo Seco Ball.

THE PLEASURE OF YOUR COMPANY IS RESPECTFULLY SOLICITED AT A

Cotillon Party,

TO BE GIVEN AT THE *PHŒNIX HOTEL*, IN CAMPO SECO, BY ARNOLD, WHITING & CO., ON THE 22D OF DECEMBER, 1854.

Invitation to Cotillon Party at Campo Seco, December 22, 1854

Courtesy of Calaveras County Archives

Returning to Campo Seco, Captain Messenger in partnership with W. C. Whetstone purchased the Cosgrove Ranch. It comprised of 1000 acres and was located between Valley Springs and Campo Seco. In the midst of fertile fields, orchards and vineyards, stands Hiram Messenger's old ranch house called the Casa Blanca. There he and his wife Harriet lived out their long and useful lives.

CAMANCHE

A boomtown of gold rush days, Camanche[6] was never as fierce as its name implies. Named for Captain Samuel W. Quay, formerly of Lynchburg, Virginia. He mined here in 1849 and was dubbed by miners "Scalp'em, Sam," and his nickname may account for the name Camanche.

John A. Lyons erected the town's first frame hotel and saloon. Martin Duffy established a trading post, which soon developed into a general merchandise store. Built by Martin Duffy, the Orleans Hotel was the first two story stone building to grace the town.

John Story, a Camanche claim owner, had his sluice boxes robbed time and again. To stop the unlawful practice he loaded his gun with buckshot and adjusted it so that one walking close to the sluices would discharge it.

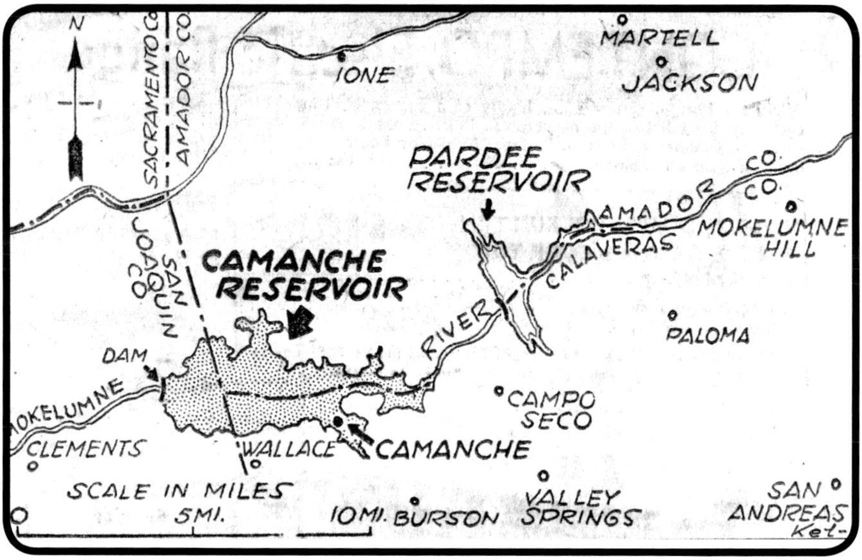

Map of Camanche and Pardee Reservoirs. Part of a newspaper clipping in Emmett Joy Scrapbook.

Courtesy of Calaveras County Archives

Only recently, Story had discharged his Chinese foreman. Shortly after the fortification of his long toms, Story wasn't a bit surprised when the boy was lying close to the gun, a dead Chinee boy, in one yellowish hand a lantern and in the other, the tools necessary for a "clean-up."

Camanche was once visited by a tornado of intense velocity and came near having its Roman Catholic Church demolished along with several others of its pioneer buildings.

Full of hope and courage were the pioneers who laid the foundation on which Camanche arose and prospered.

In Camanche no paneless window and sagging doors are to be seen. True, the pioneers are no longer there, but their descendents in several instances are in Camanche, carrying on successfully. An orderly, well-organized 1849 mining town, Camanche's record for good behavior gives written testimony to the worth of its first settlers.

LA PALOMA (THE DOVE)

Dr. Hugh H. Toland, a native of South Carolina, was tenting in Paloma in 1850. One day, with gold his objective, he followed a little gulch to its head. In his wanderings along the gulch, which soon became widely known as Lower Rich Gulch, he found a quartz vein worthy, he thought, of devel-

View of the town of Camanche before it disappeared under the waters of Camanche Reservoir in 1964. Built by East Bay Municipal District to supply Calaveras water to San Francisco Bay area homes.

Courtesy of Calaveras County Historical Society

opment. Dr. Toland's hard rock mine, from the grass roots to its lowest level, yielded gold bearing quartz rock in large quantities. His pile made, Dr. Toland disposed of his valuable property to U. S. Senator William M. Gwin of San Francisco, for a tidy sum of money. Under the new ownership the mine was developed both "up top" and "down under." Dr. Toland's discovery, for many long years, proved beneficial to Calaveras County. Once Senator Gwin was in command at this mine, Dr. Toland went to San Francisco in which city he founded the Toland Medical College, known today as the Stanford Medical School.

Dr. Hugh Toland, founder of the Stanford Medical School.

Courtesy of C.C.H.S.

In the old days, when 40 iron stamps were crushing rich rock at the Gwin mine, Paloma was a fun loving, sports minded place, for this we have Lareado Briseno's word. Lareado, whose nickname was "Let'er go Charley," worked as a "single jack" miner for several years in 'Duke de Gwin's' deep diggings. A few years back, Briseno, in his cabin between Macroni Flat and Dogtown, related to this writer a few tall tales about Paloma when it supported a racetrack. Jockey Club members, Robert Redmond and George E. Wesson and a few other lovers of horses promoted this racetrack. Wesson's fine racehorse, "Fandango Jack," lauded "Let'er go Charley" was usually first to come thundering down the home stretch, to victory.

View of Lower Rich Gulch and the Gwin Mine near Poloma, circa 1900
Courtesy of Calaveras County Historical Society

Now at Paloma there are no miners to be seen, no miners are eating cold lunches out of tin buckets to the tune of banter and good cheer. Paloma, of the gracious name, was renamed Fosteria after work at the mines was suspended some 25 years ago. Ideally situated, Dr. Toland's old campsite is frequently visited by vacationers.

ELLINGWOOD'S RANCH

This ranch, a few miles west of San Andreas, was the property of Ezra A. Ellingwood, a native of Beverly, Massachusetts. In 1849, Ezra Ellingwood, Captain Thomas Remmonds, George Whitmarsh and others formed a partnership, raised money between them and in Boston, purchased the bark called "San Francisco". This vessel was provisioned for two years' voyage for California. Besides forty passengers and the crew, the bark carried some twenty hogs, a cow, kitten, 6300 feet of planed boards, 10,000 bricks and the frames for eight wooden houses. Isaac Barker, a writer and artist, who was one of the Argonauts, while sailing to the new El Dorado, kept track of each day's happenings. The following is from a page of his sea journal:

"Wednesday morning, August 15, 1849. This morning commences

Close-up of the Gwin Mine near Poloma, circa 1906
Asa Gourley photo courtesy of Wally Motloch

with clear, beautiful weather and a fine breeze from the northwest. All the population of Beverly stirring and the streets alive with males and females, boys and girls, old and young, with ears extended and eyes sticking out a foot, they are all wending their way down Cabot Street, through Ice Alley, as if for a wager, towards Foster & Lovett's wharf to see our departure for California. Half past eight, cast off hauser and we started, exchanging cheers upon cheers with the broken-hearted shore men and women, who vainly endeavored to cheer loudly in reply and followed us disconsolately along the beach. Wind hauling to the north'd braced sharp up, and shaved off the corner of Beverly Bar, then hove to and called the role. At half past nine discharged the pilot and here we are. Goodbye Old Beverly! God bless you women at any rate!"

Ezra Ellingwood in 1850 straddled a mule in Stockton and rode to a spot near Lattimerville, his inevitable home. He took a turn at mining, but preferring a plow to a "long tom," he became a rancher. A breeder of livestock, Ezra Ellingwood represented a class of young men who had willingly left comfortable homes to help found a new empire in the Far West. A few years after the death of his friend and neighbor, George Vogelsang of Petersburg, he married his widow Dorothea, whose oldest son, Charles Vogelsang, was for many years one of California's Fish and Game Commissioners. Her younger son became an admiral in the U. S. Navy. Ezra and Dorothea Ellingwood, after living long and useful lives, died at their ranch house on the north branch of the Calaveras River and were buried in the People's Cemetery in San Andreas.

Senator William McKendree Gwin.
Courtesy of C.C.H.S.

MEDINA'S CAMP

Francisco P. Medina, a native of Peru, founded this camp in 1848. It was located between Latimerville and Double Springs. Medina's wayside tavern and trading post was a famous stopping place in its day. A "wet" diggings located on the old river road, which ran between the mines and Stockton. Its first gold hunters were Henry W. Dunning, Jay Smith Sublette, Herman Bode, James Cole, William (Pony) Denig, Peter Featherstone, Thomas Stevenson, Elijah Root, and Paul Desiren Dominque.

J. Frank Washburn, a native of Hancock, N. H., after an unsuccessful try at mining at San Antonio Camp, located in Medina's Camp in 1851. Here, near the wooden bridge, he established a butcher shop. In 1856, Washburn sold his meat business to P. H. McGurk, an Irishman, who was the custodian of the bridge that spanned the north branch of the river.

Medina, a few years later, opened a second store on the River Road, near Fanning's bridge and here; his place of business became the nightly gathering place for his neighbors. One evening, in the late 'sixties, after all except three men had returned from the store to their homes, people who lived close by were awakened by the barking of pistols and the sound of shuffling boots, indicative of a struggle.

Hastening outdoors, Medina's neighbors went to his store to find the door locked and since there was no answer to their knock, they battered it down. They entered the room, only to find it vacant but the floor was drenched with blood. A search revealed the bodies of five men, among whom was Francisco Medina. With pockets rifled and hands tied, each one had been shot through the head. Their bodies were dragged to a shallow gulch into which they were pitched headlong, one on top of the other. At this time both Tomas Rodundo (Procopio) and Tiburcio Vasquez were serving sentences in the state penitentiary, so Juan Soto, who had made it possible for banditry to continue in California without interruption, was suspected of being the leader of the gang that had turned Medina's peaceful store into a human slaughterhouse. Besides Medina those who lost their lives were Francisco Lastraella, Rosario Rodriguez, Pablo Sorreto and Henry Woodson, the latter was a Negro.

PETERSBURG

Located on the North Branch of the Calaveras River, a short distance from its junction with the main stream, Petersburg[7] was also on the road to Stockton. Charles G. Lake, a forty-niner, who was washing gold here in 1853, wrote:

Courtesy of Calaveras County Archives.

"The diggings around here have always been considered good, from $5 to $6 per hand is the average. Golden Hill is about a mile from here and the claims on it are very rich, eighteen ounces having been taken out of one cart load of dirt. The dirt, to be washed, has to be carted some distance but since Captain Pope is about to bring water onto the hill from his Willow Creek ditch, this necessity will soon be obviated. Our camp has exhibited a novel feature, of not having for the past month, a single person who has not been employed. Building is going on rapidly and permanent improvements are being made every day."

Petersburg, in the midst of alluring scenery, it is now a grazing ground for sheep and cattle. An old and picturesque adobe stands near the south bank of the river. The handiwork of Javier Salcido, a native of Mexico, is all that remains at this historic settlement, which once formed a part of the great Estanislao Rancheria.

GREASERTOWN

Greasertown[8], a short distance from Petersburg, was first called the "Merciful Camp," a name it well deserved, for its campfires once warmed a homeless, hungry, and perplexed horde of poverty stricken Mexicans, who after what was termed the "Rancheria murders" were expelled. The Rancheria murders were committed in August, 1855 at Lower Rancheria, the citizens of Amador County, by reason of the brutal slaying of so many innocent people, expelled all Mexicans from within the boundaries of their county. Men, women and children on foot, were herded to the Mokelumne River, dividing Calaveras from Amador County, where the unfortunate ones were left to shift for themselves. The people of Calaveras County, realizing their great extremity, permitted the exiles to establish a camp that ever since then has been known a Greasertown. Here, the Mexicans lived in peace and contentment with their American neighbors.

GOLDEN GATE RANCH

Beyond Lattimerville, in a northeasterly direction, was the Golden Gate Ranch, a relay station for stages running between Stockton and Mokelumne Hill. One of the best known and most popular of the many wayside taverns along the river road, it was owned and conducted by Lewis Schrack and his wife Susan.

In Paris, Texas on May 6, 1849, Lewis Schrack married Miss Susan Holman and together they started across the desert for California. Autumn came to find them in Vallejo, building a hotel in which, that year they entertained some of the members of the State Legislature. Lewis, becoming afflicted with the gold fever, followed a burro from Vallejo to the mining region with the packsaddle loaded with a gold washer's fixin's. On August 25, 1851, he encamped on a spot where afterwards arose his ranch house. Government land, he at once made application for 160 acres. There was no water, so he dug a well and pitched a tent, which after Susan's arrival at the ranch became a wayside inn.

Susan Schrack, blonde and beautiful, experienced all the hardships of frontier life. At Golden Gate Ranch, the tent she called home had canvas flaps for windows and a dirt floor that, in the rainy season, became damp and muddy. But in spite of the dampness, Susan stood, her shoes sopping wet, kneading loaves of bread and preparing food. Meals not only for her family but for teamsters, stage drivers and their passengers, miners, horsemen and footmen who might chance that way. After the erection of a frame house, a gentlewoman Susan Schrack, felt pine boards under her feet and panes of

Mrs. Susan Schrack.

Courtesy of Calaveras Archives

glass replaced the canvas tent flaps.

In 1851-1852, Joaquin Murieta and his robbers had a cave or a "hide-out" on the side of Golden Gate Peak, close to Schrack's stage station. The Mexican Chief, Murieta and a few of his favorite lieutenants frequently stopped at Schrack's for a "square meal" and whenever the bandits appeared on the scene, the kitchen help fled in terror, leaving Susan alone to prepare their food. The meal finished, Murieta invariably refused to accept any change from the gold slug he laid upon the table.

Lewis Schrack, while returning home from San Andreas one night in February 1853, was stopped on the trail by Murieta, who with drawn revolver demanded an explanation of his movements. Surprised, Lewis uttered the

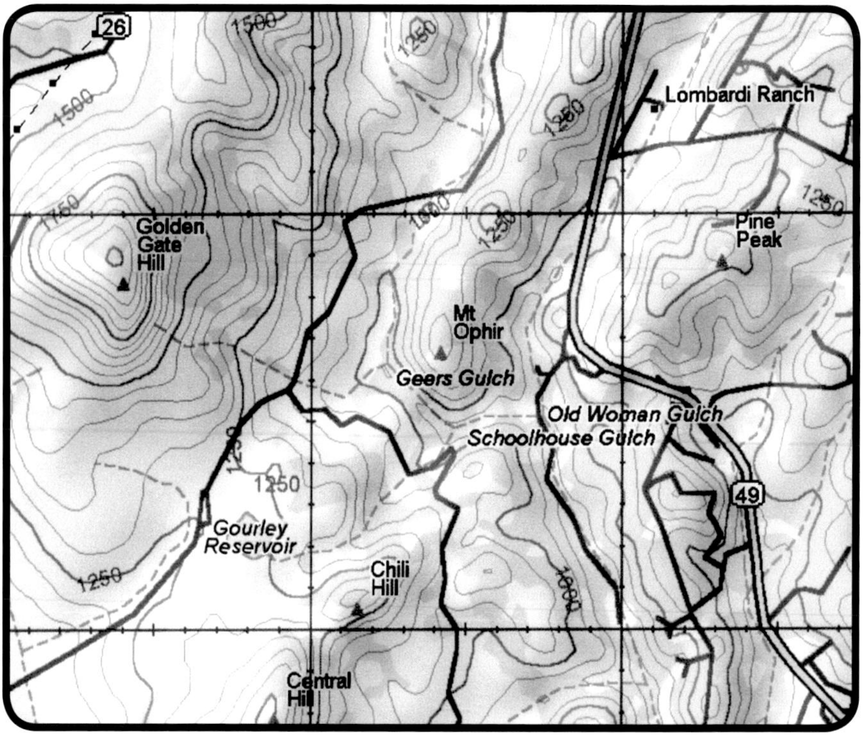

Detail of map showing the Golden Gate Hill and the Gourley Reservoir at the base of it.

Map U.S.G.S. Topo 7.5

single word "amigo". The outlaw, dismounting, expressed regret and offered the rancher a purse filled with gold and at the same time, he ordered his men to doff their sombreros to Lewis whom he called "mi amigo." Mr. Schrack declined the gold with thanks thinking that, he was lucky to have been halted by Joaquin rather than Manuel Garcia (Jack-of-the-terrible hand).

One day while Lewis was in Peek's store in Mokelumne Hill he was asked by Samuel Pearsall, a pioneer of the Hill, if he believed that the California Rangers had shot and killed Joaquin Murieta. "No," he replied with conviction, "Joaquin is living peacefully on a large ranch in the State of Sonora, Mexico, over which graze his fifty California ponies."

Lewis Schrack, born in Norristown, Pennsylvania, was educated in Philadelphia. A man of much talent, he was capable of filling any position in life. He spoke several different languages fluently. For many years he represented Calaveras County in the Lower House and left the imprint of his individuality upon the State Legislature. At one period of his career, Mr. Schrack published the San Francisco newspaper "Call" and wrote a history of Calaveras County. Lewis Schrack died at Golden Gate Ranch on February 7, 1883.

GOLDEN GATE PEAK

This symmetrical peak stands alone on the old trail that led from San Andreas to Golden Gate Ranch and furnishes beauty to the surrounding landscape. It was extensively mined in 1850, however it yielded but little gold to the prospectors. Among the miners were, Javier Salcido, Michael D. McNoble, Major James Gorman, Henry Van Bibber, W. S. Coolidge, R. Emerson, Joseph Sunderland, Columbus C. Lake, F. Dana, A. Goodhue, William Waters, James R. McKinney, John Donnallan and Peter Davis. In this locality an occasional adobe wall crumbling and desolate, is to be seen and that is all.

VALLEY SPRINGS

Valley Springs, situated in beautiful open country, though no gold harvest was ever reaped here nevertheless was a bustling town when mule trains, freighters and stages traveled between Stockton and the various mining towns and camps. It was not regarded in the light of a town, until the coming of the narrow gauge railroad. A town site of eighteen blocks, each surrounded with black walnut trees was laid out.

George Late sailed around the Horn in the bark "Kirkland" and reached San Francisco on August 22, 1849. A short time later we find him encamped at Valley Springs and conducting a trading post. In 1853, he returned to the East and married Miss Rebecca C. Shafer. A few months later they embarked, by way of Panama for California. Upon their arrival in the Golden State, Mr. Late and his bride took up residence in Valley Springs. Here, in the gently sloping hill country, this couple established a home. Their lovely house, built of squared sandstone surrounded by oleanders, fig and orange trees, is still serving. Mr. and Mrs. Late are no longer there but the roses, honeysuckle and other climbers they have planted still twine tendrils around the window frames and doors of their old home.

At Stone Corral, on the river road that led from Stockton by way of Linden and Valley Springs, was the Red House, a wayside tavern, where the drivers of the jerk line teams of Chicard & Company of Stockton, and those of Andrews & Cadwallader of Mokelumne Hill, halted for a night's rest and food. The old roadhouse no longer stands under the oak trees but its stone corral is still intact, the habitation of ground squirrels and lizards.

The Pleasant Valley House, beyond Stone Corral, on the road to Jenny Lind was a two-story frame building. It fell victim to flames that totally destroyed it. The North America House, a relay station where travelers refreshed themselves and in double quick time the fagged stage horses were replaced with fresh ones was between Jenny Lind and Valley Springs

George Late home in Valley Springs.
Courtesy of Calaveras County Historical Society

The Tremont House, built of lumber brought around the Horn, was on the river road about one and one-quarter mile southwest of the North America House. Between Valley Springs and San Andreas, near Mountain Gate, stood the Spring Valley House, a two-story frame building. The barns and corrals at this roadside stopping place provided for teamsters, horsemen, footmen, stage drivers and their passengers, quite the best to be found along this seventy-mile route.

A THUMBNAIL SKETCH OF VALLEY SPRINGS

[This article was authored by Mrs. Buckbee April 22, 1935 it appeared in Las Calaveras January 1996]

Situated in a beautiful valley at the edge of the limestone belt, Valley Springs, although as mall place, has always been an active one. In 1884, this town, throwing off its swadding clothes, moved westward to meet the railroad, and in the going, Antone Sheaton, a house mover, was killed.

In the shade of the oaks in the old days, mule trains, freighters, stages on their way from Stockton to the town and camps of the foothills, halted for the night in Valley Springs. The settlement at that date was not regarded as a town, its serenity was not disturbed until 1884, when the iron horse came whistling up the narrow guage railroad track, to the amazement of the countryside. That year a town-site of 18 blocks, each surrounded by walnut

Valley Springs Carriage Factory and Blacksmith shop built at the time the rail road reached the town in 1885. From the left, Mr. Smith who kept a stable next door, Harvey Smith, Propietor, R. Marsh workman and John Brown, blacksmith.

Courtesy of Calaveras County Historical Society

trees, was laid out and many attractive building were erected.

George Late rounded Cape Horn on the bark Kirkland and reached San Francisco on August 22, 1849. He possible was Valley Springs' first permanent settler. Miss Rebecca C. Shafer was "the girl he left behind" so in 1853 he returned to the East and on February 14, 1854 married her.

The youthful couple returned to California via the Panama route and arrived in Valley Springs the following August. Their house of limestone, quarried from a hill near town, served the Lates for many years and remains in an excellent state of preservation, although no family members still live there to enjoy the roses and other climbers that twine around window frames and doorways.

John Doak, a pioneer of 1847, located at Lunch Hill, near Valley Springs and lumber not being available he erected a canvas hotel large enough to accommodate 100 persons. Doak had the huge canvas house made in Chicago and shipped around Cape Horn to California.

Narrow guage engine of the San Joaquin and Sierra Nevada Railway on the turntable at Valley Springs in 1885.
Courtesy of Calaveras County Historical Society

The two Lillie brothers reached this place in the spring of 1850 and opened a blacksmith shop, the elder brother, an expert farrier, reportedly shod Joaquin's buckskin stallion and received not only gold but the Mexican bandit's praise for his skillful and rapid work.

Bernardo Reyna, a native of Mexico, reached Stockton September 30, 1849 and a few days later left for Valley Springs. Ramona, his daughter, married Guadalupe Celaya and they became highly respected residents. Their son, Nativo Celaya, was born and reared in Valley Springs.

Mareclino Granados born on the Calaveras River near the historic adobe of the Rancheria del Rio Estanislao, now under water, is Valley Springs' oldest citizen. His brother Lincoln, the towns butcher is his neighbor and both remember many of the old guard of Calaveras County.

They remember when Miss. Maggie McAllen of San Andreas taught the local school and when Dr. Marsh of Burson, close by, tied his chestnut sorrel mare to the hitching post near the wooded watering trough in front of Purdy's Valley Springs Hotel. A small town in the flush days, Valley Springs had saloons aplenty. Thomas J. French and F.I. Johnson were the first merchants, when it boasted a Protestant church, schoolhouse, town hall, hotel and several dwellings.

Frank Pattee, while still a boy peddled meat in the town and its immediate vicinity. Soon as an accommodation to his customers, he was carrying more groceries from Tom French's store than he was meat from the Pattee Ranch. John Pattee his eldest brother, noting this, concluded that a general merchandising business might prove more profitable that stock

Waiting for the train at Valley Springs Depot, circa 1885.
Courtesy of Calaveras County Historical Society

raising. A short time later under the banner of Pattee Brothers, John, Joseph and Frank Pattee opened a store in Valley Springs, where for many years they conducted one of the most profitable businesses in Southern Mines.

During the early days Valley Springs received water from the Mokelumne Hill Canal Company and when water no longer flowed through that concern's ditch, John Pattee supplied the town with water for all purposes from his reservoir, west of Wheat's Ranch at Double Springs.

Hiram Ashley Messenger, a discoverer of copper in Calaveras County was one of those pioneers, who believed in the iron horse. He was one of the promoters of the San Joaquin and Sierra Railroad, the terminus of which was Valley Springs. As a contractor for the roadbed construction in 1883, he did an admirable piece of road building.

No sketch of Valley Springs would be complete without some mention being made of "Pop" McClellan of Woodbridge, who for many years served as conductor on the narrow gauge train that ran between Lodi and Valley Springs. Small, slim, wiry with gray, pointed beard, Pop was ever popular in Calaveras County.

In the eighties Valley Springs was proud of "Casa Blanca" the palatial home of Hiram Messenger. That house fashioned after a famous Mexican resort below old Fort Buchanan in Arizona, stood at the head of a beautiful valley, two miles from Valley Springs, surrounded by 600 acres of land. It was one of the show places of the county.

LATTIMERVILLE

On the north branch of the Calaveras River this 1849 settlement took its name from David Lattimer who established a wayside tavern here during the above year. It soon became a top diggings and a noted relay station for stage lines running between Stockton and the hill towns eastward. A large Rancheria was once situated between Lattimerville and Double Springs and was ruled by Raphero, a Siyakumna chief. Raphero was accused by Captain Sutter of having slain one of his vaqueros and setting fire to his grain fields. He was tracked down and brought to Sutter's Fort by the scout, Kit Carson. Here, Chief Raphero was given a form of a trial and found guilty. While declaring his innocence, he soon fell under the bullets fired from the rifles of the forts men.

Walter Robie, a Tennessean, conducted a general store here in 1850 and later engaged in the livestock industry. At Lattimerville, when gold in the riverbed was plentiful, there were two hotels, two stores, seven saloons and a "Chinee" washhouse. At this once lively stage station nothing remains except a few stone foundations, rock walls and an aged fruit tree or two.

IOWA TOWN

On the river road or Antelope Trail from Stockton to the mines was the Iowa Town. It was near Double Springs some two miles west of Lattimerville. As a town it was no great shakes. It consisted only of a cluster of cabins erected in the spring of 1849 by a company of Americans. Prominent among them were A. R. Wheat, Joseph Wheat, the brothers G. and J. Rasman, D. Miller, N. Murphy, J. Bacer, C. Meyers, Starr, Ellecut and the brothers A. and T. Nash. The Americans had arrived only to find a group of Chileans at work close by. The leader of the group, known simply as Tirante, was a rabble-rouser of the first order, second only to Domingo, the leader of Sutter Creek's Chileans rebels.

Tirante, the Fra Diavolo [Devil Monk] of the New El Dorado, looked the ruffian that he actually was. Seemingly, he had a voice and a blow in every Chilean uprising in Old Calaveras. Eventually he, like Haman[9] he fell into his own mischief.

A feud about the division of the ground not only grew but also strengthened until finally, strong in number the foreign miners, dared to storm the Iowa cabins. They brutally murdered Starr and Ellecut. Overpowered, the other ten Americans who with arms pinioned were compelled to walk under an armed guard from the scene of hostilities to within the sight of the

Alabama House on O'Neil's Creek[10]. Then, by a zigzag route, the captives were marched back towards the starting place. That day, luckily for the Americans, the brothers George and Enoch, Enochs of Philadelphia, were on their way to Carson Hill and had stopped for a rest at a tent hotel just as the Americans and their guards reached the spot and halted in front of the tent's entrance. One glance and the brothers realized the seriousness of the situation. Whipping out revolvers they rushed outdoors and covered Tirante and his bedeviling rascals.

While George stood, a cocked weapon in hand, Enoch cut the rawhide throngs. Freedom regained, the Americans took over and forced the offenders back to the wrecked cabins. The news of the conflict having reached Chili Campo, Double Springs, New Town and Lattimerville, the Americans settlers shouldered guns and went to the aid of their countrymen. All Chileans were rounded up and placed on trial in the Alcalde's Court, presided over by Wm. L. Dudley.

The Chileans who fastened the crimes on three of their number made confessions. The accused trio was found guilty of the first-degree murder. The hangings took place promptly and without flurry. Eight others, including Tirante, were made to suffer the fiery sting of a blacksnake whip and then ordered to leave California under penalty of death.

A legend now, after some one hundred years, the Iowa Town went out of existence and it took its story of strife with it.

JENNY LIND

Dr. John Y. Lind in honor of his wife, Jenny, gave this settlement its name. He founded Jenny Lind on the north bank of the Calaveras River in 1850. On the river road, all eastbound teams from Stockton and San Jose passed through these placer diggings. Jenny Lind, in 1854 was without a physician. Dr. Lind received that year the appointment of an Assistant Surgeon to the U. S. Marine Hospital, in Washington, D. C.

Lacking sufficient water to wash the gravel during the dry season, June to November, in 1856, canals were under course of construction to bring in water for mining and agricultural purposes. That year Jenny Lind had two hotels, four stores, two blacksmith shops, public school, church, theater, "ten pin" alley, several saloons, two billiard halls and a large number of dwelling houses. John Chapman was the official recorder for the town of Jenny Lind and John Heckendorn acted as its Justice of the Peace.

A young child found a large lump of gold on Main Street in Jenny Lind on Christmas Day in 1859 and the find created a gold revival. Thereafter,

Jenny Lind in 1856.
Courtesy of Calaveras County Historical Society

many large nuggets were found in the very heart of the town. After the placers petered out, the hydraulic miners took over and turned the picturesque old town into a full blast mining camp and it remained this way for many years. Now, however, it is permitted to flourish, chiefly by reason of the rich agricultural land with which it is surrounded.

FISCHER'S BRIDGE

This bridge spanned the Calaveras River at a point near the San Joaquin county boundary line. Here, in 1850, arose the settlement called Bellota [acorn]. Before the building of this bridge by William V. Fischer, the Mokelumne Hill road crossed the Calaveras River at Davis and Atherton Ferry trading post and stage station, a few miles east of Fischer's bridge.

Fischer's old tavern, now a residence, stands on the present highway, near the north bank of the stream and south of the river, is a roadside store which in the old days was a social hall and a community house.

David F. Douglas, the first settler in this region, took up land between Fischer's Bridge and the Davis and Atherton Ferry. Here, in 1850, he built a shake house, one of seventeen roadhouses along the old Mokelumne Hill road. Douglas, who had arrived in California in 1849 from Mexico with Colonel Isaac Graham's Dragoons, was a member of the Constitutional Convention and was the Secretary of State from 1855-1857 under Governor J. Neely Johnson.

The old hand-hewn water trough, preserved in a rough shed, is reminder

A typical one-man gold mine operation. Miner standing next to the windlass.
Courtesy of Calaveras County Historical Society

of Bellota's days of freighters and rutted roads, muddy during the winter months and choked with powder-fine red dust in the summer.

CHILI JUNCTION

The Indians were enjoying a "big eating" on Chili Gulch when in the summer of 1848, a few men arrived there to dig fortunes. Esteban Naides and his peons, it is said, lighted the first campfires at this junction. In 1850 Hosea Allen operated a trading post at this place. A year later the whole length of Chili Gulch was considered a dangerous ground. That year, the fires of vengeance blazing in his mentally disturbed mind, Joaquin Murieta had only recently risen up in Murphys diggings and was creating a new kind of hell-without-bounds for the miners along the entire length of the Mother Lode.

In December 1851, a small group of American miners were driven from their claims by a large group of Chileans led by Dr. Concha. At Chili Gulch all American miners were strongly opposed to the method by which the Chilean leaders through their peon laborers had acquired many of the richest claims, compelling the Americans to make laws forbidding the practice.

On Chili Gulch, where hostile Chileans had once held the ground and had yelled, in the Spanish language, "Esto perpetua!" at the Americans, nothing in the way of an arrastra, adobe hut or stone foundation remains to remind one of its first settlers, except the fig trees and grapevines planted there in the days when Three-fingered-Jack's dreadful saber made the stoutest heart quake.

MONITOR CAMP

Israel Grey, a mining partner of Ezra Ellingwood, founded Monitor Camp on Grizz Grey Gulch, near Petersburg. A hunter and wrestler, Grey was tall, brawny and muscular, with almost superhuman strength. After locating on Grizz Grey Gulch in 1849, when not digging gold, Grey spent his time on Bear Mountain, hunting wild game. One day, on an excursion into the hills, he carried a single shot Kentucky rifle and near the head of Salcido Gulch, where the chaparral grew thick, he came upon a huge grizzly bear. Time was not to be lost. He leveled his rifle and fired the single shot, he missed his mark, and the bullet infuriated the savage beast. Grey was without time to reload his weapon. The grizzly, with mouth open, charged him. The hunter thrust his hand and forearm into its mouth and with his free hand, drew his Bowie knife. A fierce combat followed. Grey frightfully mangled, was able finally to plunge the blade into the animal's heart. Then, crippled and bleeding, he made his way back to his cabin on Grizz Grey Gulch. This gulch leads from the Robbers' Bend past the Horswill tunnel and onward to the Calaveras River.

Israel had a common law wife Lucy, with whom he lived happily at Monitor Camp. Lucy Grey's former husband lurked sullenly in the neighborhood; he was the father of her young daughter. One day he attempted to kidnap the girl but Grey foiled the attempt. Then, in order to legally protect the child, he promptly married her mother according to the laws of the state. One morning while Grey was at work in his claim, near Robert Redmond's store at Latimerville, William Fry, Lucy's former husband in a jealous rage, emptied a load of buckshot into Grey's body, killing him instantly. Jim Smiley, working with Grey in the claim, with the aid of a sluice-fork overpowered Fry and stayed his flight. Grey was buried in the Pioneer Cemetery.

Two miles west of San Andreas on a wooded hill side that looks down upon the gently flowing North Branch of the Calaveras River, is the oldest Christian burial place in Calaveras County, the Pioneer Cemetery. Many of the white slabs of marble that marked the graves there tell us that, the diggings men were murdered for gold.

A miner's shack, many a die hard gold miners lived their later years in such shacks. Here Peter Meyers with wife Mary. North Branch circa 1907.

Courtesy of Calaveras County Historical Society

PARTIAL PAGES -

Gold

.... Let us quote Mr. Bidwell;
"Early in March of 1844, a Mexican, working under me at the Hock Farm, a property of John A. Sutter, came to me and told me there was gold in the Sierra Nevada. His name was Pablo Guterriez. The discovery by Marshall, it will be remembered, was in January 1848; Pablo told me this at a time when I was calling him to account because he had absented himself the day before without permission. I was giving him a lecture in Spanish, which I could speak quite well in those days. Like many Mexicans he had an Indian wife, sometime before he had been in the mountains and had bought a squaw. She had run away from him and he had gone to find her and bring her back. It was while on this trip he said, that he had seen signs of gold in Bear River."

Had Pablo Gutierrez used a wooden batea [pan for washing gold] instead of a reata [whip] he, instead of James Wilson Marshall, might have been the discoverer of gold in Northern California...........

Dr. I.C. and Olive Mann Isbel were members of Captain Aram's wagon train which reached the Bear River in early fall of 1846. The prairie-soiled clothing which Olive Isbel washed in this stream was heavy with shining substance when she scattered it on the brush to dry.

"What do you suppose it is, Olive?" queried Mrs. Aram.

" I don't know, but I think it must be isinglass" responded Mrs. Isbel

Two years later she realized that she had found gold but hadn't been able to recognize it as such. She missed the chance of making an important discovery..........rest not found.

Footnotes

1 In Amador County now.

2 Now in Amador County.

3 Originally named Catts' Camp, after Samuel Catts who arrived in California with Stevenson's Regiment in 1847. The following year, Catts launched a freight line from Stockton to Sonora and established this hilltop as a camp. Later, this spot became a popular stop for travelers on the way to Mokelumne Hill. Buckbee's account is suspect.

4 Las Calaveras, January 1956 (Publication of the Calaveras County Historical Society) In an article on Campo Seco, Lila Edalgo states the cork oak was planted near the Maher home by John Mackay.

5 Las Calaveras, January 1956, "The copper mine was discovered by two Mexicans in 1859. It soon became the property of Mr. J.K. Harmon who operated it for many years. Later the Penn Mining Company obtained the mine and hauled much matt to the railroad at Valley Springs.

6 The old town of Camanche is now under of the Camanche Reservoir.

7 Petersburg is now under the Now Hogan Reservoir.

8 Greasertown is now under the New Hogan Reservoir.

9 Human was an enemy of the Jews. According to the book of Esther, he was hanged for plotting their destruction.

10 Below the junction of the McKinney and O'Neil's creeks, this part of the river is called the Calaveritas Creek today.

27

VOLCANO

Volcano reached its name by reason of the chalcedony; carnelian, cacholong, onyx and obsidian which were found there in large quantities and which the geologists thought were of volcanic origin. Gem collectors who, no doubt used them for jewelry, have carried many exquisite semi-precious and precious specimens from these diggings.

Cave in Volcano. The first five meetings of the Masonic Lodge were held in this cave in 1854.

Courtesy of Calavers County Archives

In November 1859, the strident clanging of the fire bell warned people of Volcano that fire again was threatening their homes and businesses. The blaze at this time originated in a bakery at Main and Consolation streets. No rain as yet had fallen that season. The buildings were extremely dry, making wrecking of those standing in the path of the flames, a necessity. Volcano's crack fire department made a successful effort to save their town from complete destruction. Mahoney Hall was again saved by means of wet blankets. In this second conflagration of property loss was close to $100,000.

In the spring of 1854, a huge grizzly bear was discovered in a ravine a short distance from Volcano. The animal's presence so close to town created quite a stir, especially amongst bear-hunters. A scouting party armed with sledgehammers, axes, "Kentuck" rifles and shotguns went forth to slay the monster. At the approach of the enemy the savage beast rose up on its hind legs and looked around. At once the scouts took to their heels, except for one man who had faith in his "shootin iron" which carried a ball about the size of a pea. The lone man blazed away and hit the grizzly. Infuriated, the Monarch of the Sierra rushed forward and all but de-scalped him. Suffering and bleeding the injured man crawled through the dense underbrush to his cabin. That day other men, better armed, tracked down the beast and killed it. It proved to be the largest grizzly ever seen in Old Calaveras, its length when stretched, being fourteen feet.

Each Sunday and holidays weather permitting, the citizens of the Volcano locale rallied for their favorite sport, bull and bear fighting. The gold washers from the out-lying camps knocked off work and tramped into town. Mexican, Peruvian and Chilean miners especially, relished this sport as they had been trained to the Spanish tradition of bullfighting. A bull and bear fight could always draw out the entire Hispanic-American population. Mounted on splendid horses, mules and burros the seniors, senoras [married women] and senoritas [unmarried young ladies] rode into town pleasure bent. Brilliant serapes floated carelessly from the shoulders of the seniors and the gay shawls and rebosos [big scarf] flaunted by the senoras and senoritas added considerable color to Volcano.

Bear and Bull fight.

Courtesy of Emmett Joy Scrapbook, Calaveras County Archives

Black and savage Spanish bulls were plentiful in Old Calaveras. And there were many toreadors [teases the bull] and matadors [kills the bull] in the county who could handle them skillfully. Grizzly bear, less plentiful, were not easily captured and certainly not easily handled. A grizzly, any fine specimen, was valued from $1,000 to $4,000. Therefore, the bear was usually given an unfair advantage. A Volcano Flat savant, after witnessing a bull and bear fight recorded:

"Just before the fight commenced,
The bull was lassoed.
His horns were sawed off and
The fight pretty much taken out of him
Before he was turned into the arena.
The boys got all riled up over the way the bull was sacrificed.
The cheesy devils
left him without any fight at all worth of speaking of."

A corral close to the arena contained several fierce Spanish bulls, any one of which was able and willing to help out his companero in a tight situation. So as the loud bellowings and snortings resulting from one bull being chawed and clawed increased, the eyes of the spectators focused on the bull with curved needle pointed horns. This bull inside of limited space of the corral was tearing around and storming with rage. The bull hoofed up clouds of red dust, a form of an enraged bull's of protestation.

The ticket-holders ordered the vaqueros [cowboys] to return the handicapped bull to the corral and to enforce the order, more than a hundred revolvers were drawn. The fight promoters understood that the miners meant business and they also knew that unless the order was promptly obeyed, the grizzly, most certain would be shot. With so many men, quick on the draw, flashing weapons, the promoters had no alternative but to have the bull returned to the corral and another animal brought out to finish the fight.

The gate opened and an ink black bull proud and defiant came thundering into the arena. Twirling its tail and snorting contemptuously, then with lowered head it made a charge and the fight was on. The grizzly growled and showed its fangs, these were soon fastened in the bull's neck. Aided by its strong forepaws the savage bear used its hind paws with terrible effect on the bull's rump and sides. One ear was ripped off and each gouge made by the grizzly's dreadful claws left gaping wounds. The bull, its bravery unimpaired, was utterless to inflict any punishment on its hard-cuffing adversary.

Five minutes of this one-sided fighting was time enough to convince the bull that, it was not so invincible. Its disdainful snortings quickly changed to violent rage and its last angry appeals were heard throughout Volcano.

Blinded by blood, the grizzly for a second released its hold. The bull made a charge at the brush fence that was separating the animals from the spectators. Then with sudden whirlwind fury it plunged through the fence, scattering the crowd in all directions. Down through the diggings tore the maddened bull followed by a dozen mounted vaqueros. Charging with bloody head, the retreating animal put fear into the hearts of the bravest footmen. In front of a store with bright colors on display in the windows, the bull stopped, looked and being master of the situation began to rid the establishment of red flannel shirts and bright blue serapes. With demonic fury, one after another, it demolished the panes of glass in the show windows. Its temper finally appeased, the vaqueros managed to get a lariat around its horns and legs thereby curbing all further exhibition of its varying moods of bravery and anger.

Mahoney Hall, famous structure of Old Calaveras, had a history all of its own. There was a general regret, both in Calaveras and Amador counties, when in 1865, it fell a victim to that dreaded power of fire. The "Volcano Blues," an intensely loyal military organization of Civil War days, used the old hall in 1861 as an armory. When the blaze started, Old Glory was unfurled atop the building and to the regret of the "Blues" in the hurry and general confusion it was overlooked. But the starry banner neither burned nor fell. Waving, it remained atop until the flagpole toppled carrying the flag with it. Old Glory struck the ground beyond the path of danger and was rescued by the "Blues," who carried it off to a place of safety.

Volcano drowsing in its bowl at the foot of steep hills is one of the most characteristics of all California's mining towns. The cedar, oak and pine trees are still flourishing along the creek banks, just as they did in the days of its founders. Each spring, the spotted lilies flaunt gay and waxen petals. The solid rock road above the town that brought the emigrant trains is still there. These trains while crossing the Sierra from Donner Lake through Faith, Hope and Charity valleys went over the Kit Carson Pass and Spur and down the Ram's Horn road. They all traveled past the Tragedy Springs and the Maiden's Grave marked with dreadful memories. They reminiscence of the ones who endured untold hardships and suffering in order to reach these limestone hills, placers and quartz ledges, for which this picturesque town Volcano, was and still is renowned.

The pioneer spirit of Volcano has run its course, even so the stately St. George Hotel and other buildings of the gold stampede era stand to give mute evidence of this historic town's former glory.

28

WHERE A CONDOR'S SHADOW FELL

In days of Conestoga wagons, buffaloes, oxen, wild animals and even wilder men, had reached Saint Joseph, Missouri, where they purchased mules, saddles, bridles, rifles and hatchets. Then with rolls of blankets tied to their saddles, they went along with a group of horsemen, a dozen or so in number to the Big Blue. Among other rivers crossed and followed were the Big Sandy, Platte, Sweetwater, Green, Humboldt and Truckee.

Example of a miner's camp of the early days.
Courtesy of Wally Motloch

They were outdoors under the blue sky most of the time, so when Fort Laramie was reached on the day of July 4, 1849, they were not only inured to sunshine, thunder, lightning but to wind and rain. Bob and Bill having an objective point, a purpose, regardless of weather conditions, plodded cheerfully along. The prairie with wild grain high as a man's head was often Indian swept as well as windswept. Bob's mule was stolen one night and "ham-strung" a few evenings later. The warlike Sioux Indians made off

Travel set-up of a typical miner, prospector or a surveyor.
Gourley photo courtesy of Wally Motloch

with Bill's brand new rifle, but since they were on their way to garner gold in California, they didn't permit material losses to disturb their peace of mind.

Cholera was rampant on the plains that summer. Bob and Bill helped other men dig roadside graves in which the bodies of the unfortunate ones would lie. Above each desolate grave a cross would stand. They performed other acts of mercy while serving fellow travelers and grew stronger spiritually. Bob's mount gone, they took turns riding Bill's brown mule, but mostly they walked, they didn't mind. Jogging beside them were other men, mountain men, hardy and fearless, who were given to banter, breezy persiflage and at times to vulgarity.

Down the Emigrant Trail past Truckee Lake (Donner Lake) to Emigrant Gap where in the winter of 1846 so many brave-hearted men, women and children shivered, starved and died, came Robert Edes Bradshaw and William A. Samson.

Finally in late September, when the wild grape vines festooning the cottonwoods, which flanked both banks of the Sacramento River, the West's last stronghold was reached. They came to Sutter's Fort where Captain John

Augustus Sutter and a bulldog pistol were a man's best friends.

When Bob and Bill had left the homes of their parents in Springfield, they were well equipped. But, upon arrival at Sutter's Fort, the only baggage they possessed were the clothes on their backs. Friends and neighbors since earliest childhood, the hardships of prairie life they experienced together had deepened their friendship to such an extent that the words "thine" and "mine" were no longer spoken by either of them. Now what one had he shared with the other.

Adam Asa Gourley at North Branch.
Courtesy of Irene (Gourley) Craik

Captain Sutter, as was his way with the stranger at his gate, gave them besides food, lodging, and good cheer, encouragement. The following day they purchased from Captain Sutter two saddle horses and a pack mule, in fact all articles necessary for the comfort and success of a placer miner. Shortly, with packsaddles bulging, Bob Bradshaw and Bill Samson leaped into their saddles and with Captain Sutter's admonition:

> "Make your try for gold a determined one, boys",

ringing in their ears, they soon struck the old Indian Trail leading from Sutter's Fort to the various camps in the Sierra foothills.

At least one thing is certain; they followed the old Indian Trail, sunk deep in the centuries past by the feet of countless braves, until the northern bank of Mokelumne River was reached. At Big Bar a flimsy makeshift boat ferried them across this stream. At the time of crossing they could see hundreds of gold washers standing knee deep in eddies, scooping up sand. The south bank reached, they rested for a brief time in the shade of a giant black oak tree. In the burnished leaves blue jays were strutting and cawing. While they sat in idleness, smoking and chatting, they were amused to see half grown deer running hither and yon, seemingly unafraid of the red-shirted miners washing gold in the river below.

Finally in October they reached their destination, Chili Junction, on Chile Gulch. Here, in this Calaveras locale they dismounted, lighted a campfire, staked their animals, pitched a tent fastened with ropes to trees that became their own "witness trees" within a week's time. Their camp in order, their claims located, they settled down to live life as best they knew how. Since in Chili Junction there was never anything except words of praise spoken in their favor, they must have behaved themselves exceptionally well.

There wasn't much in the way of entertainment in Chili Junction. Mokelumne Hill, a regular Goliath of a place, was the location the pleasure bent men would go in order to find a fandango, hurdy-gurdy house, saloon or gambling tent. Trained in childhood to shun evil rather than seek it, both Bob and Bill had kept right on shunning anything and everything that to their way of thinking wasn't exactly right and honest.

Rather than seek pleasure in Mokelumne Hill, Winter's Bar or Poverty Bar, these New Englanders preferred to tuck their blue denim jeans inside their boot tops, roll back the sleeves of their work shirts and while red-headed woodpeckers drummed holes in trees, would work hard and long in their claims. Each one had experienced a new kind of joy when for the first time he dug out from the ground a lump of virgin gold.

Unfortunate, sometimes is the miner who found gold in abundance. This gold-strewn wilderness was bandit ridden. If a miner was murdered in Old Calaveras, as hundreds were, a grave was hastily scooped out on some hillside and with pine boughs answering for both shroud and coffin, he was lowered to rest. Slabs of white marble are to be seen today in remote and lonely places of the Southern Mines. In most instances the inscriptions engraved thereon mutely tell of tragedies of long ago.

The newly dug fortunes of Bob and Bill were at the mercy of petty thieves and master thieves. Worse yet Joaquin Murrieta's dagger hurlers and blade slathers were forever riding to the jingle of stirrups, making the new El Dorado[1] doubly unsafe. All things considered, these partners decided to protect their treasure in the safest way possible, that is to have it transformed into money and turned over to some express company, the vanguard of the banking business in California. The express companies were the first to link the hurly-burly mining camps with the business of the wide world. Realizing this fact, Bob and Bill were soon taking advantage of this method for safe guarding their yellow metal.

Hating strife and loving peace, they desired to establish themselves in some profitable and legitimate business in a larger and more peaceable

Possibly, a visit by a surveyor to a miner's camp in the woods.
Courtesy of Calaveras County Historical Society, gift of Rosemary Faulkner.

community. The truth is they longed to return to the East, not because they had been scared out of the Junction, but simply because they had grown tired of hearing so much loud talk about blood shed, robberies and lynchings. They were acutely aware that Mokelumne Hill, maintained a permanent gibbet from which dangled a strangler's rope. In this rip roaring mining town for a whole month a man a day was executed by order of old Judge Lynch, and in almost all instances gold was the reason for the many crimes committed.

Bob and Bill agreed one day that it was one thing to mine raw gold and see that it didn't swirl and spin away into the possession of others and quite another and more difficult thing, to protect one's life while doing it.

The gold mined each day was weighed and equally divided. Bob kept his daily clean up in a buckskin sack attached to the belt buckled around his waist. When the sack became too heavy for comfort, he removed the gold, placed it in a tin can and buried it under a pine tree growing close to their tent. Bill, on the other hand, stored his portions in a strong box, which he made no effort to conceal. In the past these partners on more than one occasion had sold their treasure in Mokelumne Hill at a huge discount rather than journey with it to Stockton for transmission to San Francisco.

Conditions being as they were and since they had realized their objective, Bob and Bill thought it best to pull up stakes and pack out of Chili Junction before the month, July had drawn to a close.

Having definitely decided to shake the dust of the Chili Junction off their boots, they saddled up and galloped to Mokelumne Hill. There they left dust and nuggets worth several thousand dollars in the custody of Reynolds, Todd & Company who were the common carriers of newly mined gold in California. This express company, at the request of its owners, would deliver their gold for coinage to the United States Mint in Philadelphia. They still had in their possession a goodly amount of the yellow metal, enough and more to defray all expenses while in San Francisco and including the price of passage for two on the fast clipper, Flying Cloud.

The next day in need of supplies, they struck out together on foot for the Junction's one and only grocery store. Upon their return when near their tent the dark shadow of a California condor[2] fell on the trail in front of them. The condor was flying to its nesting place in the Lomira Hills [Bear Mountain Range] from the buttes north of the Mokelumne River. Any Mexican gold digger upon seeing this shadow would have made the sign of the cross over his heart at once, but a miner from the States would have done exactly as Bob and Bill did – attach no significance to the shadow of this monster bird of prey.

When not working outdoors, Bill spent his time inside the tent writing letters to his parents and numerous friends in Springfield. Those letters he received in return arrived at infrequent intervals after a passage around Cape Horn or via Panama, often requiring many months to reach San Francisco. Bob preferred to read books and newspapers rather than write letters, so the pleasure of receiving them was not always his. But since the Springfield friends of one were usually the friends of the other, things turned out all right for him. Bill would read his letters aloud to share them with Bob.

On that day, their gold was lying in two heaps on a rude pine table in the tent where Bill sat writing a letter to his mother. Bob, whose turn it was to prepare the evening meal, was in their small shake lean-to. Willingly and cheerfully as was his way, he defeathered the quail, pared potatoes that he had planted and dug with his own hands, and mixed the dough for saleratus [baking soda] biscuits. He poked oak sticks under the sheet iron stove, filled the tea kettle with spring water and set it on the top of the stove to boil for tea.

As he performed these chores he may have sung to the tune of "Oh, Susanna", one of his favorite songs:

"I dreamed a dream the other night
When everything was still.
I dreamed I was a-sailing
Down a gold-strewn rill"

And while Bill sat unconcerned, scribbling accounts of the wild doings over at Poverty Bar and Mokelumne Hill, Bob set the table for two outside under the leafy branches of a mammoth oak standing close to the lean-to. In summertime the stately oak was always filled with songbirds. On this particular evening it was a red-topped linnet's vesper song that had attracted and held Bob's attention and having a fondness for bird song, silenced his own voice he listened to that of the bird.

Thus far the present year, only a little more than half spent, was the cruelest and bloodiest California had ever known. Only a few months back Joaquin Murrieta, the fires of vengeance leaping in his lithe young body, had risen up in Murphy's Diggings and was now making Calaveras County a hell on earth. It was now considered the most dangerous county in all America, for whenever and wherever the Mexican chief's band of assassins rode, death invariably followed, unexpectedly, suddenly and surely. This state of affairs was fully realized by the two men planning to leave Chili Junction for safer ground. Both Bob and Bill, mere boys, strong of body and brave of heart, felt himself equal to any situation that might arise. Even so, each one kept a loaded pistol under his pillow instead of in his hip pocket.

The biscuits and quail were perfectly browned, the potatoes mashed, the gravy made and the tea brewed, ready to be poured into tin cups when Bob heard the sound of hoof beats and the jingle of silver fringe on stirrups. He turned away from the stove at once and went outdoors. There for a brief moment he stood dead still, mystified and listening.

From the back of a huge bowl beside the supper table, sprang with leopard-like agility the lynx-eyed, shabling-gaited Manuel Garcia. Garcia was known throughout the Southern Mines as Three-Fingered-Jack, the most dreaded and dastardly villain that had ever set foot upon the native soil of California. He stood for an instant, a demon from the jaws of hell, a Mexican saber uplifted in his hideous hand.

With one look at the revolting gorilla-man, the defenseless Bob Bradshaw's face went white as the dog fennel flowers beneath his feet. His time of crucifixion was short. The treacherous desperado, just as he had done to so many other gold washers, lifted his heavy saber still higher and

Wally Motloch at the Pioneer Cemetery. Located on highway 12 between San Andreas and Valley Springs

with a mighty stroke brought it down against the nape of Bob's neck, severing his head from his body.

Bill, hearing strange noises, dropped his pen, jumped to his feet and ran outdoors where he was met by other cutthroats of Murrieta's terrible gang. These bandits were soon plunging daggers into his body. His pistol beyond reach, with his bare fists, he fought the scoundrels with all the strength he was able to muster. He kept right on fighting, determinedly and courageously until finally, his valiant body was literally hacked into pieces. More than twenty blows were required to fall the brave Bill Samson. When at last he dropped to the earth, still alive, he was blood drenched from head to foot. And so it was that another page of outrage and murder in the new El Dorado was added to Joaquin Murrieta's book of infamous deeds.

A short time later quite by accident, four prospectors discovered the bodies of the unfortunate partners. Jerking a blanket off a bunk they lifted the mutilated body of their comrade and tenderly laid it on the woolen. Then these men with a corner of the blanket in each one's hand carried Bill to the store of Lake Allen at the Junction where everything humanly possible was done to save his life. All efforts failing, he died that same evening.

The description that Bill had been able to give of Three Fingered Jack not only marked him as a man of cool head and iron nerves but one possessing keenest sense of observation. While fighting desperately, he told the surgeon dressing his wounds that he had caught a glimpse of a pistol belted desperado who had raked the two gold piles off the table into a cowhide bag. The bag was brought outside the tent and turned over to two men astride the same horse.

That night after hearing the tragic news, the miners living in and around Chili Junction were thrown into a near panic. The next day armed with every weapon they could lay their hands on, they attempted to track down the murders. Failing to pick up a "hot" trail, they returned to the Junction and were soon ripping apart their sluice boxes and cradles. From the salvaged boards, two coffins were made to hold the bodies of the slain gold washers between whom there had never been any thine or mine. Their friends, and others at Chili Junction, Poverty Bar and Mokelumne Hill, were anxious to render service, made arrangements necessary for a Christian burial. Two days later a few of these men with a distressed look in their eyes, lowered Bob and Bill to rest in the same grave on a hill slope known today as the Pioneer's Cemetery[3] a short distance west of San Andreas.

Above their grave is a tombstone, which in 1854 reached Chili Junction from Massachusetts. The inscription cut deep into the white marble tells one that it was:

"Erected to the memory of
Robert Edes Bradshaw and
William A. Samson
by their loving parents
who, in Charleston, Massachusetts,
mourn the loss of their worthy sons,
who on the Chili Gulch in far away California,
July 20, 1851, were murdered for gold."

In the burial place of many of the first gold washers, the marble slab that marks their grave still stands[4]. Neither snow nor frost falling upon it each winter for ninety-one years has been able to crack or mar the stone. This memorial, better than word or pen, records the tragedy at Chili Junction, where Jack of-the-terrible-hand played another one of his blood curdling roles. But time, as time always does, eventually caught up with this arch-villain. He died, his boots on and all.

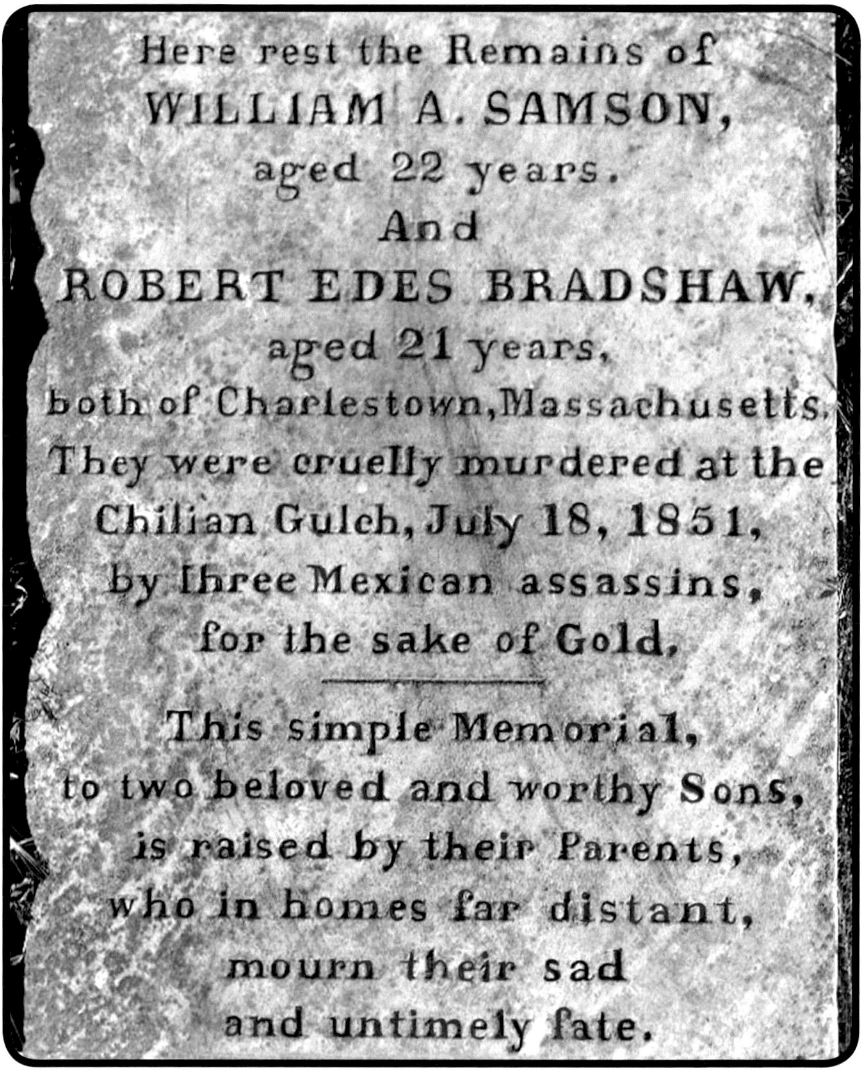

Tombstone of William A. Samson and Robert E. Bradshaw. Originally, it was located at the Pioneer Cemetery but unfortunately is no longer there. It was recently stolen!

Courtesy of Bank of Stockton Historical Photograph Collection.

Footnotes

1 New " El Dorado" does not refer to any location but is a term for a general place with gold and good fortune. Not to be confused the town or county of El Dorado.

2 It could have been a California condor but most likely in this area, it was a vulture.

3 Located on highway 12 between San Andreas and Valley Springs.

4 Unfortunately, this stone is no longer there in 2005.

Appendix A

Copy of a letter from Calaveras County to Governor Peter Burnett. Jesus Maria, May 1, 1850 (MS 264) California Historical Society, Manuscript Collection. San Francisco. (Source of original unkown)

"Jesus Maria, Calaveras County, May 1st. 1850

To His Excellency
Governor of California

Sir:
We your humble petitioners being Chilians, Sonorenos and other Mexicans apprehending some difficulty on account of our working on the gold mines, having been debarred the privilege of working at some places and now being threatened to be driven off from our present encampment, and not wishing to resist the Americans or do any act contrary to the laws of your nation, humbly beg your protection.
And should it be contrary to your laws that we work in the mines we will peaceably retire. But if it is lawful for us to remain and work in the mines we earnestly request your speedy intercession.
And we would beg have here to remark that subib?
we are about being prevented from working the mines [while] other foreigners are allowed that privilege.

Yours with much respect
Julian Abechuco
Richard Paynter
Jacinto Fernandez
Francisco Garcias
Jose Andrade
Raimundo Gonzales
Jose Duarte
Pablo Arana
Joaquin C y Verrano
Jose Maria Cota"

BIBLIOGRAPHY

Selected items from The Saga of Old Tuolumne, by Edna Bryan Buckbee.

Allsop, Robert, California and its gold miners, Groombridge & Sons, 1853.
Borthwick, J. D., Three years in California, William Blackwood, London, 1857.
Brooks, J. Tyhitt, M. D., Four months among the gold finders in Alta California,
Bryant, Edwin, What I saw in California, D. Appleton, New York, 1848.
Buffum, E. Gould, Six months in the gold mines, Lee & Blachard, 1850.
Bidwell, General John, Echoes of the past, Chico, California, N. D.
Bancroft, Huburt Howe, Works, 39 vols. H. H. Bancroft, San Francisco, 1882-91.
Buckbee, Edna Bryan, Pioneer days of Angel's Camp, California, 1932.
California gold regions, F. M. Pratt, New York, 1849.
Carson, James H., Recollections of the mines, San Joaquin Republican, 1852.
Calaveras County, illustrated and described, W. W. Elliott & Co., 1885.
Elias, Sol. P., Stories of Stanislaus, Sol. P. Elias, Modesto, Cal., 1894.
Eldredge, Zoeth S., History of California, 5 vols. Century History Co., 1915.
Foster, G. G., Gold regions of California, Dewitt & Davenport, New York, 1849.
Fremont, John C., Memoirs of my life, Belford & Clark, Chicago, 1857.
Genealogy and biography, Northern California citizens, Chicago, 1901.
Hittell, Theodore Henry, History of California, 4 vols. H. H. Bancroft, S.F, 1885.
Hutchings, J. M., Scenes of wonder and curiosity in California, S. F, 1872.
Helper, Hinton R., The land of gold, H. Taylor, Baltimore, Md., 1855.
Johnson, Theodore S., Sights in the gold region, Baker & Scribner, N. Y, 1849.
Kelly, William, A stroll through the diggings, Simms & McIntyre, 1852.
King, Clarence, Mountaineering in the Sierra Nevadas, Osgood & Co., 1872.
King, Thomas Butler, California: the wonder of the age, William Gowans,, 1850.
Lyman, A., Life in the gold diggings, E. T. Pease, Hartford, Conn., 1852.
McGroarty, John Stevens, California: its history and Romance, Grafton
Miners' Own Book, Hutchings & Rosenfield, San Francisco, 1858.
M'Collum, William, M. D., California as I saw it, G. H. Derby, Buffalo, 1850.
McIlhany, Edward W., Recollections of a forty-niner, Hailman 1908.
Patterson, L. B., Twelve years in the mines of California, 1862.
Robinson, Fayette, California and its gold region, Stringer & Townsend, 1849.
Ryan, William Redmond, Personal adventures in upper and lower California,
Shaw, Pringle, Ramblings in California, James Bain, Toronto, Canada, 1856.
Spurr, George G., The land of gold: A tale of forty-nine, Boston, 1881.
State register and yearbook, 1857-59, Langley & Mathews, San Francisco.
Taylor, Bayard, El Dorado, G. P. Putnam's Sons, New York, 1850.
Taylor, William, Life in California, Carlton & Porter, New York, 1858.
Wood, Harvey, Personal recollections of, Mountain Echo Printing Office, Angel's Camp, Calaveras County, California, June, 1878.
Yale, G., Titles to mining claims and water rights in California, A. Roman & Co., San Francisco, 1867.

Index

Places listed on the map, see next page

Map of Western Calaveras County (Gold Regions)

Numbers correspond to the list on the opposite page.

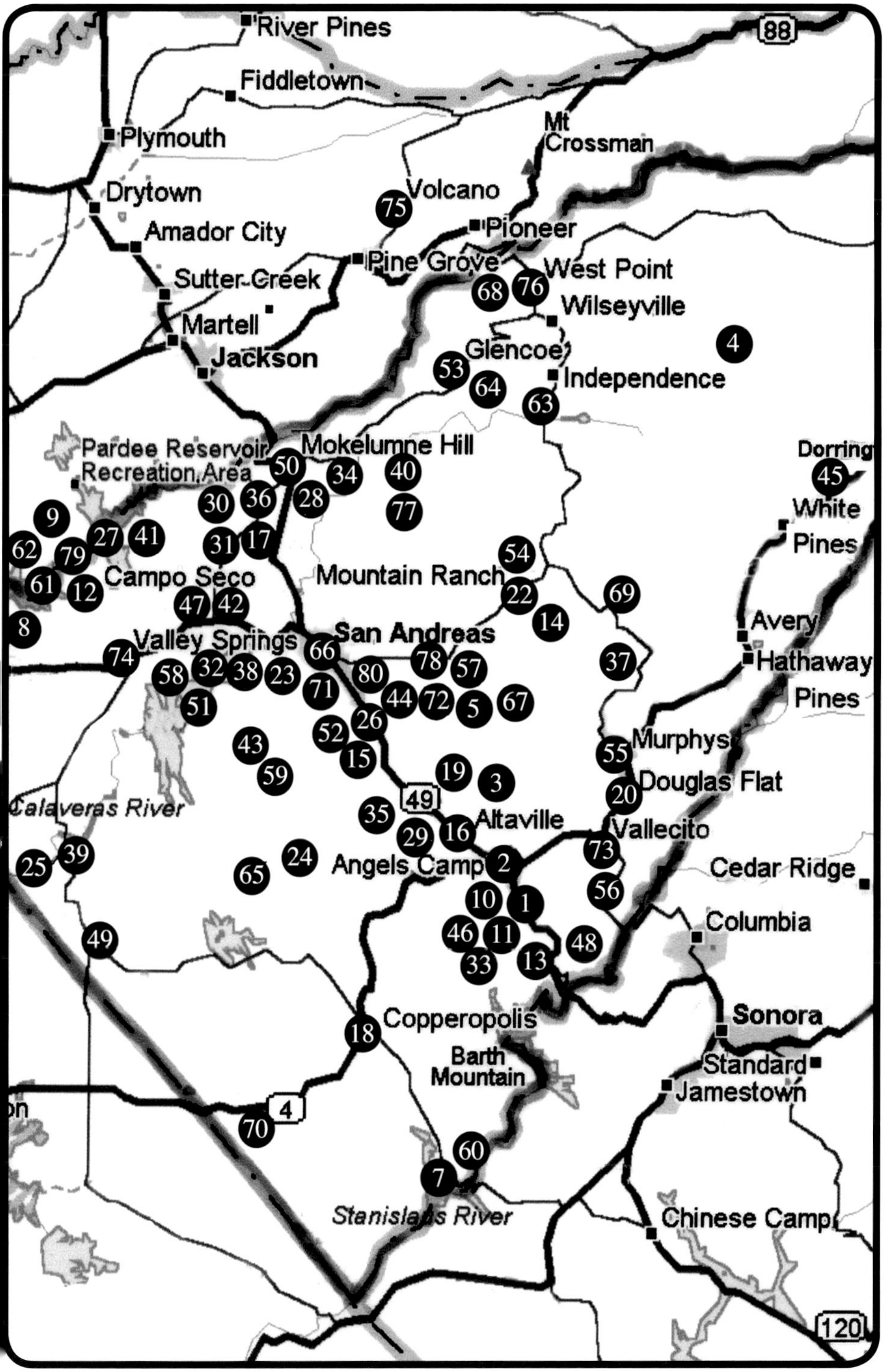